WILLIAM H. STEPHENS
THE
NEW TESTAMENT
WORLD
IN PICTURES
PAULA A. SAVAGE, designer

Lutterworth Press
Cambridge

Lutterworth Press
P.O. Box 60
Cambridge
CB1 2NT

British Library Cataloguing in Publication Data available

ISBN 0–7188–2701–5

Copyright © Broadman Press 1987
First published by Lutterworth Press 1988

This book is dedicated to Shirley, my wife, friend and lover
who trudged with me through archeological sites and museums, and
who shared the adventures of hot deserts, rough areas, and exciting,
calmer places to gather the photos and information in these pages.
Without her support, this book never would have been written.

Printed in the United States of America

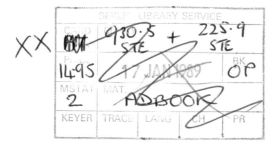

CONTENTS

CONTENTS

INTRODUCTION

This book grew out of a series of circumstances which worked together to highlight its need. The first circumstance was the constant need to identify subject areas for articles during my ten-year tenure as editor of *Biblical Illustrator*, a Bible background and archeology magazine. While much archeological data is available about histories and cultures of the Old Testament, such information related to the New Testament is sparse in comparison.

The second circumstance was the growing awareness that New Testament scholars basically are linguists. The articles these well-qualified writers submitted to *Biblical Illustrator* were based on sources almost exclusively literary. Very little of the type of hard data such as comes from archeology is used in New Testament study; that which is used is borrowed from other disciplines.

The third circumstance was my research for a novel on Paul, which was to be as comprehensive and accurate as I attempted to do with *Elijah* (Tyndale House). That research reached one dead end after another as I sought to reconstruct probable life situations for Paul's background, life, education, travels, and ministry.

The fourth circumstance was a three-month study leave granted to me by the Baptist Sunday School Board, publisher of *Biblical Illustrator*. Those weeks were spent visiting archeological sites and museums throughout the Mediterranean region and in Europe. My conviction grew both that an enormous amount of information is now available to New Testament scholars that is not being used, and that an enormous amount of work needs to be done to develop new information. The goal of this book is to stimulate interest in the study of the type of hard data which this book reflects and incorporate it into New Testament study. None of the information is new. It has been gleaned from a very wide range of material covering disciplines of New Testament study, Greek and Roman archeology and history, and such subjects as diverse as slavery, architecture, and theater.

A field of New Testament archeology does not exist. The work done in this field essentially is a gathering of information from other disciplines. Biblical archeology began as an attempt to understand more about the world of the Old Testament. Particularly in the early decades, and to some degree still, sites are identified for excavation on the basis of their Old Testament connection.

That is the kind of discipline that needs to develop for New Testament archeology. Lystra existed for only about a century, but that time frame is exactly suited to the New Testament period; Lystra is a mound on a farm. Derbe is much the same. Colossae is a large mound that entombs a very ancient city. It, too, is farmland. Berea has received some attention but it is an inhabited city and so is difficult to excavate. Alexandrian Troas, just a few miles from Troy, is a vast site with ruins jutting above the surface. Its importance was so great that it was considered for an eastern capital of the Empire. It, too, is farmland. Tarsus, Paul's home city, has been only generally surveyed and a small amount of archeology accomplished. It is inhabited, but the ancient city was much larger than the present one. Laodicea has received spot excavation only. The remains are only partially buried. Antioch of Pisidia also is essentially farmland; it has received some excavation, but a great part of this important inland site still lies buried. Patmos is growing rapidly up the mountainside, every year making more land inaccessible, yet a walk through the farms up the hill from the town reveals pottery shards with a wide range of style. What would Patmos tell us about a Roman penal colony? A systematic survey of the vast areas that make up Galatia needs to be done; such a study likely would shed light on the long-debated North and South Galatian theories.

Paul's world contrasts sharply with that of New Testament Palestine. Caesarea Maritima, Capernaum, Chorazin, Jerusalem, and other sites including many in Galilee and several sites in Jordan are being excavated. Some sites in Turkey and Greece have been under excavation for years, such as Antioch of Syria, Cenchraea, Corinth, Philippi, Ephesus, Perge, Sardis, Smyrna, and Thessalonica. Harvard University is slowly identifying early Byzantine sites for excavation.

New Testament scholars need to give priority to examining in detail the information from these excavations and museum holdings from those sites and many others for their relevance to New Testament studies. Other sites, such as Herculaneum, Pompeii, and Boscoreale, and their artifacts can reveal much about first-century life. The National Museum of Naples is a ripe field of information for New Testament scholars, as are other major museums such as the British, the Louvre, the Bode, and Pergamum; but in addition artifacts in smaller museums scattered throughout Europe and the Near East cry out for examination. Tools, clothing, furniture, paintings, mosaics, statuary, and bas-reliefs on sarcophagi need to be examined for regional differences, cultural variances, and cosmopolitan sameness for the Greco-Roman world.

Scholars in the fields of Greek, Roman, and Hittite archeology do not focus on questions or sites of interest primarily to New Testament scholars. An organized discipline of New Testament archeology would enable a systematic identification of sites to be excavated, reasons for such excavations, schedules for their excavation, negotiations with appropriate governments, fund raising, and other essentials. The process will entail a number of years, but some aggressive New Testament department in a university or seminary needs to commit resources to set out priorities for projects. The effort could revolutionize New Testament study.

Some of the crucial questions that need attention are: How much was Hellenistic and Roman culture absorbed and how much resisted in Palestine? How much did the Jewish Diaspora influence the Greco-Roman world and especially early (first-century) Christianity? How did border cities between East and West such as Tarsus amalgamate both cultures into a unity? What similarities and differences can be observed between priesthoods and other religious concepts of East and West? What regional differences existed in the first century between Macedonia and southern Greece which would explain some of Paul's writings? Many skills and disciplines are required. The task of research must be done by specialists. Generalists and broader historians then can build on that work to develop a comprehensive picture.

I am a generalist; the fact that this book has been written by a generalist may be an asset, but it may also be subject to some concerns by specialists. I have attempted to use reference material that is accessible to as wide a range of readers and users of this book as possible. To that end, I have used books in English except where I had no choice. Most books and articles were written by specialists; a few have been written by generalists with good credentials. My choices of resources generally have been not to use primary source material, though on occasion appropriate data has not been available otherwise.

I have not set footnotes, fully aware of the problems that decision might create for specialists. To do so would render the text quite difficult. The resource lists appear at the beginning of each section. Translations of ancient writings are listed first, followed by other sources listed in alphabetical order of the writers' names.

Photos have been selected for their relevance to the New Testament world. A high percentage of them date to the first century; those which date earlier or later provide insights into the New Testament world when used with discretion. Values and cautions regarding these photos are noted where appropriate.

The focus of this book is on the Greco-Roman world; the photos and information about the East, including Palestine, primarily is intended to indicate briefly how those lands were affected by Hellenism and Roman culture.

Two indexes are provided, a Scripture index and a subject index. The Scriptures listed are those which I consider relevant to the text or photo; some readers may identify other Scriptures which I missed. In addition to this index, representative Scriptures are listed at the end of the descriptive copy of most photos.

To a large degree I have used James Pritchard's *The Ancient Near East in Pictures* as a model. However, I have made some design changes. Descriptive copy for the photos appears with the photos rather than at the back of the book, and I have added instructions to each section to add to the value of the photos and descriptions. The result has been, I believe, a usable library of information for pastors and for scholars in Greek and Roman fields as well as New Testament scholars. The physical layout and design of the book is due to the unusual skill of Paula Savage, master design artist at the Baptist Sunday School Board and artist/designer for *Biblical Illustrator*.

Many museums have granted permission to photograph in their museums, and a few have generously provided their own photos. Photos 9, 114, and 555 were taken by my wife, Shirley; all of the other photos are mine except for a few furnished by museums to whom credit is given with the descriptive copy.

Credit is due a number of New Testament and other scholars who encouraged me in this project. Special thanks go to Harold Songer of Southern Baptist Theological Seminary, and Trent Butler, formerly of the Baptist Seminary in Ruschlikon, Switzerland and now with Holman Bible Publishers. These and others too numerous to name are profoundly thanked.

William H. Stephens

THE EMPERORS

The emperors immediately relevant to a study of the first-century world of the New Testament fall into 4 groups: the Julio-Claudians, those of the Civil War, the Flavians, and the adoptive emperors who followed the Flavians.

The Julio-Claudians
Julius Caesar, 49-44 BC (dictator)
Augustus, 31 BC-AD 14 (first emperor)
Tiberius, 14-37
Gaius (Caligula), 37-41
Claudius, 41-54
Nero, 54-68
The Civil Wars
Galba, 68-69
Otho, 69
Vitellius, 69
The Flavians
Vespasian, 69-79
Titus, 79-81
Domitian, 81-96
Adoptive
Nerva, 96-98
Trajan, 117-138

In one sense, Julius Caesar was the first emperor; however, his aggressive manner of asserting his power brought about his assassination. His achievements were impressive nonetheless, and his rule both signaled the end of the already-dying republic and paved the way for Augustus. The republic was dead, mostly from old age; it had lost its vitality and ability to respond to the needs of the Roman city-state which had grown into a world power.

This shift from republic to emperor rule had enormous implications for the entire Western—and

▲ 1 **Cameo with bust of Augustus**, sardonyx. British Museum. The gold diadem was added in the Middle Ages and restored in the eighteenth century. The most prominent symbol at the bottom of the cameo is the aegis, a goatskin fringed with snakes and a Medusa head, which was an attribute of Athena (see photo 479). *Luke 2:1; Revelation 12:3; 13:1; 19:12; 21:20.*

part of the Eastern—world. The stability afforded by Rome and especially by the Empire during the brilliantly administered reign of Augustus provided crucial avenues for the spread of Christianity. So important was the timing of some of the developments that New Testament scholars traditionally refer to the "fullness of time." They point to such factors as the de-

velopment of an extensive road system, the pacification of the Mediterranean Sea, the spread of the Greek language (which already had occurred widely, but continued under Rome), the religious foment which was part of the first century, and other factors.

The emperor's power grew slowly from Augustus' beginning. As one who brought order out of the chaotic Roman world, he was proclaimed a savior. He developed his power due both to skillful manipulation and genuine adoration by the people. The powers gained through these means became more formalized as the first century progressed. By the end of Augustus' reign, all of the legions but one (in Africa) were under his command, the army was made into a standing professional force (previously it had been conscripted), and he had arranged for oaths of personal allegiance to be made to him throughout the Empire. This last accomplishment was done under the guise of spontaneity, not a difficult task for such a popular emperor to arrange, and it became an annual event by the end of the first century.

During Augustus' reign the publicans were restricted as the primary tax gatherers, their function reduced to collecting only customs and inheritance taxes. The granting of citizenship accelerated (in general) with each reign. Romanization progressed rapidly; however, it did so during the first 50 years of the Empire as a natural by-product of conquest, pacification, and trade rather than from conscious effort, and it progressed more slowly in the East, which had its already-ancient civilizations.

The effect of any single emperor on the New Testament world must be studied against this greater backdrop of administration, trade, and other developments which began under Augustus. In general, the foibles and brutality of some emperors had scant effect outside of Rome and the leading Roman families. The Empire was administered in the main by a rising population of equites (knight class) and freedmen.

Augustus set the direction for the Empire; the changes and additions of later emperors only influenced directions. His impact was so great that either natural or adoptive descent from him was deemed essential for the emperorship until Nero committed suicide. These related emperors were the Julio-Claudians, taking their name from Julius Caesar.

Nero's demise brought on some 21 months of confusion and civil war, as first Galba, then Otho, and last Vitellius became emperors. The able Vespasian, conqueror of the Jewish revolution, established the Flavian dynasty which ended in the assassination of his son, Domitian.

Domitian was the last emperor to influence the New Testament world. However, the next era is important for the information which can be read from it backward into the previous decades (though this practice must be done with care). It began with Nerva, who, advanced in both years and wisdom, established a new era of peace by adopting the able Trajan as his successor.

During the span of years covered by the reigns of Augustus to Domitian several significant developments evolved: the use of client kings versus governors vacillated, but the Empire progressed during the period to favor governors over client kings; slavery produced a society in which development of some technologies were retarded due to cheap labor; against this disadvantage, slavery provided a process by which divergent cultures were assimilated into the Roman world as the slaves were freed; and citizenship was granted ever more widely.

Several areas of study in regard to the emperors are important to the New Testament and its world. The policies of each emperor in regard to the establishment of provincial boundaries, establishment of colonies, recognition of specific cities for various honors, trade policies, policies regarding the Empire's wider borders, attitude toward Eastern religions, the emperor's view and that of others regarding his deity and how that deity was honored locally, the use of the arts for propaganda, and the degree of involvement in the administration of provinces are but a few matters that should impact New Testament study.

In addition to these direct areas, each emperor's dress and behavior trickled down to be copied in whole or part by his subjects. Nero, for example, gave great impetus to the arts and sports. An emperor's favorite god or goddess was honored correspondingly by some subjects. An emperor's personal preferences could influence others to the degree that trade in those commodities would develop.

Again, each emperor's policies should be considered apart—to some degree, at least—from his personal life. Domitian, for example, is pictured as a horrible madman who caused great persecution for Christians. He must be held accountable for his atrocities, but he must also be evaluated for his administrative ability, tyrant though he was.

In addition to the emperors themselves, their reigns were impacted as much or more by their choice of advisers and aides as by their own views and policies. The evils of Tiberius' rule, for example, were due more to his right-hand man Sejanus than to himself.

The Civil War, Julius Caesar, Jane F. Mitchell, translator (New York: Penguin Books), 1976; *Fall of the Roman Republic*, Plutarch, Rex Warner, translator (New York: Penguin Books), 1958; *The Twelve Caesars*, Suetonius, Robert Graves, translator (New York: Penguin Books), 1957; *The Histories*, Tacitus, Kenneth Wellesley, translator (New York: Penguin Books), 1972; *The Annals of Imperial Rome*, Tacitus, Michael Grant, translator (New York: Penguin Books), 1971; *Cambridge Ancient History*, Volume VII; *The British Museum and Its Collections* (London: The Trustees of the British Museum), 1982; *The World History of the Jewish People: The Herodian Period*, Michael Avi-Yonah, editor (New Brunswick: Rutgers University Press), 1975; *The Capitoline Collections*, Settimo Bocconi (Rome: Museo Capitolino), 1950; *History of Rome*, Michael Grant (New York: Charles Scribner's Sons), 1978; *Twelve Caesars*, Michael Grant (New York: Charles Scribner's Sons, 1975); *Oxford Classical Dictionary*, Second Edition, N. G. L. Hammond and H. H. Scullard, editors (Oxford: Clarendon Press), 1970; *Greek and Roman Portraits*, Anton Hekler (Hacker Books), 1972; *The Roman World of Dio Chrysostom*, C. P. Jones (Cambridge: Harvard University Press), 1978; *Wars*, Josephus (*The Words of Flavius Josephus*, translated by William Whiston; London: Ward, Lock, & Co.); *Reading and Dating Roman Imperial Coins*, Zander H. Klawans (New York: Sanford J. Durst Numismatic Publications), 1982; *The Grand Strategy of the Roman Empire*, Edward N. Luttwak (Baltimore: The Johns Hopkins University Press), 1976; *The Roman Imperial Coinage*, Vol. I, Harold Mattingly and Edward A. Sydenham (London: Spink and Son, Ltd.), 1948; *The Provinces of the Roman Empire: The European Provinces*, Theodor Mommsen (Chicago: The University of Chicago Press), 1968; *Roman Literature and Society*, R. M. Ogilvie (New York: Penguin Books), 1980; *Ancient Rome*, Robert Payne (New York: American Heritage Press), 1970; *The Harvest of Hellenism*, F. E. Peters (New York: Simon and Schuster), 1970; *The New Testament Era*, Bo Reicke (Philadelphia: Fortress Press), 1964; *Rome in the Augustan Age*, Henry Thompson Rowell (Norman, Oklahoma: University of Oklahoma Press), 1962; *Roman Society and Roman Law in the New Testament*, A. N. Sherwin-White (Grand Rapids: Baker Book House), 1963; *Civilization and the Caesars*, Chester G. Starr (New York: W. W. Norton and Co., Inc.), 1965; *Coinage in Roman Imperial Policy: 31 BC—AD 68*, C. H. V. Sutherland (New York: Sanford J. Durst Numismatic Publications), 1978; *Dictionary of Roman Coin Inscriptions*, Stewart J. Westdal (New York: Sanford J. Durst Numismatic Publications), 1982.

JULIUS CAESAR

Gaius Julius Caesar was born in 100 BC into an era of enormous social conflict. As all Roman young men, he began his career as a military officer, serving in Asia (where rumors of his homosexuality began, though the evidence apparently was limited to one occurrence).

Then he served in Cilicia. He was aggressively energetic, brilliant, and daring, willing literally to gamble for the world. He spent some time studying in Rhodes and was captured by pirates, and then ransomed. He sought his captors out, killed them, and crucified their dead bodies.

After considerable political intrigue, Gaius was appointed consul. The very popular Pompey was constantly frustrated by the competition of Crassus and Caesar. The three of them formed the First Triumvirate, assigning specific benefits to each. Caesar was given special command in Illyricum and Gaul for five years, to which another five years later was added. This charge offered the greatest promise of fame. While there, he expanded his regular army with legions loyal personally to him. He used every pretext to battle with the Gaul tribes until he extended the province to the Rhine River and even invaded Britain. He put together the most awesome and effective army the world had seen up to that time. With the spoils from those battles, he was able to court popular opinion and extend his power.

Crassus' fall came with his ill-advised attempt to invade the Parthian Empire. He was killed at Carrhae (Harran) in 55 BC and lost the Roman emblems, a great embarrassment to the Roman people.

▼ **2 Portrait bust of Gaius Julius Caesar,** dates to about 44 BC, copy, Roman-German Central Museum, Mainz. The original in the Staatliche Museum, Berlin, is made from Egyptian green slate. The place of discovery is unknown, probably Italian. A piece of the toga on the right side and a piece of the right ear are restored.

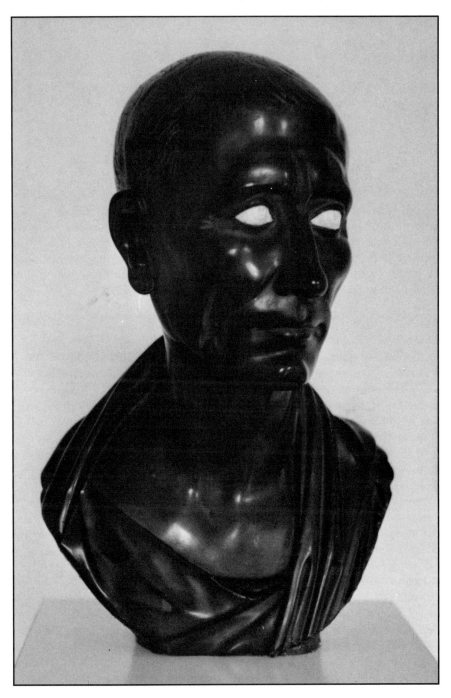

▲ **3 Coin of Julius Caesar,** issued 49-44 BC. Museum of Art and Archaeology, University of Missouri-Columbia. The elephant (obverse) is one of the most abundant type. Note the armor on legs of the elephant, which tramples a serpent. Coin also shows, on reverse, the pontificate emblems. Julius Caesar's earliest coinages date from 49 BC and were struck for his Gallic army. His image was the first to appear on Roman coins during the person's lifetime, but perhaps his innovation was acceptable since others regularly followed suit.

provinces, projecting or creating over 30 colonies, many of them in Spain. Carthage and Corinth were refounded as colonies, as were a few in Asia Minor. He intended the established communities to serve as centers of Romanization.

He undertook new building projects, including temples, a theater, public libraries, draining of marches, an extensive highway, and a plan for the Corinth canal. He wrested the Roman government from a tired and manipulated Republican base and established a dictatorship. Suetonius described Caesar as being tall, well-built, and fair, but bald and subject to epileptic seizures. He was given to luxury, and his affairs with women were notorious, but he was not a drinker. The Roman historian considered him to be as good or better at oratory and military affairs than anyone else. Suetonius recognized Caesar's good points, but listed a series of excessive honors and indulgences that he believed justified his assassination: taking titles of Imperator and Father of his Country, setting his statue among those of the ancient kings, establishing his own cult, and demeaning the Senate. Caesar's policy was designed to connect him with divinity; one of his statues even shared the temple of Jupiter. Over 60 conspirators banded together to assassinate him; he was 55 years of age and ill. His will left much of his estate to Octavius, his sister's grandson, and he adopted Octavius into his family.

Julius Caesar was buried with great honor and public mourning, Jews being prominent among foreigners. Later, in 42 BC, a temple of the deified Julius was begun and dedicated in 28 BC; its remains have been excavated.

Caesar's own extant writings include *The Civil War, An Essay on Analogy, Answers to Cato,* and *The Journey.*

Pompey, who had remained in Rome, had to act to stop Caesar's enormously increased power.

He brought together Caesar's opponents, such men as Catallus, Varro, and Cicero. Caesar's response was to begin the civil war. He crossed the small but crucial Rubicon, the river boundary between Italy and Gaul, and through various maneuvers bested Pompey, who fled to Egypt and was murdered by Ptolemy XIII. Ptolemy's act gave Caesar a pretext for declaring war, which he won against considerable odds. Afterward, he moved from Egypt to Syria to Pontus, winning victories as he went, then returned to North Africa and destroyed Scipio and his supporter King Juba.

Back in Rome, he celebrated 5 triumphs in quick succession: the Gallic, Alexandrian, Pontic, African, and Spanish. His victories brought scores of thousands of slaves, the untrained providing cheap manpower for a great many activities, the trained becoming tutors to the Romans. Celebrations, which he paid for, included gladiatorial contests and theatricals, a mock battle between 2 armies (each 500 strong plus elephants and cavalry), and a mock naval battle in an artificially built lake.

He reorganized the calendar, which badly needed revision, reformed voter registration, admitted many professionals to citizenship, sought to reform the laws (showing some desire for justice), and established a policy of moving citizens, especially soldiers, to

AUGUSTUS

The influence of Augustus on Western history is almost beyond comprehension. His skills pulled together an empire and thoroughly set the course of future centuries. His time is called the Augustan Age, from 31 BC to his death in AD 14. To be sure, the exciting progress of the time began before him and continued after him; but Augustus had the skill to use the events and movements to his and the empire's advantage.

Gaius Octavius was born on September 23, 63 BC in Rome. His family was of equestrian rank, but Gaius' father was able to marry a sister of Julius Caesar, which allowed him to embark on a senatorial career. Caesar's later adoption of Gaius was a stroke of immense luck, for it provided the future Augustus both with wealth and a propaganda base from which to build his attempt for the emperorship. Augustus' *Res Gestae* tells the story of his strategies and wars as he rose to power.

The long Roman civil wars and other causes had resulted in lawlessness. Augustus outlawed the workers' guilds, which often were fronts for outlaws, and took other measures to make roads safe for travel. He reformed many laws, seeking to favor marriage and large families; limited access to Roman citizenship by freedmen, though his changes actually made it easier to move from one class to another; and limited public freedom for women. He established 28 colonies for veterans and established a message system for keeping in touch with provinces. He improved provincial government, established the first permanent army and navy, and allowed local customs to prevail wherever possible.

▲ **4 Portrait bust, Augustus as a lad.** Roman-German Landesmuseum, Cologne. The features are similar to a larger bust of Augustus in the Vatican Museum. *Luke 2:1.*

Augustus' goals to expand the empire are debated; but whether by plan or for expediency, he set about to consolidate areas of conquest. By 25 BC he organized Spain into three provinces, Baetica, Lusitania, and Tarraconensis. He formed three provinces of Gaul: Aquitania, Lugdunensis, and Belgica. Augustus renamed southern Gaul as Narbonensis; stopped efforts to conquer Germany east of the Rhine and consolidated the area to the west; organized the area south of the Danube, part of which he included in Italy, the rest becoming provinces of Raetia and Noricum. After fierce fighting, Illyricum was organized into Dalmatia and Pannonia. He reinstituted the Delphic Amphictyony, an ancient political organization of Greek states, so that all of the Greek lands were included under its banner; however,

its powers were limited to the administration of the important sanctuary at Delphi.

His sympathies lay with the West, so he founded few colonies in the Eastern provinces. The cities of a province were classified according to the privileges they possessed. At the top were the *coloniae civium Romanorum* (almost all towns to which military settlers had been sent); then came the *municipia* or *oppida civium Romanorum* (inhabitants possessed franchise); then the *Latin* were next (citizenship could be obtained by holding a magistracy; these had an aristocracy of Roman citizens). Other cities enjoyed various special privileges, a few among them calling themselves "free" or "federate" communities, a somewhat anachronistic term.

In the East the franchise was given less freely than in the West, for Augustus had projected himself as champion of the West in his battles with Antony.

Augustus' own earlier provinces comprised, roughly speaking, Gaul, Spain, Egypt, Syria, and the more backward parts of Asia Minor; the Senate was responsible for the rest of the empire. In 22 BC Gaul Narbonensis was transferred to the Senate, and at an unknown date so was Baetica. Illyricum was transferred from the Senate to Augustus in 11 BC due to the wars there. The new provinces acquired in Augustus' reign came under his rule: Galatia, Raetia, Noricum, Pannonia, and Moesia.

The system of appointment of governors which prevailed throughout the Principate was largely Augustus' creation. When a man had held the praetorship he was qualified to become proconsul of a less important province. Of the senatorial provinces Asia and Africa were governed by consulors, the rest by praetorians.

Assignments usually were made by lot and appointments were for a year, with exceptions made. Augustus' governors were appointed by him and were answerable directly to him; he was not hampered by rigid rules. Galatia was a praetorian province. Every province may not have had a separate governor (we aren't sure).

Men of equestrian order sometimes were assigned governorships of newly conquered provinces. Except for Egypt, which had a legionary force, the equites had only auxilia. In the East, most important of these was Judea; in the West, Raetia and Noricum.

Client kingdoms were Armenia, Judea until AD 6, Thrace, Mauretania, and Cappadocia. Each province, too, had its equestrian procurator who, in the eyes of the locals, was almost as important as a governor. They were appointed by the emperor; relations between locals and governors were not friendly.

Augustus' reforms of provincial administration were good for Rome.

Taxes were equitably distributed, revenue went to Rome and not to middlemen, governors were selected carefully, and extortion charges were given a hearing.

Galatia, a client kingdom, became a province in 25 BC, and a string of client kingdoms continued to the east to the Armenian mountains. Peace was made with Parthia, while Syria and Judea were given attention for tax purposes.

Egypt, with its vast grain reserves, was retained personally by Augustus so that no ambitious senator could build a power base from there. Egypt was required to provide one-third of the annual supply of grain needed by Rome. North Africa was already organized into the provinces of Cyrenaica and Africa and the client kingdom of Mauretania.

In addition to Egypt, Augustus retained personal control of Syria, Gaul, northern Spain, Cilicia, and Cyprus. Pragmatically, Augustus allowed Herod to retain his throne and even extended his rule to include some Transjordanian cities, the Bashan, Trachonitis, and Auranitis (to support the empire's anti-Nabatean policy). When Herod I died, Augustus made Samaria, Judea, and Idumea a personal province.

Due to Tarsus' support of Julius Caesar, he granted it the status of free city with numerous benefits and honors. His rule, too, greatly benefited Bithynia. Candace, queen of Ethiopia, had some sort of diplomatic relationship with him.

Augustus' policies of consolidating the empire and making the roads safe established a "Roman Peace" (*Pax Romana*) that lasted for 2 centuries. He ordered the doors of the temple of Janus closed 3 times during his reign, an act that signified peace throughout the empire. They had been closed only twice in all of Roman history previously.

The emperor was thorough in his vision and execution. He was

▼ 5 **Portrait bust, Augustus,** dates from time of battle of Actium in 31 BC, marble, height of head is 1 foot, 2 inches (.37 m.). Capitoline Museum, Rome. He is pictured as gentle and wise. *Luke 2:1.*

skilled in administration, commerce, and propaganda, all of which were essential elements in the creation of the empire. His organization of the provinces and pacification of the travelways made possible the blossoming of commercial enterprises that extended into India and even, by extension, into China.

Businessmen traveled the world in search of new avenues for profit. He opened up administrative posts to the equestrian class, which effectively took power from the senatorial class and gave it to people who had proved their business and administrative talent.

Roman citizens were willing to give up precious liberties for the security his rule provided, and they indeed gave up much. Augustus began the *curcus publicu*, posting stations erected along trunk roads; he inaugurated a police system, set up a network of informers, accounted as treason any slight insult even to a statue of his likeness, and discouraged freedom of thought.

His discouragement of freedom of thought is ironic, for under Augustus the arts flourished as they never had among the Romans. He used the arts to accomplish his ends, which included personal propaganda and efforts to revive the Roman spirit and create pride in being a Roman.

Having learned well from the mistakes of his uncle, Augustus studiously avoided the titles and honors that led to Julius Caesar's assassination; yet he accepted and skillfully encouraged titles and honors that had real power in them. He encouraged, or at least did not discourage, the Eastern provinces to worship him as a god, usually in conjunction with Rome; such worship of rulers was common in Hellenism. The divine veneration of Augustus arose spontaneously; such practices in the East were traditional. To be the priest of Augustus in a province *(flamen)* was an

honor. In some districts, however, the government took the initiative for emperor worship, as on the Rhine.

Rome already had produced some good writers, such as Virgil, Horace, and Propertius; Augustus used them for propaganda. A major goal of the emperor was to link Rome's history with that of the Greek world.

Virgil's *Aeneid* did just that; it stated the purpose the gods had for Rome to rule the world, and it prophesied the rise of a savior (an unveiled reference to Augustus). Aeneas was Augustus' ancestor, and Aeneas' mother was Venus; thus Augustus was descended himself from Venus. Horace composed a poem about Apollo that obviously praised Augustus for taking him as his patron god.

He encouraged and supported all kinds of entertainment, including athletics, the theater, gladiatorial contests, and other amphitheater activities.

He also sought to make Rome look like a world capital, boasting, "I found Rome built of bricks; I leave her clothed in marble." Suetonius considered Augustus' best works to be his Forum with its temple of Mars, the temple of Apollo on the Palatine (the hill on which Augustus had his palace), and the temple of Jupiter on the Capitoline hill. He built a great many other buildings as well and strongly encouraged the wealthy to be patrons of such building projects.

The emperor was chief magistrate, commander of all armies, the holder of the treasury, and the chief high priest. In spite of his extensive laws and complaints against promiscuous and luxurious living, he was a notorious womanizer and gambler. He gave many dinner parties, but they were not extravagant, and he drank little. His palace was simple, much smaller in fact than most villas, and simply furnished. Suetonius pictured him as hand-

▲ 6 **Portrait bust, Augustus as high priest.** Roman-German Landesmuseum, Cologne. The head is from a togate statue. The emperor has the edge of his toga pulled over his head, the manner in which a high priest offers a sacrifice. The portrait thus pictures him as the highest priest of the Empire. His hairstyle is similar to that portrayed on the Ara Pacis in Rome. He maintained this hairstyle up to near his death. *Luke 2:1; 1 Corinthians 11:4-15.*

some and graceful but negligent of his personal appearance. He was superstitious and paid attention to omens. Tacitus described him as power hungry and ruthless. He died on August 19, AD 14 at 75 years of age.

TIBERIUS

Tiberius Claudius Nero was born in 58 BC and named after his father; his mother was Livia, whom Augustus later married. Suetonius tells that Tiberius' childhood years were difficult ones in which his father and mother had to flee often from Augustus during the Civil War years. Later, he spent 22 years as a commander of armies, serving longer than any Roman patrician of the period, and with great distinction.

He married Agrippina, daughter of Augustus' right-hand man Agrippa, a union that proved to be a happy one. Agrippa was married to Augustus' daughter Julia. When Agrippa died, Augustus forced Tiberius to divorce Agrippina, whom he loved dearly and who was pregnant with their second child, and marry Julia, whom he strongly disliked. Historians debate the effect this tragedy had on Tiberius, but it surely affected him deeply.

At the height of his career he retired abruptly to Rhodes, some 6 years after his marriage to the notoriously promiscuous Julia, perhaps to escape an unhappy marriage, perhaps not to appear as a rival to Augustus' 2 grandchildren for the throne. When he later sought to return to Rome, Augustus refused him permission; Tiberius found himself in exile on Rhodes. Only after 7 years away from Rome was he allowed to return, after continued intervention by Livia.

Within 3 years, Gaius and Lucius, Augustus' grandsons who were his candidates to follow him, died. Even so, Augustus still had reservations about Tiberius' character for the office, so he forced him to adopt Germanicus, Tiberius' nephew. The reality was apparent, however, that Tiberius was the only real alternative as the next emperor, so Augustus adopted him and began systematically to elevate him publicly. Tiberius had to take to the field again to combat the Illyricum revolt. When he returned he was given joint control with Augustus of the provinces. He was, in fact, responsible for maintaining stability of the empire during Augustus' last years. By AD 13 Tiberius' powers were equal to those of Augustus, who died one year later.

Tiberius' character indeed did not suit him for the emperorship, not because he was incapable but because he did not have Augustus' sense of the opportune. Tiberius was secretive and a poor communicator; he disliked the public

▼ 7 **Bust, Tiberius,** Capitoline Museum, Rome. The features represent Tiberius when he was young; he wears a characteristic melancholy expression. *Matthew 22:17; Luke 3:1; 20:22-25; John 6:1; 21:1.*

games, and he admittedly disliked the burden of being emperor.

At first he acted circumspectly, rejecting flattery and honors, and he refused to punish slanderers. Indeed, he was a republican at heart and had little stomach for the direction Augustus had been taking Rome. Yet he knew that he had no choice but to continue the direction.

Gradually, though, his policies revealed a heavier hand. He cut down on public entertainment, issued edicts against behavior he considered to be frivolous, exiled men and women who resigned from their class in order to pursue careers and activities otherwise unacceptable, abolished foreign cults at Rome and exiled Jews of military age to unhealthy climates, crushed public riots without mercy, abolished the traditional right of sanctuary, and began to force the execution of many accused of treason on the flimsiest excuse.

Tiberius was a good fiscal administrator in spite of his faults. He governed the provinces carefully, cutting back on expensive building programs and other costs. He advised his governors, "You should shear my sheep, not flay them." The empire as a whole continued in peace and prosperity. The road system was expanded across North Africa, city planning began in Antioch, and previous defeats at the hands of Germanic tribes were avenged. He reduced the client state system by annexing Cappadocia, Commagene, and Hierapolis-Castabala; and he detached the undeveloped part of Cilicia (Cilicia Tracheia) and assigned it along with Lycaonia to the deposed ruler of Cappadocia. In Galilee, Herod Antipas built and named Tiberias after him. In an attempt to limit the bleeding of provinces, Tiberius required longer tenures of his governors.

His greatest mistake came when in AD 20 he took Sejanus, head of

▲8 **Coin of Tiberius,** bronze as, issued in Rome, AD 14. Milwaukee Museum of Art. The coin is a portrait of the deified Augustus, which Tiberius regularly issued. Augustus is shown wearing the aureus; the radiant signifies deification. The coin is struck off center. Lettering running up right: DIVVS AVGVSTVS PATER = Divine Augustus Father (of his country). Asses were issued only at intervals during Tiberius' reign. A denarius (not shown) sometimes is referred to as the famous "tribute penny" of Luke 22:24 because it was issued during Tiberius' reign. The obverse of a denarius had either the quadriga (4-horse chariot) or the head of the deified Augustus, and on the reverse an enthroned female with the attributes of Pax and Justitia, sometimes identified as Livia. *Texts: See photo 7.*

the Praetorian Guard, as his principal adviser. Sejanus took every opportunity to enhance his position, and it was after his appointment that the treason trials became frequent. To compound the problem, Tiberius moved to the island of Capri off the coast of Naples, never to return to Rome. Tiberius tried to govern, but his obscure writing style made the process of governing from Capri impossible.

Suetonius wrote appalling stories of Tiberius' sexual deviancy on Capri, but most historians discount their accuracy. Eventually he came to realize Sejanus' ambitions; he had him executed and every remembrance of him was removed. The treason trials increased, however, after Sejanus' death, and the last 6 years of Tiberius' reign were terrifying ones for Roman politicians.

He died at Misemum on March 16, AD 37 at the age of 79 after appointing Caligula as his successor. He had reigned for 23 years. Tacitus provided an extensive account of Tiberius' career, including much about Sejanus. His concluding paragraph describes Tiberius as a person of competence, with some good qualities, so long as people lived who restrained him. But in the end his "perversions" were revealed, "then fear vanished, and with it shame. Thereafter he expressed only his own personality—by unrestrained crime and infamy."

CALIGULA

Gaius was born in AD 12 at Antium (Anzio), Italy to the very popular Germanicus, whom Augustus had forced Tiberius to adopt. Caligula, meaning "little boots," was Gaius' nickname, given to him because he wore little army boots while an infant in Germany with his parents. Germanicus died, perhaps by poison, when Gaius was 7, and subsequently his mother and 2 brothers met their deaths in Tiberius' political intrigues. Tiberius summoned him to Capri when he was 18, apparently to groom him for the emperorship. In AD 37, at Tiberius' death, Caligula was acclaimed emperor; he was 25 years of age.

Caligula restored the honor of his family members who were executed during Tiberius' reign by such acts as placing their images on coinage. One of his earliest acts was to banish from Rome all male prostitutes; he even threatened to drown them all. He completed the temple of Augustus and Pompey's theater begun by Tiberius, began an aquaduct and an amphitheater in Rome, and completed several other projects in the empire, including the Didymaean Apollo's temple at Ephesus. He also surveyed the Corinth isthmus for a canal.

However, Suetonius recorded his contributions rather quickly and then cryptically stated, "So much for the Emperor; the rest of the story must deal with the Monster." The account continues with an account of one of the most sadistic spirits ever described in literature, including a variety of bizarre and dehumanizing sexual practices and incredible bloodthirstiness.

Though his reign began propitiously enough, his zeal soon waned. He spent little time in ruling; as a result Greek freedmen gained significantly in power. Many of them were from Alexandria and were prejudiced against the Jews; they were able to influence Caligula. Ironically, Jews were pleased with him at first. His unification of the tetrarchies of Philip and Herod Antipas under the kingship of Agrippa I and appointment of a pro-Jewish governor of Syria were positive moves for the Jews.

But through the Alexandrians' influence, Jews were persecuted in Egypt. Then, Caligula's determination to be treated as a god coupled with his ill will toward Jews caused him to order his statue in the guise of Zeus to be set up in the Jerusalem Temple. Agrippa I and the governor of Syria, one Petronius, were able to postpone enactment of Caligula's order for a time. With his assassination the danger ended, but not before several uprisings in Judea had taken place in protest.

Caligula was passionately devoted to entertainment, often participating as a dancer or gladiator. Suetonius found very little positive to say about Caligula and a great deal to abhor. His bloodthirstiness was as bizarre as his sexual deviancies. He is reputed to have been incestuous with his sister Drusilla. Because meat was too expensive he fed criminals to the wild animals to be used in the circus; Suetonius enumerates a number of such examples. His expenses were so enormous as to drain the treasury, causing him to tax and take possession of property so ruthlessly that he drove the robbed citizens to suicide. Part of his reason for these economic actions was to obtain funds; his extravagances depleted the state treasury even though Tiberius had left behind the enormous sum of 27 million gold pieces. He may have had epilepsy and may have known that he was mad, and he suffered from insomnia. He was both irreligious and superstitious.

While he did not believe in the gods, he felt his own deification was a useful political tool. Augustus and Tiberius were careful to avoid the Eastern image of imperial ruler; Gaius impatiently declared, "Nay, let there be one master, and one king!" and he insisted on being treated as a god. He had a temple erected to himself and in it was placed a lifesize gold statue of himself. Every day the statue was dressed in clothes exactly like the ones he wore. He talked directly to the gods, even speaking in the ears of their statues and, according to Suetonius, was overheard threatening Jupiter.

Gaius reversed Tiberius' policy regarding client states; he restored Commagene to the deposed king and added Cilicia Tracheia to the king's territory. He assigned Pontus, Lesser Armenia, half of Thrace, and Ituraea (Golan Heights region) to kings or tetrarchs, all of whom had been his playmates (Agrippa I was one of them); and he annexed Mauretania.

Caligula's assassination was accomplished during a theater intermission when the emperor was talked into taking a walk with some friends. He was stabbed repeatedly, his body half-cremated and buried in a shallow grave. His wife and child were also murdered. Caligula was 29 and had reigned for just less than 4 years.

▼9 Bust of Caligula. Glyptothek, Copenhagen. The portrait is an approximate likeness but is a typical emperor style. Gaius was bald and was extremely conscious of it. He wears a diadem and crown and is dressed in a cuirass with an image of the sun god.

▲10 Coin of Caligula. Sesterces, AD 39-41, the temple of the deified Augustus. Roman-German Landesmuseum, Cologne. The depiction served as propaganda for Caligula to be identified with Augustus and his divinity. Caligula used coins in a manner similar to that of the Eastern kings, adding divine attributes to himself or otherwise associating himself with divinity. He used coinage, too, to bolster his standing with the army, which was a major support for his emperorship. To that end, he issued coins of himself addressing troops. On the coins, he is shown bareheaded, wearing a toga, and speaking from a platform.

CLAUDIUS

▲ 11 **Bust, Claudius,** Capitoline Museum, Rome. The emperor is shown in an idealized form, yet his features basically reflect his likeness. *Acts 11:28; 18:2.*

Tiberius Claudius Nero Germanicus was born on August 1, 10 BC in Lyon. His only experience in government was a consulship given him by Caligula. Both Augustus and Tiberius had passed over him because of his physical handicaps, about which his family had been embarrassed and because of which they treated him with scorn. Deprived of a political career, he filled his time with scholarly studies and the writing of some significant history books.

When Caligula was assassinated in AD 41, Claudius was the only surviving member of the Julio-Claudian family. The army was strongly attached to that family, so the Praetorian Guard proclaimed him emperor at age 50. But his studies apparently had good effect, for he understood the past and made some good judgments.

Claudius gave attention particularly to the judicial system, hearing many cases himself. Suetonius accused him of being inconsistent, sometimes showing a strong sense of equity, sometimes acting in haste; yet Claudius seemed genuinely to have been concerned about those who were weak. Once, for example, he found that some sick slaves had been abandoned to die by their owner; he freed them. He extended the law courts, held previously only during the summer and the winter, to include the entire year. He softened the ban on guilds to allow such groups for purposes of common worship or burial. His most significant public work was the building of a major harbor, thus shifting Rome's major seaport from Puteoli to the much closer Ostia. He added major roads to the Empire's system, in addition to major projects close to Rome.

Claudius continued Caligula's return to the client king system, making a few provident changes in kingships; he also extended Agrippa I's rule to include Judea and Samaria. When Agrippa died, however, Claudius made Judea a province once more, which it remained until 66. In AD 50 he gave Agrippa II some minor territories. Claudius administered the provinces with great care and involvement. He affirmed the rights of Jews once again, but with some cautions. His decision to make Judea a province in 44 renewed the Zealot movement but also was an asset to the Christian missionary movement.

He sought to extend Roman citizenship more widely into the provinces and opened the Senate a bit to people from the Western, but not Eastern, provinces. He also extended the Roman frontier to include southern and central England to create the province of Britannia.

Claudius' act most famous among modern Christians was his expulsion of Jews from Rome because of "continuous disturbances at the instigation of Chrestus." Scholars speculate that "Chrestus" is a misspelling of "Christus"; if so, the event may indicate conflict between Christians and Jews of Rome and may have been the occasion when Priscilla and Aquila left Rome.

Claudius, without a background in the army or politics, had few friends among the ruling class whom he could depend on. Consequently, he used freedmen to aid him in the administration of the empire; one of these, Felix, was made governor of Judea. He had two freedmen in his service who were his right-hand men, Narcissus and Pallas. Narcissus suppressed a plot to seize power by Claudius' third wife, Messalina, who was executed.

Perhaps the plot by Messalina was the cause of Claudius' increasing concern about plots; he was guilty of executing 35 senators and 200-300 knights. After Messalina's execution, Claudius married his niece, Agrippina (the younger), who gained more and more power as Claudius became more infirm by age and overwork. She was aided by Pallas, who became her principal adviser. Agrippina was the mother of the next emperor, Nero, whom in AD 50 she convinced Claudius to adopt with the intention that he should be the next ruler, at the expense of Claudius' own son Britannicus. Agrippina was exceedingly aggressive; for the first time in Roman history authority was concentrated in the hands of a woman. She even was called Augusta, a feat no other wife of a living emperor had been able to accomplish.

Suetonius described Claudius as one who gave splendid banquets and championed many games, was a notorious womanizer, was given to gambling, was exceptionally absentminded, had disagreeable physical traits and habits due to his illness, but nevertheless "had a certain majesty and dignity of presence." Most scholars feel that he was the most timorous and suspicious of any of the emperors, possibly due to his physical condition.

Claudius died in October, AD 54, at 63 years of age. The most widely publicized version of the cause of death was that Agrippina had poisoned him. Nero was 17; Agrippina was in effect regent.

▲ **13 Coin of Claudius,** with his likeness. Museum of Art and Archaeology, University of Missouri-Columbia. The lettering is: TI CLAVDIVS CAESAR AVG P M TR P IMP P P = Tiberius Claudius Caesar Augustus Pontifex Maximus Tribunicia Potestas Imperator Pater Patriae. The reverse of the coin, not shown, has Minerva. Some of Claudius' coins clearly demonstrate the collapse of republican ideas and the codification of the Principate as an institution; they have the legend "Imperial Liberty" (Libertas Augusta) and the figure of the goddess of liberty, which had last been seen on the issues of Brutus. Claudius thus proclaimed himself as the protector of liberty but sealed authority in the principate. A new imperial virtue is commemorated on the coins of his reign, right from the very beginning: it is Constantia, personification of perseverance. With the successful southern Britain campaign, Claudius minted gold and silver coins with advertisements of the victory. Museum photo. *Acts 11:28; 18:18; Galatians 5:1-13; Ephesians 6:18.*

▼ **12 Marble bust, possibly Antonia,** as she sometimes has been identified. British Museum. She was Claudius' mother, the daughter of Mark Antony and Octavia, and was famous for her beauty. She described her son as a monster. The bust rises from a flower.

NERO

Lucius Domitius Ahenobarbus was born on December 15, AD 37, at Antium. His mother was the notorious Agrippina; his father was Cnaeus Domitius Ahenobarbus, of an ancient and noble Roman family, but one whom Suetonius accused of cruelty and dishonesty. His childhood years saw him grow up in difficult circumstances; his mother was exiled by Caligula and his father died the following year.

Claudius recalled Agrippina from exile and later married her in AD 49. Seneca became his tutor; Claudius adopted him as the future emperor in AD 50, at which time Nero's name became Nero Claudius Drusus Germanicus. When Claudius died in 54, Nero became emperor at age 17. Agrippina in effect became ruler of the empire; the first coins issued during Nero's reign had her image beside his, with hers in the favored position. But her ascendency did not last long. Within a year her position began to decline while Seneca and Burrus gained power. In 59 Nero had his mother put to death, fearing that she was guilty of subversion.

After Agrippina's death, Seneca and Burrus found Nero harder and harder to control. During the early years, however, he ruled well. Extortion by provincial governors was curtailed, and reforms were made at Rome. He abhorred the frequent deaths that the empire's traditions made necessary, such as the killing of gladiators in the arena and the slaughter of all an owner's slaves if one killed his master.

Apparently at some time classes of crimes performed by Roman citizens could be punished by provincial governors with no right of appeal to Rome; these innovations may date to Nero. Nero deferred the hearing of cases to his princeps, whose opinions he then confirmed unless he had a particular interest in a case. Paul may have appeared before a princep rather than Nero himself. The emperor also had the Isthmus at Corinth surveyed for a canal, but work barely began on it before it was abandoned.

Nero probably should not have been an emperor; he was much more interested in the arts and personally performing in them. He was interested, too, in rowdy living, dinner parties, sexual activities, and luxury. One of his dinner parties could last 12 hours. With his art and his parties, he had little time to rule. The Empire outside of Rome was little affected, however; the administration continued hardly abated.

When Burrus died in 62, Seneca resigned; Nero replaced them with 2 praetorian prefects, Faenius Rufus and Gaius Ofonius Tigellinus. The latter exerted great influence; one of his actions was to aid Nero to divorce Octavia and to marry Poppaea, the wife of the later emperor Otho. Later he kicked her to death while she was pregnant and ill.

In 64 Nero began his public appearances as a performer, debuting at Neapolis (Naples), whose inhabitants were Greek (he was decidedly pro-Greek). Nero's reign thus would be thought to be one when the arts were encouraged, but Nero was too jealous of rivals for that to happen.

AD 64 also was the year of the Great Fire of Rome. Historians are not agreed on Nero's complicity, but at the time he was suspected of setting the fire to make room for his planned Golden House, an incredible project in size, extravagance, and expense. (The magnificent structure did not last long; it was destroyed right after his death.) To divert blame for the fire from himself, he blamed the Christians. Tertullian claimed that laws outlawing Christianity dated back to Nero; the laws stayed in effect, with varying levels of enforcement, until the reign of Severus. Both Peter and Paul suffered martyrdom under him.

Nero embarked on a massive propaganda campaign through the use of coinage. His images that appear on them combine his true features with features of grandeur, while the inscriptions list his great contributions to the people. He supported his artistic performances on coins as well—they were severely criticized as unbecoming an emperor—by depicting references to Apollo (the lyre-playing god) and to military operations (for his chariot-racing).

Nero avoided unnecessary military operations, but some important actions transpired. He put down a revolt in Britain; war with the Parthians was concluded with a treaty favorable to Rome; and Vespasian was dispatched to Judea to deal with the rebellion there. The kingdom of Pontus was ceded to him as a province by King Polemo, and the province of the Cottian Alps reverted to Rome upon the client king's death. He assigned Pontus and Lesser Armenia to the province of Galatia, which made the new boundaries very extensive.

A conspiracy to assassinate Nero developed in 65 which involved many well-placed Romans. It was discovered in time, and 51 people were charged. Many of them were executed, including Seneca, while others were banished. The discov-

▲14 Julio-Claudian, probably Nero, veiled as a priest. Corinth Museum. In this head and neck portrait, Nero has a light beard down his cheek and under his chin. Since beards were not in style for Romans during the first century AD, he was expressing himself. His hair comes onto his brow some- what as Augustus wore his, which was a common style. With his toga pulled over his head, he appears as the Pontifex Maximus—the high priest of the Empire—who was the bridge between the gods and the people. *1 Corinthians 11:4,7,13-15.*

ery of the event was celebrated with a coin inscribed SECVRITAS AVGUSTI (the safety of the emperor). The following year other plots, or alleged plots, were uncovered and a reign of terror toward the Roman nobility began. During these dangerous times, Nero was on a triumphal tour of Greece, appearing on stage and in chariot races. He was awarded 1,808 prizes for his performances! In return, or perhaps for his love of Greece, in 67 he granted the province of Achaea freedom from taxation.

The tendency toward revolt grew, and Nero returned to Rome after much coaxing. Unable or unwilling to respond to the growing threats, including Galba's declaration in Spain of himself as emperor, his supporters left him until he committed suicide by stabbing himself in the throat. The date was June 9, AD 68. He was 31 years old, the last of Augustus' line. Suetonius described him as of average height, with light blond hair, blue eyes, a squat neck, pretty but not handsome, with a protuberant belly and spindly legs. Suetonius furthered the belief that Nero really did not die but would someday reappear and confound his enemies. The myth has been connected by some to Revelation 3:18.

▲ 15, 16 Two coins of Nero (obverse and reverse of same type), AD 64-68, gold aureus. Roman-German Landesmuseum, Cologne. Photo 15 has the head of Nero wearing the radiant crown. The lettering is: NERO CAESAR AUGUSTUS. His new coinage portrayed him as a man already bloated with self-indulgence. Photo 16 shows the temple of Vesta; the perpetual fire of Rome was kept in the circular temple. Nero is said to have experienced an inexplicable terror within its walls in AD 63, which may account for the coin type. The temple was destroyed in the fire of AD 64. The effigy of the goddess is clear in the temple, but Ovid claimed that no effigy stood in the temple in Nero's time. Other coins, showing him with radiating crown, identify him with various gods: Apollo, Hercules, and Helios.

▼ 17 Coin, temple of Janus, bronze dupondius, ca. AD 66-68. Milwaukee Museum of Art. The lettering is: PACE P R TERRA MARIQ PARTA IANUM CLUSIT, plus S C (by order of the Senate) on either side of the temple. The inscription refers to the doors of the temple being closed, indicating peace. The obverse (not shown) has a radiate head of Nero, with the lettering: IMP NERO CLAUD CAESAR AVG GER P M TR P P P; Imperator Nero Claudius Caesar Augustus Germanicus Pontifex Maximus Tribunicia Potestate Pater Patriae. *Matthew 5:9; 10:34.*

▲ 18 Coin with Poppaea, Nero's wife. Billon tetradrachm, from Roman Egypt. Milwaukee Museum of Art. Poppaea was Nero's wife from AD 62-65, before which date she was his mistress. At her instigation, Nero murdered his mother Agrippina in AD 59 and in AD 62 divorced and killed his wife Octavia. In AD 65 Nero killed Poppaea in a fit of rage by kicking her in the stomach while she was pregnant.

GALBA, OTHO, VITELLIUS: THE CIVIL WARS

In March, AD 68, a period of civil war began which saw 3 emperors within a span of 22 months.

Servius Sulpicius Galba was born about 3 BC, so was about 70 when he declared himself representative of the Senate and people of Rome in opposition to Nero. He was governor of Nearer Spain at the time. At the end of May the Senate offered him the throne. The new emperor began a slow march from Spain to Rome, during which time support for him continued to grow. He arrived at Rome in October, but some precipitous acts quickly made him unpopular. He had a reputation as a competent though severe ruler during his governorships, but his rule as emperor was disastrous.

Scholars tend to contribute his shortcomings to his age, which resulted in considerable power being placed in the hands of 3 advisers, only 1 of whom had potential, and all 3 of whom fought among themselves. The austerity Galba had to inaugurate because of the condition in which Nero left the treasury was unpopular with the people, too. Though the people were used to undisciplined morals by their emperors, Galba's homosexuality with older men was especially frowned on; the practice was better accepted when the partners were boys and young men.

The power of provincial armies, as evidenced by actions against Nero and in favor of one candidate or another for emperor, was a new force to be reckoned with, and it was Galba's undoing. The army of Upper Germany toppled Galba's

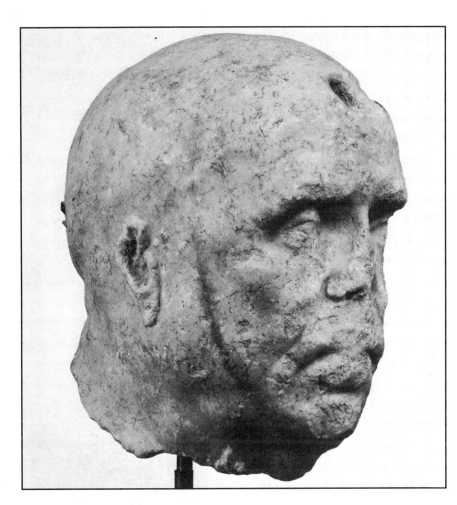

▲**19 Galba,** bust from Asia Minor; height 11³/₈ inches (28.7 cm.). J. Paul Getty Museum. The identification is not certain. The head is a little larger than lifesize. Originally it had a bronze imperial crown attached at the neck and forehead.

statues and declared support for the Senate.

Galba quickly adopted Piso as his heir, but the choice was unpopular with all the armies. The legions of Lower Germany declared Vitellius, who was their governor, as emperor (January 2, AD 69), an action that caused disquiet among

other legions. Moreover, Otho, who supported Galba and supposed that he would be his successor, moved to have himself declared emperor by a small group of guardsmen. On January 15, Galba went to the praetorians to disperse to them bonuses which he previously had refused them; they attacked him and hacked him to pieces. Piso was beheaded. Galba had reigned 7 months.

Marcus Salvius Otho was born on April 28, AD 32. He was an intimate friend of Nero's, who sent him to govern Lusitania (western Spain) so he would be free to marry Poppaea, who may have been Otho's wife (their marriage is debated). Otho was the first notable person to support Galba. He was 36 when declared emperor, a declaration soon supported by several other legions. But Vitellius, himself declared emperor, was marching toward Rome.

The legions loyal to Otho were too far away to render help; his support was inadequate to meet Vitellius, with whom he tried to negotiate to no avail. Moreover, he was not well liked by the noble class because his life-style, dress, and vanity were too much like Nero's. The decisive engagement was the battle of Bedriacum. When Otho heard the news of his army's defeat he committed suicide, ostensibly to avoid further bloodshed. He had reigned for 95 days.

Aulus Vitellius was born in AD 15, the grandson of a knight and the son of Claudius' adviser and good friend. The army of Lower Germany hailed him as emperor on January 2, AD 69; the next day Upper Germany's forces joined his cause. After Otho's defeat, the Senate recognized Vitellius on April 19. His hopes were high, but by the time he reached Rome in July the legions in the east and in the Danube had committed to Vespasian, who was governor of Judea.

Vitellius was very tall, with a crippled thigh due to a chariot accident, and with a large stomach due to excessive drinking and overeating. His rule was moderate; indeed, he avoided the usual kinds of punishment of those who had opposed him. Suetonius, however, depicted him as arrogant, offensive, extravagant, and cruel, but his view may have been preju-

diced. Vitellius' downfall came partly because he was ignorant of military matters; he depended on Caecina and Valens as commanders.

Like Otho, he reacted too slowly to the approaching armies of Vespasian. The place of engagement was the same; Vitellius' forces were defeated at the Second Battle of Bedriacum. He retreated to Rome where he tried to abdicate but was not allowed to. When Primus (Vespasian's commander) entered the city Vitellius was savagely murdered at the age of 56.

▼ **20 Bust of Vitellius.** Capitoline Museum. The age of the head is disputed; it has been considerably worked over and set on a bust it does not belong to.

VESPASIAN

Titus Flavius Vespasianus founded a new dynasty, the Flavian, which included Titus and Domitian. He was born in Reate in central Italy on November 17, AD 9. His father was a knight, a tax contractor. He had a military career, serving in Germany, then in Britain with distinction. He was awarded the governorship of Africa (Tunisia); amazingly, he apparently did not enrich himself. In fact, he afterward went through a period of poverty and became a mule dealer.

But then he was appointed governor of Judea, with the assignment of suppressing the revolt of the Jews against Rome. (Ironically, Suetonius told of a "superstition" current in the East that out of Judea would come the rulers of the world; he applied the belief to Vespasian.) When Nero committed suicide, Vespasian began maneuvering for the emperorship, gaining support from provinces of Syria, Egypt, Judea, and the Danube. He left his son Titus to complete the conquering of Jerusalem, while he moved to Egypt to cut off Rome's grain supply. Meanwhile, his commanders moved his armies toward Rome. The commander of a legion of the Danube region, Primus, defeated Vitellius at the so-called Second Battle of Bedriacum. Vespasian became emperor in AD 69 and very soon was awarded a triumph for the victory in Judea.

Vespasian commemorated his incredibly good fortune by issuing coins with the goddess Fortuna and the letters AVGVSTI added, "the Fortune of the Emperor." Josephus, the Jewish general who surrendered quickly at Sepphoris, became an apologist for Vespasian, and others pointed out that astrologers had predicted his rise. After the civil wars, the people were ready to believe.

As emperor, his tastes were plain and modest. He drank in moderation, and his sex life was temperate by court standards. A widower, he lived with a freedwoman mistress until she died; afterward, he took a concubine to his nap every day. He was good-natured, with a bawdy humor.

He was aided by the former governor of Syria, Mucianus, who was better born, much richer, and more diplomatic than Vespasian. People were ready for peace, and Vespasian's simple style was a reminder of the more ancient Roman tradition. He built the Temple of Peace to commemorate his gift of peace; it was beautiful enough to be called by the elder Pliny one of the Wonders of the World.

The new emperor had to satisfy legions who had developed a taste for electing emperors; his success in accomplishing this feat was a major reason for the internal peace the empire was to know almost until AD 200. He also accepted the office of censor, a signal that he intended to control the Senate, and he advertised the fact on his coinage. He appointed his supporters, many of them from Italian and other provinces, to replace the aristocratic families who had been decimated by the frequent purges ordered by previous emperors.

He extended the citizenship more openly to the provinces, a move that broadened the base of the Empire away from its domination by Italy to a more open society. He made the free communities of Achaea, Lycia, Rhodes, Byzantium, and Samos, and the kingdoms of Trachian Cilicia, Lesser Armenia, Sophene, and Comma-

▲ 21 **Coin of Vespasian,** with his image. The Archaeological Museum of The Southern Baptist Theological Seminary. The lettering is: IMP CAES VESPASIAN AVG COS, plus unreadable numbers that indicate his years as consul. The meaning is Emperor (Imperator) Caesar Vespasian Augustus Consul.

gene into provinces. He combined the territories of Galatia, Pontus, Cappadocia, and Lower Armenia into an enormous province of Galatia (12,000 square miles). The province of Cilicia was enlarged.

He was a hard worker, conscientious, thrifty, and tolerant. He began construction of the Amphitheater at Rome (the Colosseum) and inaugurated other building projects to replace the unsightly ruins and vacancies of the fires of the civil war years. He also rebuilt various cities in the empire that had been destroyed or damaged by earthquakes, and he was a patron of the arts (though he had to expel some or all philosophers from Rome for a time because of outspoken opposition to him). Titus had served beside him as his deputy, so when Vespasian died at age 69 on June 23, AD 79, the transition was smooth.

TITUS

Titus Flavius Vespasianus was born in AD 39 in Rome "in a small, dingy, slum bedroom" (Suetonius). He was educated, however, with Nero's stepbrother Britannicus and they were close friends. Suetonius lauded him as good at music and verse as well as every art of war. He served admirably in wars in Germany and Britain, spent some time in Rome as a rhetorician (lawyer), then went with his father Vespasian to Judea. There he captured the well-fortified cities of Tarichaeae and Gamala. He was instrumental in negotiating a pact between his father and Mucianus, governor of Syria.

When Vespasian went to Rome to claim the emperorship, he left Titus in charge of the war in Judea. Titus began his siege of Jerusalem in May, AD 70; the city fell 4 months later. Jerusalem was leveled and the Temple destroyed in the process. Josephus, who became a collaborator with the Romans, claimed that Titus tried to keep the destruction to a minimum. Josephus also disclosed, however, that he arranged games in Caesarea

▲ **22 Portrait head, Titus,** Glyptothek Museum, Munich.

▼ **23 Coin of Titus,** AD 79-81. Museum of Art and Archaeology, University of Missouri-Columbia. The coin (obverse) shows his head. The lettering is: IMP TIIVS CAES VESPASIAN AUG P M. It translates: Imperator Titus Caesar Vespasian Augustus Pontifex Maximus. The reverse of the coin has a dolphin and anchor. Museum photo.

Martima after the war in which Jews were set against wild beasts, in which combat 2,500 Jews were killed either by beasts or by being burned alive. Titus then repeated the event in Berytus, Phoenicia.

When Titus returned victorious to Rome, Vespasian shared the triumph for the Jewish war with his son. Titus then became his colleague in ruling the empire. Suetonius painted a sordid picture of his character; he wrote that Titus was thought to be profligate, cruel, immoral (including homosexual), and greedy.

He had a tempestuous affair with the notorious Berenice, sister of Agrippa II. Having collaborated against the Jews in the war between the Romans and Jews, a war she was strongly opposed to, she joined him later in Rome. In fact, had she not been an Oriental queen and reminiscent of Cleopatra and Antony, Titus might have married her; instead, he sent her away when opposition became unbearably strong.

When he took the throne, then, people expected the worst. They were delighted when he turned out to be pleasant and generous. His building projects included the completion of the Flavian Amphitheater (Colosseum) and adjoining baths. It was during his reign that Mount Vesuvius erupted (AD 79), burying several towns, including Pompeii, Herculaneum, and Boscoreale. He did all he could to aid the survivors and the families of those who died. The next year a great fire struck Rome; he spent from his personal fortune and stripped his own holdings of statuary to rebuild.

But Titus had a terminal disease, and he knew it. He complained that his life was being snatched from him, and for only one reason that he could think of. Historians have proposed all kinds of possibilities for what he had in mind; one suggestion is that he did not eliminate the possibility of Domitian, his brother, succeeding him. He died at age 41, after a rule of only 2 years and 2 months, in the same country house where his father had died.

While Christians in the early centuries of this era believed that Titus' destruction of Jerusalem was judgment on the Jews' refusal to accept Jesus as Messiah, Jews believed that Titus' early death and the natural disasters of his reign were God's judgment on him for destroying the Temple.

▲ **24 Coin of Titus,** shows thunderbolt on square seat. Museum of Art and Archaeology, University of Missouri-Columbia. The lettering is: TR P IX IMP XV COS VIII PP. It translates: Ninth Tribunician Power, Imperator 15 (year), eighth consulship, Pater Patriae (Father of His Country). The obverse (not shown) is a head of Titus. Museum photo.

DOMITIAN

Titus Flavius Domitianus, Titus' younger brother, was born on October 24, AD 51. While Titus had grown up during the time the family was more prosperous, Domitian was a boy during the difficult years. He was in Rome during the civil war and narrowly escaped death when the capitol was set afire. He was jealous of his older brother, and some of his actions raised suspicions that he might be scheming to inherit the throne instead of Titus. Consequently, he was held in check by the assignation of little responsibility of substance. To fill the void, he turned to poetry. Domitian assumed the throne in AD 81. He had thought out his path of rule carefully, and he systematically set out to be an absolute ruler. His wife was the powerful Domitia, daughter of Corbulo, Nero's general.

The emperor instituted laws against loose morals, but he himself was notorious for his sexual behavior, which included mistresses, prostitutes, eunuchs, and a variety of demeaning eroticisms. He had great reverence for the old Roman religions. Minerva was his favorite goddess. Since she was identified with the Greek goddess Pallas Athena, he used her to demonstrate his appreciation for Greek culture. He had no close friends except one or two women, was secretive, and had a frightening sense of humor. His excesses equaled those of the worst emperors.

Suetonius described Domitian as large, tall, and well-made but with hammer toes. Later he developed baldness, a paunch, and spindly legs. He was rigid and severe, but he also was a superb administrator. Suetonius wrote that he "kept such a tight hold on the city magistrates

▲ 25 **Coin of Domitian,** AD 81-96. Museum of Art and Archaeology, University of Missouri-Columbia. The image shows the laureate head of Domitian. The lettering is: CAES AUG F DOMIT COS II; Caesar Augustus F (several meanings) Domitian Second Consulship. The reverse (not shown) depicts Domitian on horseback. Images on his coinage show him as stern, proud, and aristocratic. Other coins commemorate the defeat of the Germanic tribes, his triumphal arch, and illustrate the Secular Games of AD 88. Most were devoted to Minerva, though some show Jupiter. *Acts 14:12-13; 19:35; Revelation.*

and provincial governors that the general standard of honesty and justice rose to an unprecedented high level." His reign, in fact, is the dividing line between independence of the proconsuls and control of them. He was responsible for such building programs as a forum (finished by Nerva) in Rome, the temple of Capitoline Jupiter, and a grand palace on the Palatine Hill. His lavish games and shows included women in gladiatorial contests and foot races.

To finance his vast expenditures,

he resorted to meticulous taxation. He mercilessly continued the taxation on the Jews, begun by Vespasian, that required them to pay the amount that once was their own Temple tax to his treasury; those Jews who tried to keep their Jewishness secret to avoid the tax were prosecuted. At the end of his reign, in 95, he condemned his cousin and his cousin's wife on a charge of atheism. They are sometimes thought to have been Christians but most likely had become enamored with Judaism.

He directed a good bit of his attention and resources toward the empire's borders in England and along the Rhine to the neglect of the eastern provinces, a policy that may have contributed to his unpopularity.

Domitian's determination to be absolute monarch was clearly announced when he took the title "Perpetual Censor." The office of censor originally was assigned the task of controlling public morals and leasing public areas and buildings. It grew in power since the censors had the right to determine those they considered unworthy to serve as knights or senators. Other emperors had used the office to their advantage, but none had usurped it permanently. Domitian intended to rule by force in the manner of Hellenistic kings. In that vein, he was willing to have his divinity openly declared. He developed a cult for worship of his father and brother and related it to Jupiter, the highest Roman god. He made the house where he was born into a temple to the Flavian family. Gold and silver statues of him were set up in profusion in Rome; a massive temple with a huge statue of himself was built in Ephesus; subordinates referred to him as Master and God in their edicts.

His fanatical support of Roman gods caused him to take action against Christians, Jews, and others who did not worship Roman gods. He sent philosophers into exile, first from Rome in 88-89, then from all of Italy in 95; they were guilty, he thought, of seditious writings. Stoic philosophers were especially suspect.

The support of the army was essential for an emperor. Since his father and brother had denied him any opportunity for military exploits, he sought the soldiers' favor by raising their pay and spending considerable time among them. He sought to do more; in 83 he led in further battles in Germany and succeeded in completing the conquest of territory between the Rhine and the Danube. Agricola, his governor of Britain, extended Roman rule into Scotland. But when Domitian sought to conquer Dacia (above the Danube) his armies suffered two severe defeats in 87 and 89.

Back in Rome, he heard before long of a revolt by one of the German legions, led by the governor of Upper Germany. Domitian acted quickly; the revolt collapsed and he punished the offenders involved severely. Afterward, Domitian became more suspicious. He reinstituted treason trials such as those of Tiberius; senators once again lived in perpetual fear. His fears increased rather than abated, and others fell under his scrutiny.

In 95, when he moved against leaders of the praetorian guard, their successors began to plot his assassination, with the involvement of Domitia. On September 18, 96 a freedman named Stephanus, who was a Christian, stabbed him to death; he died at the age of 44 in his fifteenth year of reign. His death was met with great rejoicing in the Capitol; the senators removed his statues and otherwise purged his memory.

▲ 26 **Coin of Domitian before a temple.** Museum of Art and Archaeology, University of Missouri-Columbia. The reverse is shown (obverse has Domitian's head). Clothed in a toga, he stands before a round altar and appears to be pouring a libation. A figure stands near and behind the altar blowing a double flute; another figure is at left playing a harp. The temple is decorated with a wreath in the gable and has 6 columns. SC at bottom means by order of Senate. The lettering is: COS XIIII LVD SAEC FFC, with SC at bottom. Museum photo. *Matthew 9:23; 1 Corinthians 14:7; Revelation.*

▶ 27 **Coin of Domitian, inscribed altar.** Museum of Art and Archaeology, University of Missouri-Columbia. The reverse is shown. The altar and inscriptions are encircled with a wreath. The altar inscription is CVD SAEC FFC; on either side is stated the consul years: COS VIII. The obverse, not shown, has a head of Domitian. Museum photo. *Revelation.*

NERVA

Marcus Cosseius Nerva was 66 years old when in AD 96 he was elected by the Senate to replace Domitian. His reign marked a new era in Roman history. In the 2 years he reigned, he reformed the method of succession. An emperor's son, natural or adopted, no longer received the throne automatically. (Some scholars believe this process was not foreseen.)

Nerva instituted the process of adopting the most able person to succeed him. Other reforms corrected many of the abuses of Domitian and other predecessors, and he legislated the support of poor children at the state's expense. The oppression of literary efforts loosened during his reign, and his successors continued the policy. He adopted Trajan as his son and successor in October 97 and died 3 months later.

► **28 Nerva,** bust, marble, height 13 inches (33 cm.). J. Paul Getty Museum. The head was recut from a head of Domitian, whose memory had been condemned by action of the Senate after his assassination. The action resulted in every likeness being defaced or reshaped to expunge any memory of him.

TRAJAN

Marcus Ulpius Trajanus, a Spaniard, was 44 years of age when Nerva adopted him. He was at the time military commander on the Rhine. His 19-year rule was progressive and stable. He was a careful administrator, not hesitating to take a hand in provincial or city affairs when he felt he should; but he lightened taxes in the provinces. He left behind an array of public buildings, but they were functional ones and not self-indulgent.

As the first emperor from a province, his reign demonstrated that educated and successful men from outside Italy could rise. His reign, too, can be said to mark the time when Italy ceased to be the center of influence in the Empire, for wealth, population, and power all were flowing in the direction of the various provinces. Previous emperors had virtually eliminated the ancient ruling families.

Trajan enlarged the army and introduced various innovations; he extended the boundary of the empire to the Danube, making Dacia a province; he invaded Parthia (with limited success) and made Arabia a province in the process. He was a totalitarian dictator despite his popularity. He took the title *optimus*, which linked him with Jupiter.

Trajan also reinstituted the persecution of Christians, though not as vigorously as did his successor, Hadrian. Much of what we know about his policies toward Christians comes from letters written to him by Pliny the Younger, whom Trajan appointed governor of Bithynia. He died in 117 at the age of 64 before he could return from the Parthian war, having adopted Hadrian just before his death.

▼**29 Portrait bust of Trajan,** AD 108, marble, height 29⅛ inches (74 cm.). Capitoline Museum. The nose, part of the left ear, the chin, right shoulder, and pedestal are all restored. The bust is an official piece of propaganda that portrays Trajan as a gentle, wise, and effective military leader and sovereign. It was carved on the occasion of the tenth jubilee of his reign. He does not wear a cuirass but rather his upper torso is naked except for the paludamentum, held with a clasp, and the band from which hung his sheathed sword.

THE MILITARY

The size and organization of the Roman army changed from emperor to emperor. When Augustus completed his conquest he slashed in half the 60 Roman legions and settled retired veterans in new colonies. At his death there were 25 legions, though not at full strength, numbering perhaps 115,000. They were gradually increased thereafter to about 150,000 by Trajan's time. But in addition to these legions, other soldiers could be called in from provincial auxiliaries, local militias, and armies of vassal kings.

The Roman army consisted of three parts. The first part was that stationed near Rome, including the Praetorian Guard and other troops. The second part was the 28 or so legions, which comprised about 50 percent of the armed forces. The third part was the auxilia, or auxiliary forces.

The praetorian guard, which consisted of 9 cohorts of 500 each, was established first by Augustus in 27 BC. The guard gained in strength as the years went by, until by the time of Claudius they were strong enough to establish him as emperor.

A legion consisted of about 6,000 men, of whom 5,120 or 5,280 were foot soldiers and about 120 were cavalry, plus various troops that supported the headquarters. It was divided into 10 cohorts, which in turn were divided each into 6 centuries. The legion commander (legate) was a Roman praetor; he had 6 tribunes on his staff, who were men in an early

▲30 **Roman Imperial Eagle,** about AD 300. J. Paul Getty Museum. It is from a sanctuary of the Roman army.

stage of their political careers.

The centurions were the chief leaders in battle; they were professional soldiers who generally had risen through the ranks. The chief centurion served on the legate's staff; the second centurion was over the administrative staff. The centurion could receive as a decoration a special golden crown for being the first over a wall; another decoration was the silver spearshaft.

The legion was made up of citizen volunteers who served for 25 years. The common legionnaire was paid 225 denarii per year. Their retirement consisted of land grants, a monetary grant of 3000 denarii (in AD 5), and various privileges. A centurion, moreover, could amass a considerable amount of money.

In AD 23 the legions were deployed in this manner: 8 along the Rhine, 3 in Spain, 2 in Africa (province), 2 in Egypt, 4 in Syria, 4 along the Danube, and 2 in Dalmatia. The 4 legions in Syria were the V Macedonica, VI Ferrata, XV Apollinaris, and the X Fretensis; the last named was the most dominant in Palestine and remained alone after the destruction of Jerusalem in AD 70.

The Roman soldier (and provincials as well) were not allowed to marry. They often, however, lived with common-law wives, had families by them, and married them upon their retirement. The soldier below the rank of centurion was eligible for 3 decorations: necklaces, armbands, and embossed discs worn on the corselet. A higher status of soldier, the *evocati,* could also be granted a plain gold crown.

In the second century BC the legion heavy infantry included 3 classes: hastati, principes, and triarii. The hastati and the principes were armed with composite oval shields, swords, and pilum (a heavy throwing spear). The triarii were armed with the hasta (long thrusting spear). The light infantry (velites) were armed with swords, small shields (parmae), and a short, lightweight javelin. The two-foot, double-edged Spanish sword (gladius) was introduced to the Roman army in the first century BC, as was the pilum (throwing spear).

The legion forces also included ballistic equipment, the stone-throwing catapult, the catapult that shot arrows or bolts, and siege engines. A bolt was a very large arrow, as much as 6½ feet long and 1½ inches thick, with a heavy metal point, designed to pierce armor. The catapult stones weighed 11-55 pounds. Catapults for stones varied in design and size. Smaller ones could be similar to arrow catapults or might follow other design concepts. Larger ones were more like the overhand-arm type so familiar in story and drawings. This latter type came into general use after the New Testament period, though it was known earlier.

The Roman cavalry was a weak point. They had no stirrup, which made them effective only against undisciplined troops. However, they did not normally charge the enemy; rather, they were formed into two contingents. One contingent, mounted with lances, forced the enemy to remain in tight formations, while the other contingent rained arrows from horseback onto the tightly formed enemies. The auxiliaries, however, filled this tactical void well, while Roman cavalry was used to pursue fleeing enemy troops. The cavalryman might dismount to engage the fleeing enemy in hand-to-hand combat.

Another weak point in the Roman army was that its soldiers could cease to be soldiers during times of extended peace. When war was eminent the legions had to be purged of unfit soldiers, and severe training steps sometimes had to be taken to bring the rest up to par.

The auxiliary were made up of noncitizens; they complemented the legions when needed. Their forces included cavalry and light infantry. They numbered about the same as the legion forces, but were organized into smaller units.

Some of the auxiliaries had special battle skills lacked by the Roman armies, and enlisted to good use by them, such as archers (mounted and unmounted) and slingers. They served 26 years, after which they were awarded Roman citizenship. Their ranks were not open to everyone, however, such as the general Egyptian population. They did not serve in their native lands.

The Roman soldier might carry 80 pounds on an all-day march, then have to construct defenses at the end of the day. When the army stopped for the night, it set up a protected camp. The soldiers set about digging a ditch and heaping the dirt from it up toward the camp site. On top of the heap thus built, a palisade of pointed poles, much like an American frontier fort wall, was erected. Inside the wall the legion erected its tents, made of leather, according to a prescribed pattern.

Trajan's Column in Rome shows a series of scenes that spiral from the bottom of the column to the top; they reveal much about Roman army life and battle tactics in the early part of the second century AD. Indeed, the legionnaire was a construction worker as well as a soldier, and he carried in his gear a multipurpose pickaxe called a dolabra. The legionnaire also built roads, dug quarries and canals, and made their own roof tiles and pottery.

The colonies settled by retired legionnaires became an effective means of pacifying areas which tended toward revolt or lawlessness. Though not intended for the purpose, they also became effective in the spreading of Roman culture.

When a Roman camp was established anywhere in the empire, it followed much the same pattern. Walls with watchtowers surrounded a tightly packed compound that contained the commander's quarters, a treasury, a shrine, rows of barracks, quarters for centurions, granaries, kitchens, ovens, horse stalls, latrines, cells for punishing offenders, a hospital, shops, and a parade ground; if times were peaceful other houses and buildings might be built outside of the walls, such as baths, an amphitheater, and merchant areas. Settled by legions on the borderlands of the empire, they were under the direct authority of the emperor, though they could and did choose to support contenders for the throne from time to time.

The Roman soldier had considerable freedom of religion; however, he was encouraged to worship the standards under which he marched. The eagle was especially venerated. By the first century AD it was made of gold, or silver gilded with gold. During the Empire, medallions with the images of the emperors were added to the standards. The soldier also worshiped the gods whose festivals were celebrated on the regular annual calendar, plus non-Roman gods whose worship was encouraged by military units. To these were added the worship of unofficial cults such as local deities. Two widespread cults that were mainly military were Jupiter Dolichenus, associated with iron, and Mithras.

Rome at War, Peter Connolly (Englewood Cliffs, New Jersey: Prentice-Hall, Inc.), 1981; *Engineering in the Ancient World*, J. G. Landels (Berkeley: University of California Press), 1978; *Life in Egypt Under Roman Rule*, Naphtali Lewis (Oxford: Clarendon Press), 1983; *The Grand Strategy of the Roman Empire*, Edward N. Luttwak (Baltimore: The Johns Hopkins University Press), 1976; *Ancient Rome*, Robert Payne (New York: American Heritage Press), 1970; *Saalburg, Roman Fort* (Homburg: Saalburgmuseum), 1980; *Glanum*, François Salviat (Paris: Caisse Nationale des Monuments Historiques et des Sites), 1977; *Führer durch das Landesmuseum Trier*, Von Reinhard Schindler (Trier: Selbstverlag des Rheinischen Landesmuseums Trier), 1980; *Roman Britain*, H. H. Scullard (London: Thames and Hudson), 1979; *The Roman Soldier*, G. R. Watson (Ithaca: Cornell Univ. Press), 1969.

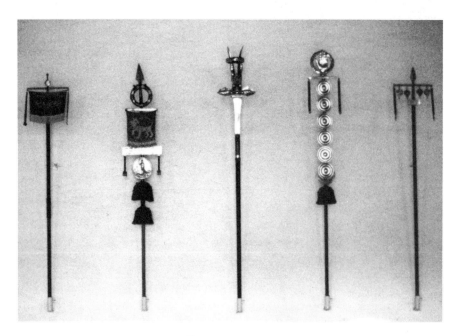

▲31 Legion standards. Saalburg Fort Museum, Saalburg, Germany. The eagle and other standards were placed in a special chapel (sacellum) in every legionary headquarters. The eagle standard, which was carried by all legions, is the center one. The eagle's wings are upraised and encircled by a wreath. This reconstruction is based on an image on the tombstone of Gnaeus Musius. During most of the Empire period the eagle was of gold. It stayed in the camp unless the entire legion moved. The standard to left of the center one is the signum, the symbol of one of the centuries. It is an upraised hand inside a circle of wreath. Six discs and a bell continue down the shaft. The standard right of center carries the emperor's image (imago) on the disk (its display caused riots in Judea), a crossbar above the image which has the letters COH VII RAET, and a zodiac sign of a lion above the crossbar. The flag on the right is a vexilla; one was carried to identify the legion and one the detachment. The standard at the far right resembles a spear shaft with symbols hanging from a crossbar. The reconstructions do not show that standards were pointed for thrusting into the ground and had handles with which to pull them up. They were such important religious symbols that their loss usually resulted in the dismemberment of the unit. They were carried by bearers dressed in animal skins with the animal heads over their own. *Matthew 8:5-13; Revelation 14:9-11.*

▶32 Layered armor, cuirass, AD 90-100, copy. Roman-German Central Museum, Mainz; the original reconstruction by H. Russell Robinson is in the Museum of Antiquities, Newcastle-upon-Tyne, patterned after a discovery of (von) Corbridge at Hadrian's Wall in England. Of iron, bronze, and lead, it is the hook type called *lorica segmentata*. It is hinged where the shoulder and chest units join, while the other pieces are riveted to leather straps running vertically. The style existed in the first half of the first century. *Romans 13:12.*

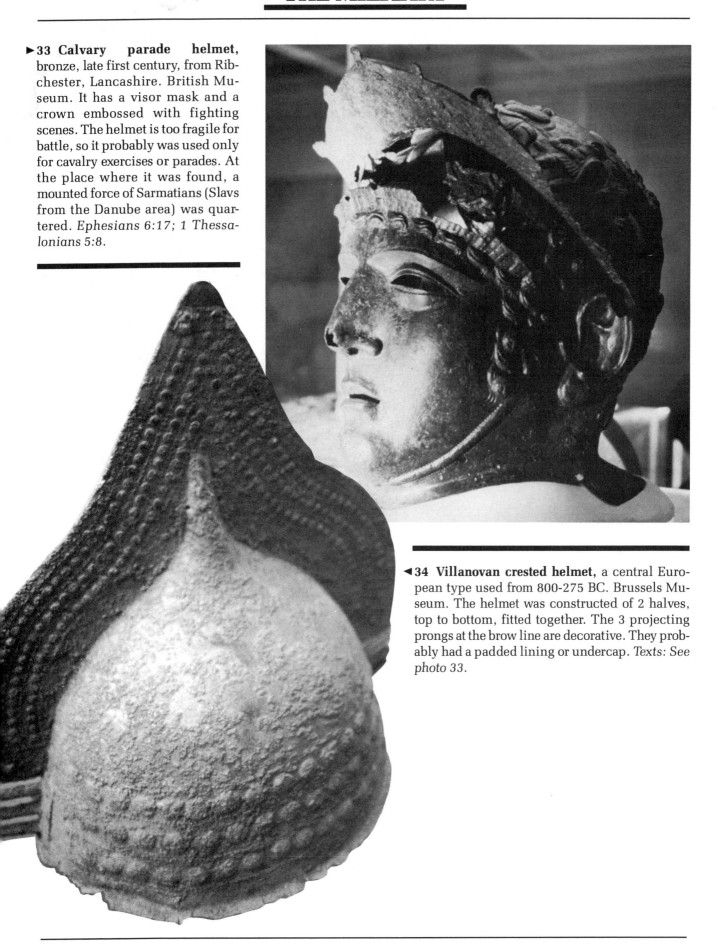

►33 **Calvary parade helmet,** bronze, late first century, from Ribchester, Lancashire. British Museum. It has a visor mask and a crown embossed with fighting scenes. The helmet is too fragile for battle, so it probably was used only for cavalry exercises or parades. At the place where it was found, a mounted force of Sarmatians (Slavs from the Danube area) was quartered. *Ephesians 6:17; 1 Thessalonians 5:8.*

◄34 **Villanovan crested helmet,** a central European type used from 800-275 BC. Brussels Museum. The helmet was constructed of 2 halves, top to bottom, fitted together. The 3 projecting prongs at the brow line are decorative. They probably had a padded lining or undercap. *Texts: See photo 33.*

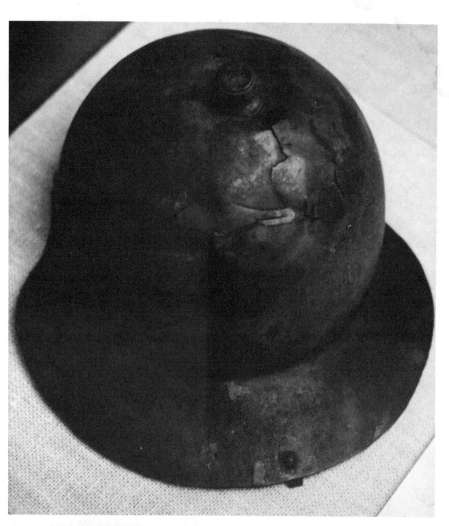

▼ **35 Bronze Montefortino type helmet,** Gallic, third-first centuries BC. Brussels Museum. *Texts: See photo 33.*

▲ **36 Bronze legionary helmet,** first century AD. British Museum. It was found in digging the canal between Tring and Berkhamsted. *Texts: See photo 33.*

◄ **37 Roman helmet, from Asia Minor,** Montefortino type, first century AD. Roman-German Central Museum, Mainz. The helmet has a spear-type point on top and a narrow deflector at back. The simple Montefortino type was used much during the transition from Republic to Empire, when soldiers had to pay for their own armor. Cheaply built armor was produced by workshops, which sometimes attached the cheekpiece by only one rivet. *Texts: See photo 33.*

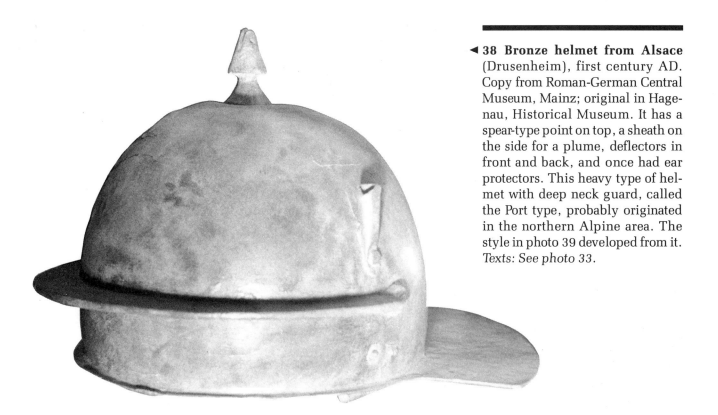

◄ **38 Bronze helmet from Alsace** (Drusenheim), first century AD. Copy from Roman-German Central Museum, Mainz; original in Hagenau, Historical Museum. It has a spear-type point on top, a sheath on the side for a plume, deflectors in front and back, and once had ear protectors. This heavy type of helmet with deep neck guard, called the Port type, probably originated in the northern Alpine area. The style in photo 39 developed from it. *Texts: See photo 33.*

► **39 Helmet, Imperial Italic type,** iron with bronze, first to second centuries AD, from the region of Hebron, Israel. Copy from Roman-German Central Museum, Mainz; original is in the Israel Museum, Jerusalem. It has deflectors in front and back and ear protectors. Crescents form designs in each quadrant formed by the crosspieces. This style was the standard infantry helmet from the mid-first century AD. The cheek pieces are better and the reinforcing strip across the front deflected downward sword blows. The flange above the ear is a second-century AD addition to protect the ear. The helmet was held on by 2 straps which ran from the neck protector to cross under the chin and tie to the cheek pieces. *Texts: See photo 33.*

▼ 41 Grave monument for Flavius Bassus, end of first century AD, found in Gereon Street, Cologne, Germany. Roman-German Landesmuseum, Cologne. The inscription reads: "Titus Flavius Bassus, son of Mucala Dansaler, rider in the Northern Ala division of Fabius Prudens, deceased in old age, 46 years after serving 26 years. His heirs erected this monument." He is running his horse over an enemy and is about to thrust his pilum into him. The sword at his waist is of a common type of the first century, with a large ball-shaped pommel. Except for a simple helmet with neck flange, he is depicted in the nude, as is the man behind him. The horse is fitted with a fancy girth and hangings at his neck and flanks. The fallen soldier holds on to his oblong shield. *Acts 23:23,31-32.*

▲ 40 Infantry legionnaires in battle, limestone bas-relief, first century AD. Roman-German Central Museum, Mainz. The legionnaire carries an oblong shield, a short double-bladed sword, and wears a helmet similar to the one in photo 39, embossed with a fish or dolphin. The helmet sometimes had a plume at the top. The sword of the Republic had a curved blade. Its design was in transition during the first century, but basically the straight dagger shape was common by then. The blade was 20-22 inches (50-56 cm.) long. During the first century AD the blade was shortened to 17-21 inches (44-55 cm.). The deceased is dressed in a sleeveless tunic rather than armor. His companion carries a throwing spear (pilum) and wears a similar helmet and a sleeved tunic. Roman soldiers did not carry long thrusting lances; the pilum was an extremely heavy weapon which was thrown at close quarters; its iron head was 4½ feet (137 cm.) long. The spear used for long distances was the jacula, thrown by means of a twisted thong. *Acts 21:32; Ephesians 6:11-17.*

43 Roman legionary, bronze statuette, first century AD. British Museum. He wears a cuirass made of overlapping bands of metal (see photo 32). He wears a kilt of leather or metal-plated strips. He also wears a crested helmet, greaves, and boots, which had metal studs on the soles. The centurion's dress was much the same but his parade uniform, at least, was more ornate. He also wore a cape attached to his shoulders. Greaves were worn by Roman soldiers from early times, but under the Empire they became a mark of distinction for the centurion.

42 Roman soldier with rectangular scutum shield, sword, and spear. Saalburg Fort Museum, Saalburg, Germany. The shield had a linen and hide cover over laminated wood strips and is decorated with a large boss in the center, which was an insignia. His helmet is crested and has cheek pieces. Note the long spearhead on the pilum. His sword, of similar design to the one in photo 40, is hung by a strap over his shoulder. His armor is mail, and he wears greaves, with protectors on his thighs. (Greaves had fallen out of general use by the first century but were worn by centurions as an insignia; his armor also was silvered.) *Matthew 10:34; 27:54; John 19:34.*

▲ 44 **Statue of Trajan, closeup of cuirass.** Olympia Museum. Heavily embossed, it has Helios' head at the top, with horses ridden by Victories the dominant figures, with dolphins under them. The leather scallops each have a figure attached: Jupiter (Zeus) in the center, bounded by lions or monsters, elephant heads, etc. The "muscled" cuirass was common among officers, though not always so ornate. A leather tunic, with extra leather strips over the shoulders and thighs, probably was worn under the cuirass. *Revelation 9:9,17.*

▼ **47 Roman soldier on horse,** marble. National Museum, Naples. The rider carries a small round shield that was typical for Roman cavalrymen. His short sword is carried in a scabbard strung from his shoulder and hanging on his left side. This fact is one indication that he was a centurion. He would carry a dagger on his right side; the legionnaire wore his weapons on the opposite sides. He wears a helmet with cheek pieces and a plum running crosswise; the plum arrangement is further indication that he is a centurion. He also wears a cuirass, pleated kilt, greaves, and sandals.

▲ **46 Sarmatian Rider,** relief from victory monument of Trajan, about AD 105. Saalburg Fort Museum, Saalburg, Germany. The rider wears close-fitting trousers, shoes, and carries a lance (contus). He has a swordbelt across his shoulder. His horse's mane is cut short, and the saddlecloth is decorated with tassels. The cavalryman in the Roman army wore either mail or scale armor. The Sarmatians along the Danube confronted Rome with fully armored riders late in the first century AD. Rome afterward used them as auxiliary troops.

▼ **49, 50 Battle scenes from Glanum monument of the Julii** St. Remy (see photo 893). On the west side (photo 49) is an infantry combat, with a struggle around a dead warrior. Short swords, pilum spears, shields, cuirasses, kilts, and a variety of helmet styles can be seen. At the top of the scene are heavy garlands, at the top of each swag is an Eros, and on top of each garland is a head of Old Silenus and satyrs. On the north side (photo 50) is a cavalry battle. The figures are helmetless, wear capes, and fight with pilum spears. A double-bladed axe is seen on the far right. The same decoration is at the top of the scene. The east panel is a combat against the Amazons; the south is a chase of wild Calydonian boar. (East and south panels not shown.) *Matthew 24:6-8.*

▲ **48 Wooden long shield with iron boss,** reconstructed, found a few miles east-southeast of Neumagen. Landesmuseum, Trier. The shield is of the Germanic culture of the region during 450-250 BC. The Roman shield *(oval scutum)* was similarly rectangular and made of wood and leather with a metal boss in the center. *Ephesians 6:16.*

51, 52 Battle scene between Greeks and Galatians, 2 sides of a sarcophagus. Capitoline Museum. The Greek armor is similar to that of the Romans, and they fight with heavy spears. The Galatians in photo 51 are shown naked to emphasize their uncivilized state; the one bound and sitting on the left has a heavy necklace around his neck. In photo 52 a Galatian naked except for a cape is about to strike a cavalryman whose horse is falling. The captured Galatian at lower right wears a loincloth and a heavy necklace. *Acts 16:6; 18:23.*

▲ **53 Entablature showing Roman soldiers,** bas-relief from southern France. Musée Lapidaire, Arles. The figures exhibit a variety of dress, visible somewhat in spite of the weathered condition: kilts, platelet mail, tunics, plumed helmets, and three-tiered kilts. *1 Thessalonians 5:8.*

▶ **54 Bronze horse's bit,** found in Pompeii, first century AD. Field Museum. *James 3:3; Revelation 14:20.*

◀ **55 Bridle bit,** typical Romano-Celtic type. British Museum. *Texts: See photo 54.*

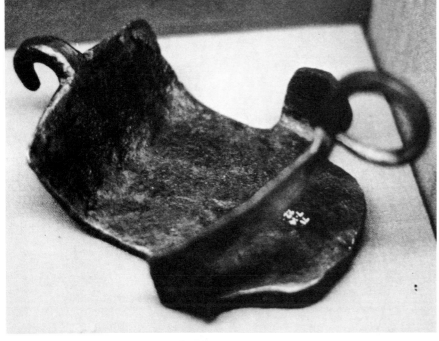

◄ **56 Hipposandal** (temporary horseshoe), found at Bishop's Gate, Greater London. British Museum. Its use is debated; one possibility is that it was used only for draught animals.

► **57 Caltrop,** strewn in path of enemy cavalry. British Museum.

► **58 Roman arrowhead** (far right). The Archaeological Museum of The Southern Baptist Theological Seminary.

▲ 59 **Five lead sling bullets,** Greek, fifth-fourth centuries BC. Museum of Art and Archaeology, University of Missouri-Columbia. Inscribed slingstones such as these were used in antiquity throughout the Greek world. The inscriptions usually refer to a city or ruler who issued the bullets or to a commander of a battalion of slingers. Left to right, the lettering reads, in Greek: XENOKRATES; ANDRON; DASOU; a thunderbolt, symbol of Zeus; and another thunderbolt of the same style.

▶ 60 **Catapult stones,** used by Romans in conquest of Masada. On site at Masada, Israel.

▲ **61 Greek battering head,** the only surviving example, fifth century BC. Olympia Museum. Note figure of ram's head at back.

▼ **62 Model of Vindonissa, legionary camp** east of Basel, Switzerland. Vindonissa Museum. The long buildings on the right are barracks, 21 of them plus 3 more just inside and west of the South Gate. The East Gate is on the far right; running clockwise from it are the South, West, and North (far right) Gates. Each gate has two towers, and other guard towers are situated between them. The headquarters building is at the end of the road that passes through the East Gate; it is built around a large courtyard. The complex extends north to include 2 smaller courtyards and their surrounding rooms. Four sets of officers' quarters are lined up to the west of the headquarters building. Between them and the south wall are storehouses. The 4 long buildings to the north of the officers' quarters are shops and stores. Still moving north, there is the gymnasium, then the surgery. The next building to the north, set among the barracks, is the hospital; it also is built around a courtyard with a temple in its center. The arsenal is located in the farthest-north abutment; just south of it are the stables. *Revelation 20:9.*

▲ **63 Troop barracks of centuria,** reconstructed. Saalburg, Fort Museum, Saalburg, Germany. *Mark 15:39,45.*

▶ **64 Bricks with Roman legion stamp,** from the Praetorium in Cologne, Germany. The stamp is: LEG I M P F (Legion I, Minerva, Pia Fidelis).

▲ **65 Military discharge certificate,** 2 parts, engraved in Latin on bronze plates. British Museum. It grants the usual privileges (Roman citizenship, the right to marry, or the legal recognition of a relationship already contracted) to the time-expired men of 13 cavalry regiments and 37 infantry battalions stationed in Britain, and is dated the equivalent of July 17, AD 122, during the reign of Hadrian. This particular diploma was issued to one Gemellus, a native of Pannonia, a lance-corporal of the first Tampian regiment of Pannonian horse; one plate gives the names of 7 witnesses. Gemellus obviously returned from Britain to Pannonia, as his diploma was found at Brigetio, on the Danube, 50 miles west of Budapest.

◄ **66 Military discharge certificate,** bronze. J. Paul Getty Museum. It was issued under Domitian, ca. AD 88-89. 1 Timothy 2:9-12; 1 Peter 3:3.

THE PEOPLE

Both the unity and the diversity of the Roman empire are of interest to the New Testament scholar. The unity was due to the long process of Hellenization which was inherited and emphasized in varying degrees by Rome. The diversity must be taken into account in the study of various passages. The world to which Paul wrote his letters was not a singular world. Macedonia, for example, had a culture different in significant respects from the Greek areas in the south. Moreover, the Western provinces were quite distinct from the Eastern. There is a constant tendency in New Testament studies to apply Roman customs uncritically to the eastern provinces which comprised the world of most of the New Testament.

The Eastern provinces were essentially Greek in character. They were generally content with Roman rule, but likely regarded Rome's civilization with contempt. The Western peoples mixed a Latinized Hellenism with their local customs; the Eastern provinces continued to speak Greek. Peters locates the East-West line somewhere in present-day Yugoslavia. Further, those ancients committed to Hellenism perceived the culture to be a blanket which covered much of the world they were concerned with. It was, rather, something of a Diaspora instead, a network of cities that had power and influence but which did not succeed in replacing local languages and customs. Many people became bilingual; many local gods and goddesses combined into local-Greek (and Roman) forms, but local traditions continued.

The similarities grew out of the Hellenization which was vastly accelerated by Alexander the Great and his successors. The interlocking of political administration, commerce, and culture produced the need for a common language. The form of Greek that emerged was *koine*. Non-Greek regions were bilingual, and Rome came to use both Latin and Greek.

To the Hellenization process in play for 3 centuries, Rome added its influence through colonies. Rome had a long history of establishing colonies, but they had been close to home and their purpose was defense. The century before Augustus saw the establishing of colonies for the purpose of providing land to Rome's poor, a policy which drifted toward such colonies being settled by retiring army veterans. Augustus used the practice to release happily the army which won the empire for him. But he innovated in establishing colonies in Syria and Anatolia and inland. All of them were military in character and intended for defense.

Ancient Civilizations and Ruins of Turkey, Ekrem Akurgal (Istanbul: Haset Kitabevi), 1978; *Atlas of the Biblical World*, Denis Baly and A. D. Tushingham (New York: The World Publishing Co.), 1971; *Turkey Beyond the Maeander*, George E. Bean (Totowa, New Jersey: Rowman and Littlefield), 1971; *Guide to Boğazköy*, Kurt Bittel (Ankara, Turkey: The Publications of the Ankara Society for Promotion of Tourism, Antiquities, and Museums), 1975; *Syria as a Roman Province*, E. S. Bouchier (Oxford: B. H. Blackwell), 1916; *Atlas of the Roman World*, Tim Cornell and John Matthews (New York: Facts on File, Inc.), 1983; *The Archaeology of the New Testament*, Jack Finegan (Princeton: Princeton University Press), 1969; *From Alexander to Cleopatra*, Michael Grant (New York: Charles Scribner's Sons), 1982; *The Hellenistic World and the Coming of Rome*, Erich S. Gruen, 2 volumes (Berkeley: University of California Press), 1984; *The University of Missouri Studies*, "Cappadocia as a Roman Procuratorial Province," William Emmett Gwatkin, Jr., Volume V, Number 4, October 1, 1930: *The Early Greeks*, R. J. Hopper (New York: Harper and Row Publishers, Inc.), 1976; *The Cities of the Eastern Roman Provinces*, A. H. M. Jones (Oxford: The Clarendon Press), 1971; *The Roman World of Dio Chrysostom*, C. P. Jones (Cambridge: Harvard University Press), 1978; *Journal of Roman Studies*, LXI, 1971, LXVI, 1976; *The Greeks*, H. D. F. Kitto (Baltimore: Penguin Books, Inc.), 1957; *Life in Egypt Under Roman Rule*, Naphtali Lewis (Oxford: Clarendon Press), 1983; *The Grand Strategy of the Roman Empire*, Edward N. Luttwak (Baltimore: The Johns Hopkins Press), 1976; *Slaves, Citizens, Sons*, Francis Lyall (Grand Rapids: Zondervan Publishing House), 1984; *Roman Rule in Asia Minor*, Volume I, Magie (Princeton: Princeton University Press), 1966; *The Provinces of the Roman Empire: The European Provinces*, Theodor Mommsen (Chicago: The University of Chicago Press), 1968; *MVSE: Annual of the Museum of Art and Archaeology*, Number 5 (Columbia, Missouri: University of Missouri), 1971; *Art and Thought in the Hellenistic Age*, John Onians (London: Thames and Hudson, Ltd.), 1979; *The Harvest of Hellenism*, F. E. Peters (New York: Simon and Schuster), 1970; *The Museums of Israel*, L. Y. Rahmani (New York: Rizzoli International Publications, Inc.), 1976; *Roman Britain: Outpost of the Empire*, H. H. Scullard (London: Thames and Hudson), 1979; *Roman Imperial Sculpture*, D. E. Strong (London: Alec Tiranti, Ltd.), 1961; *Hellenistic Civilization and the Jews*, Victor Tcherikover (New York: Atheneum), 1975; *Museum of Anatolian Civilizations*, Raci Temizer (Ankara, Turkey: The Publications of the Ankara Society for Promotion of Tourism, Antiquities, and Museums), 1975; *Roman Imperial Art in Greece and Asia Minor*, Cornelius C. Vermeule (Cambridge University Press), 1968.

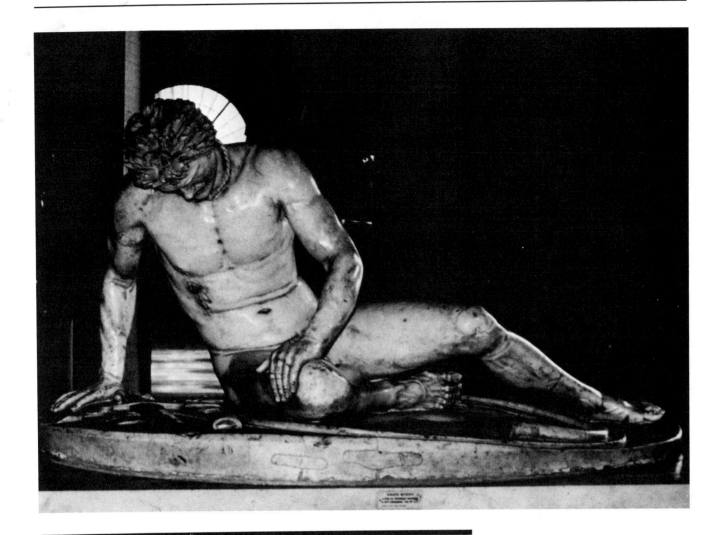

▲ 67 **The Dying Galatian,** Roman copy of an original of about 200 BC. Capitoline Museum. The original statue was produced by the Pergamum school and was part of a group that originally was set up at Pergamum, or possibly at Athens. They reflect the heroic art style of Pergamum (see photo 96). The several figures, all defeated, represent peoples who had been significant enemies of Greece. Attalus, king of Pergamum, placed his defeat of the Galatians at the same level of historical importance as earlier defeats of the Persians and Amazons. The nearness of death each figure approaches may represent how far back into history the peoples were a threat. The Giant lies dead, flat on his back; the Amazon is dead or almost so; the Persian still shows signs of life; and the Gaul (photo 96) is in much the same position as the Galatian. In fact, the 2 statues almost surely represent the same people. *Galatians; 1 Corinthians 16:1.*

GREECE

The origin of the Greeks is lost in antiquity. They were culturally linked to the Minoans on Crete; the Mycenean culture obviously was an outgrowth of the Minoans'. The Minoan civilization was destroyed about 1400 BC by sea raiders who were part of a migration that included the Sea Peoples. The Mycenean Age ended during the latter part of the twelfth century BC. The Dorians then appeared on the scene as marauding tribes who ushered in 300 years of Dark Ages. The Ionians, who may have come out of a people called the Pelasgians who were indigenous to Greece, fled to the west coast of Turkey.

Only the Athenians remained on the Greek mainland as a Greek civilization. Across the sea they established a number of major cities, added to some Mycenean-related cities already there.

Over the next several centuries civilization increased in the region. The classical period began about the middle of the seventh century. The Greeks as we know them were an amalgamation of the 2 strains that came to inhabit the Greek lands: the Dorians and the Ionians.

Alexander the Great began a new era called the Hellenistic Age. He was from Macedonia, which was considered inferior by the Greeks to the south. Parts of Macedonia had been settled early by Greeks, but they probably had mixed with local Illyrians and Thracians. The Macedonians considered themselves, however, to be one people. Alexander's father, Philip II, united the people of Macedonia and Greece partly by conquest and partly by diplomacy. Alexander's routing of the Persians from Asia Minor united

▲68 **Portrait head, lady of first century BC.** Olympia Museum. Her hair is tightly curled in front, and she wears a tiara-type headdress, whose ties hang down her neck. *Texts: See photo 69.*

the Greek-speaking peoples in spirit if not always in peace.

Though Alexander's vast empire was divided among his generals after his death, all of them but Ptolemy gave themselves to the spread of Hellenism. That process and its results is a complex and important study which caught up all of the lands of the New Testament, including Palestine. The modern understanding of how the Greeks viewed barbarians, however, is wrong. As much as they believed they had found the way to live, they admired much in the Eastern civilizations which they considered superior to theirs in age, develop-

ment, and luxury. The Greek word *barbaros* simply refers to people who make noises like "bar bar." The term included those who fit the modern definition, but also referred to citizens of one of the luxurious civilizations such as Persia or Egypt. The term did not necessarily imply contempt.

The Romans conquered Macedonia in 168 BC; in 148 BC it was made into 1 single province. The conquerors laid the Via Egnatia over ancient routes. The province was generally peaceful during the whole of the Imperial period. The interior remained a village economy; Greek culture was limited largely to the coastal areas. The cities were allowed considerable freedom and retained their Greek customs. Thessalonica remained the capital, and the Roman colonies established by Augustus were previously existing cities. Rome apparently gave no special care to Macedonia; it was much more fertile and economically stronger than Greece proper.

The Greek regions to the south fought among themselves, using Rome and being used by Rome until Rome's armed interventions brought both peace and subjection. Augustus separated the Greek areas into the 2 provinces of Achaia and Macedonia; he further reestablished the ancient institution of the Delphic Amphictyony. Though he limited its function to the administration of the revenues of Delphi, the act provided a religious structure that embraced virtually all of the Greek lands. Achaea and Macedonia were reunited into 1 province from AD 15-44, then separated again.

The Greek cities were accorded a high degree of freedom, including self-administration in accordance with Greek structures. However, the Romans modified the Greek city laws when they felt the need to do so, and every city lived under the threat of losing its freedom if its citizens did not handle it well, as "well" was perceived by Rome.

The claim that Rome conquered Greece politically but that Greece conquered Rome intellectually is close to the truth. Romans hired Greeks (or enslaved them) to teach their children, cure their ills, carve their monuments and statuary, and lecture in their halls. Greek writings were loved and Roman writers sought to copy their style. Yet Romans also had a great disdain for much that was Greek. Greeks were considered to be undisciplined, effeminate, immoral, and too luxurious by many Romans.

Greece indeed had much to give to Rome. Yet Romans amalgamated Greek learning, art, and culture; they did not adopt it. Their drive for efficiency and functionability improved on much of what was Greek.

Jews had dispersed to Greece at least by the second century BC but, according to Tcherikover, their presence was not very important.

Paul's travels in Greek lands reflects the terrain of those lands. His work was along the coast of Macedonia and extended as far inland west as Berea. To travel south to Athens, he chose the sea route. The east part of Greece (Thessaly) is a series of mountain ranges divided by valleys that run to the sea; travel by land would have been difficult. We have no record of Paul visiting the west parts of Greece; that region (Epirus) is separated from Thessaly by the Pindos Mountains, which run south right down to the Gulf of Corinth. Paul did not visit the southern Peloponnese; the central part (Arcadia) was the most remote and primitive of any Greek lands, though Sparta was an ancient city there.

▲ **69 Statue of Poppaea Sabina, wife of Nero,** full-length. Olympia Museum. Her hair is in the Claudian style, with the chignon in the back and fine waves of hair in front, tightly curled, with long ringlets hanging down her neck. She is dressed in Greek style, with a thin tunic; it is the undergarment that touches her shoes. She wears a diplax over it (which in a less ample form is called a peplum), which is wound once around her body and under her arms, then again, thrown over her shoulder and arranged in a sleevelike pattern. It is held with a clasp at her waist. *1 Timothy 2:9-12; 1 Peter 3:3.*

▼ **70 Domitia,** headless statue. Olympia Museum. She wears the same type clothing as in photo 69 except it is more open and the folds are draped over her arm. *Texts: See photo 69.*

ASIA MINOR

Asia Minor includes the Turkish peninsula roughly from the Euphrates River to the Aegean Sea, which included Asia, Bithynia, Pontus, Paphlagonia, Galatia, Lycia, Pamphylia, Cilicia, and Cappadocia. The westernmost part, principally Asia, was dominated by ancient Greek city-states; Greeks also had established important cities on the shores of the Black Sea and the Mediterranean, but the regions beyond those coastlands remained provincial and rustic.

Much of the peninsula shared the history of the Seleucids; however, some regions were isolated enough to retain their own lands. Bithynia never submitted to Alexander. Cappadocia, Commagene, and Lesser Armenia continued to be more oriented culturally to the east than to Rome.

Broad river valleys opened much of Asia to the west, while mountain ranges cut off the Black Sea and the Mediterranean coasts from the interior. Deciduous forests follow the Black Sea coast; the Western coasts are low and fertile; the Mediterranean coast is dense mountain forest; open forestlands surround the west, north, and east sides of Anatolia, the central portion of Asia Minor, which consists of high plateau steppe. A massive mountain range, the Pontic, shuts the entire Black Sea coast off from the interior, while another, the Taurus, shuts off the Mediterranean coast. Rainfall declines as one moves inland from any of the coastal areas.

Pamphylia is a narrow, fertile coastal plain that is closed off from the interior by the Taurus Mountains. The unhellenized portion of Cilicia blocks the east, Lycia the west, and Pisidia the north. Three difficult but important routes in an-cient times allowed access to Pisidia. Because it was the southern gateway to the Western and Eastern kingdoms, the Hellenistic kings sought to control it. Due to its isolation and the presence of many small harbors, it became a domain of the pirates who dominated parts of the Mediterranean during the 80s and 70s BC. These mountain ranges were peopled by pastoralists who, in hard times, turned to banditry and even revolt.

Rome controlled these areas with colonies: Lystra, Parlais, Antioch of Pisidia, Cremna, Comana, and Olbasa. Eastern Asia Minor was bound by Syria on the south, Armenia and Parthia on the east.

Several client states existed in Asia Minor. Lycia, an isolated region on the Mediterranean just south of Asia, was a client state referred to as a free league. Cilicia Tracheia lay east of Lycia, on the coast below Galatia. Next to and east of it was the Teucrid Ethnarchy on the coast below Cappadocia. Still farther east between Syria and Cappadocia were the kingdoms of Tarcondimotid and the amazing Commagene. The temple kingdom of Comana lay between Pontus and Bithynia. In AD 17 Tiberius annexed Commagene and assigned it to Syria. In the same year he assigned Cilicia Tracheia and Lycaonia to the son of the deposed ruler of Cappadocia. Gaius reversed Tiberius' action and restored Commagene to client status and added Cilicia Tracheia to it. Pontus and Lesser Armenia also became client kingdoms again.

The colonization of Pamphylia began in the eighth century BC; Side and Phaselis were the first 2 cities built. Croesus of Lydia conquered Pamphylia, and it fell into the hands of the Persians when Lydia was conquered in the sixth century. Alexander the Great captured the area in 334 BC. After his death the region was subject to Alexander's successors, principally the Ptolemies. Then it was a dependency of Pergamum until that kingdom was willed to the Romans. In the first century BC, however, Pamphylia was bound to Cilicia. This Cilicia (Cilicia Campestris) was the flat plain area which included Tarsus. Pompey made it a province in 64 BC to serve, along with Syria, as a buttress against Parthia and Armenia.

What portions of these areas were assigned to what provinces in the early empire is debated. Pisidia was not a province proper until Diocletian, but it was a well-known geographical concept. Augustus founded the colonies of Comama, Cremna, Olbasa, Parlais, and others for the purpose of colonizing southern Asia Minor. Antioch likely was established as a colony on a much older base about the same time that Galatia was made a province, about 25 BC. The other colonies were founded during the last decade of the first century BC.

Antioch of Pisidia was ideally located for both military and commercial purposes. It dominated the region. The city occupied about 115 acres; thus it was a colony of moderate size. The temple of Men Askaenos stood on a mountain peak, but the Romans broke the god's power. By the time of Claudius, at least, Antioch had an influential Jewish community.

Lystra also was founded in 25 BC, on a flat plain 24 miles south of Iconium. The mound, probably the town's acropolis, occupies only about 16 acres. Lystra lies to the

east of the outermost of the mountain ranges that form the Pisidian triangle; thus it was cut off from the other colonies. Obviously, it had the primary role of controlling the Homanadenses. They were a tribal people who had not been subjugated and who were a principal cause of Augustus' establishing the colonies. As part of the preparation for the coming war, he had a road built in 6 BC, called the Via Sebaste, to connect the colonies. Antioch was its pivot, and from there the branches encompassed the Pisidian triangle.

The war lasted 2 to 3 years; when it was won 4,000 male prisoners were distributed among the neighboring tribes. For the next 300 years Pisidia was peaceful, though trouble occurred later in nearby Isauria, Lycia, and Cilicia Tracheia. The road system, which connected with Side on the southern coast,

also became a major link to the east-west trade route.

Jewish emigration into Asia Minor is recorded first in the time of Antiochus III; he ordered that 2,000 Jewish families be moved to Lydia and Phrygia from the Tigris-Euphrates region. During the Hasmonean period, records exist of Jews living in many cities and regions of Asia Minor.

ASIA

The province of Asia had a long history of Greek culture, over which had been superimposed the rule of Persia (547 BC) until Alexander the Great drove them out in 334 BC. Shortly after the Trojan War, Aeotolian Greeks settled between Troy and Smyrna; Ionian Greeks settled from Smyrna to the

▲ 71 **Prisoners in chains:** bas-relief from Smyrna, third century AD. Asmolean Museum, Oxford. The first figure, bearded, wearing a helmet and a light tunic, leads 2 prisoners bound by chains attached to neck rings. They are unbearded, with short hair, and are naked except for small loincloths. *Luke 21:12; Acts 12:6; 28:20; 2 Timothy 1:16.*

Maeander River; Dorian Greeks settled south of the Maeander and on Rhodes and Cos. The cities of the Ionians became the most highly developed. The southern part of Asia, south of the Maeander River, was ancient Caria, allies of the Trojans according to Homer's *Iliad*, whom he calls "barbarous of speech." The Carians were closely associated with the Lelegians. The 2 peoples established a number of cities throughout the region. Greek colonization touched only the coast; the interior remained Carian and was composed primarily of villages. Caria was a satrapy under Persian rule. The satrap ruled virtually as a king and had as a major goal the Hellenization of Caria, though his efforts did not reach into the interior.

Four rivers run west through Asia into the Aegean Sea: the Caicus, on which Pergamum is located; the Hermus, on which Smyrna is located; the Cayster, on which Ephesus is located; and the Maeander, on which Miletus is located.

After Alexander, Asia was caught up in the attempts of the Ptolemies, the Seleucids, and other Greek kings to control Asia Minor. As Rome's power grew and that of the Seleucids declined, smaller kingdoms came to the fore. Rhodes controlled much of the southern coast, while Pergamum controlled Asia down to Caria. Rhodes, in fact, was given both Caria and Lycia by the Romans in 190 BC, the rest of western Asia Minor to Pergamum. A few years later the Romans decreed Caria and Lycia to be free. In 129 BC Caria was added by Rome to the kingdom of Pergamum.

The Attalid dynasty of Pergamum was by far the most significant on the mainland. Three kings—Attalus I (241-197), Eumenes II (197-159), and Attalus II (159-138)—built a kingdom whose boundaries included ancient Phrygia and Lydia and exercised sovereignty over the Greek cities of the northwest coast; and they were able to hold the Galatians in check. Over the years they created a brilliant culture which included the famous library of Pergamum with its 200,000 volumes and the invention of parchment (pergamene). Pergamum's wealth was based on silver mines, wheat, and stockbreeding, coupled with good management. The last king, Attalus III,

died in 133 BC and willed his kingdom to Pergamum's long-time ally, the Romans. Asia's future, however, was to be stormy for a time. The next year Attalus' brother tried to incite a rebellion against Rome; in 130 it was crushed. Mithridates destroyed and sacked Asia's cities in an anti-Roman bloodbath (88 BC). The Roman general Sulla mounted a counterattack in 87 and a year later swept Mithridates out of western Asia Minor.

During the civil war that led to Augustus' emperorship, Caria suffered greatly under the rule of Brutus. The region was rewarded by Augustus; thereafter Caria knew a long period of peace in which its industry and affairs could develop. The region became prosperous.

Christianity was slow to make headway in the area, except for Laodicea and Colossae on its northern fringe.

GALATIA

The population of the north of the province of Galatia was ethnically Gaulish; the people were Gallic in origin, having conquered the territory around 280 BC. For more than a century the Celts had been moving unseen into the region. They retained their identity; indeed, Jerome found that the language spoken there in his day was understandable in Gaul.

The central highlands of the Asia Minor peninsula, weak from Hellenists' warfare, was overrun by Gauls, who were part of a large-scale migration. Fearsome marauders, they were feared for their barbaric cruelty in war. Used by one of the Hellenistic kings in the continuing wars among the competitors, they were rewarded with a region around Pessinus and Ancyra and became mercenaries for whoever would hire them.

The king of Pergamum, Attalus I, defeated them in 230 BC in a bat-

tle that was decisive enough to hold them in check; he was hailed as savior by the Greek states. The dynasty used their victory to good advantage, attributing their annexation of territories to their ability to protect Hellenists from the Galatian incursions.

The king of Bithynia, Nicomedes I, had brought the Galatians into a treaty in 278 BC to make no alliances without his approval. The Galatians, organized into 3 tribal units, conquered the area east of the Halys and made Tavium (21 km. southwest of Boğazköy) their capital. Boğazköy, once a major city and fortress of Phrygia, became a village, whose scanty remains of the second and first centuries BC have been excavated; other remains that date to the Roman Empire have been discovered on Buyukkale and in the Great Temple I.

Ancyra became the capital of 1 tribe. The god Men and the goddess Cybele were worshiped there. These 3 communities apparently were the only ones in Galatia proper; thus the region was basically settled in villages (other cities sometimes mentioned were in areas later attached to Galatia).

By 44 BC a certain Deiotarus had gained control of all three regions. After his death in 41, Amyntas became king. In 36 BC Antony gave Galatia, along with Pamphylia, Pisidia, and Lycaonia, to Amyntas. The regions had been in virtual anarchy for decades; Amyntas had to conquer much of the kingdom for himself.

In 25 BC Augustus annexed Galatia upon the death of king Amyntas, who apparently had succeeded in pacifying the areas. Some scholars believe that Augustus' Galatian province was essentially coterminous with Amyntas' kingdom. To the south, it included at least Attaleia. Central Pisidia remained a part of the province at least until the reign of Vespasian.

Its territory varied in patterns that are unclear, though during Paul's day it generally included Galatia proper, Lycaonia, Pisidia, parts of Pamphylia, Paphlagonia, and parts of Pontus.

Galatia was governed usually by senior consular legates until AD 6; during Tiberius' reign the legates apparently were praetorian, attended by the decline of Galatia's military and administrative importance, which was transferred to the Balkans. Sagalassus was a principal city located in central Pisidia. A temple to Augustus and Roma were built on the site of the Galatian temple.

▲ 72 **Battle scene between Greeks and Galatians,** AD 150-170. Capitoline Museum. The relief is on a marble sarcophagus found in 1829 in the Vigna Ammendola on Via Appia. The height is 4 feet, 4⅝ inches (1.25 m.), while the base is 6 feet, 11 inches (2.11 m.). Debate exists as to whether the figures are Greeks and Galatians or Romans and Gauls. The scene is closely modeled on Greek prototypes; the victorious soldiers are Greeks with an admixture of Roman detail; barbarians were depicted in stock fashion during the period, naked, bearded, and with heavy necklaces. *Texts: See photo 71.*

PHRYGIA

A destruction level at Troy (VII b 2) represents a cultural break and the arrival of new people with affinities with eastern Europe; they may later have become the Phrygians, who ultimately settled in Anatolia. They were Indo-European-speakers; their language probably was related to Thracian. After a period of semi-nomadism, they formed the Phrygian state with its capital at Gordion. They were one of the Sea Peoples who brought about the disintegration of the Hittite Empire; they came to rule the area from Afyon to the Sivas district. Some pottery details connect them with Romania.

The Phrygians were in contact with Assyria; excavations of Gordion reveal extensive buildings and tombs of outstanding importance. They attained a high level of technical skill and culture, especially in wood inlay and metalwork, by the end of the eighth century BC. They were, in fact, more advanced culturally than the Greeks during this period. Homer referred to them in *The Iliad* as inhabitants of Troy. They looked toward expansion into eastern Anatolia and northern Syria. They may have obtained their alphabetic system of writing from the east independently of the Greeks; their writing was similar to that of the Greeks. They had connections with the Urartians (in the Lake Van region).

The Phrygians acted as a buffer between the eastern powers and the Greeks. Thus, their art shows affinities with both east and west. The nomadic Kimmerians (Gimirrai of the Assyrians; Gomer of the Old Testament; they may have been the Scythians) and the rising power of Lydia brought the decline of the Phrygian kingdom. In 650 BC they accepted the rule of the Lydians, after which, from the mid-fifth century, they were dominated by Persia. From this time on their art shows orientation toward eastern Greek.

They occupied the area in west-central Anatolia of the middle and upper Sangarios River and the great bend of the Halys. They held some of the former Hittite sites: Alaca Hüyük, Boğazköy, and Alişar; other cities were Pazarli, Kültepe, and Ancyra. They had entered Asia Minor from the west.

▲73 **Phrygian captives, a father, mother, and child** on statue base. Corinth Museum. The father, bearded and with long hair, wears a cape and trousers and has a brooch around his neck; his hands are tied. Two shields and a helmet are stacked to his right. His son wears a tunic; his seated mother wears traditional Greek dress with her head covered. The bas-relief is on a base of the statue in photo 76. Most scholars believe the work celebrates the Roman victory over the Parthians either in AD 165 or by Septimius Severus, but the dress is standard Roman treatment of barbarians, using Phrygian motifs. *Acts 2:10; 16:6; 18:23.*

Two important sites are located in the upper valley of the Sangarios: Midas City and Gordion (Yassihüyük) west of Polatli. The Greeks knew the names of the Phrygian kings Gordios and Midas (known to the Assyrians under the names of Mushki and Tabal). The Kimmerians defeated the Phrygians and sacked Gordion at the end of the eighth century. Subsequently Phrygia recovered culturally but not as a great power.

Their patron goddess was Cybele, who inherited ancient qualities of a local goddess, Kubaba.

Laodicea, Apamea, and Synnada were Phrygian provinces, detached from Asia in 56 BC and added to Cilicia.

Dio Chrysostom, a prolific writer born in the middle of the first century in Bithynia, recorded a speech he made at Apamea (probably) in Phrygia late in his life. Apamea was a prosperous city, set as it was at the meeting of several major routes and in a large, fertile region; it also was an administrative, judicial, and tax-gathering center for Rome.

Jews had lived in Anatolia from the time of Antiochus III (242-187 BC), who brought them there from Babylon to serve in part of his military force.

▼74, 75 Phrygian grave markers. Roman-German Central Museum, Mainz. Each bas-relief shows the deceased standing in a niche. Photo 74 is for Alexandros and his wife Valeria; it dates to about AD 165. The columns are scrolled, with capitals in the form of upturned leaves. A bird sits on each head, their beaks meeting in a kiss at center. The male and female hairstyles are similar, the woman's having occasional curls in front. He wears a tunic with designs above the chest and held by a wide waistband. A shawl is draped around his shoulders in such a way as to cover his right arm in a manner of a himation. His shoes are enclosed. She wears a tunic with designs, and a wide band binds her body from breasts to hips. Her short boots are flanged at the top. She holds an instrument of some kind that appears to be broken off; part of it appears to have been resting in her left hand. Photo 75 is of the Aurelios Trophimos family; it dates to about AD 250. The designs on the column are cruder. Simple lines at the top meet and separate Greek words, over the man, *etous*, over the woman, *tae*. The man's hair is curled, the woman's longer, straight, and parted in the middle. He wears a short-sleeved tunic with border at the neck and hem and has bracelets on his wrists. He holds a pruning hook. She wears a sleeveless tunic that has bands falling from her shoulders to the hem. Spinning tools are at her waist and left leg. A comb and hand mirror is engraved below the column beside her. Both figures hold their right hands across their chests. The child between them wears his father's hairstyle and a tunic of the same design. His hands are placed much like his father's. *Texts: See photo 73.*

▲76 Phrygian captive, colossal statue. Corinth Museum. The statue formed part of a column that was on the north boundary of the Corinth agora. He is clean shaven, his hair long and curly, and he wears a Phrygian cap. He wears a long-sleeved tunic (or perhaps, in keeping with Phrygian custom, a long-sleeved vest), over which he wears a loose tunic with slits in the sides for his arms. It is pulled up at the waist and draped over a belt. A cloak is fastened across his shoulders with a brooch. His legs are protected with heavy wrappings, and he wears closed shoes which are tied at the top. The capital, with some similarities to the Corinthian style, has leaves rising upward to bands that end in small scrolled ornaments. (See photo 73.) *Texts: See photo 73.*

CAPPADOCIA

Cappadocia lay in the eastern part of Asia Minor, bounded on the east by Armenia, on the north by the Black Sea, on the west by Galatia, and on the south by Commagene. It was a rugged and isolated tableland whose crops were meager and temperatures extreme. However, its pastoral economy produced horses, sheep, and mules.

During Persian times, Cappadocia was ruled by a Persian satrap; afterward the Seleucids ruled briefly. In 301 BC Ariarathes II regained the throne, though he and his successors maintained alliances with the Seleucids. When Rome conquered the Seleucid Antiochus III the Great, Cappadocia shifted its alliance to Rome and became a client kingdom. Its neighbor Commagene to the south remained a client kingdom until AD 72.

The Roman capital was Mazaca, also called Caesarea (Kayseri). Strabo noted that only 2 cities existed in Cappadocia proper, Tyana in Tyanitis and Mazaca in Cilicia. A number of other cities existed, however, in the province. The local peasants had never risen above a tribal organization. Hellenization was slow; only the capital attempted to maintain a semblance of Greek culture, which spread slowly through the area. Even in the fourth century AD the native Cappadocian still was spoken.

The kingdom was annexed in 17 AD. Along with Lesser Armenia (a small area in the northeast corner of Cappadocia) and Commagene, both of which were attached to it, Cappadocia was oriented toward Syria and the east more than toward Greece and Rome.

The politics of Cappadocia during the first century BC were bound up with Pontus and Mithridates on the west and Armenia on the east, caught up in Mithridates' wars with Rome. From AD 17 until AD 72 Cappadocia was administered as a province along the lines of Egypt; but there were only 2 cities in the country, so the administration was feudal. Many Cappadocians were sold into slavery. It was noted for its temple-states, especially those of Comana, Venasa, and Zeus Dacieus.

PONTUS AND BITHYNIA

The kingdoms of Pontus and Bithynia came into being as the Seleucid empire disintegrated. They were combined into 1 province by Pompey when Mithridates of Pontus was finally defeated.

When Rome inherited the kingdom of Pergamum from Attalus III in 133 BC, the 3 feudal kingdoms of Bithynia, Paphlagonia, and Pontus dominated inner Anatolia. The kings of Pontus ruled from a fortress at Amasia; from there they controlled the trade that moved along the southern coast of the Black Sea. The ancient Greek cities of Sinope, Amisus, and Trapezus lay in their territory. The villages, however, spoke some 22 languages.

In 120 BC Pontus passed by assassination into the hands of the 11-year-old Mithridates VI Eupator; by age 20 he had killed his mother and brother to gain control of the kingdom. His imperialistic ambitions brought years of warfare to Asia Minor. Before he was curtailed, he defeated the Roman army, devastated the cities of Asia, and instigated an anti-Roman pogrom in which Romans all over Asia were massacred. Though Pompey brought him temporarily to bay and made a province of Bithynia and Pontus, Mithridates' efforts to forge an empire continued for several more years, including a retaking of his old kingdom. When the Romans finally took control of Pontus, the northern portion was incorporated into a joint province with Bithynia; other portions were doled out to various client kings.

The city of Comana, at the juncture of the old border between Pontus and Bithynia, was made a temple state by Pompey for the Anatolian Great Mother, Ma (identified with Cybele). It was one of several powerful temple-states in Pontus.

Bithynia, the name of which came from a Thracian tribe, was the westernmost of the 3. Essentially a feudal state, it claimed both shores of the Bosporus and the Propontis, along with the mountainous regions to the south. During the second century BC Bithynia was bound by treaty to Rome; however, its king Nicomedes became involved in the imperialism of Mithridates of Pontus, dividing Paphlagonia between them. Bithynia later joined Rome in an unsuccessful effort to curtail Mithridates. Eventually, though, Mithridates was pressed back inside Pontus and Rome's power began to grow in the region. Nicomedes IV willed Bithynia to Rome upon his death in 74 BC. In addition to Apamea, Rome established the colonies of Heraclea Pontica and Sinope. Other principal cities included Chalcedon, Prusa, Nicomedia, Nicaea, Prusias and Hypium, Claudiopolis, Tius, Amastris, Abonuteichus, Pompeiopolis, and Amisus.

The wealth of Bithynia and Pontus brought an influx of Romans to the region, which in turn brought about the rapid Romanization of the area. Nicomedia became the center for Bithynia's emperor worship. The enlarged province was allowed to be governed by proconsuls chosen annually by lot from among qualified senators; it seemed to have been cursed with an unusu-

▲ **77 Woman playing dice,** small terra-cotta found in Bithynia. Roman-German Landesmuseum, Cologne. Gambling with dice (see photo 588) was a favorite pastime among women in the Empire. A number of terra-cottas similar to this one have been found (two women would be in pairs). The pastime is also portrayed on Pompeii's walls (see photo 590). She is dressed in the typical Greek himation but also wears a skullcap. *Matthew 27:35; Acts 16:7; 1 Peter 1:1.*

ally repetitive pattern of maladministration and profit-taking by the governors. It was a difficult province to administer for other reasons as well, and the emperors kept a close watch on it, sometimes appointing legates answering directly to them for periods of time. Pliny the Younger was a legate so appointed.

CILICIA

Cilicia lay west of the northeastern curve of the Mediterranean Sea. The plains area in the eastern part, Cilicia Pedias, was a region of strong cities, fertile soil, and strong commerce. The mountainous area in the western part, Cilicia Tracheia, was more isolated; its life was that of the village and tribe, and its chief value was timber. The people were called Cetae, a name that resembles Kedi (see p. 64).

The isolated coastline of Cilicia Tracheia harbored pirates as Pamphylia's did. Rome became involved in Cilicia as a result of the Roman attempt to eradicate piracy, which after all arose as a result of their own policy that limited the sea power of Rhodes and other kingdoms who traditionally had kept the sea lanes safe. The piracy wreaked havoc on both the commerce and population of Cilicia Pedias, many of whose citizens were kidnapped and sold into slavery.

During the first century the region was considered unready for direct Roman rule, a country of "unruly tribes and robber chiefs." Part of the region was assigned by Augustus to the Teucrid king, the other part to Amyntas. When Amyntas died, the western part of his kingdom was assigned to the province of Galatia, the rest to the king of Cappadocia. Its assignments varied with the deaths and fortunes of various kings until annexed by Vespasian and assigned to Pamphylia.

The history of Cilicia is somewhat obscure during the late second and early first century BC. In addition to the attempts by Rome to solve the piracy problem, which involved Cilicia, Dolabella apparently was governor of the region in 80-79. Cilicia at the time was part of the Pisidian zone. However, during Dolabella's time Cilicia became a regular governor's assignment, a province with an army. As he and his successors succeeded in expelling the pirates from the coastal areas and the tribal chieftains from the interior (particularly the Isaurians between Pisidia and Iconium), Lycaonia was attached to Cilicia. Then, with the rising threat and power of Mithridates, Cilicia became a military strongpoint for Rome against the Hellenistic king.

Lycia was an ancient kingdom whose history in the century before Roman control was tied to the kingdom of Pergamum.

Cilicia Pedias lay on one of the ancient world's most important trade routes. Two gates opened from Cilicia through the mountains into the interior and on the west: the Syrian Gates (north of Antioch of Syria, modern Belen Pass) and the Cilician Gates above Tarsus. The region appears in Egyptian records of the thirteenth century BC by the name Kedi (or Kode). Sometime after that it was apparently involved in the massive movement of peoples that involved the Sea Peoples. During the eighth century the name Cilicia first appears. The Cilicians may have been an Aegean people; ancient legends abound that the cities were founded by Trojan War heroes.

The several important cities of Cilicia included Mopsuhestia, Mallus, Soli, Issus, Myriandus, Seleucia on the Calycadmus, Aphrodisias, Adana, Castabala, and Tarsus. Issus and Myriandus lost their importance after the Persian

period and possibly were combined into the one city of Alexandria. During the first century cities were formed in the north of Cilicia Pedias: Augusta, Livia, Neronias (the eastern Irenopolis), and Flaviopolis. This region was less civilized and was attached at times to Commagene.

Ancient legend had Tarsus founded by one of the Argives. Sennacherib of Assyria rebuilt Tarsus in imitation of Babylon in 698 BC. During the Persian period Greek influence was strong; the coinage of the city was inscribed in Greek rather than the Aramaic used by most cities of the region. Xenophon had been there some 400 years before Paul; he found there the palace of a King Syennesis, which was a titulary name. During the Hellenistic period, Cilicia was contested by the Seleucids and the Ptolemies, but the region remained generally Seleucid. During this period, Tarsus bore the name of Antioch upon the Cydnus.

Antiochus Epiphanes probably settled Jews there as colonists in 171 BC. Tarsus was loyal to Pompey and he made it the capital of the region; then the city shifted its loyalty to Julius Caesar. Its connection with Antony is famous from his meeting there with Cleopatra; Antony made Tarsus a free city.

From 56-50 BC the province (not strictly organized as a province) stretched from Laodicea to the Syrian Gates. After 50, however, its importance declined in favor of Asia. In 49 the three Phyrgian areas were returned to Asia, and after a few obscure years, Cilicia Pedias was attached to Syria. It was not to become an independent province again until Vespasian was emperor. Thus, when Paul wrote of his travels in Syria, he was in his own political province.

Strabo wrote that Tarsians had an enthusiasm for philosophy and for education generally. Nearly all the students in Tarsus were natives,

who often afterward went abroad to study. Strabo further wrote of Stoic studies flourishing. Scholars have pointed out Paul's familiarity with Stoicism. It was a "free city" from Antony's time; as such, it paid no tribute and had self-government. Dio Chrysostom spoke of workers in sailcloth (*Appian, B.C.,* v. 7) and of their repute for being many in number and disorderly in ways and of their uneasy position in the city. Tarsus shared the region's wealth with the other cities of the plains. The Cilician Gates, which was the creation apparently of Tarsus in ancient times, provided much trade through the city. The soil produced cereals, grapes, and flax, the latter providing the base for the linen industry for which the region was famous. Tarsus was aggressive and was reprimanded by Dio Chrysostom for constantly feuding with and suing its neighbor cities.

Among the feuds the cities engaged in was the attempt to outdo one another in the games they sponsored. Tarsus celebrated the Epinicia, Olympia, Actia, Coraea, Demetria, various games held in honor of emperors, and others. During the first century, Tarsus was undisputed leader of the region. Strabo noted that the River Cydnus flowed hard by the young men's gymnasium. Plutarch described the coming of Cleopatra to meet Antony (*Life of Antony,* c. 25).

The 2 great languages of the nearer East were Greek and Syriac, to which the Aramaic of Palestine is closely akin. Tarsus stands where the 2 met, a frontier town. Westward, thought and speech were Greek; eastward, thought and speech were Syriac. Writers have speculated for a very long time about Paul's background and training in connection with Tarsus in Cilicia and his Pharisaic training in Jerusalem and perhaps earlier. The answers have been anything but conclusive.

THE EAST

The province of *Syria* comprised some of the choice areas of the Seleucid kingdom. The region was civilized long before Rome was, and the people went on about their business with only a cloak of Romanization. They added Roman names to their gods, but the adjustment was primarily cosmetic. When the Romans arrived they found in Syria Greeks and Macedonians who had settled there in the years since Alexander's conquest.

The Aramaeans in the north took their name from Mesopotamia and had spread throughout the region of Syria outside of Phoenicia and Judea. The Phoenicians occupied their ancient homeland along the Mediterranean. Their language was dying out here (though not in such ancient colonies as Carthage), and they were speaking Greek and Aramaic.

Greek descendants existed in all the chief towns, especially Antioch, Apamea, Seleucia, Chalcis, Laodicea (of Syria), Damascus, and Palmyra. Antioch was settled with people from Athens and Macedonia, to whom Antiochus the Great added other Greeks and Cretans. The city also contained a large Jewish community. The other cities also were settled with Europeans.

Aramaic continued in popular usage and was the primary language, though Greek was used in commerce. Many cities had both Greek and Aramaic names, as did many people. Syria accepted Roman rule quickly and adopted Roman weights, measures, coinage, and calendar; and many spoke or at least wrote Latin. They accepted, too, Roman amusements, such as chariot races and theaters.

Syria came under Roman domination through the efforts of Pompey in connection with his war against Mithridates. The province dates from 64 BC, but it was small at that time, relying on the municipalities and native princes in a client system. No organized colonization took place there before Augustus. From 57 BC onward a proconsul commanding a powerful army made his headquarters at Antioch. Pompey and then the first governor of Syria, A. Gabinius (57-55 BC), freed the Greek cities conquered by the Hasmoneans and restored the Greco-Syrian cities of Samaria, Scythopolis, Dora, and Gaza which had been destroyed by the Hasmoneans.

After Augustus gained the emperorship, Syria in 27 BC was made an imperial province due to its important location bordering on Parthia, Armenia, and Judea. A few colonies of veterans were founded in Syria, and many towns were enlarged and beautified. The period from 30 BC to AD 66 was one of peace and greatly increased prosperity. Bouchier called it the chief province of the empire.

Judea sometimes was a client kingdom, sometimes a province. Its history is well known; for that reason and to allow space for less well-known regions, its history will not be reviewed here. Photo 111 provides an overview of a model of Jerusalem; in addition, the Pilate Stone is included, along with several photos intended to indicate the impact of Hellenism and Roman culture on Judea.

Jews, in addition to Palestine, were dispersed far and wide in the east. Though the Babylonian captivity had much to do with the dispersion, their spread predates that climactic event. They had colonies in China from early times; they were in India, Yemen, Persia, Africa (in addition to Egypt), and throughout Syria.

Arabia conjures up quite a different image today than is appropriate for the first century. Then it was the kingdom of the Nabateans, a people who had migrated forcefully northward to force the Edomites west across the Arabah rift. The Edomites carved out a region for themselves in the Negeb and became known as the Idumeans. The Nabateans appear in history first in 312 BC; evidence indicates an aggressive commercial involvement in the transporting of spices and perfumes during the third century. By the first century AD their kingdom was firmly established, with an important city, Bostra, in the north. Some cities of the Decapolis lay within the boundaries of the Roman province of Arabia: Philadelphia, Gerasa, Dium, and Adraa. They controlled the Hauran, Median, the Negeb, the northwest part of the Arabian peninsula, and the Sinai. Their cities of 'Avdat and Kurnub in the Negev have been thoroughly excavated. Petra was another major trade city. While Bostra became the capital of the province, some debate exists as to whether it or Petra was the capital of the kingdom.

The Nabateans were enemies of the Hasmoneans and later of Herod I. Their kings during the first century were: Aretas IV (8 BC—AD 40), whose reign marked the Nabateans' golden age; Malichus II (40-70); and Rabbel II (71-106), at the end of whose reign Arabia became a Roman province. The movement of spices and perfumes was transferring from Nabatean control to Egypt, however, so during the first century the Nabateans were settling down and learning agriculture. The discovery of some papyrus documents which were the personal papers of a Jewess named Babatha reveals the easy intermingling between the Jews and the Nabateans.

Palmyra, earlier called Tadmor, was a caravan city that lay on a route between the Euphrates River and Damascus. It sought to remain independent between the antagonists of Parthia and Rome, but gradually came more under Rome's influence. In AD 18 Tiberius incorporated it into the province of Syria but it remained semi-independent.

▲ 79 Judaea Capta coin of Domitian. The Archaeological Museum of The Southern Baptist Theological Seminary. A weeping Jewess sits under a palm tree and on the other side the conqueror's shield leans against the tree. Some coins show a Roman soldier along with the shield and also add to the simple IVDAEA on this coin the additional words CAPTA or DEVICTA ("defeated"). The Flavian emperors minted this type of coin, which became the means of exchange for the occupying X Legion, and thus a constant reminder to the Jews of their defeat and the strength of Rome.

▲ 78 Bust, woman of Roman period, Judea, 63 BC-AD 130. Rockefeller Museum, Jerusalem. She is dressed in the Greco-Roman style with an inner tunic around which is wrapped a peplum or diplax. Her hair is pulled straight back without a part and hangs down her neck almost to her shoulders. The Roman style was not as full as this, though it sometimes hung down the neck in wavy tresses. The raised portion on top appears to be braids of her own hair. *Acts 2:5.*

81 Pilate Stone, Caesarea Maritima. Photo is of copy on site; the original is in the Israel Museum, Jerusalem. Its height is 2 feet, 7½ inches (.8 m.). The stone was found in secondary use as a step in the theater. Originally it was a dedicatory inscription for a building, perhaps a temple to Tiberius. Only part of the inscription remains; the conjectured part is in parentheses:

(CAESARIEN) S (IBUS)
TIBERIEVM
(?? PON)TIVSPILATVS
(?? PRAEF)ECTVSIVDA(EA)E

The translation is:

To the people of Caesarea
Tiberium
Pontius Pilate
Prefect of Judea

"The Prefect of Judea Pontius Pilate erected the Tiberium in honor of Tiberius Caesar."

The stone is the first epigraphical reference to Pilate, governor of Judea in AD 26-36. *Matthew 27:2-65 and parallels; Luke 3:1; 13:1.*

80 Herod the Great, reproduction of bust. The Archaeological Museum of The Southern Baptist Theological Seminary. Romans did not wear beards during the first century; Herod thus followed the Eastern style in this regard. *Matthew 2:1-20; Luke 1:5-21.*

82 **Funeral statue, North Syrian woman,** limestone, AD 165-200. Height 2 feet, 6 inches (76 cm.). Museum of Art and Archaeology, University of Missouri-Columbia. She wears a tunic with sleeves that reach to the wrists and are cuffed. It is bound by a cloth belt under her breasts. She has a fringed shawl, or mantle, over her head and shoulders and wrapped around her upper arms. She holds it at her hip with her left hand. She wears sandals, identical bracelets adorn each wrist, and she wears a necklace with a crescent. Her pose is copied from the Greek-style statue called the *pudicitia*. Costumes were brilliant in color and richly jeweled. Linen, or silk for the rich, were preferred to wool. Women regularly wore veils which often formed the only headdress, sometimes brought round the head like a hood, thus resembling the izar still worn in Syria. They wore frontlets or jewels fixed on the forehead, necklaces, pearl earrings, anklets, and a girdled chiton which overflowed with an Oriental character. Sometimes the statues exhibit tattooing on the chest. *Acts 15:23,41; 18:18; Galatians 1:21.*

▼83 Bust, Syrian woman, set in a niche, AD 96. Museum of Art and Archaeology, University of Missouri-Columbia. She wears a shawl or mantle over her head and shoulders and wrapped around her right arm. The garment under it is crossed in front. She wears a bracelet on each wrist, earrings, and a choker-type necklace. She holds a small bottle in her left hand. Her hair is fixed with side curls just in front of the ears. Under the veil she wears a sort of turban and a wide headband. The Greek lettering at the bottom reads: "Farewell, noble Leouitha, free from pain, year 408." *Texts: See photo 82.*

▲ **84 Funeral stone from Palmyra,** limestone, second-third century AD. Field Museum. The man's sideburns reach to his chin; his hair, mustache, and whiskers are curled. He wears a tunic, visible at the neck, and over it a pallium wound over his left arm and shoulder, around his back, over his right shoulder, under his arm, and thrown back over his left shoulder. His style of wearing the pallium is the pudicitia (meaning modesty), found in tomb statuary. He holds a sprig in his left hand. The inscription over his left shoulder is in Aramaic. The right arm using the himation as a sleeve was a traditional pose of dignity. The style shows the influence of Rome in the east, at least among upper classes.

▲ **85 Funeral portrait of a man named Nardos Chalbos.** Syrian, second century AD, limestone. Roman-German Central Museum, Mainz. His hair is longer and straighter than in photo 84, and he is bearded, but his attire is the same. He holds a rod or more likely a scroll in his left hand. *Texts: See photo 82.*

▼ **86 Funeral portrait, Syrian woman,** second century AD. Roman-German Central Museum, Mainz. She wears a tunic with sleeves to the wrists, over which a shawl is draped over her head and shoulders. A bracelet adorns her wrist, and she wears three necklaces: a choker with hanging ornaments, a lower band from which hangs a crescent, and a still lower one with a shell design. *Texts: See photo 82.*

EGYPT AND NORTH AFRICA

When the seventh Cleopatra committed suicide with the bite of an asp in 30 BC, the long period of Ptolemy rule ended.

Egypt had particular problems of government. Augustus conquered Egypt personally and retained it as a personal province. With its vast wealth, to assign a potential competitor as governor would run the risk of providing him a power base. Egypt's Hellenistic administrative structure was retained, and by policy few cities were established. Augustus chose to keep Egypt agrarian in order to maximize the produce Rome could drain from the province. Recovered Roman records reveal how thoroughly and systematically Rome sought to exploit the wealth of Egypt, which was assigned the task of providing one-third of the grain supply for the city of Rome.

Augustus and his successors followed the style of the Ptolemies; they built in the Egyptian style and carved their likenesses in the form of pharaohs. The social structure remained somewhat the same, but with the Romans on top. Pyramid in style, the base of the social structure was the Egyptians, a mass of people who were rich and very poor, artisans and peasants, townspeople and villagers. They had varying degrees of benefits, but none of them had benefits to approach those above them on the pyramid.

The next layer up was the Greeks and Jews (the Jews lost their place in the Jewish War of 66-70); and on top were the few Roman citizens— 2 legions of soldiers, transient Romans, and permanent Romans. The Greeks and Jews were exempt from the poll tax, allowed to purchase public lands, exempt from various

▲87 Funeral painting, woman from the Fayyum, Egypt, second century AD. Field Museum. The portrait is fixed onto the wood with paint-impregnated wax which was heated. The plaque likely hung in her home while she lived and then was wrapped over her face in the mummification process. She appears to wear a light tunic and a choker. Her hair is short. *Matthew 2:13-22; Acts 2:10; 21:38.*

types of service, and eligible to serve in Roman legions which gave them Roman citizenship immediately upon enlistment.

The Egyptian class included the descendants of the Greeks who had settled in Egypt during Ptolemaic times. They were subject to numerous restrictions and fines for violation; they bore the labor burden; and they paid taxes, assessed on the people, their land, and virtually every aspect of their lives. Appar-

ently Augustus singled Egypt out for reprisals because of their support for Antony. Rome isolated Egyptians into a sort of apartheid.

Egypt had only 3 Greek cities: Naukratis in the Delta, Ptolemais up the Nile valley, and Alexandria. The latter remained an important intellectual and commercial center. It was a cosmopolitan city, with many ethnic groups, including a large population of Jews (Philo claimed one million).

When Claudius assumed the throne in AD 41 delegations of both Greeks and Jews petitioned him to rule in their favor. The occasion was tension brought on by pressure from Jews to be accorded Alexandrian citizenship and anti-Jewish actions by the Greeks. Riots broke out when Caligula was assassinated.

In North Africa Carthaginian influences still were strong; the Punic language was spoken by many. The province of Africa included all of the Mediterranean coastland outside of Egypt and Cyrenaica. The Romanization took place over an ancient city structure that was oriented to the East; Carthage, for example, had been a colony of Phoenicia. Cyrenaica consisted of five cities called the Pentapolis, Apollonia being the most important, that occupied a well-watered coastal ridge. It was administered together with Crete by a proconsul appointed by the Senate.

Africa ran from Cyrenaica to just west of modern Casablanca. A number of important cities flourished: Lepcis Magna, Thapsus, Neapolis, and Carthage being a few. The region produced a number of literary figures, lawyers, and politicians. Its economic base was olive oil and corn.

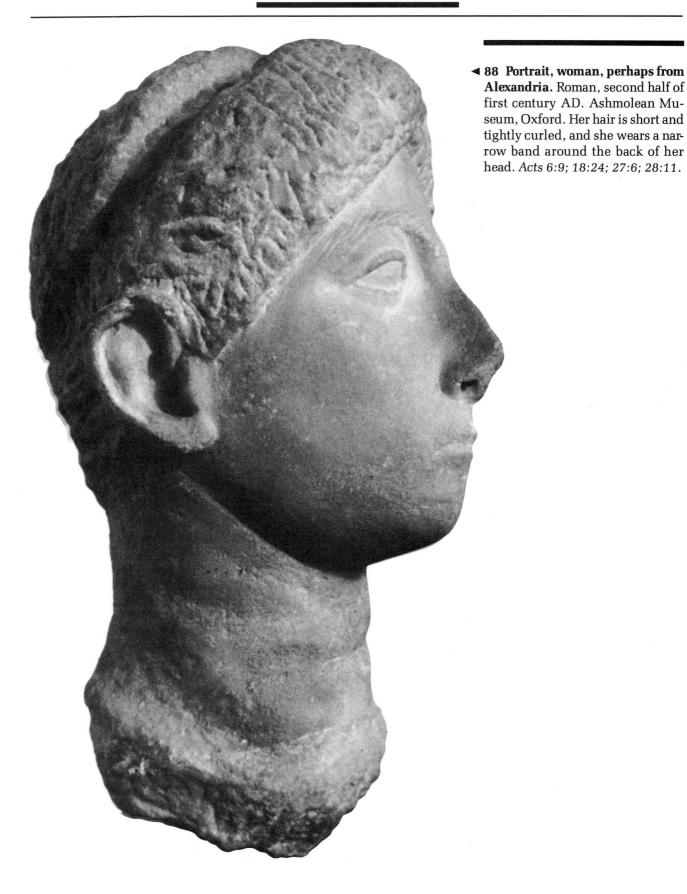

◄ 88 Portrait, woman, perhaps from Alexandria. Roman, second half of first century AD. Ashmolean Museum, Oxford. Her hair is short and tightly curled, and she wears a narrow band around the back of her head. *Acts 6:9; 18:24; 27:6; 28:11.*

▲ **89 Plaster funeral mask, Greco-Egyptian burial,** first-third centuries AD. Field Museum. His hair is short in the Roman style; he has sideburns and a short goatee. *Texts: See photo 87.*

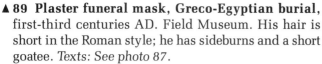

◄ **90 Plaster funeral mask, Greco-Egyptian burial** of first-third centuries AD. Field Museum. Her hair is short and tightly curled in the Roman style. *Texts: See photo 87.*

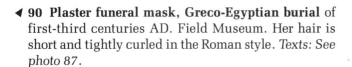

► **91 Plaster funeral mask, Greco-Egyptian burial** of first-third centuries AD. Field Museum. Her hair is fixed in an intricate Roman style, with the main portion parted in the center and combed to the sides in waves, the portion next to her forehead in short, tight ringlets, and capped with a headdress. *Texts: See photo 87.*

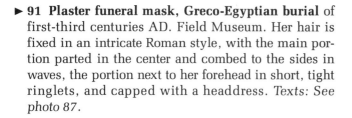

▼ 92 Portrait statue of woman, marble, found in the temple of Aphrodite at Cyrene. Roman, AD 130-150. British Museum. She wears a tunic, seen at the neck and at bottom, over which she has wrapped her himation. The himation was held in place only by its own weight and the nature of its being wrapped; clasps were never used for it. Her sandals are thongs. Her hair is bound up severely; it is pulled straight back from her forehead, and the long tresses are braided and wrapped around her head. *Matthew 27:32; Mark 15:21; Luke 23:26; Acts 2:10; 6:9; 11:20; 13:1.*

◄ 93 Female bust from Carthage, terra-cotta, second century AD. British Museum. Her garment appears to be a himation. Her hair is parted in the middle, perhaps rolled, and pulled tightly back around her ears. It is held into place either by a braided band or braids of her own hair.

► 94 Anthony of Egypt, funeral relief. The Archaeological Museum of The Southern Baptist Theological Seminary. The tombstone art shows decline as the Byzantine period approached; the figure is lifelike and natural enough, but the folds on his tunic lack refinement, the columns and altar are simple, and the dog is a caricature. The man wears a sleeveless tunic with a belt arrangement at his hips and has a himation or shawl hanging from his shoulder and draped across his arm. His hair is full and he is beardless. *Texts: See photo 87.*

EUROPE

Europe begins west of the Black Sea and Asia Minor. This section will treat those regions briefly; except for Macedonia they were not involved directly in New Testament history. However, Rome favored the west; those regions were quicker to adapt to Roman culture, they received favored treatment from Rome in regard to the franchise, and Rome had historic links to Gaul. Gaul was the scene of Julius Caesar's greatest victories and the base he built from which to capture the emperorship. Paul traveled to the borders of Illyricum (Rom. 15:19) and he wanted to—perhaps did—travel to Spain.

The reign of Augustus was a period of consolidation. Spain was occupied completely by 25 BC and organized into 3 provinces: Baetica, Lusitania, and Tarraconensis. Wars in Germany were only partly successful; Rome finally settled for the Rhine as its northern border, the Danube as its eastern. The territories included southern Europe from the Black Sea to the Atlantic below the Rhine and Danube. The area that now is Bavaria, Switzerland, and western Austria was organized into 2 provinces called Raetia and Noricum. The areas to the east became the provinces of Illyricum, Moesia, Macedonia, and Thrace. Illyricum rebelled and brought on a costly 3-year war which thwarted Augustus' plans to conquer more of Germany. When the region finally was subdued, it was divided into 2 provinces: the coastal area became Dalmatia, the interior Pannonia. Britain was invaded in earnest in AD 43 and the southern part lying closest to France was conquered.

Southern Gaul had been under Roman influence from the Republi-

▼ **95 Bas-relief from sarcophagus.** Glyptothek, Munich. The photo shows part of a scene of the myth of Orestes before Iphigenia, but the clothing is anachronistic. The figure on the right is a native Taurian tribesman (modern Crimea). He wears barbarian trousers and a Phrygian cap. His long sleeves probably belong to a vest, which is covered by a loose tunic. His pantaloons are of the same material as his vest. They fit somewhat loosely around his thighs, tighter at his ankles. His hat is of the Phrygian type, with its top bent forward and flaps hanging to his shoulders. It sometimes was hard, sometimes soft and pliant. He carries a large sheathed sword. *Acts 28:2; Romans 1:14; 1 Corinthians 14:11; Colossians 3:11.*

can period, but they had their own civilization which they did not want to lose. This region was renamed Narbonensis, while the northern portions of Gaul were reorganized into 3 provinces: Aquitania, Lugdunensis, and Belgica.

Germany became Romanized faster than Gaul north of Narbonensis, since the Germanic people were not organized as successfully as were the Gauls; but the influence worked both ways. The Romans, who essentially were soldiers who manned the forts and remained in Germany after they retired, also were Germanized.

Thrace, the eastern neighbor of Macedonia, was made up of tribespeople much like those of Illyricum.

▶ **96 Gaul warrior,** marble, two-thirds lifesize. National Museum of Naples. The height is 3 feet (.914 m.); the width of the plinth 6 feet, 1 inch (1.85 m.). The statuary is from the Pergamum School. The statue is a copy of one of a series done by Epigonus of Pergamum that Attalus I dedicated in Pergamum (or possibly Athens) about 200 BC to emphasize the significance of his victory over the Galatian Gauls. The Pergamum School shows unusual emotional intensity, a preoccupation with the theme of violence, suffering, and death. The vigorous style is sturdy rather than refined, a bit heavy in general effect. The warrior sinks toward death from a mortal wound. He is seated on the ground, leaning heavily on his right arm, his legs bent in pain. The artist has given him a natural dignity. The Dying Gaul in the Capitoline Museum, Rome, is in a similar pose but has no helmet (see photo 67). These sculptures were brought to Rome at the end of the second century BC, where they had great influence on Rome's interest in Greek art. *Texts:*
See photo 95.

◀ **97 Fragment of heads of Gauls,** limestone architectural frieze, first century AD. Musée Lapidaire, Arles. The fragment was used later in a rampart. The technical detail is unusual. A trepan (sort of awl) was used to outline the head, pupils, eye sockets, lip corners, and ear channels. The hair is cut short in the Gaul style. *Texts: See photo 95.*

▼ **98 Bearded head, northern Germanic area.** Brussels Museum. The head is unusually realistic, the skin light and the hair dark, the hair and beard medium length and well trimmed. *Texts: See photo 95.*

▲ **99 Horseman attacking a Gaul,** bas-relief from an alabaster burial urn, from Chiusi, Etruria, Italy, third-second centuries BC. Field Museum. The horseman wears armor and holds a lance. The Gaul, depicted nude, holds an oblong shield in his left hand and thrusts a sword into the horse's belly with his right hand. Another Gaul, nude but for a belt and cape, grasps the blade of the horseman's sword. He also appears to hold a shield. The horseman's hat appears to be of the hard Phrygian type with the forward fold at its peak. A winged female demon holding a sword watches the combat. She wears boots and a sleeved tunic pulled up and bound under her breasts and again at her hips. She holds another object, perhaps a sword, in her right hand. Her hair is pulled back in a bun. *Texts: See photo 95.*

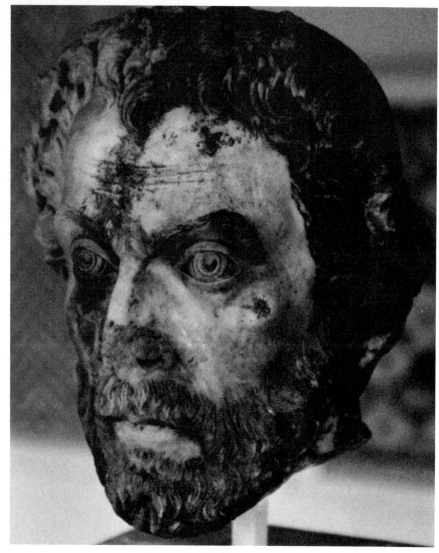

►**100 Marciana in Herculaneum style Roman dress,** full statue, second century AD. Glyptothek, Munich. She wears a tunic, visible at the neck and legs, and over it a himation. The himation is wound around her body, under her right arm to enclose it, and thrown back over her left shoulder. The first wrapped portion is pulled up over the back of her head. The corners are clearly marked by tassels. Along with the folds in her left hand, she holds two poppy capsules and an ear of wheat, which represent Demeter. This addition was used to portray women of noble descent who were officers or priestesses of Eleusinian temples. Her right hand probably held a torch. Her hairstyle is Trajanic, consisting of 1 small and 2 larger rolls of hair. The small roll is triple braided.

▼**101 Portrait head and neck, bearded man, northern Germanic area.** Brussels Museum. His cap covers a ring of hair and itself is comprised of 2 rings, 1 on top of the other. *Texts: See photo 95.*

THE CITY

The Roman Empire essentially was an association of about 1,000 cities ruled by Rome. Most of those related to New Testament studies had ancient or at least Hellenistic origins; a few were established by Rome as colonies.

Rome did not in most cases impose a new system of rule onto the cities but rather used the prevailing patterns. Greek cities were administered by an order of city councillors made up of aristocratic families. Rome did not replace them; indeed, the Empire's policy was to enhance their old positions as the best way to ensure order.

These local magistrates maintained order, watched over finances, and dispensed justice. Rome became involved in matters of taxation if necessary, if the all-too-common disputes between Greek cities began to get out hand, or if the public peace was threatened. This semi-autonomy was a far cry from the heavy-handed rule of previous conquerors even if the cities were not truly free, and the policy accounts for the fact that the old Greek cities welcomed Rome as a liberator.

The city-state was the ancient pattern of the civilized portions of Greece and Asia Minor. Even under the Persian rule and later under that of Alexander and his successors, a sense of nationalism never developed. Allegiances were to cities until well beyond the New Testament period, however valuable and appealing Roman citizenship was.

The world of the New Testament, too, was centered around the cities.

this in spite of the fact that about 90 percent of the Empire's 60-80 million inhabitants lived outside the cities (according to modern estimates; Karl Christ, p. 81). Most of the cities had populations of 10,000 to 15,000; some were smaller, and only a few were larger.

The cities for the most part were situated along the seacoasts or navigatible rivers; occasionally one existed as a religious center or on an overland trade route. The interiors of the Empire—such as in Syria or Asia Minor—held only a few cities at the beginning of the Empire. Rome then created a few, most of town size. Some of them were colonies; others had populations made up of native people who came to be educated in the ways of city life and commerce.

Roman colonies were more common in the West, outside of the New Testament world (Spain, Gaul, Britain, etc.) than in the East. Even so, colonies were established early in the Empire in Greece, northwestern Asia Minor, Galatia, and Pisidia. (See pp. 53, 56.)

The city was a great common denominator of the Empire. A traveler could find himself comfortably familiar in most towns and cities, somewhat as today the frequent traveler becomes accustomed to the sameness of shopping centers. This commonality made travel easier, but it also hastened the spread of the Greco-Roman culture. The regions which previously supported other civilizations were giving way quickly during the first century to the Empire's influence. The Greek

successors of Alexander already had started this process through Hellenization. New towns were established to serve as royal residences or old towns were refounded and embellished.

City planning had a long history before the period of the Empire. Rome's famous well-ordered design was an ideal rather than a reality for most cities. The design was feasible only when a new city was established, and the Romans had the common sense to adapt to the terrain or existing city layouts. The origin of the grid plan probably did not derive from the military camp but rather evolved from an ancient grid concept perfected by Hippodamus of Miletus (fifth century BC).

The forum was the only real requirement for the formation of a Roman city, though a city was not considered one unless it could boast certain other amenities. The forum ideally was situated in the center of the city at the point where 2 principal roads met: the *cardo* (north-south) and the *decumanus maximus* (east-west), which preferably were oriented toward the compass points. This concept, however, had to accommodate the realities of pre-existing cities and rapid growth which often caused the city to spread far beyond its walls. Theaters, amphitheaters, stadia, and baths often were outside a city's walls, and districts grew up around them.

New construction was based on Roman architectural models, with local influences modifying the designs. Rome did not impose the architectural concepts, but admiration for Rome had great influence. In Greek cities, the agora had long existed; it served essentially the same function as the Roman forum. Both had market areas, sacred festivals, porticoes, townhalls, arches, temples, odeons, and other civic structures. The architecture from city to city reflected similarities, but the trained eye can detect significant differences that reflect both time and region. The austere white ruins seen in travel today do not depict the ancient reality. Landscaping with flowers, trees, and other plants was extensive, while buildings and statues were brightly painted. The forum areas generally were barred to wheeled traffic except at night. Certain types of markets, shops, and trades often were confined to specific buildings or areas.

The largest cities became teeming masses of inhabitants. Ancient writers have described the noise and tumult of Rome. However, the more typical cities such as Pompeii or Ostia were more pleasant places to live. The cities sought to become well equipped to serve their citizens. Adequate water supply and proper drainage were priorities; and buildings were built to meet the civic and religious needs of the populace. Most of these public works were provided by wealthy citizens in return or as a condition of their election as magistrates or to other leadership positions. Cities competed fiercely with one another for official Roman recognition as the first city of the region and for various levels of recognition; such honors could bring great commercial rewards. Peace was kept in the Greek cities by the *Eirenarch*, who was a policemaster in command of a corps of town-soldiers whose repute was not very high.

Economic advantages as well as political involvement centered in the cities. The attendant values resulted in local efforts to create

▲ **102 Forum street, Herculaneum.** The street was called the Decumano Macimo, the Main Street, and was reserved exclusively for pedestrians. Herculaneum had no forum; this street probably served that purpose. Some of the most beautiful houses of the city faced this street, such as the House of the Bicentenary. Shops and artisans' workshops, with painted signs, lined the street as well. A public fountain is at lower right in the photo, a hitching-post to its left. The provision market for meat and fish (macellum) is on the right of the street and the triumphal arch at the end. *Matthew 11:16; 20:3; 23:7; Acts 16:19; 17:17.*

cities or to enhance a city's position in the Empire (see p. 13).

(see p. 13)

Ancient Civilizations and Ruins of Turkey, Ekrem Akurgal (Istanbul: Haset Kitabevi), 1978; *Discovering Jerusalem*, Nahman Avigad (Nashville: Thomas Nelson Publishers), 1980; *Aegean Turkey: An Archaeological Guide*, George E. Bean (New York: Frederick A. Praeger, Publishers), 1966; *Römisches Alltagsleben in Stadt Köln*, Hugo Borger (Römisch-Germanisches Museum der Köln), 1975; *Ostia*, G. Calza and G. Becatti (Rome: Instituto Poligrafico dello Stato), 1976; *Daily Life in Ancient Rome*, Jerome Carcopino (New Haven: Yale University Press), 1940; *Herculaneum: Italy's Buried Treasure*, Joseph Jay Deiss (New York: Harper and Row, Publishers), 1985; *The Architecture of Ancient Greece*, William Bell Dinsmoor (New York: W. W. Norton and Co., Inc.), 1975; *The Archaeology of the New Testament*, Jack Finegan (Princeton: Princeton University Press), 1969; *Cities of Vesuvius: Pompeii and Herculaneum*, Michael Grant (New York: Penguin Books), 1971; *The Roman Engineers*, L. A. and J. A. Hamey (Cambridge: Cambridge University Press), 1981; *Jerusalem Revealed*, Israel Exploration Society (Jerusalem: Shikmona Publishing Co.), 1975; *Corinth and Its Environs in Antiquity*, Savas E. Kasas (Athens: Savas Kasas), 1974; *Waterworks in the Athenian Agora*, Mabel Lang (Princeton: American School of Classical Studies at Athens), 1968; *Nimes*, V. Lassalle (Paris: Art et Tourisme); *Greece: History, Museums, Monuments*, Leonidas B. Lellos (Athens: L. B. Lellos), 1972; *The Roman Forum and the Palatine*, Giuseppe Lugli (Rome: Bardi Editore), 1970; *The Mute Stones Speak*, Paul MacKendrick (New York: W. W. Norton and Co.), 1983; *Römermuseum und Römerhaus Augst*, Max Martin (Basel: Römermuseum Augst), 1981; *The Mountain of the Lord*, Benjamin Mazar (New York: Doubleday and Company, Inc.), 1975; *Roman Ostia*, Russell Meiggs (Oxford: The Clarendon Press), 1973; *Nimes, Arles, Orange, Saint Remy*, Roger Peyre (Paris: Librairie Renouard), 1910; *Pergamon Archaeological Guide*, Wolfgang Radt (Istanbul: Turkiye Turing ve Otomobil Kurumu), 1978; *A History of Greek Art*, Martin Robertson (Cambridge University Press), 1976; *Glanum*, Francois Salviat (Paris: Caisse Nationale des Monuments Historiques et des Sites), 1977; *The Glory that Was Pompeii*, Patricia Vanags (New York: Mayflower Books, Inc.); *Roman Art*, Helga von Heintze (New York: Universe Books), 1971; *Roman Art and Architecture*, Mortimer Wheeler (New York: Oxford University Press), 1964; *Greek and Roman Technology*, K. D. White (Ithaca: Cornell University Press), 1984.

DESIGN AND LAYOUT

▲ **103 Scale model of Pompeii ruins,** 1:100 scale, located in the National Museum of Naples. An overview of the southwestern portion of the city as it was in AD 79. The long building on the lower right is the Basilica. Just to its left is the Sea Gate and its street, which runs into the Forum. The large courtyard and temple just below the Forum is that of Apollo. Various houses and villas lie below and to the left of the temple of Apollo. The block structures at the entrance of the Forum (right) are commemorative arches; others can be seen next to the steps and just above the back corner of the temple of Jupiter, which lies at the opposite end of the Forum. Magistrates' offices and the Council chamber once were just outside the Forum gate. The square just above the Forum's entrance and arches was the voting hall (*comitium*). Across the street to its left is the Cloth Traders' Hall (*Eumachia Building*); next left is the temple of Vespasian; next is the Sanctuary of the City Lares (small structure with apse); next to it is the larger Provisions Market (*Marcellum*). The Cereals Market lies behind the upper back corner of the temple of Jupiter. The somewhat larger structure below it and just behind the Forum is the Forum Baths. The temple of Fortuna Augusta lies just above the baths and to the right of the vertical street. To the left of the vertical street but indistinguishable in the photo are the houses of the Tragic Poet, the Faun, the Vettii, and the Gilded Amorini; Insula (Block) VI, 13; and the Fullery. All of those structures lie below the long street which, though not distinguishable, can be imagined on a horizontal line from above the theaters at the upper right corner of the photo. The Stabian Gate is at the right end of this street; along and below it are the theaters, temple of Isis, and Stabian Baths. The street ends at the other side of Pompeii at the Vesuvius Gate. Above the street lies the house of the Menander, the Centenary, and the Silver Wedding; and the Stabian Baths. The Herculaneum Gate lies outside the photo at the end of the wall that runs left in the center of the photo. *Matthew 9:35; 12:25; Acts 9:25; 12:10; 16:12; 19:29-41.*

104

105

106

 104, 105, 106 Model of public district of Miletus, Bode Museum, Berlin. 104 looks east, shows the harbor at the north, far left, with small and large harbor monuments. A quay made of marble, which dates to Roman times, curved around the harbor. The size of the Harbor Stoa, running vertically in the photo, is evident by comparison with the ships at dock. Built in Doric style during Hellenistic times, it stretched 160 meters and contained 30 shops. The large rectangle attached behind it at the east end is the North Agora (Forum). The smaller square just below it in the photo is a smaller marketplace with shops. Both were built in classical times and enlarged during the Hellenistic and Roman periods. The Delphinion, Miletus' chief religious center, where Apollo was worshiped, is the square building with the circular shrine in its center, located beyond the Harbor Stoa. The Harbor Gateway is between the 2 structures. It opened onto the Processional Way, which runs alongside and east of the North Agora. Opposite the North Agora on the other side of the Processional Way is the long Ionic Stoa erected during Claudius' reign. Behind it lie the Capito Baths at the north end and the Gymnasium at the south end. The baths were built during Claudius' reign. The gymnasium dates from the second century BC and consisted of a large gate entrance (propylon), a palaestra, and 5 rooms for study. It likely was Miletus' principal gymnasium. The Processional Way continues to the North Gate (Miletus Gate), which dates to the second century AD and opens to the large South Agora. The Nymphaion, also built during the second century, borders the open space in front of the gate on the east side. On the west side is the Bouleuterion (Senate house), which dates to between 175-164 BC (see below). To its north, the small temple may be Aesculapius, and a sanctuary for the Imperial cult may have been in front of it toward the Way. 105 looks up the Processional Way from south to north. A portion of the enormous South Agora (538 x 633 feet; 164 x 196 meters), built in Hellenistic times and enlarged during the Roman period, is in the left foreground; the Ionic Stoa is on the right, the North Agora on the left, the Harbor Gateway at the end. The Gymnasium design is clearly seen on the near side behind the Ionic Stoa. The Capito Baths lie beyond and include the 2-storied columned courtyard and the structures behind it. 106 looks from east to west. The Delphinion is at the right of the photo, the Capito Baths to its left, the Harbor Stoa above it, and the North Agora behind the Harbor Stoa. The small temple to Aesculapius(?) is just to the left of the North Agora, and left of it lies the Bouleuterion. It was entered by a propylon which opened into a columned courtyard in Corinthian style, beyond which was a roofed auditorium that would seat 1,500 in seats built in a horseshoe shape as in a stadium. It was built in the Hellenistic period at the order of Antiochus Epiphanes (175-164 BC). *Acts 20:15-17; see also photo 103.*

▼**107, 108, 109, 110 Model of Pergamum acropolis,** Bergama Museum. The lowest part in photo 107 on the right (south end) is a double balustrade which supports the theater terrace. Above it rises the steep theater. The famous Zeus altar is to the south of the theater, and south of the altar lies the Upper Agora. The temple of Athena is just above (east) of the theater, the temple of Trajan above to the northeast. The royal palaces are east and the barracks northeast of Trajan's temple. The enclosed area on the north is the arsenal (military magazines). 108 shows the theater, its terrace, the Zeus altar (right), and the temple of Dionysus at the left

end of the terrace. The terrace is the longest promenade on the citadel and was entered from the south. A long Doric stoa (columned porch) borders the west side, a shorter one on the east. The building beside the theater facing west likely was used by actors. The retaining balustrades are 5 stories high in places and were an impressive architectural achievement. The theater, divided by stairways into 3 sections, could seat 10,000. During the Roman period theater performances were shifted to a new theater in the lower city and a stone podium was erected to serve as a speaker's platform. The Zeus altar is described in photo 439. Photo 109 shows the

107

108

temple of Athena, who was the city's goddess, above the theater. The temple proper sets at an angle near the theater and inside a temple complex which consists of a courtyard surrounded by 2-storied stoas. The temple, which housed the art collections of the Pergamenes, is the oldest in Pergamum. During Roman times a bronze statue of Augustus probably stood in the temple court. The stoas were built during the second century BC. Eumenes II probably built the library, which is the complex attached to the north stoa. Ancient reports claim that 200,000 scrolls were kept here. The discovery of parchment, which is a variation of the name Pergamum, was invented here. The library, however, was carried off by Antony to Egypt in 41 BC. In it stood a smaller copy of the Athena statue of the Athens Parthenon. The narrower complex of buildings to the south of Athena's temple and above the Zeus altar is the Heroon, the sacred precinct of the cult of the rulers. It was entered through the columned openings on the west and consisted of an antechamber where special meals of worship likely were eaten. The temple proper lies on the east. Photo 110 shows the temple of Trajan (nearest), surrounded by stoas, and the royal palace with its barracks. The palace complex begins on the right behind the temple of Athena. The palaces are built on the peristyle plan. The barracks (building with square tower) was converted for use by citadel troops from the earliest palace built by Philetairos (281-263 BC). From north to south, the next 3 palaces are conjectured to be those of Attalos I (241-197), Eumenes II (197-159), and Attalos II (159-138). In Roman times the city moved far down into the plain. A road connected the Aesculapion (see photo 113) to the acropolis. *Revelation 1:11; 2:12-17; see also photo 103.*

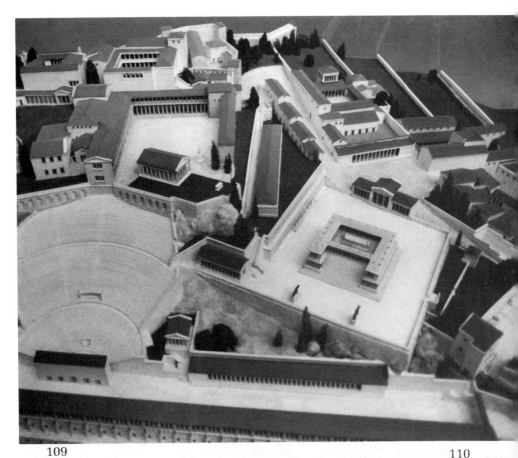

109   110

▲ 111 **Model of first-century Jerusalem,** Clear Creek Baptist Bible Institute, Clear Creek, Kentucky. Location of the city walls is based on probabilities. The Temple Mount is the city's most prominent feature. Solomon's Porch runs along the eastern (nearest) wall, which contains the Golden (Shushan, Persian) Gate. The Royal Porch runs along the southern wall. That end of the Mount was approached from a large terrace which held mikhveh (ritual washing) pools, then up a massive stairway and a series of doors which gave entry to tunneled stairways that opened onto the Temple Mount beyond the Royal Porch. The stairway at the east end of the Royal Porch, with its stairway and wall extension, is conjectural and did not exist. A stoa also ran along the west wall. The gateway seen in the photo led onto a landing and stairway that turned south to descend into the Tyropean Valley (rather than connecting with the palace area as was formerly believed and as is shown in photo). The north wall, with its Damascus Gate, gave entrance from the less protected north. The double pool outside the Damascus Gate is the Pool of Bethesda. To the south of the Mount can be seen the stadium (Hippodrome) situated in the Tyropean Valley. East of the Hippodrome and south of the Temple Mount is the ancient Ophel, the site of the original Jerusalem and the city of David. During Josephus' time it served as a residential quarter; part, if not all of it, constituted the Lower City. The Gihon Spring lies below the waist of Ophel; the Siloam Pool is inside the southeast wall line near the toe of the hill. The Tyropean Valley was much deeper in the first century; it ran along the western wall down to the Hinnom Valley to the south. Markets lined it on the north end. The Xystos, a Hellenistic gymnasium that was used as an open court in the first century, was north of the gate that exited the Temple Mount on the west. The Upper City (Western Hill) was heavily populated with residences; its excavations, which have included some homes of important priestly families, are reported in *Discovering Jerusalem* by Nahman Avigad (Nashville: Thomas Nelson), 1983. The location of the stadium shown in photo is unknown but is speculated to have been on the Western Hill, possibly farther south. The towers that can be seen along the western city wall mark the location of Herod's Royal Palace. Residential areas continue to the north of the Western Hill and west of the Pool of Bethesda. The wall line on the north-west probably is accurate based on fragmentary finds; the current wall, which would enclose the area inside the L, is of a later date. Thus, the place of Jesus' crucifixion and tomb likely was near the city wall inside the L, most likely the site of the Church of the Holy Sepulchre. The Hinnom Valley can be seen at the far left of the photo, the Kidron Valley at bottom. They joined southeast of Ophel. Gethsemane and the Mount of Olives lie east and are not shown. *Matthew 4:5; 21:1 to 28:15; see also photo 103.* **See color photo 409.**

▼ 112 **Jerusalem Temple** proper and part of courtyard from model at King David Hotel, Jerusalem. *Biblical Illustrator* photo/Ken Touchton. The tall rectangular building houses the holy place and the holy of holies. The altar was situated between its door and the gate just in front of it in the photo. Rooms were built into the walls which surrounded the Temple; they were for the use of priests. Three doors on each side gave them access to the Court of the Priests. The gate near the altar is the Nicanor (Corinthian). Just inside it on the Temple side was the Court of the Men of Israel (see below), where men stood to participate in the sacrifices. The court was marked probably by a line on the floor, beyond which only priests were allowed. The Nicanor Gates opens onto the lower Women's Court, accessed by a series of 12 steps. This court is the rectangular area with towers at the corners. The name does not indicate that only women could go into it but rather that women could go no farther. Actually, most public celebrations in the Temple occurred in the Women's Court. Choirs stood on the steps of the Nicanor Gate to sing. The rooms and porticoes which can be barely seen in the photo houses storage rooms for priestly vestments, precious vessels, oil, wine, and other items relevant to worship in the Temple. The Women's Court is accessed by doors on each side which open from the general Court of Israel. It consists primarily of 14 steps and a platform. Thus, the succeeding sanctity of each court is marked by raised platforms. The low wall seen at the foot of these steps is the *bel* or *soreq;* it marked off the limits of the Court of the Gentiles. The warning signs were set in the walls at the entrances to the *bel.* The Court of the Gentiles was some 250 yards (231 meters) on the longest side. The 268 columns on Solomon's Porch (near wall) rose 35 feet (10.67 meters) in height; the Royal Porch (south, left of Temple) ceiling was 92 feet (28.04 meters) in height, the center portico 50 feet (15.24 meters), supported by 162 columns.

FORUMS, STREETS, AND SHOPS

◄113 **Sacred Way, Pergamum** (the Via Tecta), which leads from the Aesculapeion southwest of the city to the acropolis. Lined with shops, it was almost .62 miles (1 km.) and ran to the theater. For about 487.5 feet (150 m.) on the Aesculapeion end (shown) it was lined with splendid stoas on both sides, ending at the propylon (built in the second century AD) of the Aesculapeion. Looking from the Aesculapeion, the theater is seen left of the end of the road; it rises steeply up the side of the acropolis. A sacred way was a common element in ancient Greek cities. *Revelation 1:11; 2:12-17.*

► **114 Substructures of forum area, Thessalonica.** The marble paving can be seen at the top, laid over rectangular blocks, in turn laid over brick subpavement. The agora consisted of a large court which measured 292.5 feet (90 meters) east-to-west and 227.5 feet (70 meters) north-to-south. The agora is built over remains of Hellenistic Thessalonica. The shape of the bricks and their structure can be seen in the right side of the photo. Note the closed arch at the lower middle of the picture. A drainage canal and its opening is in the lower right corner. *Acts 17:1; Philippians 4:16; 1 and 2 Thessalonians; see also photo 102.*

115

116

117

118

115, 116, 117, 118 Trajan's Forum, Rome, the last and largest of Rome's fora, built AD 108-117. The photos are of the market that adjoined the forum on the northeast. Architecture, already monumental by Greek standards, became more so beyond the first century. Apollodorus of Damascus, a famous architect, designed the forum into 3 separate areas that totaled 1, 083 by 607 feet (330 by 185 meters): a porticoed piazza, which included a gigantic basilica, a colossal equestrian statue of Trajan, and the market area; the famous Column of Trajan, with its story-telling spiraled bas-reliefs; and the porticoed sanctuary with Trajan's temple. Photo 115 shows the northeast part of the square with the 5-storied market. It was built in red brick and not covered with marble or stucco as many earlier buildings had been, following instead the form seen often at Ostia. Statuary stood in the niches. The first-level rooms were framed in travertine: the second-level windows are arched and were framed with pilasters. The road (photo 116) runs above the second level. Photo 116 shows the shop-lined street that rises to the second level of the market (compare the lower floors at lower left with photo 115). Photo 117 is a view of the inside of the market looking from the mezzanine down to the lower floor, similar to modern shopping centers. Photo 118 shows a walkway in the market with shops on each side. The rooms are arranged with a variety of accesses, using both internal and external communications. Some rooms have drains. The complex had 150 shops, plus offices and open areas. *Acts 19:21; 28:15-16; Romans; see also photo 102.*

◄ **119 Tower of the Winds, Athens,** near the Roman Agora, built in the first century BC. Each face of the octagonal marble structure had carved on it an allegorical representation of the appropriate wind from its direction, 3 of which are visible in the photo at top of tower. Each face also had a sundial. A water clock (clepsydra) built by Andronicus of Cyrrhestes was inside the tower. It may have been the first phase of Julius Caesar's building scheme for the Roman Agora, which was completed in 10 BC. The tower is 25 feet, 8 inches (7.9 m.) in diameter and 47 feet (14.46 m.) high (to top of finial). The roof is made of 24 triangular marble slabs, their tops carved to resemble roof tiles. The finial on top was a Corinthian capital and supported a weathervane in the form of a bronze Triton whose rod pointed into the wind. It had 2 entrances and apparently was open day and night. *Ephesians 5:16; Acts 17:15-34.*

◄ **120 Forum of the Corporations, Ostia.** It lies behind the theater and contained 70 offices of the various associations (see photo 150). These corporations functioned somewhat like a combination stock exchange and chamber of commerce. Each organization chose patrons from among the powerful, and each elected magistrates who served 5 years. Such associations were strictly licensed and regulated. Their members might be local or traveling businessmen, and might be Latin or of various other cultures and nationalities.

▶ 122 Fortune Street, Pompeii. Ruts from wagon wheels can be seen between the long stepping-stones in the foreground. It crossed Stabian Street going east and became Nola Street and Decumanus Major, which ran to the Nola Gate; going west it became Terme Street. Nola Street and its continuations was a maximum of 28 feet (8.53 m.) in width, thus was among the wider streets of Pompeii (Mercury, at 30 feet [9.14 m.] was the widest). Other streets were 10 to 20 feet (3 to 6 m.) wide. As the others, Fortune Street was paved with polygonal blocks of basalt fit with great care. They were bounded by raised curbed sidewalks which here are paved with small stones; other walks were concrete or beaten earth. The water ran on the streets.

▲ 121 Political graffiti, Pompeii. The whitewashed walls all along Pompeii's streets served as signs for all purposes. Appeals to vote for a certain person for office, business advertisements, amusements such as gladiatorial games, and other graffiti abound.

▲ **124 Shop, Herculaneum.** Many such shops have been found in Herculaneum and Pompeii. This one was a wine shop or snack bar. Its counter is faced with irregular pieces of marble and 5 large jars are inserted into the countertop, with at least 2 in a counter behind. The wine was kept cool by the stone that held the jars, and the counters contained snacks such as cheeses, walnuts, almonds, dates, figs, raisins, and cakes. Two shallow counters are at the end of the short leg of the L, and another large jar stands on the floor near the door on the left. These shops were attached to living quarters. The shops and their houses varied in quality then just as they would today.

WATER SUPPLY

▶125 **Fountain at Aesculapeion, Pergamum.** It was 1 of 3 fountains attached to the Aesculapeion, 1 of which was sacred, available for drinking water, bath treatments, and mud packs. In its present state, it dates to the second century AD. Many cities had sacred fountains; often the most sacred were the most ancient ones; they had been the domains of nymphs or other lesser deities. The Sacred Pool was the central point of the sanctuary of Aesculapius at Pergamum. The building which housed it was simple, and its veneration is attested by ancient writers, Aristides being perhaps the best known. He claimed that eye problems were cured by bathing in it; by drinking its waters one could have cured asthma, chest disorders, foot problems, and speech impediments. The pool shown is near the theater and was unroofed. It probably was used by patients whose prescriptions involved cold baths. Mud packs used in treatments often were washed off in the pools, especially the Sacred Pool or one near the incubation rooms. This pool more often was used for cold bath treatments. *John 9:6-7; Revelation 1:11; 2:12-17.*

▼126 Fountain of Peirene, Corinth. It consisted of 6 hewed, deep dipping basins (beyond the openings) which would hold almost 350 gallons (1,325 liters); they were filled by an underground reservoir. In antiquity it was considered the most healthful water in all of Greece. The original structure dates from the time of Periander. During the third century BC the fountain house was marbled in the style of an Ionic porch. After the Romans destroyed Corinth, then resettled it later, they rebuilt the structure with a double colonnade of poros; the upper story was Ionic, the lower Doric. The court was marbled as well, and a descent was built down to the central basin, into which water flowed from mouths placed in the back and sides of the basin. Paintings of fish, dating from Roman times, have been found on a basin side wall. Marble facing was added during the first century, and further improvements were made by Herod Atticus (AD 101-177). *Revelation 7:17; Acts 18:1-8; 1 and 2 Corinthians.*

▲ **127 Fountainhead, Judea.** Rockefeller Museum. Such devices received water and dispersed them into larger fountains through spouts. Here the mouths of Phrygian-capped heads, with hair shaped into ringlets, form the spouts. Lion bodies which merge into oversized feet support the fountainhead on its base. In smaller towns and villages, wells were used. Then, as today in such villages, they were a gathering place. Wellheads sometimes were quite well done, sometimes simple, but they operated with the rope and pulley principle attached to a frame above the wellhead. *Revelation 7:17.*

▲**128, 129 Castellum, Nimes.** Once the water reached its destination from river springs 31 miles (50 km.) away, it had to be distributed. First it passed through settling tanks, then was channeled into a castellum to be distributed. Lead pipes took it from there to baths, fountains, industrial establishments, and private users. Oftentimes the water was boiled for purification, for algae and other impurities were a problem. The natural pools which many cities dressed up into fountains were all the more popular for their pure water. The Nimes castellum shown has an inside diameter of 22 feet, 6 inches (6 m., 88 cm.). The basin inside it is 18 feet (5 m., 50 cm.) wide and 3 feet, 3 inches (1 m.) deep; its pavement is 7 feet, 3 inches (2 m., 20 cm.) wide. The waters entered by a canal that was 4 feet (1 m., 20 cm.) wide. Ten lead pipes in the round openings in the basin's side distributed the water to different parts of Nimes. Three sluice gates allowed for emptying and for overflow. A curved metal screen could impede the flow. The remains show clearly how the system worked. The upper part of the building has disappeared, but the threshold to its entrance can be seen at the right of photo 128 and at top center of photo 129, a small rectangular room followed by steps.

130 Stone water pipe, Judea. Rockefeller Museum, Jerusalem. The sections were part of an aquaduct that came to Jerusalem from Solomon's Pools. The pipe section, of which these segments were a part, ran for 1½ miles (2.5 km.) near the so-called Rachel's Tomb during New Testament times. It was part of a massive effort to furnish Jerusalem with water; some segments of this pipe bear inscriptions of commanders of Rome's Tenth Legion.

131 Caesarea Maritima aquaduct, the one nearest the sea. Another low-level one, also approaching Caesarea from the north, lies a short distance east and runs parallel part of the way. It is about 3 miles (4.83 km.) long. The higher one shown in the photo originates at Mount Carmel some 4½ miles (7.24 km.) northeast of Caesarea. It was built by Herod the Great and extensively repaired during the second century by the Tenth Legion at Hadrian's command. *Acts 8:40; 9:30; 10:1-22; 18:22; 21:8-16; 23:23 to 25:1.*

133

132

132, 133, 134 Pont du Gard. Aquaducts carried water by gravity; thus the slope was carefully measured so the water would flow neither too fast nor too slowly. This stretch is one of the most spectacular of the many remains of aquaducts. It is the Pont du Gard near Arles, France. The builder probably was Veronius, whose name is engraved on an interior face of the eighth arch from the right bank and the second tier. It brought water from the spring at Eure to Nimes over a distance of 31 miles (50 km.). The massive structure, 884 feet (269.44 m.) long at the top level, rises 159 feet, 8 inches (48.7 m.) above the Gard River and crosses 6 more bridges before the water arrives at Nimes. The arches rise on 3 tiers to span the river gorge. The lower one is the shortest and most massive; it has 6 arches, the longest of which spanned 70 feet, 6 inches (21.5 m.), the others 63 feet (19.2 m.) and 51 feet, 8 inches (15.75 m.). A modern road is built on the ancient roadbed of the bridge. The second tier has 11 arches, with each support in the center springing from the one below; thus the spans are the same. The third tier has 35 arches, each with a span of 14 feet, 3 inches (4.35 m.). Only this third upper smaller tier carried water; its interior is seen in 133, a tunnel almost high enough to allow standing. The water-carrying portion is the actual aquaduct; all else is designed to maintain the proper slope for the water to flow at the proper speed. Sometimes lead and earthenware pipes were used, but Romans preferred masonry. Sometimes aquaducts were cut out of solid rock. The aquaduct portion of the Pont du Gard is formed by dressed blocks on the sides above the small arches and topped with flat stones. Variations included curved arched ceilings and pointed arched ceilings over the water channel made by leaning the ends of flat stones against one another and covering them with dirt to hold them in place. Every means was taken to avoid theft of water. Blocks were left protruding (134) to support scaffolding for repair work.

134

▶ **135 Public latrine, Ephesus.** It was located next to the brothel and next to Scolastica's Baths. People sat on all 4 sides of the rectangular structure. A continuous flow of water ran in a sewer deep below the seats to provide flushing. The seats are of marble. A narrow canal runs inside the perimeter in which water ran continuously. While the wealthy constructed latrines of their own—which sometimes were served by water from aquaducts and sometimes by cess trenches serviced by manure merchants—the average people relied on public latrines. Even the middle-class apartment dweller did not have access to a drainage system. The cost of using a public latrine was low, and a great many of them existed. It was completely public, where people met, talked, and exchanged dinner invitations. They often were pleasingly, even ostentatiously decorated with statues of divinities, figures of dolphins, and sculpted fountains. Passersby and the very poor used

jars which fullers placed in front of their shops to catch the urine necessary to their trade, and the people emptied their house pots in locations provided. These locations were the dungheaps where un- wanted babies were left exposed to die or to be rescued. Sometimes the chamber pots were dumped out directly into the street. *Acts 18:19-21,24-26; 19:1-41; 20:16-17; Ephesians.*

◀ **136 Limestone toilet seat,** found at Tell el-'ajjul. Rockefeller Museum, Jerusalem. The seat was carved from limestone and then plastered.

HOUSES, DWELLINGS, AND ARCHITECTURE

◄ **137 Glanum Gate, the triumphal arch,** located at St. Remy in southern France. Monumental gateways into cities or important structures were part of the architecture of Greek and Roman cities. This arch was on the main road from Italy to Spain and is the oldest of several arches in the area of the Narbonnaise (Orange, Carpentras, Avignon), dating to just after the Julii Monument (see photo 893). The top is destroyed, but would have been rectangular. Fluted columns in relief frame bas-reliefs, and square columns at the opening rise above their capitals to an ornate masterpiece of sculpture that has bountiful garlands and fruit. The underside of the arch has a geometric design in relief. Flying Victories, now fragmented, adorn the upper arch on each side. The reliefs between the fluted columns are of Gaul captives, both men and women. *Matthew 7:13-14; Acts 9:24; 14:13; Revelation 21:21; 22:14.*

◄ **138 Tour Magne, Nimes.** The name means "big tower." Its base is 65 feet, 7 inches (20 m.) wide and is polygonal; it is 110 feet, 10 inches (33 m., 80 cm.) high. The lower tier has deep niches; above it is a blank zone; above it is a register decorated with Tuscan pilasters, all seen best from the southern side. The top structure seen in the photo is a tubular structure which served to lighten the inside masonry. The tower was part of the wall defenses; it had a ramp and a staircase for access.

▶ **139 Miletus Gate,** built about AD 211, marble. Pergamum Museum, Berlin. The height without the pediment is 46 feet (14.02 m.). The structure was the monumental north entrance to the South Stoa of Miletus. Some comparisons can be made with the ornamentation of the Maison Carée at Nimes (photos 390-392). The basic Greek style was influenced by Flavian art, just as was the Celsus Library at Ephesus (see photo 550). Fluted columns support 2 stories with pediments. Both Doric and Corinthian design are combined in the capitals. Each story boasts 3 arches separated by *aediculae* which stand out from the walls, while side wings provide a strong frame effect. The roofline is broken for effect. The architecture is somewhat more monumental than that of the first century and has been influenced by the stage designs of the theater (see photo 540) which were common even in the first century. A large nymphaeum with statuary was near the gate, so that the effect of the open space added to the monumental design. *Acts 20:15-17; see also photo 137.*

▶ **140 Terra-cotta lamp holder in shape of town house,** about 150 BC. British Museum. It probably was the type built in Alexandria. It is 2-storied, with a wide entrance on the first floor and windows on the second. The top peak is for attaching a handle; however, similarly shaped pigeon houses often were built on roofs in Egyptian houses. *Acts 6:9; 19:24; 27:6; 28:11.*

▲ **141 Shepherd by grass hut** holding ram in Good Shepherd style. Pio-Christian Museum, Vatican. Other sheep graze or watch him. He wears a tunic bound at the waist, with one shoulder bare, and boots. His house is a round thatch hut; its door stands open. The row of huts continues behind the near one. *Matthew 18:12-13; Luke 2:8-20; John 10:1-16; 21:16-20; 1 Peter 5:2-4.*

▶ **142 Soul house from Egypt.** Field Museum. These model houses were placed in tombs, the practice having evolved from more simple model offerings of food. The soul was believed to dwell in these houses; in some of them a small figure of the deceased can be seen inside the doorway. They were in use from about 2000 to 100 BC. The style of housing likely reflects the style actually lived in. Photo 140 shows a similarity of style. Here, steep stairs reach unporched second floors, whose doors are on either the side or front. *Matthew 2:13-22; Acts 2:10; 21:38.*

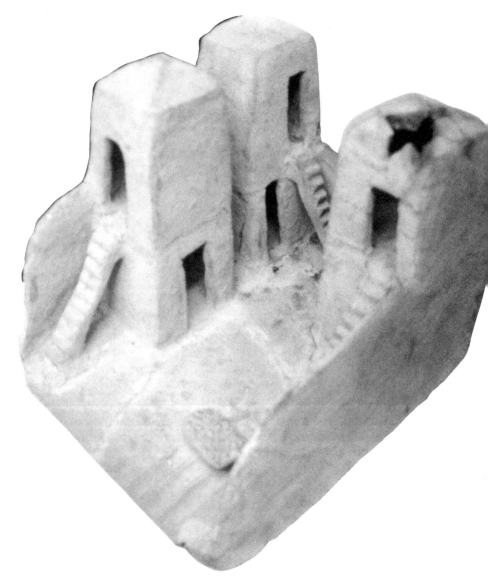

► **143 Trellis House, Herculaneum.** Its construction is a wooden skeleton of square frames, each square then filled in by stones held together by mortar. The interior walls are cane laths with a thin coating of plaster. Such houses were quickly built and economical but were not strong, were damp, and were susceptible to fire damage. This house was designed for 1 family on the ground floor with some upstairs space and another family on the second floor. The two families shared a cistern and a courtyard which provided light and ventilation. The upper apartment had an independent stairway. The front measures 22 feet (6.71 m.). The rooms are small, and one room on the street level was a shop. The contents of the house—furniture, utensils, gods, glassware, and even wool—was protected by the lava mud. Many houses of this economic level existed in Herculaneum; they provide an indication of how the growing housing shortage of parts of the Empire was met. *Acts 9:17; 16:15; 17:5-9; 18:7; 20:8-9; 1 Corinthians 11:22.*

► **144 Villa at Augst,** rebuilt to house the Römerhausmuseum. It is an authentic reconstruction of a Roman house, combining the living quarters with the shop. Augst, Switzerland was founded about 44 BC as Augusta Raurica, a Roman colony in the territory of the Gallic Raurici. A portico runs across the front of the house and partway down each side. Facing the portico, the workshop is on the left, the entrance on the right, and the shop is between them. In typical Roman style, an enclosed courtyard lies behind the workshop and shop and is surrounded by other rooms: a kitchen (see photo 831), dining room (see photo 836), baths, and bedrooms. The courtyard is a peristyled gar-

den. The typical Roman house was built around its atrium, which was not an open courtyard but a room with an open skylight and, directly below it, a pool. Rainwater fell into the pool to furnish the water supply. A main reception room *(tablinum)*, a dining room *(triclinium)*, and bedrooms surrounded the atrium. Under Greek influence, the rooms came to be built around an open court which was encircled by a covered walkway, or peristyle. The atrium was retained in various ways, and the courtyard became a pleasant garden. *Acts 16:40; 1 Corinthians 16:19; see also photos 147, 148, 151.*

◄ **145 Doorway to small shrine, Courtyard of Dionysus, Ostia.** Inside, a small terra-cotta statue that may represent Isis was found. The door facing is of the type that adorns more prosperous entrances in Ostia. The architectural feature is done in brick plastered over to appear to be concrete or marble columns with simple capitals. *Revelation 3:20.*

▼ **146 Stairway, House of Menander, Pompeii.** Second stories often were added to the atriums of villas to convert them to apartment houses or for shops to be placed on the lower floor. The spaces to the left of the stair are for storage.

▲ **147 House of the Poet Menander, Pompeii, atrium vestibule.** The house takes its name from a portrait of the poet painted on the walls of an *exedra* opening off the peristyle. It occupies the greater part of a block. It belonged to a member of the family related to Nero's wife Poppaea. The room's pavement is made entirely of fragments of colored marble set in a ground of black tesserae. Window glass has been found in some excavations, usually from small windows opening onto gardens, but it was not common. Ordinary dwellings had only shutters, which were opened in good weather and closed in bad, leaving the room dark. *Hebrews 3:3-6; see also photos 144, 148, 151, 158.*

► **148 Courtyard in House of Antes, Glanum.** The house plan is rather irregular; the house was entered through an area supported by rectangular pilasters which opened onto an interior courtyard situated on the south. The house plan was arranged around this courtyard, which had as its dominant feature a rectangular pool surrounded by columns. The square pilaster seen in the background beyond the peristyle is one that was part of the entrance; it has shallow fluting and is surmounted by a Corinthian capital. The supports around the pool are smooth and the capitals are flat. The house likely had 2 floors; a stairway existed at the southwest corner. The plan of this rich residence is comparable to that of the Greek Hellenistic houses, of the type well known at Delos. Mosaic floors of the *opus signinum* style

have been found at Glanum (St. Remy), which consists of lumps of marble and stone, sometimes with figured designs, in tesserae. This style later was replaced by black and white patterns.

◄ **149 Pergola in House of Stags, Herculaneum.** The ledge in front was in ancient times the edge of the marina, which the house overlooked. The garden of the house lies beyond the pergola, where the palm tree is, and beyond that was the outer portal of the dining room. Its walls were decorated with mosaics. An original 3-legged table with a bowl on it can be seen inside the pergola, which is flanked by 2 rooms designed for afternoon naps. The house was built around a rectangle more than 142 feet (43.28 m.) long; it dates to the time of Claudius or Nero. *2 John 10; see also photos 144, 147, 148, 158.*

See color photo 410.

▲ **150 Via della Fontana, Ostia.** The Forum of Corporations is on the right, the Insula of the Child Hercules and the Insula of the Painted Ceiling are on the left, and the Laundry is at the end of the street. This area was rebuilt during Hadrian's reign. On the far right (south) shops open onto the street; they are connected with houses that open onto the Via della Corporazioni a block to the right. In the center area of the photo, the system is reversed, with houses opening onto this street. The nearer area is industrial. The 3 or 4 upper floors are reached by independent stairs from the street. The tenants had to draw their water from a cistern in the street. Ostia was the seat of a large organization called the Annona; it was charged with supplying Rome with food. Consequently, the city had many organizations of various types of laborers, proprietors, and merchants (see Forum of Corporations, photo 120). The laundry had a large room with central basins for

water; along its walls ran a series of jars, partly buried, in which laundrymen trod the cloth with their feet (see photos 278-281). A courtyard was used for drying clothes, and other rooms existed for other needs. Much can be learned about the middle-class Roman from Ostia. The population included merchants and artisans from all over the Empire, especially from Africa and the East. The city grew rapidly after Claudius made it the major port of Rome (beginning construction in AD 42; it was inaugurated 12 years later by Nero). Housing innovations developed to meet the need, some of them similar to the developments in Herculaneum (see photo 143), some different. Genuine apartment houses developed in Ostia; they were 3-storied, well-designed apartment complexes. While the Pompeian houses looked inward to a peristyle, the Ostian houses drew light from large windows that opened onto the main street, the larger ones supplemented by inner courts. However, the windows were paned with selenite and mica; good transparent glass was only then becoming available for windows. The brick facades were not plastered, and the arches were painted. The dwellings had balconies, supported by a continuous row of barrel vaults or by other decorative means, such as by wood supported by beams in the walls, or by a lunette-shaped projection. Some of the apartment complexes had the lower floor in shops. The placement of stairways to allow independent access to apartments, placement of courtyards, and arrangement of apartments is a change from the normal Latin style. Ostia also had its villas.

▲ **151 Rebuilt Roman villa.** J. Paul Getty Museum, photograph by Julius Shulman. The villa, which houses the museum, is a reconstruction of the Villa of the Papyri near Herculaneum. It overlooked the Bay of Naples. The main peristyle and the rooms which house the museum are shown. The same type of trees, flowers, shrubs, and herbs that grew in the ancient garden have been placed in the villa; and the bronze statuary in the gardens are casts of originals, now in the National Museum of Naples, that once graced the original villa. *Philemon 2,22; see also photos 144, 147, 148. 158.*

▶ **152 Mural of landscape,** National Museum, of Naples. In the foreground is a round gazebo attached to a small sanctuary. They are built on a platform which is reached by 4 steps in front. A statue of a divinity can be seen in the sanctuary window, and a large tree grows behind the structure. A dim figure to the left may be fishing. Several figures walk along the quay; the first one carries a long pole with a burden at each end, while the third figure is bent over and walking with a cane. The last figure is taller than the rest. A boat is in the water beside the quay. The large structure on the hill in the background may be a villa. It is columned with towers at each end. *2 Timothy 2:20.*

◀ **153 Palace gardens, Palatine.** Private apartments looking out onto gardens in the huge Imperial Palace of the Caesars in Rome. The apartments, though part of a complex that included state rooms and halls, were arranged in 2 stories secluded around a sunken garden. The garden area was furnished with baths, and with niches and pedestals for statues. A door in the bottom wall gave access to an exedra that allowed a front view from the whole building toward the Circus Maximus. The whole was decorated with marbles, statues, golden ornaments, paintings, mosaics, and carpets. *Philippians 1:13; 4:22.*

154

155

▲ **154, 155 Hadrian's Tivoli Palace,** built between AD 118-134. The buildings cover an area of about 500 yards (457 m.) by 1000 yards (914 m.) and consisted of halls, baths, libraries, terrances, fountains and other buildings. The dining room is 77 feet (23.5 m.) long; an island villa may have been Hadrian's private retreat. The estate signals a period of great creativity in the Empire. The buildings in photo 154 are: At the upper right, the taller building with gardens behind is the Praetorium, and at the lower right is the palaestra. The long building running to the left of the palaestra is the slave quarters. The building behind and slightly left of the palaestra is the baths structure, and more baths are to the right across the small courtyard and above the slave quarters. At the left of the photo, the building with 3 semicircles is an odeon. Behind it is a dining hall; beyond the hall a stadium, and beyond the stadium one of several palaces. The buildings in photo 155 are: The round building at the upper right is the Theater Maritimo; above it is a garden area consisting of a large pool surrounded by porticoes. Below the theater are 2 large palaces with gardens and dining rooms; another palace is at top left, the building fully in the photo. Directly left of the theater is the Heliocaminus (baths) and left again are guest rooms. A pavilion is at the far left. Many of the buildings were connected by a series of underground tunnels called cryptoporticoes; they were primarily for the use of servants, who by using them could remain out of sight. Statuary from Hadrian's villa is on display in a number of museums.

▼**156 Mosaic from a synagogue in Apamea, Syria,** AD 391, below. Brussels Museum. The design is composed of clusters of circles crisscrossed with a narrow leaf shape arranged in a geometric pattern. Designs that did not include figures of humans or animals were common in synagogues. *Acts 13:5,14,42-43; 15:21-23; 18:18; Galatians 1:21.*

▲**157 Marble tile floor in house at Ostia,** above. The design is the use of squares and triangles set in small designs inside a large design. Many middle-class and wealthy homes had marble tile floors; the art of mosaic and tile floors had been popular in Greece for several hundred years.

◄**158 Pavement in Roman villa, Malta,** Room B, left middle. It dates to the early first century BC Hellenistic period. The center portion is paved with lozenge-shaped black and white marble tiles and soft green stone. The interlocking pattern creates an optical illusion. The wide border mosaic is an interlocking geometric pattern. The reconstructed villa houses the Malta Museum. *Acts 28:1-10; see also photos 144, 147, 148, 151.*

◄**159 Mosaic from synagogue in Apamea,** left. Brussels Museum. The scene shows a lion attacking a young deer. The inner border is of interlocking spirals, the outer border a geometric pattern. *Texts: See photo 156.*

160, 161 Two ends of large floor mosaic from synagogue, Apamea, Syria. Brussels Museum. The mosaic is a series of hunting scenes interspersed with trees and bushes. In photo 160, at top, a hunter on horseback kills a deer with bow and arrow, while a lion is attacking the hunter. A bear lies speared beneath the horse and lion. The next register down shows a bowman on the left shooting the attacking lion, while a caped hunter on foot attacks a lion armed only with a small spear and round shield. Photo 161 shows, in the bottom register, a rabbit hunter at right holding in his right hand a game bag and what appears to be 2 spears. He works with 2 hunting dogs who chase 2 rabbits that balance out the mosaic at bottom left. Next to the rabbits, a hunter attacks a tiger with a light spear and round shield. A wild boar either is being attacked by the tiger or is poised to charge the hunter. A lion is shown devouring a deer after the kill. A middle register, not shown, connected the 2 ends. It has 2 hunters on horseback attacking a tiger which is protecting its own kill. *Texts: See photo 156.*

162 Nile mosaic, from House of the Faun, Pompeii, second century BC. National Museum of Naples. The mosaic was located in the same room as the mosaic of Alexander at Issus (see 408); Nile scenes were very popular from the second cen-

▲163 Architectural fresco, National Museum of Naples, first century BC-first century AD. The style is baroquely ornate, with the center-piece being a spiral-wrapped column which is reminiscent of the later Byzantine period. Two gilt bowls set on ledges. Such designs do not represent true architecture of the period, but rather are a whimsical and delightful expression.

tury BC to well into Imperial times. The design is of Hellenistic origin and perhaps comes from a Greek city of southern Italy or Sicily. As was common in Roman art, the artist has set various animals in conflict. The center has a hippopotamus facing a crocodile; at lower left a mongoose confronting a snake; and at lower right two ibeses lock beaks (they may be courting rather than fighting). The conflicts are in contrast to the ducks, which swim peacefully, and the perched birds. The hippopotamus was a symbol of the Nile River, and the crocodile was a symbol of Egypt. The ibis was sacred to Isis, who had strong influence in Pompeii and Herculaneum.

▼164 Architectural fresco, first century BC-first century AD. National Museum of Naples. This design is even more whimsical than in photo 163, with thin, dainty lines on which are suspended mythological figures.

◄165 Outside peristyle, Villa of Mysteries, Pompeii. The brick columns support a peristyle of the country type which opens onto the countryside rather than into an inner court. The construction technique is clear in the damaged columns. They are brick covered by a thick plaster that is fluted to look like marble. The tiled roof is supported by rafters which rest on a rough style called *incertum*, which in turn rests on a large beam supported by outside columns.

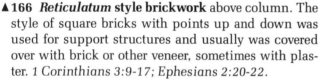

▲166 *Reticulatum* **style brickwork** above column. The style of square bricks with points up and down was used for support structures and usually was covered over with brick or other veneer, sometimes with plaster. *1 Corinthians 3:9-17; Ephesians 2:20-22.*

▲167 *Reticulatum* **style Roman brick construction, Jericho.** The room is a rectangular area south (toward the wadi) of the frigidarium. The turned bricks form the inner core of the wall; over them is laid brick in conventional pattern. The face of the outer brick then was either plastered (as here) or covered with marble. The style developed during the first century, as at Ostia, of leaving the bricks exposed. *Texts: See photo 166.*

▲168 **Stone arch inside 3-story Roman house, Avdat,** in the Negeb. The arch was fashioned from native stone dressed roughly into rectangular form. Pebbles were pressed into the cracks from above as fill to help form the arch. Stone fill also is in the space between the arch and the wall, and stone beams rest on the arch to support a stone-slab floor above. Remnants of the plaster that covered the structure still are present along the lower wall. Avdat was founded in the third or second century BC by the Nabateans to serve a caravan route. The city takes its name from Obodas (Abdat) II, who was contemporary with Herod I and who was buried here. Trajan annexed the Nabatean kingdom in AD 106. The house is in the Roman quarter south-southeast of and near the acropolis. It is built fortress style, with dressed stones. Floors are made of flat stones. *Acts 2:11; Galatians 1:17.*

◄ **169 Roman brick construction, Tivoli.** The inner brick, seen at lower right of doorway, is the *reticulatum* pattern with alternating long brick layers. It is covered with the same brick style but with a very smooth face. The large holes in the brick show where marble facing was attached, which covered the wall. The doorway—both sides and shallow arch—are of long, wide, thin bricks. *Texts: See photo 166.*

► **170 Roman brick construction, Insula of Serapis, Ostia.** The insula (block) was given its name because of a figure in colored stucco in the courtyard which served several apartments. Part of the mezzanine is preserved; windows looking onto the courtyard were under the high arches. A bath was attached to the courtyard. The columns and walls were plastered. The arches are built in the style of the one in photo 169. The brick style, with stacked brickwork much as is done today, is the *testaceum* style. *Texts: See photo 166.*

▲ 171 **Closeup of roof tiles,** from building shown in photo 121. The style is flat clay tiles with overlapping half circles at each edge, in contrast to the use of half-circle tiles that alternately invert and overt one another. The tile of the next course above overlaps the one below.

▲ 172 **Roof tile structure.** The ancient tiles were placed recently to protect the wall. The photo shows the way the tiles alternated to provide drainage, though originally the tiles were closer together.

▼**173 Window lattice in House of the Bronze Head, Herculaneum.** The heavy frame is modern. The brick style is *testaceum*; the heavy iron lattice reveals the need for security, a reflection of life in the area.

▲**174 Temple of Diana, Nimes,** late first to early second century AD. The area shown is the central room. The vaulting is peculiar to the Nimes area; it consists of large arches juxtaposed (see top of photo). The richness of the room is almost baroque. Three niches, of which there are 12, alternate with arched and peaked pediments. Columns once separated them. The name of Diana was attached to the structure, but its use or exact date of construction is unknown. It was part of a large complex. *Texts: See photo 166.*

◄**175 Basalt door, Jerusalem,** Rockefeller Museum. Such doors sometimes were used on tombs of the third-fourth centuries AD. They reflect the style of Roman stone doors which imitated the style of metal strips, heavy nails, and pull ring. Projections at the top and bottom (one remains at top) fit into sockets. *Matthew 25:10-11; Luke 12:36; 13:25; John 18:16; Revelation 3:8.*

176, 177 Pantheon, Rome. The original structure of the temple to the 7 planetary deities was built in 27 BC by Agrippa, but his building is gone. The present structure dates to the time of Hadrian, between AD 118 and 128, but the entablature above the columns with Agrippa's name was retained. The interior determined the design of the exterior and is the important part, made to represent the all-containing cosmos. The building consists of a rotunda, a portico, and a vestibule with 16 Corinthian columns and barrel vaulting. The height from the floor to the top of the dome equals the diameter, 142 feet, 4 inches (43.4 m.). The 29 feet, 6 inch (9-m.) hole in the center of the dome provides the only light. The dome was one of Rome's contributions to architecture, made possible by the development of concrete (second century BC). The portico and vestibule is 109 feet, 7 inches by 42 feet, 8 inches (33.4 by 13 m.); it was added later. Around the walls in the interior are alternate semicircular and rectangular niches, with columns and pilasters. Between the niches were statues and aediculae. In the second story is a complex yellow marble molding, and above that are porphyry pilasters and openings like windows. The ceiling is coffered and originally was covered with gilded bronze plates. Hadrian used it as an audience hall; it magnified his imperial might and made his visitors seem small, but it also symbolized his concern for all lands and peoples. *Texts: See photo 166.*

178 Head of Agrippa, builder of the original Pantheon, 23-13 BC. Boston Museum of Fine Arts. He was Augustus' right-hand man and probably would have followed him as emperor had he lived. His name still is inscribed on an entablature above the entrance. From a bas-relief found at Athens, dates to 23-13 BC.

BUSINESS

Commerce in the Roman world was a mixture of far-flung supply sources with local ones, with all of the attendant support systems necessary to an economy. Perishable goods, with some exceptions, were obtained locally; but with the Pax Romana the commercial tentacles of enterprising businessmen extended to distances that to the modern mind are surprising.

One storehouse uncovered in an excavation in Tomi, a site on the Black Sea, contained 100 amphorae. They held a wide variety of goods: resin, dyes, bitumen, iron ingots, anchors, candlesticks, weights, and a bronze statue head.

The image of crowded bazaar streets in the towns and cities of the ancient world partly applies to the Roman world. However, the well-designed marketplace (Greek *agora*, Roman *forum*) became commonplace to every city of adequate size. The shops that lined the streets or markethalls generally were small such as those in a bazaar of today. They sold every type of provision, just as would be expected in a modern shopping center. The types of commerce, though, tended to be grouped into sections: a section for leather goods, one for vegetables, one for bakeries, etc. Numerous bas-reliefs, often from grave monuments, reveal the nature of these shops.

The workers and shopkeepers were organized into guilds. They were not labor unions; their chief functions were social and religious, and often they were burial societies which assured adequate funerals and burials for members. Sometimes a guild, or *collegium/ collegia*, became prosperous enough to build its own temple, called a *schola*.

Tradesmen traveled the world over to obtain supplies for sale; during the heady days begun by Augustus, entrepreneurism blossomed. Making money by buying and selling goods, however, was looked down on by the nobility. They believed in the noble endeavor of farming and would allow for investment through lending. The fortune-making through commerce fell to the knights and classes below them. Indeed, many a freedman became wealthy.

The supplies came by land, more by sea, from all directions. From Britain came copper, tin, lead, and gold. Spain supplied silver, lead, tin, and copper. Gaul provided iron, copper, lead, and zinc. Silver and gold came from Pannonia and Transylvania; the once-famous gold mines of Macedonia, along with those of Asia Minor, had played out by the first century. All mines belonged to the state. They were worked by contractors who received a share; his workmen consisted of slaves and criminals, along with free persons who signed up for 6-month stints.

Shipping by sea was by far the most practical, cheapest, and fastest method and was used whenever possible. Harbors, then, were of prime importance to a city's economy. Heroic measures were taken to dredge and otherwise maintain harbors when necessary. Any such port complex consisted of quays, warehouses, and other necessary additions.

It is not surprising that trade was developed west and north of Italy, for those regions were conquered territories. Commerce spread east as well, however; after all, the East had a much longer history and culture than the West. Travel by merchants extended as far as China, or at least trade did; the Far East withheld knowledge of its land and sea routes as long as it could.

China provided silk, popular with those who could afford it. Ebony, teak, rice, precious stones, and spices came from India; perfume from Arabia; luxury goods and dyes from the Tyrian coast; glassware from Syria and Palestine; marble from Greece; porphyry (a red marble) from Egypt; fur from north of the Empire; and exotic foods from both East and West. Several ports on the African coast of the Mediterranean distributed goods received from the interior of Africa, especially slaves, wild animals for the circuses, horses, mules, cloth goods such as blankets, dates, and figs.

While commerce was a major factor in unifying the Empire, and while the dynamics it created resulted in some possibility of moving up the social scale, the society was quite rigid. Slaves were set free not because of a better ethic but because keeping them was not economically justifiable. Movement into citizenship through military service was a bait which encouraged enlistment, but the rewards were long in coming. Roman society was a hierarchical structure; the poor were not pitied but despised; loyalties were more to one's family and city than to society at large. Class distinctions were rigidly maintained both by law (adapted to the needs of the time) and by custom. Wealth did not bring one into nobility; the nobility considered the manner of its gain to be of paramount importance. With all the far-flung commerce, village life continued much as before, with the majority continuing to receive their livelihood from the soil.

The Ancient Economy, M. I. Finley (Berkeley: University of California Press), 1973; *Everyday Life in the Roman Empire*, Joan Liversidge (New York: G. P. Putnam's Sons), 1976, chapters 5 and 7; *Ancient Rome*, Robert Payne (New York: American Heritage Press), 1970, pp.217-221; *A History of the Roman World From 30 BC to AD 138*, Edward T. Salmon (London: Methuen and Co., Ltd.), 1957, pp. 253-262.

179 Scenes of business and movement of goods, so-called Circus Grave Marker, found at Neumagen. Landesmuseum, Trier. The fragments on top show wine amphorae wrapped in rope for cushioning for long-distance travel, while the rowers on the fragment on the left are carrying wine in barrels for river transport. The panel below shows tenants standing in line to pay their rent while a man seated behind a desk keeps records. *Acts 3:4; 27:2-43; Revelation 3:17.*

TRANSPORTATION

Sea travel was hazardous. Romans had no compasses, so sea captains had to navigate by stars and landmarks. Sailing was avoided during 5 winter months of the year. Late March through May and late September until early November were risky months, especially the latter; safe travel was from June to mid-September. Even then, the hazards were significant.

Much was known, however, about the world's geography. Ancient travelers by Roman times already had gone through Gibralter into the Atlantic, had circumnavigated Britain, and had gone some distance farther north. Trade to India was common, and by 120 BC the West had learned the monsoon secret previously guarded by Arabs and Indians. Alexander, of course, had gone as far east as Mongolia and the Punjab. By the Roman period the Red Sea and Indian Sea were being sailed as far south as Africa's easternmost point. The Roman trade world extended into northern Europe, the Atlantic, south to Zanzibar, and east to Indonesia. Even Chinese silk was included among Rome's luxuries.

The merchant ships could sail at about 4-6 knots. A merchant ship could make the journey by sea from Italy (Brindisi) to Alexandria in 18-20 days, a faster boat in about 9 days; the return trip was longer, 40-65 days. Grain ships made regular runs from Alexandria to Rome; from Lucian (second century AD) we have a description. The *Isis* was 182 feet (55.47 m.) long, its beam was over 45 feet (13.72 m.), and its height from deck to bilges was 44 feet (13.41 m.). It could hold about 1,200 tons (1088.4 m. tons) of cargo. The size is exceptional but not unique.

Harbor regulations banned ships of less than 70-80 cargo tons (63-73 m. tons), later under Claudius 65-70 tons (59-63 m. tons). The small merchant ship more generally had a cargo capacity of 120-150 tons (109-136 m. tons) and was perhaps 60 feet long (18.3 m.) and 20-25 feet (6.1 to 7.6 m.) at the beam. Not uncommon were ships of 400-500 cargo tons (363-454 m. tons).

Grain was shipped either in sacks or loose, liquid in amphorae. All kinds of goods were shipped, of course, from marble building materials to artworks. Contracts, which provided insurance for the voyage, were drawn up between the merchant and the ship owner, plus the banker if he were involved.

Land transport was not common in ancient times, excluding the caravans of the East. The rivers of the West afforded barge traffic, which was much cheaper and faster. The ox was the beast of burden for heavy transport, a slow animal indeed; oxen could complete only 5-12 miles (8-20 km.) per day, depending on obstacles. The mule, donkey, or human porters (for very short distances) could move faster but their loads were light. The mule, much to be preferred, could cover about 50 miles (80.5 km.) in a day. Contractors maintained troops of mules or donkeys and rented them out.

Wagons, described further in photos below, had use of the famous Roman road system. The Greeks had their roads, too, on a much smaller scale. They tended to cut grooves into the stone to make a tramway for wagon wheels. Ancient wagon axles were of a standard gauge to fit these tramways; some such stone roads had unfinished surfaces except for the grooves, a great labor-saving device.

The great Roman roads were: The Via Appia ran from Rome to Brindisi, the Italian port that was the sea gateway to the East; the Via Flaminia ran from Rome to Fano in the north of the Italian peninsula and on the Adriatic; the Via Aemilia ran from the end of the Flaminia on to Milan; the Via Aurelia ran from Rome along the west coast to Genoa (all of these were completed by the end of the second century BC); the Via Egnatia ran from Durazzo (the port in Greece opposite Brindisi) to Thessalonica and thence to Byzantium; and a road across North Africa from Alexandria to Algeria (all of these were completed by the first century AD).

The Roman road system connected with earlier systems built by the powers that preceded them. In the East, the Assyrians, Persians, and Greeks had built roads that crisscrossed Asia Minor and ran on into Mesopotamia and through Palestine to Egypt. Roads in the West and North joined with roads developed earlier by such peoples as the Gauls. In the East, Rome settled on Pergamum, Ephesus, and Apamea as highway hubs.

Plutarch described the Roman road as running straight without deviation. He was correct in general, but the Romans were efficient people and ran their roads straight because it generally was most feasible to do so. They did not hesitate to deviate from the straight pattern when the terrain required it.

The Roman engineers used terrain appropriately, too, in constructing a highway. When a road was to hold light traffic, gravel was used; when the travel was heavy, polygonal or rectangular stones were laid. Often a roadbed was essential to hold the paving, but sometimes the stones could be laid directly on leveled ground, such as the well-known stretch near Antioch in Syria.

Vitruvius described the ideal road as consisting of 4 layers: the *statumen* (foundation of rammed stones), *rudus* (smaller rammed stones or clay), *nucleus* (gravel), and *pavimentum* (pavement). However, his description was based on the roads he knew; the variations were many and were based on the terrain. The Romans had a number of tools for surveying and measuring distances: the dioptra and chorobates were levels which used water, the groma was a surveying instrument with plumb lines hanging from each end of crossed rods, and the hodometer was a wheeled vehicle which dropped a pebble into a cup at every mile it traveled.

Trade was so active after Augustus brought order to much of the world that many cities had what amounted to business consulates in Rome to aid their traveling businessmen.

But trade was not the only reason for travel. Tourism was in vogue, and many people traveled for health reasons to the major hospitals attached to the temples of Aesculapius: Epidaurus, Cos, and Pergamum. Others traveled to learn the words of the oracle centers whose leaders, from very ancient times, claimed to prophesy the future: Delphi, Delos, Clarus, Didyma, Praeneste, Cumae, and a number of others. Sports events were held in major cities and drew enormous crowds.

However, passenger ships did not exist in ancient times; travelers had to go to the waterfront and search for a merchant ship going their direction; in some larger ports various cities had offices to support their interests and would provide information about ships for their areas. Such ships provided no ser-

▲180 **Cilician Gates above Tarsus.** The pass may date to prehistoric times in the form of a footpath. At least by 401 BC and probably many centuries earlier, the Tarsians cut a road from the sheer rock walls of the narrow gorge. The Cilician Gates became a primary base for Tarsus' wealth, for it provided the only access from the Cilician Plain and the northeastern portion of the Mediterranean Sea into Anatolia where its road connected with the great overland trade route. Paul's city, then, truly was "no mean city." *Acts 15:40-41.*

vices; travelers took their own servants and food, plus the utensils for cooking and eating, their own bedding, etc.

The land traveler's clothes consisted of heavy shoes, a broad-rimmed hat, and hooded mantles for various weathers (see photo 286), a purse, perhaps a pocket sundial (see photo 215), and all the amenities for cooking and personal care. A leather tent might be taken for camping, but the major roads had inns about every 25-35 miles (40-56 km.; average day's travel). They varied in quality from those which could accommodate high government officials in comfort (*cursus, mansiones* or *stationes*) to those of minimum standards (*mu-*tationes), generally set between the *stationes*. A fully equipped inn was comfortable, affording food and shelter, change of vehicles and animals, repairmen, and even prostitutes. Lists of inns and maps were available to the traveler.

Travel in the Ancient World, Lionel Casson (Toronto: Hakkert), 1974; *Biblical Illustrator*, "Tarsus: No Mean City," George L. Kelm (Summer, 1977); *The Roman Engineers*, L. A. and J. A. Hamey (Cambridge: Cambridge University Press), 1981; *Engineering in the Ancient World*, J. G. Landels (Berkeley: University of California Press), 1978, pp. 133-185; *Führer durch das Landesmuseum Trier*, Von Reinhard Schindler (Trier: Selbstverlag des Rheinischen Landesmuseum Trier), 1980 *Greek and Roman Technology*, K. D. White (Ithaca: Cornell University Press), 1984, pp. 91-156.

◄**181 Roman mileage markers.** Römerhausmuseum, Augst. They were set up every 5,000 Roman feet (about a mile minus 95 yards) along roads throughout the empire. They gave the distance from the city or highway intersection from which the measurement was made. Sometimes other distances were added, such as important cities and the principal city of the region. The name of the person who built the road or erected the marker and the emperor's name who reigned at the time often was added. *Acts 9:1-8,27.*

▼**182 Model of military bridge,** made of wood. Landesmuseum, Trier. Julius Caesar described in his *Gallic Wars* how he constructed a similar bridge over which he moved his troops over the Rhine. First, timbers 1½ feet thick were sunk into the riverbed at an angle that brought them together at the top. They also were set at an angle against the current. After the opposite pair was set, additional pilings were driven straight into the riverbed (see row on left of hoist). Two-feet-thick beams were laid across the pilings as in photo; then long beams were laid lengthwise across them and planks laid across the beams. The hoist at right is floating on pontoons and was for lifting the pilings into place and pile-driving them into the bottom by positioning the upright channel around the log and driving it with the weight seen in its center. Caesar's bridge was a variation of this; he used braces on each set of angled piles to hold the cross-logs rather than additional pilings, and he buttressed the bridge with downstream pilings set at an angle against the structure.

▲183 **Permanent Roman wood bridge,** set on stone and mortar abutments, model. Landesmuseum, Trier. To allow access to the riverbed for building the abutment's foundation, 2 coffer dams were built, 1 inside the other as in photo, and clay was tamped down between them. The water inside the dam could be pumped out by use of waterscrews and waterwheels. Often the coffer dams were made of wood pilings, sometimes of stone. Once the structure was completed above waterline an adequate distance, the rest of the abutment was finished by use of scaffolding. The bridge in the photo is built of finished wood beams. The spans are given additional strength with wood braces that are attached to beams, then mortared into the abutment. Crossbeams rest on the spans a short distance apart on the spans. Across them, other beams run lengthwise and across them tightly fitted beams run crosswise. The rails are of smaller dressed beams. The Romans' wide use of the arch allowed them to build stone bridges, too, which were common throughout the empire. Romans perfected the arch.

▲184 **Freight wagon** *(plaustrum)* **pulled by ox,** funeral monument from Neumagen. Landesmuseum, Trier. The only lubricant for its wheels was olive pressings or animal fat. The squeaking added to the city's din. The wine keg is tied onto the flatbed by a rope. The faint outline of a man can be seen by the ox's head, and the wagon disappears inside an arched area. The scene likely is of a wine delivery or loading connected with the commercial scene in the upper panel.

◄ **185 Four-wheeled travel wagon (redda).** Vatican Museum. Two persons ride on a soft seat at the back while another man drives a team of horses. The *reda* often was pulled by mules. This was one of the sturdier traveling wagons, used for larger groups or for travel over difficult roads. A similar wagon but covered was popular for travel. Called a *carruca*, its cover was of leather or cloth and was in appearance somewhat like the familiar covered wagon of the American West. They, and other types of wagons, could be hired at livery stables located at city gates. *Revelation 18:13.*

► **186 Reconstruction of Roman travel wagon.** Roman-German Landesmuseum, Cologne. Made mostly of wood, it contains only a few iron parts; the decoration is of bronze. The body is self-contained and is supported on the wheel-frame by leather straps that both tie it down and provide some cushion. The straps can be seen on the side, looped through iron rings. The iron rings are decorated with bronze figures of divinities. The bronze statuettes at the top front of the wagon are Bacchus with half-animal companions. Two female panthers face each other on the parapet in front where the driver sat.

▶ **187 Two-wheeled passenger wagon drawn by mules.** Landesmuseum, Trier. The yoke rests on the upper necks of the mules and is attached with a strap around its neck near the head. A padding rests on the mules' back to protect from chafing by the yoke. On this relief, the yoke does not appear to have the strap from the pole running under the body just behind the front legs which was normal; thus, the conveyance was meant not to carry much weight. (The more efficient yoke was not developed until the ninth-tenth centuries AD.) Two passengers ride on the wagon (*cisium*); the one on the left holds a whip. Faint scenery can be seen in the background, including a building of some sort. The column at left behind the wheel indicates the scene is in the city. *Acts 8:28-29,38; 1 Peter 4:9.*

▶ **188 Two-wheeled passenger wagon (*cisium*),** pulled by one horse which is driven by a bearded man. Landesmuseum, Trier. The wheels are smaller and stouter than those in photo 187, while the wagon is much the same design. A seat cushion is visible behind the arm brace, and the footrest is clearly seen. The yoke arrangement is the same as in 184 except that the horse has no cover to protect its sides; the pole is attached only to a neck yoke which, if an appreciable load had to be pulled, would choke the horse. A milestone is visible ahead of the horse, far left. *Texts: See photo 187.*

◄ **189 Relief of a cultwagon**, ivory, third century AD, place of discovery unknown. Roman-German Central Museum, Mainz. The images are of Jupiter under the front gable and the Dioscuri with their horses on the side. The cart's 2 wheels are decorative. The manes of the high-spirited horses are braided, and the hitching straps run around their chests and under their ribs; the buckles can be seen on their sides. Four horses are visible, but their arrangement, with a lead horse half a length ahead, suggests a fifth horse. *Acts 14:12-13; 19:35; 28:11.*

▲ **190 Sculpture of wine ship**, either from a grave monument or a building of a wine trader, Neumagen. Landesmuseum, Trier. Six oarsmen sit on each side, but the 22 oars indicate that the artist carved the 6 for detail to represent many more rowers and so a much larger ship. The headless figure of a rowing foreman is at the bow; a steersman sits in the stern with his hand on a rudder whose outline can be seen extending down the stern. Four wine casks, which number also is artistic license to represent many more, are shown as cargo. Animal heads are prominent at the bow and stern. The point of the lower bow is made to represent a dolphin's snout by the addition of eyes painted above. The ship was for river traffic. *James 3:4; Revelation 18:17.*

▲ 192 Working with cargo on boat, monument of a wholesale wine merchant, from Neumagen. Landesmuseum, Trier. The workmen, wearing sleeved tunics, are wrapping or unwrapping clay wine amphorae in rope. All are bearded. On the far right is a leg which shows a nail-studded sandal. The next man advances with a boat hook, presumably to attach the boat to the dock for unloading. A tow- or hold-line is tied to the mast of the boat. The head of the man on the far right has an aquiline nose; he likely is the boat's captain.

▲ 191 Transporting of goods by water and land, funeral monument, second century AD. Landesmuseum, Trier. The top panel has a galloping team of horses pulling a loaded wagon, though the nature of the load is unclear. The faint lines of the pole and yoke appear traditional for the period, with the yoke attached at the lower throat and a supporting band running around the animal's chest just behind the front legs. The reins are clearly seen in the hands of the driver, who sits on a forward seat. The load cannot have been very heavy due to the yoke, so the relief indicates speed. The sailship in the lower panel has a shiphand handling a cloth sail, probably of flax, while a second man, seated, fortifies himself with a drink. Almost all ancient cargo ships were under sail. The sail was square, as in the photo, as opposed to more recent sails that run fore and aft. The mast fitted into a socket and was held by 2 ropes that ran to the bow; other ropes ran from the yard ends to the stern. The sail could be moved fore and aft, and tilted. *Acts 27:17.*

▲ 193 Wine amphorae ready for shipment, from the top of the so-called Circus Monument, from Neumagen, early third century AD. Landesmuseum, Trier. (See photo 179.) Fencing holds the cargo in place. Each amphora, which narrows to a point at the bottom (see photo 871), is wrapped in rope for cushioning and stacked in pyramid style. The wine is from Mosel, a deep valley of western Germany to which the Romans introduced wine growing; it became a major source of wine for the empire. From the grave monument of 2 wine traders. *1 Peter 4:3; Revelation 14:8; 18:13.*

194 Wine amphorae and casks, from Neumagen. Landesmuseum, Trier. The photo is another view of scene in photo 193, showing the same wrapped amphorae and, on the far right, wine casks. The pieces are not all from the same monument. Appropriately for a shipping monument, stylized sea monsters with trident-tails occupy the top frieze. Nymphs, along with Poseidon/Neptune, ride the monsters. Sailors were very much concerned with sea gods, for shipping was a high-risk venture in the Roman period. *Texts: See photo 193.*

195 Bas-relief of harbor scene with divinities. Vatican Museum. Five small boats, 4 of them manned, are pulled up alongside larger boats or by the dock (in center). The larger boats are manned by rowers; a steersman with his hand on the rudder pole is visible in the boat at right. A small dock is in the bottom center of the photo, with 2 small boats pulled up to it; it opens onto a small temple. The large figures are gods, goddesses, and lesser divinities. Buildings, including temples, rise tier on tier above the harbor and give an idea of the bustle and congestion of the ancient port. The rowers and workmen in the boats and on the docks are nude. *Acts 16:11; 20:38.*

COMMERCE

▲ **196 Clay "piggy bank,"** perhaps from Hungary, second-third centuries AD. Roman-German Central Museum, Mainz. The inverted shape of the top of the money box would make it difficult to take money out.

▼ **197 Tax or rent payment scene**, relief from Circus Monument. Landesmuseum, Trier. A clerk bends over a pile of coins while a man to his right carries a sack of coins across his shoulder. The tapestry hanging and tied back behind the clerk indicates an office. The desk does not have a kneehole. See photo 198 for a similar scene with full detail. *Matthew 17:25; 22:17-21; Romans 13:6-7.*

▶ **198 Business scene, tax collection or sale of goods,** relief from the Circus Monument (see photo 179). Landesmuseum, Trier. The tapestries, as in 197, indicate a well-appointed office, perhaps located in a stoa. The seated man wears a long-sleeved tunic, is bearded, and makes entries in an account book (see photos 228, 230 for book types). The standing man next to him apparently has completed his business and is ready to move on. The next man has his hands around an open bag of coins; perhaps he is the next in line or is counting money in concert with the seated man who enters the amount. Another man stands behind him. The man standing at the desk opposite the seated man holds what also appears to be an account book. A tied bag of money is on the desk in front of him. While the previously described men wear tunics, as does the man at far left, this man wears a hooded mantle, which probably indicates that he is a farmer or traveler. The man behind him also has a hood. He holds an empty money-bag and talks with the man at far left, who holds a bag of coins over his shoulder. The scene is more likely a time of tax-gathering or rent payment than a sales transaction. Such scenes are a common theme on grave monuments from the region. *Texts: See photo 197.*

▲ **199 Rent payment scene,** bas-relief from Neumagen. Landesmuseum, Trier. Three office clerks are occupied with coins and account books. Behind and among them are 4 tenants who wear hooded mantles. The tenant on the far right holds a staff in one hand while his other hand rests on the leather strap of a money purse in which he brought his rent payment. A pile of money lies on the table, a wicker basket is full of more coins, and a multi-paged account book stands beside it. The rentmaster holds a coin he has picked out of the pile, while an embarrassed farmer holds his head down, apparently caught in the act of cheating. The 2 men at the table are beardless. *James 4:13; 1 Peter 1:18; Revelation 13:17.*

▶ **200 Rent payment scene,** 1 of 3 bas-reliefs on a grave monument. Landesmuseum, Trier. One tenant empties a money sack onto the desk while another tenant approaches with a full money sack across his shoulder. The bookkeeper sits behind the desk with his account book open. *Texts: See photo 199.*

◀ **201 Two tax officials and two farmers,** relief from Neumagen. Landesmuseum, Trier. A fifth figure stands behind the seated man, who sits in a wicker chair and holds an account book. He has his hand raised in conversation, while his eyes are fixed on the book. The figure of the first farmer is damaged, so his expression is unknown. The farmer behind him wears a hooded mantle and holds a moneybox, which apparently contains his rent payment. A leather strap across his shoulder holds a purse. *Texts: See photo 197.*

▶ **202 Entrance to Epagathiana Warehouse, Ostia.** One of the best-preserved buildings in Ostia, this warehouse belonged to 2 eastern freedmen, Epagathus and Epaphroditus. Their names are inscribed on the marble plaque above the doorway shown. Through the door and vestibule beyond, a courtyard is entered which is surrounded by a 2-storied arcade; the areas were storage for the many goods which passed through Ostia. The doorway shown is an ornate one which drew inspiration from classical styles. *Revelation 18*.

WEIGHTS AND MEASURES

Except for the elite, who had large houses with a multitude of lamps of every description and servants to tend them, the effective part of the day was daylight. The ancient world focused its sense of time on the daylight hours. Hence, each sunrise to sunset was divided into 12 hours regardless of the time of year. Hours were longer in summer than in winter.

Romans had sundials, however, which they borrowed from Greece in the third century BC, and about 100 years later they imported water clocks from Greece. These time devices, though, clashed with the traditional manner of living through the day, since they divided the hour up evenly; in addition, they were only marginally accurate.

The Roman calendar began on January 1 (the old calendar on March 1). Their months were much like ours, but each month was divided into 3 parts—the Kalends, Nones, and Ides—in an irregular system that was nonetheless plain to them.

The coinage system was based on the number 12 rather than 10, which made division into 3s and 4s quite simple. Banking, moneylending, and credit operated within the empire. Temples often were used as depositories for funds. Moneychangers were found throughout the empire; they not only changed coins of varying denominations but checked coins for forgery.

Roman pound (libra)	= 12 ounces (373 grams)
Roman foot (pes)	= slightly more than 11½ inches (29.3 cm.)
Roman pace (passus)	= 4 feet, 10¼ inches (1.48 m.)

▲ 203 **Workman using balance scale.** Landesmuseum, Trier. The Romans had 2 types of balances, the simple *libra* and the steelyard (*stratera*). The Greeks used only the *libra*; the Romans used both. The *libra*, or balance scale, consisted of a pen suspended from each end of a bar. Commodities were placed in 1 pan, weights in the other. This type is not shown in photos, though pans shown are common to both types of scale. The bas-relief shows a bearded workman with apron sliding a weight along the arm of a steelyard balance scale. A larger weight is nearer the fulcrum. The load apparently is a bale of wool. *John 12:3; 19:39; Revelation 6:5; 16:21.*

Roman mile	= 1,000 paces (1,618 yards; 1,479 m.)
Roman land measurement (iugerum)	= 2109.5 square yards (2523.34 square meters), the amount a team of oxen could plow in a day
Roman dry measure (modius)	= almost a peck (8.732 liters)
Roman liquid measure (hemina)	= about 5¾ pints (3.275 liters).

British Museum: Guide to the Exhibition Illustrating Greek and Roman Life (London: Order of the Trustees), 1908; Life in Ancient Rome, F. R. Cowell (New York: G. P. Putnam's Sons), 1980, pp. 45-51; A History of Technology and Invention, Vol. I, edited by Maurice Daumas (New York: Crown Publishers), 1962; The Picture History of Inventions, Umberto Eco and G. B. Zorzoli (New York: The Macmillan Co.), 1963; Reading and Dating Roman Imperial Coins, Zander H. Klawans (New York: Sanford J. Durst), 1982; Führer durch das Landesmuseum Trier, Von Reinhard Schindler (Trier: Selbstverlag des Rheinischen Landesmuseum Trier), 1980; Coinage in Roman Imperial Policy, C. H. V. Sutherland (New York: Sanford J. Durst), 1978; Dictionary of Roman Coin Inscriptions, Stewart J. Westdal (New York: Sanford J. Durst), 1982.

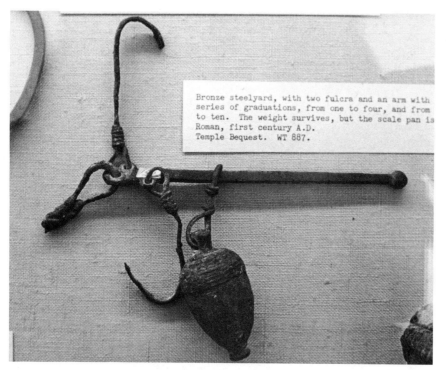

Bronze steelyard, with two fulcra and an arm with
series of graduations, from one to four, and from
to ten. The weight survives, but the scale pan is
Roman, first century A.D.
Temple Bequest. WT 887.

◄ **204 Bronze steelyard with weight,** first century AD. British Museum. The scale was hung by the upper hook (see photo 203). Loads to be measured were hung from the ring below the fulcrum; a larger weight was hung from the hook. Measures of weight were based on the duo-decimal system of the pound *(li-bra, pondus)*, which equals 10.528 ounces (327.45 grams). The Roman ounce *(uncia)* was $1/12$ of a pound; the *scrupulum* was $1/24$ of an ounce. The balance arm has 2 sets of gra-dations, one from numbers 1-4, the other with numbers 5-10. *Texts: See photo 203.*

▼ **205 Bronze steelyard with 2 hang-ers** for the material to be weighed, Roman period. Field Museum. The

weight is in an acorn shape. See de-scription for use in photo 204. *Texts: See photo 203.*

▲ **206 Bronze balance scale with 2 hangers** as in 205, used through-out Roman period, copy of an origi-nal. Roman-German Central Mu-seum, Mainz. See photo 202 for de-scription of use. The scale has 5 notches on the weight end. *Texts: See photo 203.*

▼**207 Bronze balance scale,** used throughout Roman period, copy of original. Roman-German Central Museum, Mainz. The scale has 1 hook for load to be measured and a hanger for weights to be hung. *Texts: See photo 203.*

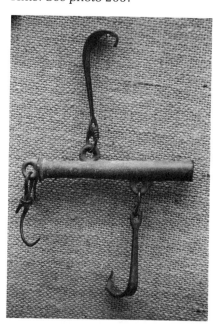

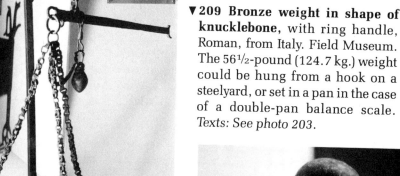

▲**208 Bronze balance scale with pan,** from Etruria, Italy, Roman period. Field Museum. The scale works in the manner described in photo 204, except that a pan is attached for the merchandise to be weighed. *Texts: See photo 203.*

◀**210 Bronze weights in shape of sitting goats,** from Pompeii. Field Museum. Each piece of the set is inscribed with its weight: P I, P III, P IIII, P V, P X (1, 3, 4, 5, 10 Roman pounds respectively). *Texts: See photo 203.*

SET OF ROMAN BRONZE WEIGHTS
Each weight is in the form of a recumbent goat on a pedestal, its weight being inscribed as P I, P III, P IIII, P V, P X respectively, signifying that the weights are 1, 3, 4, 5, and 10 pounds.
POMPEII, ITALY

▼**209 Bronze weight in shape of knucklebone,** with ring handle, Roman, from Italy. Field Museum. The 56½-pound (124.7 kg.) weight could be hung from a hook on a steelyard, or set in a pan in the case of a double-pan balance scale. *Texts: See photo 203.*

▼**211 Measure for liquids,** Roman, from Italy. Field Museum. The handle has a slot which is inscribed with a graduated scale. The measure was hung from the chain attached to the handle. Weights were attached to the ring on the end of the handle for more precision. The weight desired probably was attached first, then the liquid added. *Luke 16:6-7.*

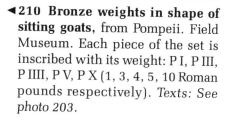

▲ 212 Bronze dry measure, Roman, first century AD, from the Rhineland. British Museum. The capacity is .639 quarts (.605 liters). A *sextarius* was .613 quarts (.580 liters), so this measure was used by a tax collector to add a 5 percent tax from the producer of the commodity being measured. *Luke 13:21.*

▼ 214 Pocket sundial, bronze with silver plate, soon after AD 134; copy, from Roman-German Central Museum, Mainz; original in Staatssammlung, Munich. Hour gradations are valid for the Province of Pontus and Bithynia in Asia Minor. From a medallion with portrait of Antinous from Claudiopolis of Bithynia. *Texts: See photo 213.*

▼ 213 Sundial from Rome, marble, first century AD. Copy from Roman-German Central Museum, Mainz; original in Staatliche Museum, Berlin. Sundials evolved from the gnomon, which was a perpendicular stick that cast a shadow on the

appropriate gradation. The sundial design shown here and in photo 215 was a considerable advance. The dial is of the *solar quadrant* type. A stylus is at the top of the base. The hour-lines on the quadrant are designed in such a way that the direction of the stylus' shadow was the same on any given hour of the day whatever the season. The *equatorial quadrant* (not shown) is a variation in design. The *universal quadrant* (not shown) used a compass to determine how to set the stylus, so it was portable for traveling. The solar quadrant dates to about 1000 BC and was in use by Greeks by about 500 BC, by Romans by about 200 BC. *Matthew 20:3-9; 24:36; 27:45-46; John 4:6; Acts 2:15.*

▲ 215 Fragment of sundial, with Greek lettering. Vatican Museum. The lines and lettering inscribed onto the concave surface indicated the time of day from a shadow cast from a pin that projected up from the center point of the sundial above the vertical line. See photo 211 for sundial details. *Texts: See photo 213.*

▶ **216 Fragment of a calendar,** second century AD; copy, from Roman-German Central Museum, Mainz; bronze original in Stadt Museum, Salzburg. The astrological months are stated in Latin with the German names above them (the writing is modern) on a reconstruction of the shape of the calendar. The top 2 rows are months, the third row is weekdays, and the bottom row is for days of the month. Pegs were placed in the holes to identify the proper month, weekday, and day of the month. The upper fragment is a representation of the Andromeda and Perseus legend; the bottom fragment has 2 figures, the 1 on the right holding a wand.

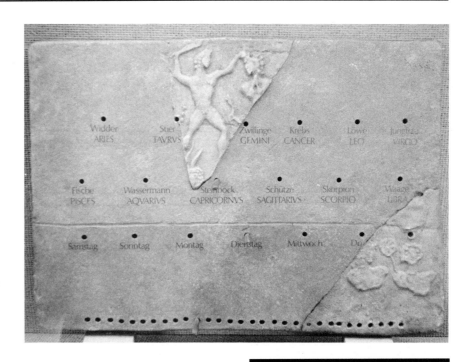

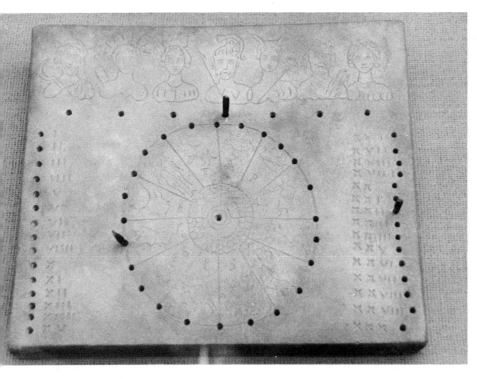

▲ **217 Stick calendar.** Reconstruction (clay) after a discovery found in Rome. Roman-German Central Museum, Mainz. The top row consists of weekdays. Twelve astrological months, each indicated by the animal sign and each divided into halves, are indicated by the circle. Days of the month are indicated by 15 days down each side marked by Roman numerals. The pegs indicate: Tuesday, August 22 (lion).

218-224 Coins and their values. All from Roman-German Central Museum, Mainz.

Table

4 sestertius	= 1 denarius
8 dupondius	= 1 denarius
8 semis	= 1 denarius
16 as	= 1 denarius
64 quadrans	= 1 denarius
25 denarius	= 1 aureus

The denarius was the standard coin of the empire; first issued about 187 BC, it remained in use until about AD 296. From the time of Nero on, it was periodically debased in percent of silver until it contained about 40 percent during Caracalla's reign (AD 211-217). At that time Caracalla introduced a new coin, the antonianianus. The dupondius (221) is difficult to distinguish from the as. The sestertius, the large coin of the empire, is known as the large or grand bronze; originally it was a silver coin worth one-quarter of a denarius. The semis, mostly of bronze with slight amounts of silver, were of various types and sizes. The aureus appeared with Julius Caesar and gradually declined in weight until abolished in the fourth century.

▲ **218 Gold aureus.** CAESAR AUGUSTUS DIVI F PATER PATRIAE. After 2 BC.

▼ **221 Brass dupondius** (half sestertius). IMP CAES NERVAE TRAIANOAUS GER DAC PM TR P COS V PP.

▼ **219 Silver denarius,** about 27-26 BC. *Matthew 18:28; 20:2-13; 22:19-21; Mark 6:37; 12:15-17; Revelation 6:6.*

▲ **222 Copper as.** IMP CAES DOMIT AUG GERM COS XIIII CENS PER P P. *Matthew 10:29; Luke 12:6.*

▼ **224 Double sestertius.** IMP C M Q TRAIANUS DECIUS AUG.

▲ **220 Brass sestertius.** IMP CAESAR TRAIANUS HADREANUS AUG.

▼ **223 Copper semis.** NERO CAES AVG IMP.

PROFESSIONS AND TRADES

◄ **225 Pastoral mosaic,** from floor of Roman villa. Corinth Museum. It likely is a copy of a fourth-century BC painting by the Greek Pausias. The herdsman is naked, his skin or clothing hanging from his neck. His full hair is curly, and he happily plays a flute while cattle graze contentedly. A pot with a handle stands below the tree.

► **226 Bakery, Pompeii.** Three mills for grinding (see 274) and a large brick oven can be seen. A similar bakery, that of Modestus, when excavated from the lava flow yielded 81 carbonized loaves still in the oven, its iron door closed. The loaves were round and patterned into 8 segments. Some 40 bakeries were discovered at Pompeii. The odor around them was unpleasant, since they threw their bran outside onto the street to be eaten by pigs. These mills could have been turned by horsepower or, if the room was cramped, by slaves by means of wooden poles inserted into each side of the waist of the upper stone.

WRITING INSTRUMENTS

Black writing ink was made from soot, resin, pitch, octopus ink, juice of the cuttlefish, or other compounds. Pens were of reed or feathers similar to those of our not-too-distant past. The stylus was made from wood, ivory, reed, or metal. The implements could be carried around in a small case called a *theca*.

Writing materials included waxed double-leafed boards, papyrus, and parchment. The wax set in the boards often was darkened to make the inscriptions show up better. They were inscribed with the stylus, which had 1 pointed end for writing and a flat end for smoothing out (erasing) the inscription. The ones shown below are 2-leafed and are called diptychs, but additional boards could be added, called triptychs and polytychs.

Sometimes board was used without wax and written on with ink and pen; these, of course, provided permanent records. Rolls made from either papyrus or parchment were written (usually) on one side in columns 2-3 inches in width. Mistakes could be corrected by rubbing them out with a sponge. Parchment was more expensive and, though common with the well-to-do, was likely too expensive for many commoners. A full-size scroll (book) could not be any longer than one of the longer Gospels. Though difficult to handle and limiting the reader to the text before him, several could be carried around. Each was wrapped in its own parchment wrapper; an attached ticket stated the contents.

Education in Ancient Rome, Stanley F. Bonner (Berkeley: University of California Press), 1977; *Life in Ancient Rome*, F. R. Cowell (New York: G. P. Putnam's Sons), 1980, pp. 163-65; *Daily Life in the Time of Jesus*, Henri Daniel-Rops (New York: Hawthorn Books, Inc.), 1962, pp. 272-276; *Römisches Alltagsleben in Köln*, Inge Linfert-Reich (Romisch-Germanisches Museum der Stadt Köln), 1983.

◄ **227 Man writing with stylus in tablet,** from Neumagen. Landesmuseum, Trier. The bas-relief depicts a man in a loose tunic writing beside a pillar on which a lamp can be faintly seen. An arch is carved into the background. The man on the right has his hand poised in the same manner and may have been writing the same way. See photo 228 for the type of tablet.

▶ **228 Folding wax tablet with bronze stylus,** first century AD. Roman-German Central Museum, Mainz. The stylus is a reconstruction. Each wood frame holds a layer of wax into which the stylus was used to write notes or figures. The wax then could be smoothed out and the tablet reused. The 2 leaves are held together by leather thongs.

▼ **229 Folding title record with seals, below.** Reconstruction, of wood and wax from a find at Pompeii. Roman-German Central Museum, Mainz. The record is written in Greek and shows the sale of a dyeworks. It is wrapped with a string sealed with five seals, each with a different imprint. *John 3:33; 2 Corinthians 1:22; Revelation 5:1.*

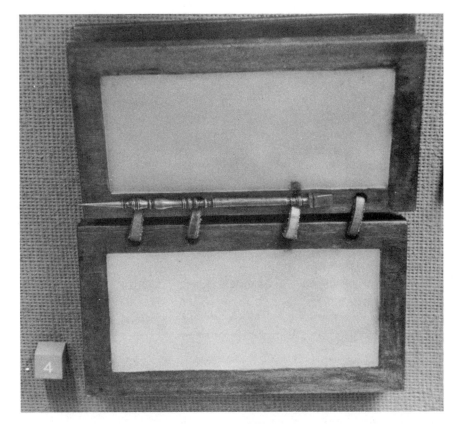

▲ **230 Wooden cover for writing tablet,** first century AD, found at Walbrook, London. British Museum.

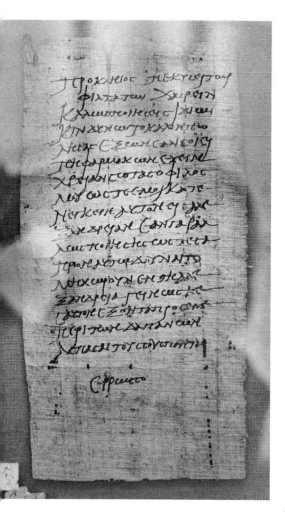

▲ **233 Pottery inkwell,** early third century BC. Agora Museum, Athens. *Texts: See photo 232.*

▲ **232 Pottery inkwells,** from Pompeii, first century AD. Field Museum. *2 Corinthians 3:3; 2 John 12; 3 John 13.*

▲ **231 Letter written on papyrus,** from Alexandria, first century AD. British Museum. The letter is written in Greek: "Prokleios to his good friend Pekysis, greetings. You will do well if at your own risk you sell to my friend Sotas such drugs of good quality as he will tell you he needs, for him to bring to me at Alexandria. For if you act otherwise, and give him rotten stuff, unsaleable in Alexandria, know that you will have to deal with me about the cost. Greet all your family from me. Farewell." (Translation from museum identification.) *Luke 1:3; Acts 1:1; 9:2; 15:30-31.*

▲ **234 Alabaster inkwell,** Roman period, provenance unknown. Roman-German Landesmuseum, Cologne. *Texts: See photo 232.*

◄ **235 Bronze inkwell with silver-plate cover.** Roman-German Landesmuseum, Cologne. The plate is inscribed with ornamentation and the words "Servandus wants to live!" *Texts: See photo 232.*

▲ **237 Bronze pen,** Roman, found in Tiber River. British Museum. *3 John 13.*

▼**238 Bronze pen,** Roman, from Athens. British Museum. *3 John 13.*

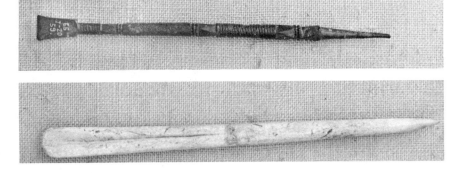

▲ **236 Faience inkwell with three holders,** fourth-first centuries BC, Ptolemaic. Milwaukee Museum. *Texts: See photo 229.*

▲ **239 Bone stylus,** Roman, from Lyons. British Museum. *3 John 13.*

◄ **240 Abacus,** bronze, reconstruction. Roman-German Central Museum, Mainz. The ancients had a system of fast counting on the fingers. The fingers of the left hand represented single-digit numbers (1-9) and tens; those of the right hand represented hundreds and thousands. The abacus shown was built on that hand method of counting. The abacus has 9 slots on the bottom, 6 on the top. From the left, slots 1-7 and the corresponding slots on the upper row allow counting from 1 to 1 million. Slots 8-9 and the right upper slot are for fractions. The tiny balls are counters. From 1-7 of them could be placed in each lower slot, from 1-4 in each upper slot. *Luke 14:28; Acts 19:19.*

ART AND ARTISTS

The art of the first century in the world of the New Testament is a composite of Greek and Roman. Art scholars assign the period just preceding Augustus to the Hellenistic period, but point out that the Greek models were continually influenced by Rome. This period began with the conquest of Corinth by Mummius in 146 BC. (The process of ransacking works of art and transporting them to Rome began long before, however.) At that time, Mummius carried off Corinth's bountiful art to Rome, where their presence made a profound impact.

Demand for Greek art grew rapidly, and Greek artists and artisans migrated to Roman centers of influence to meet the demand. Many of the classic Greek works became favorites of artists and copies have appeared at several sites. Artwork included not only the well-known marble and bronze statuary, but mosaics, frescoes, coinage, reliefs, intaglios and cameos, jewelry, glassware, silverplate, ornamentation on all kinds of objects; in short, art was as extensive as it is today.

These works of art are important as art, but they also are important because of the commerce generated by the demand and effort to supply that demand. The result impacted the warp and woof of the Roman world, with traveling artisans, interest in art, development of mass production techniques, shipping, and other factors related both to business and general culture. Moreover, the artwork produced in the West functioned as trade commodities for products from the Far East such as silk.

While statuary could be built in shops and shipped to the customer, some art had to be done on site. Mo-saics, set both in floors and walls, were popular; and painted murals adorned the walls of those who could afford them. Murals which remind the viewer of Pompeii's walls have been uncovered in the Upper City of Jerusalem.

Works of art adorned the fine homes and villas of the Roman world; lesser works were cherished by the less fortunate. In addition, public buildings—temples, baths, fountains, stoas, streets, forums—displayed works of art for all to see and enjoy. The pattern was so pervasive that a traveler could feel at home in any significant city in the empire. The subjects were from Greek and Roman myth, gods and goddesses, animals, historical scenes, and public officials (especially the emperor).

A great deal could be learned about culture of the first century in the various regions of the empire through a study of the art produced in those regions, for regional pecu-liarities are observable; each area added its own touch to the general trend. Moreover, official art—which was used for propaganda as effectively as other media is today—had its own style.

The Capitoline Collections, Settimo Bocconi (Museo Capitolino), 1950; *Greek, Etruscan, and Roman Art*, George H. Chase (1950), revised by Cornelius C. Vermeule III (Boston: Museum of Fine Arts), 1963; *Great Treasures of Pompeii and Herculaneum*, Theodore H. Feder (New York: Abbeville Press), 1978; *Roman Art*, Helga von Heintze (New York: Universe Books), 1971; *Greek and Roman Sculpture*, A. W. Lawrence (New York: Harper and Row, Publishers), 1972; *The National Museum, Naples*, Bianca Maiuri (Instituto Geografico de Agostini), 1959; *Biblical Illustrator*, "Workmanship: Early Examples," Paula A. Savage, Fall, 1983; *Guide to the Vatican* (Monumenti, Museie Gallerie Pontificie), 1973; *Roman Art and Architecture*, Mortimer Wheeler (New York: Oxford University Press), 1964.

◀ **241 Portion of Battle of Issus mosaic, from Pompeii.** National Museum of Naples. The portion shown is a closeup of Darius at the moment of defeat at the hands of Alexander. It is the largest and most intricate of the Pompeii mosaics; the full piece measures 9 feet (3.28 m.) by 17 feet (5.18 m.) and was inset into a floor in the House of the Faun (see color photo 408). Darius is about to turn his chariot around to flee to safety. He is gesturing toward a fallen comrade, obviously of some importance for he is dressed in a gold tunic, while his chariot driver behind the king is madly whipping the horses. It is a work of the second century BC, probably based on an original painting, perhaps by Philoxenus of Eretria who lived about 300 BC.

▶ **242 Venus di Milo,** an original Aphrodite of the second century BC found on the island of Melos. The Louvre. The missing arms were carved separately and the body was formed in 2 pieces from Parian marble: the torso and head, and the draped legs. The statue is taller than life, 6 feet, 8 inches (2.03 m.). Intended to be viewed from a three-quarter angle to the right, the left side of the face and torso is less carefully worked. Though the best known of Greek classics, the workmanship is not as good as some other pieces. Nonetheless, the balance is good. The statue represents the Greek ideal of feminine beauty; her sensuality comes from the sense of motion and dignity. The lost right arm likely held the polished shield of Ares, god of war. The sculptor is not known; various parts of the work reflect the influence of Phidias, Lysippus, and Praxiteles. *Revelation 18:12.*

◄ **243 Discus-thrower (Discobolus)** by Myron, wrongly restored as a warrior. Capitoline Museum. Myron was one of the 3 greatest sculptors of ancient Greece, along with Phidias and Polyclitus. Myron was able to freeze great moments of action with his mastery of details of the anatomy. Myron's frequently copied original Discus-thrower was in bronze. Of this copy, only the torso is original. The head, arms, and legs were restored by Monnot (1658-1723), who owned it at the time. He misinterpreted the design and his restoration has become famous. A comparison of this statue with a proper restoration (see photo 624) reveals the plausibility of his error. The torso itself, however, demonstrates great skill in muscular rendition. *Revelation 18:12.*

► **244 Lion killing sheep.** Vatican Museum. The sculpture, along with many other animal statuary of Greek and Roman origin, was restored so fully by F. A. Franzoni (1775-1818) that it may be considered his work. The frequency of such themes, however, along with the graphic nature of the subjects, illustrates a type of visual that was seen often in public places of the Empire.

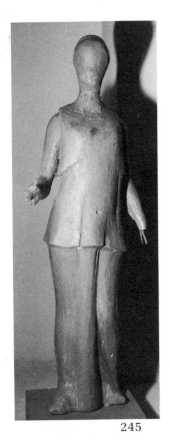
245

246

247

248

▲ **245-249 Stages of "lost wax" process,** from models in National Museum, Athens. The ancient artist in bronze used the process of carving his work in wax, making a mold around it, draining off the wax (hence, "lost"), and filling the mold with bronze. 245: A clay model of approximately the size and shape of the desired work was made. The piece shown is small; for larger pieces an iron frame supported the wax. 246: The clay model then was covered with wax. The artist carved the detail into the wax in the form he intended for the finished piece then added another layer of clay over it. 247: The form was inverted and wax tubes (runners) were set into place, running from a funnel, through which to pour the molten metal. Other tubes (risers) were also added to serve as vents for the passage of fumes. Iron dowels were inserted into the piece to hold a clay covering (inverted). 248: The invested model was then placed into an oven and fired. The wax melted and ran off, thus leaving a hollow space between the original clay approximation and the outer clay investment. The final outer surface, of course, was set in reverse inside the investment layer. The molten metal was poured into the funnel and through the runners to fill up the hollow space. When the whole structure cooled, the outer clay layer was broken away and the runners and risers (filled with metal) were cut away. Any irregularities in the metalwork were corrected; then the piece was smoothed and burnished (249). As much of the inner clay as possible was extracted; the remainder was left inside the finished piece. *Revelation 18:12,22.*

249

PHILOSOPHERS

Philosophy was both a profession and an avocation. Some of those described below were politicians or otherwise followed careers. For some, however, philosophy was the means of livelihood. Philosophers sometimes made their living by teaching, but all teachers were not philosophers (see Home and Hearth, Schools). Some well-educated men became enslaved during the early empire period and so became tutors to children of the wealthy.

Philosophers did much to challenge the wrongs of society. In times of political stress they were vulnerable because they were apt to speak out. Domitian had some of them put to death because of their declamations of tyranny, as other emperors before him had done. They exerted personal influence, lectured in public, and taught itinerately from house to house.

Some of the more fortunate, or better, established schools and were employed by schools in the cities. The best-known ones were Athens and Alexandria, but previous persecutions in Egypt had scattered the philosophers so that by the Empire period, cities all over the Aegean basin could boast schools. Pergamum, Delphi, and Rhodes were considered the best. Rhodes, in fact, was quite popular; Tiberius studied there while in exile and Cicero had preceded him. As the Pax Romana became a reality, the ravaged lands of Asia recovered and renewed their lead in education. By the end of the first century AD Cos, Pergamum, Ephesus, and Smyrna had strong schools.

Philosophers could be employed by their cities as envoys to appeal to Rome on any matter of importance;

they were logical choices because of their skills at argument and knowledge of the world—the better ones among them, at any rate.

The wandering philosopher found his way to the forum or other public place and harangued the passersby. The Cynic philosophers made this approach a way of life.

Education in Ancient Rome, Stanley F. Bonner (Berkeley: University of California Press), 1977; *Greek and Roman Portraits: 470 BC-AD 500* (Boston: Museum of Fine Arts), 1972; *Greek, Etruscan, and Roman Art,* George H. Chase, revised by Cornelius C. Vermeule III (Boston: Museum of Fine Arts), 1963; *Euripides, Ten Plays,* introduction by Moses Hadas (New York: Bantam Books), 1960; *History of Rome,* Michael Grant (New York: Charles Scribner's Sons), 1978; *The Classical Mind,* W. T. Jones (New York: Harcourt Brace Javonovich, Inc.), 1970; *A History of Education in Antiquity,* H. I. Marrou (Madison, Wisconsin: The University of Wisconsin Press), 1956; *The Harvest of Hellenism,* F. E. Peters (New York: Simon and Schuster), 1970; *Roman Literature and Society,* R. M. Ogilvie (New York: Penguin Books), 1980; *The Complete Plays of Sophocles,* Sir Richard Claverhouse Jebb, translator, Moses Hadas, editor and introduction (New York: Bantam Books), 1967; *Xenophon: The Persian Expedition,* Rex Warner, translator (New York: Penguin Books), 1961.

◄ **250 Homer, Roman copy after a Hellenistic prototype.** Boston Museum of Fine Arts. The head is 16⅛ inches (41 cm.) in height. The form was copied and imitated many times. It is a creation of the ideal Homer, intended to reflect his blindness and poverty. The eyebrows are lifted, the eye sockets recessed, the lids thin. The face is age-wrinkled; yet the overall impression suggests intelligence. No one knows for sure when Homer lived; all students of Greek and Roman history are agreed that his figure loomed over the history of the region for centuries. His great writings, *The Odyssey* and *The Iliad*, formed much of the basis for education in the Greek and later the Roman world (see Education). Ancient scholars analyzed the manuscripts of Homer's works with the same intensity as the Bible manuscripts are analyzed today, to determine what words and phrases were or were not authentic to Homer. His writings were used not just to teach history but to teach morals; when the ancient Homeric myths no longer fit the culture, they were adapted as allegories, while his outdated picture of the Olympian gods and goddesses was nimbly presented to accommodate the updated views. Virgil's *Aeneid*, which gave Rome a claim to Greek descent, was built off of Homer's story. *Romans 1:14; 1 Corinthians 1:19-26; 2:1-6; 3:18-20.*

► **251 Statue of Homer, fourth-third centuries BC.** National Museum of Naples. He wears a tunic (*chiton*) and over it a pallium. Philosophers often abstained from wearing a tunic as a measure of austerity. His cap is simple and rimless, and he carries a walking stick. A bundle of scrolls is on the ground by his foot. *Texts: See photo 250.*

▼ **253 Sophocles** (496-406 BC), from a Greek original of the fourth century BC. Capitoline Museum. Only 15 years older than Euripides, he lived during the time of Pericles' leadership, the years of Athens' greatness. His writings are of the ancient classic style, reflecting serenity and order. His tragedies were widely popular in his day and he received many prizes for them. He composed over 120 plays, yet the fact that only 7 have survived in completeness, contrasted with 19 of Euripides who wrote fewer, indicates a lack of later popularity. He believed the gods to be powerful, yet he did not assume that they lived by the same standards as humans; each realm had its own way of life. He depicted humans "as they should be." *Texts: See photo 250.*

▲ **252 Head of Socrates,** discovered in the palace, Ephesus. Ephesus Museum. Though sometimes considered to be the father of philosophy, Socrates (469-399 BC) carried on a tradition of philosophy which already had a long history. He established the teaching method of asking the probing question, which has come to be called the Socratic method. The story of his death is well known; he was condemned because his questions—often caustic—seemed to call into question the existence of the gods. We know of Socrates through his pupil, Plato, who pointed out in *Theaetetus* that his teacher spent his life purposely mystifying and making sport of his fellowmen. Socrates spawned the Cynic school, street philosophers who felt it their calling to chide and harangue society for their inconsistencies. *Texts: See photo 250.*

▼ **255 Panyassis, the poet.** National Museum of Naples. The fifth-century BC composer of epic poetry was from Halicarnassus. He was an uncle of Herodotus. *Texts: See photo 250.*

▲ **254 Euripides** (480-406 BC), bust found in Anatolia, Roman period. Bergama Museum, Athens. Born in Salamis, he wrote 92 plays, of which 19 are extant. His plays introduced characters with poor morals and characters, for which he was criticized in his day; but he became one of the most popular of the Greek dramatists. Unlike the classic style of his day, his plays could be understood by the common people. Not surprisingly, scenes from them were depicted often in Greek art. He has been called the ancestor of European drama. *Texts: See photo 250.*

▲ **256 Xenophon** (fourth century BC). Bergama Museum, Bergama (Pergamum), Turkey. Greek historian who kept a diary of Alexander the Great's campaign to free Asia Minor and into Persia. In addition to the value of his writings for historical data, he revealed much about the Greek culture and lifestyle of his day. His history was one of the primary sources consulted in the ancient world. His biographical style provided a model for the several ones written during the Roman period.

► **257 Demosthenes** (384-322 BC), a copy from the Roman Imperial period of an original. Vatican Museum. He was a moderate who sought to restrain Athens' revolt against Alexander the Great and then joined the revolt. Earlier he had encouraged the Athenians to take action against Philip of Macedon. The famous orator has been called the last great defender of Athenian freedom. He was 1 of 4 ancients whose writings were basic study in Greek schools, the others being Homer, Euripides, and Menander. *Texts: See photo 250.*

► **258 Epicurius** (341-270 BC), bust found in the piazza of Maria Maggiore in 1742. Capitoline Museum. Born on the island of Samos, he founded the philosophy of Epicurianism. He moved to Athens in 306 BC and quickly became very popular. He believed that the end of life was pleasure, but he also taught that the enlightened seeker of pleasure will live simply and keep his life under control to avoid the unpleasantness of some after-effects. He distinguished between pleasures that are necessary (food and sleep) and those that are unnecessary (sex, exotic foods, ostentatiousness); the unnecessary pleasures are impossible to fulfill satisfactorily, so the wise man will not attempt to do so. His lack of reconciliation of those acts which may be right even though they do not produce pleasure, and his lack of taking into account differing needs and tastes of persons left his philosophy open to the excesses which followed among his spiritual heirs. He developed his philosophy along scientific lines, as perceived in his day. The universe is constituted of nothing but atoms and void. When atom impulses strike us, we are stimulated accordingly. Consequently, death is simply the dissolving of life; pleasure or lack of it is the result of those sensations. The chief Roman Epicurean was Lucretius (94-55 BC?). He believed man's greatest fear was death and that religion was responsible for that fear and other superstitions that plagued mankind. Roman Epicurianism called for a passive attitude. Virgil was among other Romans influenced by Epicurius. *1 Corinthians 15:32; 1 Timothy 6:20.*

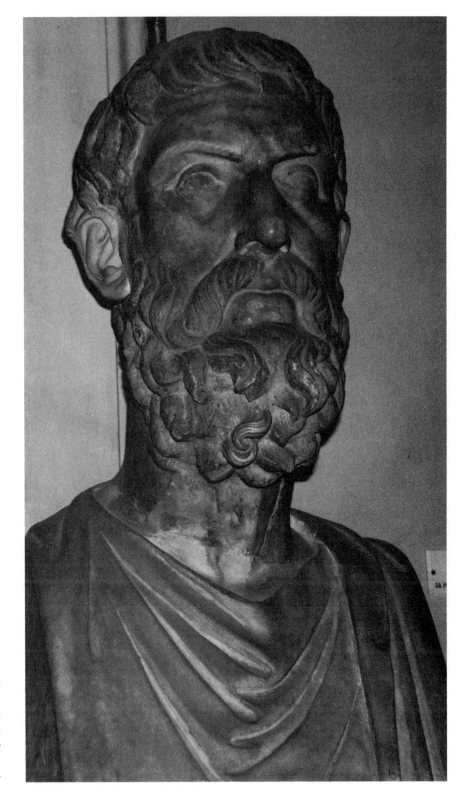

▲ **259 Philosopher, possibly Cleanthes,** the Stoic. Roman copy of a Greek original of about 250 BC. British Museum. He was a successor to Zeno, the originator of Stoicism. He taught that the sun is the central organ of the universe and guides it just as the mind guides the body. His writing, *Hymn to Zeus*, was the Stoic's anthem to the one god they believed ruled the world, called by many names; but whether Cleanthes believed that Zeus was the highest, most all-powerful god above all other gods or that Zeus was the only God is difficult to tell. *Colossians 2:8; see also photo 250.*

▼ **260 Mosaic of philosopher,** Landesmuseum, Trier. He wears the traditional garb of a philosopher, a himation without a tunic underneath.

▼ **262 Bust of philosopher, from Samaria.** Rockefeller Museum, Jerusalem. Judea had a great deal of Hellenistic and Roman influence, as reflected in the remains of theaters and other buildings in the Decapolis, Caesarea Philippi, Caesarea Maritima, Samaria/Sebaste, and other locations. This philosopher's bust from Samaria indicates the influence of philosophy which later produced Justin Martyr from the same city.

▲ **261 Cicero** (106-43 BC), Capitoline Museum. He was born into an undistinguished family, but his skill at oratory—the basis of training in Roman society—caused him to be selected by the nobility to put down a threatened revolt by Catiline. As a result, he was named consul. He amassed considerable wealth, including collections of Greek art. His oratorical and writing style became the dominant model of Roman literature and laid the foundation for later European style. Fifty-eight of his speeches survive, along with some 800 letters to friends, and he composed 16 philosophical works. He was a Stoic and believed in the basic dignity of all people, based on the idea that all people are part of a "divine fire." Stoicism had been brought to Rome by Panaetius (ca. 180-110 BC) whose works Cicero reflects. He believed the world was subject to terrible conflagrations periodically; with Panaetius he revived the old Greek view that the soul was composed of 3 parts. *1 Timothy 6:20.*

◄ **263 Seneca the Younger** (4 BC-AD 65); bronze, from Herculaneum. National Museum of Naples. One of the great figures of Roman literature, early church historians attempted to connect his thought with that of the apostle Paul. The man himself, however, failed to live up to the ideals of which he wrote. His elder brother was adopted by Junius Gallio and was the governor of Achaea in 51-52 AD (Acts 18:11-17). He hid himself in his studies during the reigns of Tiberius and Caligula, was exiled to Corsica from AD 41-49; then Agrippina had him brought back to Rome to tutor the young Nero. His influence during the first 5 years of Nero's rule was enormous; he and a military commander named Burrus effectively ran the empire. Then Nero took charge, murdering his mother in the process. Seneca went into retirement to avoid Nero's jealousy, but eventually he was accused of conspiracy to assassinate Nero and in AD 65 was ordered to commit suicide. His extant writings include 9 tragedies, 124 letters on philosophy, 7 books on science, a short satire on Claudius, and 12 essays. His writings reveal much about Roman society and alternately have been praised and condemned by critics. The statue is referred to as Pseudo-Seneca. Its identification with him is compatible with the face, which reflects anguish: his hair is disheveled, his cheeks hollow, the skin of his neck loose, and his eyes troubled.

OTHER PROFESSIONS

▲ **264 Tile of tax collector,** London, first or second century AD. British Museum. The inscription reads: Pp. BR. LON = Tax-gatherers of London in the province of Britain. The perception of the Roman citizenry was that they should not pay taxes, but that those who were conquered by them and/or received the benefits of Roman rule should pay taxes. During the second century BC Rome established the policy of tax collection which resulted in the publicans (*publicani*). Rome put tax collection in the province of Asia up for auction to the knights. As time went on the knights formed companies and this method of tax collection spread. Direct taxes included the tax on all throughout the empire who occupied land, and a poll tax collected in certain provinces such as Egypt and Syria (including Palestine). Augustus thoroughly reorganized the tax collection system, however, and eliminated the collection of direct taxes by publicans; but they continued to collect indirect taxes such as customs, harbor taxes, and the like. As emperors extended their influence into more areas, their own agents collected taxes by set systems. By Hadrian's time publicans are rarely mentioned. *Matthew 17:25; 22:17-21; Romans 13:6-7.*

Ostia, G. Calza and G. Becatti (Instituto Poligrafico della Stato), 1977; *An Economic Survey of Ancient Rome*, Tenny Frank (Baltimore: The Johns Hopkins Press), 5 vol., 1940; Grant, *History of Rome*, 157, 174, 261-3; Grant, *Cities of Vesuvius; Greek and Roman Sculpture*, A. W. Lawrence (New York: Harper and Row, Publishers), 1972.

▼ **266 Lamp with fishing scene.** Roman-German Landesmuseum, Cologne. One man fishes from a boat with line and pole; another uses a net from the shore. Their tunics are pulled down to their waists and up from their legs to form a type of loincloth, and they wear Italian, broad-rimmed hats. The city rises across the river in tiers that probably indicate a steep bank. *Texts: See photo 265.*

▲ **265 Lamp with fisherman.** Roman-German Landesmuseum, Cologne. He wears a floppy, pointed cap of the Phrygian type, a loose tunic, and holds a basket. He has just caught a fish. He likely is fishing for recreation rather than professionally, but his cap indicates that he is a common man. Fishing was a major food industry throughout the Empire, and it took place in rivers, lakes, and seas. Some entrepreneurs built artificial ponds. Fish from the Jordan River and the Sea of Galilee were popular. The Roman government claimed fishing rights in all waters and charged for concessions, which they granted to unions and societies in the Near East, including Egypt and Palestine. *Matthew 4:18-22; John 21:2-14.*

▶ **267 Rock anchors.** Museum of Archaeology, Nimes. Such anchors were common in the ancient world for use with small boats. A rock was roughly shaped and a hole was drilled through it to hold a rope. Slightly more advanced versions had sticks stuck through other drilled holes; they held to the bottom better. Larger boats used iron anchors much like modern ones. *Texts: See photo 265.*

◀ **268 Shepherd with dog, sheep, and goats.** Capitoline Museum. The balding, bearded shepherd is feeding his dog. He wears a loose tunic clasped on his left (near) shoulder, with the fold at his waist covering a belt or sash. He wears sandals. Reclining and frolicking goats and sheep surround him. *Luke 2:8-20; John 10:1-16; 21:16-20; 1 Peter 5:2-4.*

▼269 **Lamp with shepherd**, first century type. Brussels Museum. The bearded shepherd wears a belted tunic with short sleeves. He has a sheep pelt tied around his neck, the hooves still attached, and he leans on a straight shaft. Two sheep graze while 2 goats nibble at tree leaves. A bird is perched in the tree above its nest. The Latin behind the shepherd is TITURUS. *Texts: See photo 268.*

▶ 270 **Statue of the Good Shepherd.** Vatican Museum. The good shepherd theme was common in antiquity from the seventh century BC onward. This Christian statue of the third-fourth century is patterned after the Greek Classical style and so is rare for its period. The shepherd is young, beardless, and has curly hair with long locks. He wears a sleeveless tunic caught at the waist and carries a shepherd's bag. His sandals are thongs and have leggings attached. *Texts: See photo 268.*

▶ **271 Plowing scene relief,** funerary monument. Museum of Archaeology, Nimes. The tomb likely belonged to a landowner who represented himself with the humble scene. His wife is shown with him. In the lower register, the farmer wears a tunic, and the plow is pulled by 2 oxen. The relief technique is raised in part and in part is cut into the stone. *Luke 9:62; 17:7; 1 Corinthians 9:10.*

▲ **272 Reaping machine relief,** reconstructed based on 2 funerary reliefs found at Arlon and at Buzenol in Belgium, and also on a caisson of the arch in Rheims known as the Porte de Mars. Landesmuseum, Trier. A box supported on 2 wheels catches the heads of grain; long teeth on its edge hold the heads of grain so that the workman with a long-handled tool can quickly press the grain loose from the stalks. The bucket is supported by two 8-spoked wheels and is propelled by a mule attached at the lower neck with a halter. A bridle is connected to the halter, and stout poles connected at their back ends by a crosspole run alongside the mule. The back side of the poles and also a second workman guiding the mule from behind are out of the picture. The wheels and part of the bucket are reconstructed. *Matthew 6:26; 9:30-42; 25:24-26; 1 Corinthians 9:10; James 5:4.*

◄**273 Farmer driving cow into town,** about AD 50. Glyptothek, Munich. In the ornate bas-relief, the farmer passes various roadside shrines as he arrives at the town gate. He is taking the cow to market, along with 2 sheep slung across the cow's back and tied by their feet, a hare hanging from a pole across his shoulder, and a basket of goods he holds in his hand. The farmer wears a short tunic, a hat, and has a moneybag across his shoulder and under his arm. The roofed shrine at upper left on the rocky ledge is of Priapus, whose figure is in the door. The large circular shrine the farmer passes has a pillar sticking up from inside that is sacred to Diana. An arched gateway has been built over an old, perhaps sacred, oak tree.

◄**274 Bas-relief of functioning mill.** Vatican Museum. The grain was poured into a opening at the top of the mill. The upper mill part is shaped to fit over an inverted cone. As it turned, here by horsepower, the grain was ground into flour against the lower cone which was stationary and fell onto the floor or an apron below. A workman wearing a tunic on the far right holds a container for the flour. A portion of another mill is at the left and a hen is perched above and between the mills.

►**275 Lamp with butchery scene,** Roman, first half of first century AD. British Museum. One man, clothed only about the hips, holds the animal's legs while a man wearing a tunic wields a knife. Found at Petra where it was made by one lampmaker named Faustus.

▲ **276 Fishmonger's shops, Ostia.** Their entrances are on the main street; behind them is a market area. A marble table separates 2 mosaics of fish, 1 of which can be seen at lower center. A marble-faced tank is behind the table and another table is to the right of the tank.

▶ **277 Wine shop with customers at table,** relief from a small grave column, second-third centuries AD. Landesmuseum, Trier. The photo shown is the top register of the monument which contains the relief in photo 184. It depicts a wine shop owned by the deceased. Customers sit at a table while the proprietor waits on them. Shelves behind him hold goods, and on the floor is a wine amphora still plugged and wrapped in rope, and a barrel of wine with a dipper handle protruding from it. Other goods hang along the top of the relief.

278, 279, 280 Laundry in Ostia. It was identified by numerous terracotta jars half-buried in the ground beside 3 central tanks, and by a large terracotta basin used for dyeing and washing materials which then were hung to dry on wooden beams, the points where they were inserted into the walls still being visible. The extensive finds of whorls and frequent references to spinning and weaving in the home lead us to conclude that a great deal of clothing worn was made in the home. Fulleries developed extensively in the cities, however, which indicates that the home-spun material often was processed commercially, sometimes for local consumption and sometimes for commercial distribution. The fullery of Stephanus in Pompeii contained a system of vats for washing, cleaning in a mixture of water and lye, hanging, and room for displaying. Dyers might combine their work with fulleries or might operate independently. Vats were used as treading-tanks. Some tanks were heated. Cloth manufacturing, dyeing, and fulling have been found throughout the Empire, including Palestine. Laodicea gained much wealth from the cloth business, which had to include fulling, using the Hieropolis mineral waters across the valley. Fullers finished cloth by beating it with mallets when they wanted the texture tighter, or by combing it to raise the nap, which then was trimmed. Photo 278 shows 4 basins, with brick columns running along each side. The near basin has a gutter for filling it. Photo 279 shows the third basin with some of the plaster intact. Beam holes may be seen on the upper rear wall. Photo 280 shows the last basin, with an inverted terra-cotta jar. *Mark 9:3.*

◄ **281 Fullery in Ostia,** east of the Courtyard of Dionysus. The room is a long rectangle with a basin running along 2 long walls and a short end one. The walls and basin once were plastered, with portions of plaster remaining. The channels were for laundry use. *Mark 9:3.*

▼ **282 Two workmen tying a bundle,** relief. Musée Lapidaire, Arles. The bundle apparently is ready to be hoisted, perhaps for loading. The bundle itself is tied with rope: one workman braces against the bundle as he works. Both men wear sleeved tunics belted at the waist and open sandals. *1 Corinthians 3:9; Colossians 4:11; 1 Thessalonians 4:11.*

▲ **283 Lamp with manufacturing scene.** Roman-German Landesmuseum, Cologne. A workman works at a bellows, pumping air with his foot while he holds a tool in the fire of the small furnace. He is surrounded by tools of his trade. He wears a hat and a kilt, which is bound by the sort of straps worn by a charioteer.

SLAVES

Slavery in the ancient world, including the Roman Empire, is not fully understood in spite of the many references to it in ancient literature and many artistic representations.

In Roman eyes slaves were absolutely subject to their masters, though from time to time they were legally protected from extreme harshness. Slaves could be bought and sold, were unable to marry, and could be branded in the face if they were suspected of considering escape.

Yet this rigid legal denial of rights clouds very real distinctions. Slaves ranged in skill from the most menial to teachers and philosophers. Many doctors were slaves. Freedmen sometimes married slave concubines. Slaves and freedmen often worked at the same trades and belonged to the same collegia. Domestic slaves at Rome were freed often at age 30 or at the death of the owner. No evidence exists that slaves were identifiable by clothing, hairstyle, or such. Even so, strong feelings existed among both Greeks and Romans about the inferiority in every way—mentally, morally, physically—of slaves to free persons. The attitude of free toward slave makes Paul's Galatians 3:28 all the more remarkable.

Slaves were brought into the Empire in various ways. The many wars Rome fought provided the largest number, especially from the end of the Punic Wars on. Piracy, which included kidnapping, was a strong supplier of slaves. Only those who could afford a ransom could have any hope of freedom after being caught this way. Babies abandoned at birth could be rescued and raised as slaves. If they could prove later that they had been born to Roman citizens, they could claim their freedom, in theory.

Romans were much more liberal toward freeing slaves than the Greeks had been, and Greek slaves made up a much larger percent of Athens in her heyday than at Rome later. Some scholars even view slavery as a process by which disparate peoples were Romanized and absorbed into the Empire. Yet slavery continued throughout the Empire's history. The physician Galen (second century AD) indicated that of Pergamum's 120,000 adult population, 40,000 of them were slaves. Tax lists from Egypt indicate a lower percent.

Free persons sought to demonstrate their wealth by the number of slaves they had, and the more slaves owned by a household the more specialized was each slave's task. Since each household sought to be as self-sustaining as possible, every necessary skill was sought, either by purchasing slaves already skilled or by teaching some already owned. This emphasis should not overstate the case, however. Most people could not afford a slave, or only 1 to 3 at most.

Daily Life in Ancient Rome, Jerome Carcopino (New Haven: Yale University Press), 1940; *The Ancient Economy*, M. I. Finley (Berkeley: University of California Press), 1973; *Greek and Roman Slavery*, Thomas Wiedemann (Baltimore: The Johns Hopkins University Press), 1981.

284 Tablet devoted to Feronia, bronze, Roman, second century AD. British Museum. The goddess was worshiped by freedmen and freedwomen. Inscribed by one Hedone, a maidservant of M. Crassus. *Acts 22:28; 1 Corinthians 7:21-24; 2 Peter 2:19.*

286 Slave with lantern, bronze, from Herculaneum. Roman-German Landesmuseum, Mainz. He wears sandals and has a heavy outer mantle pulled up over his head. As he waits, he rests his head on an arm under the mantle. Mainz Museum, Germany. *Texts: See photo 285.*

▲ **285 Young reveler leaning on his slave,** terra-cotta from Alexandria, Roman period, after 30 BC. British Museum. The young man's head is crowned with oak leaves, and he wears a peplum or mantle over a tunic and sandals. His slave, who is a Negro, wears only a tunic caught at the waist and sandals. He carries a lantern of the type seen in photos. *Matthew 20:27; 26:51; Revelation 18:13.*

◄ **287 Statuette of slave,** bronze. Brussels Museum. He wears only a cloth, perhaps a tunic or loincloth, tied around his waist. A necklace hangs around his neck, and originally he held some object in his hands. He is thin but not emaciated. *Texts: See photo 285.*

TOOLS

CRAFTSMEN TOOLS

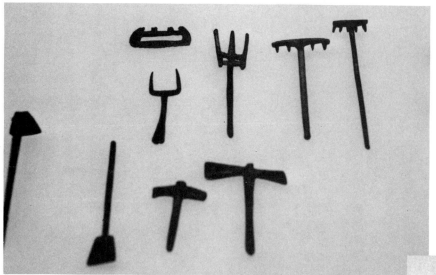

◀ **288 Votive offerings of tool models,** bronze. Roman-German Landesmuseum, Cologne. The tools appear much as they have until recent years. A hoe, shovel, metalworking tools, pitchfork, rakes, and ladders. Such offerings, tiny replicas of the real objects, were purchased in nearby markets and stalls and given to the god or goddess being implored, sometimes thrown into sacred wells, to invoke the deity's blessing.

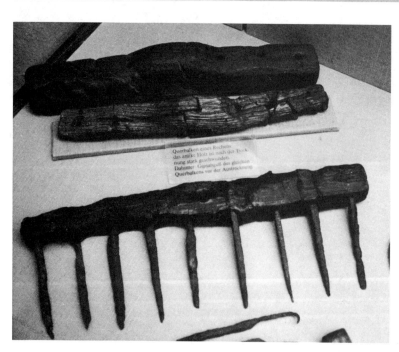

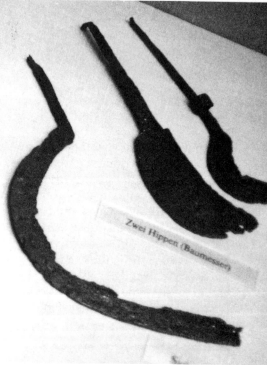

289, 290 Tools from Saalburg, Roman fort. Saalburg Museum. Photo 289 shows 3 wooden rake heads, 1 with iron teeth. Photo 290 shows a curved sickle and 2 pruning knives. They were discovered in the now-reconstructed Roman fort of Saalburg, which existed from about AD 83-260. The objects likely are from the later period. *Revelation 14:14-19.*

British Museum: *A Guide to the Antiquities of Roman Britain* (London: By order of the Trustees), 1922; *British Museum: A Guide to the Exhibition Illustrating Greek and Roman Life* (London: By order of the Trustees), 1908; *A History of Technology and Invention,* Vol. I, edited by Maurice Daumas, translated by Eileen B. Hennessy (New York: Crown Publishers), 1969; *Daily Life in the Time of Jesus,* Henri Daniel-Rops (New York: Hawthorn Books), 1964; *A Short History of Technology,* T. K. Derry and Trevor I. Williams (New York: Oxford University Press), 1961; *Greek and Roman Technology,* K. D. White (Ithaca: Cornell University Press), 1984.

▶ **291 Iron rake with 6 prongs,** from Boscoreale, first century AD. Field Museum.

▼ **292 Iron sickle** found at Boscoreale, Italy, first century AD. Field Museum. Wood remains still adhere to the cutting edge. *Revelation 14:14-19.*

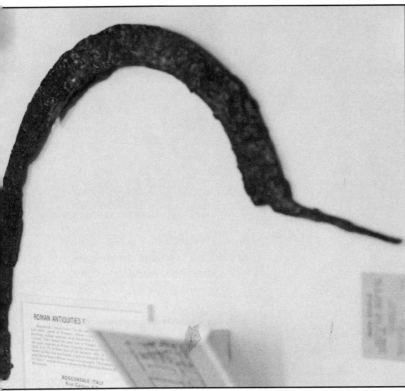

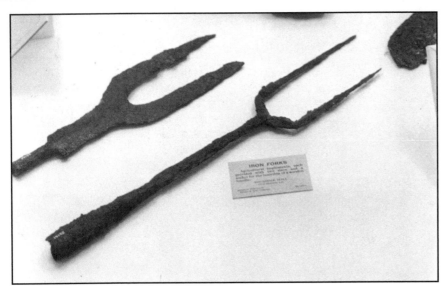

▲ **293 Heavy iron pitchfork,** from Roman fort at Saalburg. Saalburg Museum (see photos 289-290). *Matthew 3:12; Luke 3:17.*

◀ **294 Iron forks, 2-pronged,** first century AD, found at Boscoreale, Italy. Field Museum.

► **295 Iron hoe,** first century AD, found at Boscoreale, Italy. Field Museum.

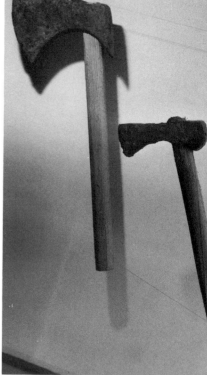

▼ **296 Bas-relief with tools.** Musée Lapidaire, Arles. From left to right: square, adze, level, axe or hammer. The level is an A-frame with markings on the crossbar. When a surface is level, the plumb bob hangs at the center mark. *Matthew 3:10.*

▲ **297 Two iron hatchets with handles replaced.** Museum of Archaeology, Nimes. *Matthew 3:10.*

▲ **298, 299 Two Roman plumb bobs.** The one in photo 298 (above) is bronze and has a hole in the top to hold a cord. From Italy, Field Museum. The one in photo 299 (right) is bronze and has the owner's name inscribed in dotted letters: BASSI-belonging to Bassus. Roman period, British Museum.

▼ **300 Roman foot rule (below),** from Italy. Field Museum. The markings divide it into 12 equal parts. The length of the foot was 11.64 inches (29.57 cm.); the *uncia* was 1/12 of a Roman foot; the *finger* was 1/16 of an uncia, or .73 inches (1.85 cm.). Thus, the units of 12 and 16 were commonly used in measurement and in coinage. The ruler is hinged in the middle for folding. *Revelation 11:1.*

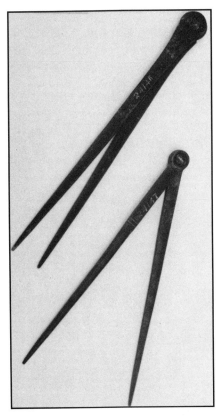

▲ **302 Roman inside calipers,** bronze, from Italy. Field Museum.

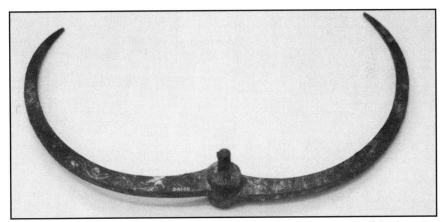

▲ **301 Two Roman compasses,** bronze, from Italy. Field Museum.

▲ **303 Roman outside calipers,** bronze, from Italy. Field Museum. The arms are decorated with a spray of ivy inlaid in silver.

◄ **304 Iron chisel (left),** from Egypt, Greco-Roman period. Field Museum.

► **305 Iron reamers,** from Egypt, Greco-Roman period. Field Museum. The handle of the reamer on the right is of bone; that of the one on the left is of wood. Field Museum.

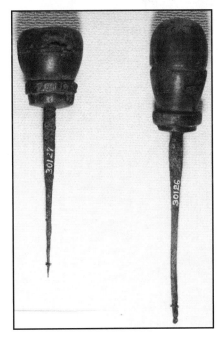

◀ **306 Plane,** Roman period, from Roman fort at Saalburg. Saalburg Museum, Germany. The near level is authentic; the one behind it is reconstructed using the ancient one as a model. The wood brace that holds the blade in place and the rear handle missing from the ancient one have been replaced on the reconstruction.

▲ **307 Carpenters' planes.** Roman-German Central Museum, Mainz. One plane has the blade inserted; it has been lost from the other one.

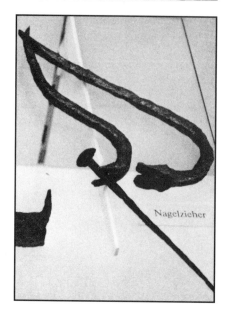

▲ **308 Two nail-pullers,** iron, with iron nail, from the Roman fort at Saalburg. Saalburg Museum, Germany.

▲ **309 Squared nails** from southern France, Roman period. Museum of Archaeology, Nimes. *John 20:25.*

▲ **310 Round nails** from Lake Nemi, Italy, Etruscan. Fourth-first centuries BC. Museo di Villa Giulia, Rome. *John 20:25.*

▶**311 Drawings of tools:** The saw had been developed by Roman times; it was of various sizes and shapes. The top 3 drawings are saws. The 2 on the right are shaped like knives but with toothed edges. The bow saw on the left was a small one held at the top or end. This type also was made large enough for 2 men to draw and pull. Romans also developed the off-set teeth that allowed cutting on both push and pull motions. The brace and bit drill on the left worked much as a modern one except that the shaft had an awl-like point rather than a screw. The bow drill was ancient and worked by the entwined string around the spindle turning the drill as the bow was pushed and pulled by the handle.

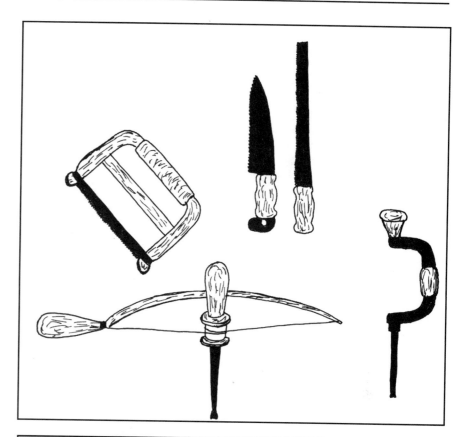

▲**312 Metalworking tools,** from the Roman fort at Saalburg. Saalburg Museum, Germany. The squared anvil weighs 7.78 pounds (35.7 kg.); it has a hole at the near left corner. The sledge hammer on top of the anvil weighs 8.55 pounds (3.875 kg.). The double-edged hammer is designed for the blacksmith's work. The piece beside it is unfinished.

▲**313 Metalworking tools,** from the Roman fort at Saalburg. Saalburg Museum, Germany. From top: tongs for forge use, small hammer, file, and lockplate. Basic tool designs lasted into modern times.

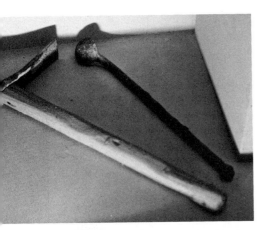

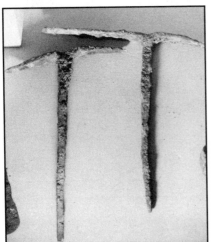

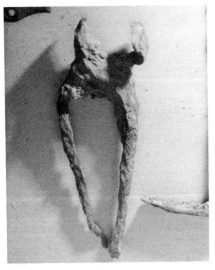

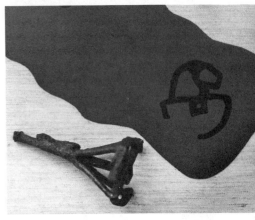

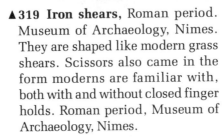

◄ **317 Two iron hammer heads** (2 photos left). Greco-Roman period, from Egypt. Field Museum.

▼ **318 Iron file (below),** probably of Greco-Roman period. Field Museum. Such files were ancient. A similar one that dates to the Assyrian conquest of the seventh century BC was found at Thebes.

▲ **320 Bronze branding stamp.** British Museum. Though this stamp dates to the eighteenth dynasty in Egypt (1375-1300 BC), it demonstrates that cattle control in ancient times included the use of "branding irons." The shape (simulated on the leather) is approximately that of a pair of ox's horns. Found at el-Amarna, it likely was used on the estates of Pharoah Akhenaton.

▲ **314, 315, 316 Metalworking tools,** Roman period. Museum of Archaeology, Nimes. Photo 314 shows a metalworking hammer and small dipper for molten metal. Photo 315 shows tongs for forge use. Photo 316 shows metalworking hammers.

▲ **319 Iron shears,** Roman period. Museum of Archaeology, Nimes. They are shaped like modern grass shears. Scissors also came in the form moderns are familiar with, both with and without closed finger holds. Roman period, Museum of Archaeology, Nimes.

HOUSEHOLD TOOLS

► **321 Heavy iron knives,** various shapes, mostly choppers, from the Roman fort at Saalburg. Saalburg Museum, Germany. The handles are replaced.

▼ **322 Iron knife** with shaft for handle. Found in the London Wall excavations. Roman period. British Museum.

◄ **323 Two iron knives.** Field Museum. The top one, without a handle, likely is pre-Roman. The bottom one, square-ended and with a handle, likely is Roman. Both are from Egypt.

► **324 Iron knife with bone handle and ring.** British Museum.

◄ **325 Iron knife with decorative bone handle.** From Egypt, probably first-second centuries AD. British Museum. The scene is of hunting, a hound chasing a deer.

▲ **327 Knife blade,** iron, Roman. Museum of Archaeology, Nimes.

▲ **326 Folding knife,** probably first-second centuries AD. British Museum. The iron blade is hinged into a groove at the rear of the bone handle. The handle is in the form of a herm (see photo 495).

▲ **328 Silver distaff for wool weaving,** Roman, first century AD. British Museum. The wool, when separated into strands (roves), was wound onto the distaff from which it was drawn as it was spun into yarn. From a tomb at Bursa (northwest Turkey).

► **329 Loom-weights,** found on Cnidus, Hellenistic period. British Museum. A weight was tied to the bottom of the yarn which was being twisted as it was drawn from the spindle. The weight added to the spin as well as kept the yarn taut. The spindle was held high with one hand as the other hand twisted the wool into yarn. All 4 of those shown are stamped with the head of Athena (see photo 478), probably with a signet ring. They likely belong to a set.

▶ **330 Three needles,** Roman period. British Museum. From top: of glass, bone, and bronze. *Matthew 19:24; Mark 2:21; 10:25; Luke 18:25.*

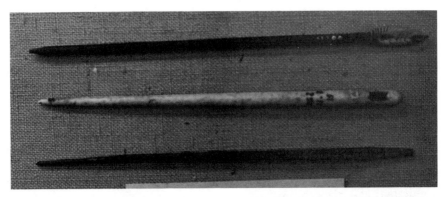

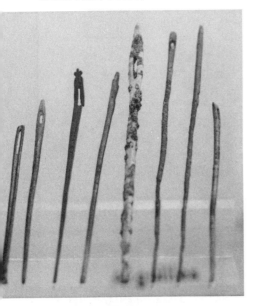

◀ **331 Collection of needles.** Museum of Archaeology, Nimes. The needles are made of bronze and are of various sizes.

▶ **332 Four thimbles,** bronze. Museum of Archaeology, Nimes. All of the thimbles have closed ends and resemble modern ones.

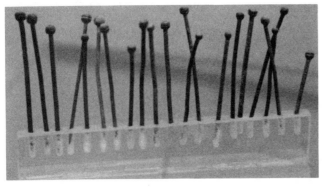

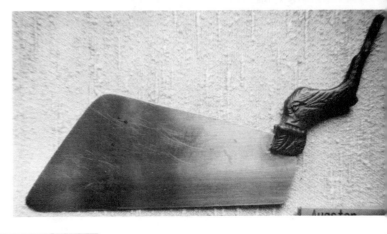

▲ **333 Collection of pins.** Museum of Archaeology, Nimes. The design is much like those today, except the shafts are thicker and the heads larger.

▶ **334 Bronze razor.** Field Museum. During the New Testament period Romans wore their hair short and shaved their faces. Barbershops arose to meet the need and became popular gathering places. The razor shown is a primitive design which had been used for centuries and still was in use in the first century. Other designs included a squared-off shape such as a spade and a hatchet-shaped blade; they could, however, take quite a sharp edge.

▲ **335 Razor,** from Augst. Römerhaus Museum, Augst. The bronze handle is in the shape of a dolphin. The blade is a modern facsimile. The Roman town of Augst is in western Switzerland.

LOCKS AND KEYS

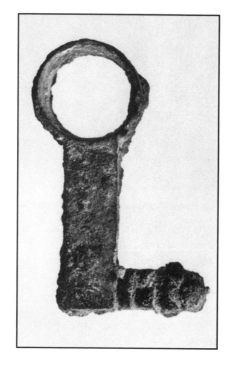

► **336, 337 Roman pin key and ward key (right),** bronze, fourth century AD. Museum of Art and Archaeology, University of Missouri-Columbia. The 2 keys represent the most common types in the Roman world. The key on the left is the pin type, the one on the right the ward type (see photo 342). The pin type is an advance on the elbow ring, which sometimes was very large. One with a wooden handle measuring 7.87 inches (20 cm.) was found at Masada; it probably was for a door on a public building in Engedi. This type of key has teeth spaced to fit corresponding holes in a bolt. The bolt was fixed on the inside of the door, and pins held the bolt into place. The key was inserted through a hole in the door below the pins that held the bolt and then "elbowed" up to fit the teeth into corresponding holes in the bolt. A spring above the pins held them into place, so the key had to be raised up to force the pins out and above the bolt; then the key was used to pull the bolt to the side. The pins were retained in place in a receptacle. Museum photos. *Matthew 16:19; Luke 11:52; Revelation 1:18; 9:1; 20:1.*

◄ **338, 339 Roman keys, pin type and combination,** bronze. British Museum. Photo 338 is a pin type. The 5 pins face downward in the photo and are perpendicular to the shank (3 can be seen on one side; 2 others are on the opposite side). The key in photo 339 combines both methods. Four pins face upward, perpendicular to a rectangle with a slotted configuration. This type of key was turned or slid after being placed in the lock, then raised to complete the release. The spring and pin arrangement of the locks of the Roman period were more finely made than earlier ones, but the principle was the same. *Texts: See photos 336, 337.*

▼**340, 341 Two bronze finger keys (below),** Roman. Roman-German Landesmuseum, Cologne. Small keys, such as for padlocks, sometimes were made into fingerrings for convenience and to avoid losing them. 340 is inscribed with the letters VITA = Good life! *Texts: See photos 336, 337.*

▲**342 Roman latch and ward keys.** British Museum. The key on the left is designed to raise a latch by fitting corresponding configurations. The key was inserted, then raised (see photos 336, 337). The key on the right is a ward key and works on the modern principle of insert-and-turn. *Texts: See photos 336, 337.*

▲**343 Roman padlocks.** British Museum. The one on the left has a chain attached, the last link of which was fastened inside the box. The lid was closed and locked with a secret catch, a sort of riddle which the Sphinx head on the cover indicates was difficult. The one on the right is in the form of a circular box. It has a hinged handle, the free end of which was fastened inside the box by pin bolts, released by a secret catch underneath. The key is rusted into the lock; it is the projection under the handle. One other padlock, not shown, worked on a barb principle. Straight leaf-spring type barbs inside a cylinder spread to catch against a surface. A key was inserted into the end of the cylinder opposite the spread prongs and slipped up the pronged shaft to press the prongs together and so allow the lock to be pulled open. Seal locks, too, were still in use. This type consisted of a wooden block held to a doorjamb by a pivot. When the door was closed, the block was raised like a latch across the door and held into place by a metal loop or other device. A cover then was slid along the top surface to keep the loop or catch from being manipulated. Then wax was put onto the surface behind the cover and a seal pressed into the wax. The cover could not be moved without breaking the seal, which entailed dire consequences from authorities. *Texts: See photos 336, 337.*

▲ **344 Heavy hinges,** bronze. Saalburg Museum, Germany. Found in the debris of the Curia, they probably were attached to the main door of the town hall of the Roman fort at Saalburg. Each hinge half has closely fitting double rings, the one on bottom complete. The top 3 have 2 drilled holes on each half; the bottom has 1. *Matthew 25:10-11; Luke 12:36; 13:25; 18:16; Revelation 3:20.*

▼**345 Hinges,** bronze, probably from Boscoreale. Photo courtesy of Kelsey Museum of Archaeology, The University of Michigan. Their shape is much like modern ones. The bottom one has 2 holes on each half; the top one has 1. Iron nails remain in the top hinge. *Texts: See photo 344.*

MILLS AND PRESSES

Grains with husks were pounded with mortar and pestle; grains without husks were ground into flour in mills. The poor ate bread made from barley, the rich from wheat. Barley was coarser and heavier, and it required more yeast to make it rise. Much of the flour, especially that of the poor, was ground at home, usually by women. For cakes and for liturgical purposes, extra care was taken to grind the grain into a finer flour.

Hand mills (querns) were essential to the life of a family, unless in an urban area they could avail themselves of the bakery. The lower stone was made from harder material than the upper one. By the first century, the long process of improving mills had resulted in the concave and convex design which both allowed for grinding and for the flour to work itself out to the edge of the mill. Strictly speaking, the result was not fine flour but coarse meal. The rise of the professional mill did not result in better flour. The flour had to be obtained by filtering the substance. Papyrus and rush were used to make sifters in Egypt; the Gallic Romans developed horsehair, while linen was used in Spain.

Due probably to the low cost of labor in the early Roman empire, the water wheel did not come into use until after the New Testament period.

In addition to mills, presses were used for olive oil and wine. For wine, 3 steps were necessary: treading, pressing, and fermenting. Treading was done in the vat, with drains for the juice to run off into tanks or recesses. Once that was accomplished, the residue was strained and placed into baskets that could be crushed without ruining them.

Three types of presses were used. In the lever press, the pulp was placed in a holder, above which 1 end of a long, heavy beam pressed a flat cover onto the baskets of pulp, which were shallow and stacked several baskets high. Pressure was applied on the other end of the beam by various means: heavy weights such as rocks, a screw process, or a winch process being most common.

The screw press was more advanced, and there were variations of it. One style was similar to an early printing press, while other styles combined features of the lever press.

The wedge press was an upright mechanism with several shelves which could move up and down inside a beam frame. The lower shelf pressed onto the pulp. Wooden wedges were placed between the shelves, the whole mechanism perhaps comprising 3 levels of shelves and wedges. The wedges were driven in by hammers, which widened the space between the shelves and consequently pressed the bottom shelf lower onto the pulp, squeezing the juice out.

Another type of press, the edge runner, sometimes was used for milling, but it tended to crush the grain rather than grind it; it was used primarily for crushing ore.

Oil production was more difficult because the pit of the olive had to be removed. The problem was solved by turning wheellike stones inside a circular rimmed mortar. Various shapes were used, but the upper stones—wheels which ran in opposing pairs—had to be suspended in order to leave room for the pits to survive without being crushed while separating the skin from the pits. The stones, heavy as they were, were suspended from a central column on which they turned. The stones in the photos below solved the problem by being slanted, thus riding on their own edges but pushing the pits out. This method probably crushed some pits more than the opposing-wheel method, but it was more efficient in that the stone wheels did not have to be adjusted. It also allowed for different size pits.

▼**347 Quern (hand mill)**, on grounds, Capernaum, Israel. Made of basalt, a dark porous stone, this quern is operated in the same manner as photo 346, except that an upright handle was used. It was inserted into the hole seen in the projection at the stone's lower right edge. Sometimes 2 women worked together to turn and feed the mill (Matt. 24:41). *Texts: See photo 346.*

▲**346 Quern (hand mill)**, from Boscoreale, first century AD or earlier. Field Museum. The principle of operation is common to mills of all sizes. Both upper and lower stones were made from porous volcanic stone for effectiveness in grinding. The lower stone was firmly anchored, sometimes by partially embedding it into the ground. Grain was poured into the bowllike recess at the top, from where it ran slowly through the center hole to be ground between the stones. The lower stone was stationary; the upper stone was turned by means of handles inserted into holes, 1 of which can be seen. The grinding at mills was a common early-morning sound. *Matthew 24:41; Luke 17:35.*

▲ **348 Edge-runner mill,** on grounds, Tabgha, Israel. This sort of mill would not be satisfactory for grinding flour; rather, it was for olives. The upper wheel was rolled around inside the rim of the base. A vertical pole extended from the center of the base, whose hole can be seen in photo. A second pole passed through the hole of the wheel and connected to the stationary upright pole. The wheel then was turned by human or donkey power. The slant on the wheel's running edge caused the pits to be pushed outward as the skins were separated; if it were flat the pits would be crushed and the olive oil would not be as good. *Matthew 18:6; Mark 9:42; Luke 17:2; Revelation 18:21.*

▼ **350 Small press (below),** on grounds at Capernaum, Israel. It was used for olives or grapes. The juice was caught in the circled groove and directed to the cuplike hole in front. Pressing was done either by screw or beam. For the former, a frame consisting of 2 upright beams and a crossbeam would straddle the press. A screw descended from the crossbeam to the top of the press; it was attached to a plate that pressed against flexible woven bags that held the olive pulp or grapes. As a handle on the screw was turned, the produce was squeezed. The beam press worked with the same type of woven bags holding the produce, but rather than a screw above them, a long beam extended out from above; pressure was exerted on its long end. *Matthew 21:33; Revelation 14:19-20; 19:15.*

▼ **349 Fragments of grain mills,** 2 sizes, on grounds at Kurnub (Mampsis), Israel. Both of the larger pieces are portions of upper stones of mills, the 1 on the left being much smaller. The 2 projections from which turnpoles extended can be seen. One pole fragment extends from the right side of the larger millstone. The full millstone was set on the round base. *Texts: See photo 348.*

▲351 Olive or winepress, on grounds at Chorazin, Israel. The press is larger than the one in photo 350, but it worked the same way. This one has the beam holes cut into each end. The juice or oil ran into the plastered hole in the ground. *Texts: See photo 350.*

▼352 Mills at Chorazin, Israel. Two types can be seen: an edge runner is in the center; the mill shown in photo 351 is barely to be seen at the left; another beam- or screw-press is at right. The area is well arranged for the crushing of olives from their pits on the edge-runner press; then the juice is extracted by use of the other 2 presses. The press at right has slots rather than square holes cut for the uprights. The millstone to which Jesus referred was not the lower stone but the upper one, as in photo 348. *Texts: See photos 348, 350.*

▼353 Fresco of cherub at boiling pot. National Museum of Naples. The cherub stirs a perfume mixture made from flower petals whose juice was pressed on a wedge press (see color photo 411). *Revelation 5:8; 18:13.*

▼354 Winepress complex at Avdat. Three winepresses were found at Avdat/Eboda, all similarly constructed. They date to the Byzantine period. The one shown has a square treading area, each side of which measure 18 feet, 8 inches (5.7 m.; the area surrounded by stone blocks). Nine cubicles of various sizes fan out and slope upward from the treading area, each of which has an opening into the square. Harvested grapes were stored in baskets placed in the cubicles and were easily moved to the treading area because of the slope. The floor of the treading area was 2 feet (.6 m.) below the openings. It was coated with thick plaster and paved with stone flags, and it sloped from all sides so that the juice would run down to a sump in the center. From there a pipe carried the juice to the collecting vat (photo 355). *Texts: See photo 350.*

▼355 Juice collection vat connected with the winepress complex at Avdat. The remaining grape skins would sink to the bottom of the vat. *Mark 12:1; see also photo 350.*

See color photo 411 for wedgepress.

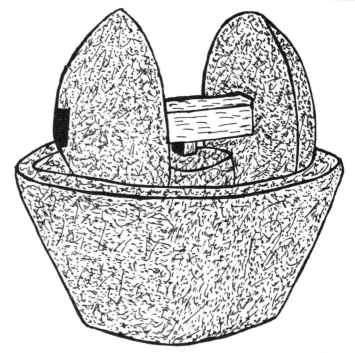

▲356 Drawing of wheelpress called a trapetum. The 2 convex millstones fit into a concave bowl but were suspended so that they did not touch the bowl. A horizontal beam passes through both millstones and once extended outward on each side for turning the stones. The beam rested on a center stone strong enough to carry the full weight of the beam and millstones, allowing the stones to turn freely inside the bowl. Just enough room remained between the millstones and bowl walls to keep from crushing olive pits as the skin was torn off. The space between the millstones and the bowl was regulated by the length of the post on which the horizontal beam rests. This type provided finer results than the edge-runner. *Texts: See photo 350.*

MEDICINE AND ITS TOOLS

Medicine in the first century was a mixture of science and religion; though primitive, its practice was at a surprisingly high level, as the tools below will indicate. Medicine in the sense we know it had its primitive form in Greece. Hippocrates (born 460 BC), of course, is considered to be the father of modern medicine.

Medicine advanced little after Hippocrates for a long time. Indeed, a major shift in thinking developed after 300 BC. Earlier medicine had been studied from a physics (and metaphysics) perspective, but it essentially became a subtopic of ethics. Ethics was the touchstone of knowledge. Hippocrates indeed emphasized ethics; much of his celebrated writings dealt with matters such as when to call in a consultant, taking into account a patient's ability to pay, and behavior when visiting a patient. But as a subbranch of ethics, research suffered.

Ptolemy I's efforts to establish Alexandria as the learning center of the world gave medical research new life. He brought Herophilus of Chalcedon and Erasistratus of Iulius, Cos to the new city. The 2 doctors used dissection to learn about the human body (sometimes, it was claimed by ancient writers, dissecting the bodies of living condemned criminals). They learned and wrote much about anatomy in general, eyes, gynecology, pediatrics, the blood system and the brain.

Without the microscope some basic assumptions were wrong, but much of their work was sound.

After this heyday of Alexandrian medicine, theories degenerated into competing schools which essentially stagnated research: the Empirics rejected research and based their opinions on experience; the Dogmatists used reasoning to arrive at conclusions; the Methodists believed diseases resulted when the body's ducts were wrongly open or closed; and the Pneumatics identified the vital principle as the pneuma, building on an ancient concept.

The Romans learned their medicine from the Greeks. In the early empire, when mistrust of Greeks still was high among many Romans, they applied the most bizarre concoctions imaginable for cures: powders and potions were made from dung and urine, blood, parts of the human body, and anything that sounded so repulsive that it just might work.

Doctors caught on quickly with the rise of the empire, however; Julius Caesar even granted citizenship to practicing physicians. Beginning in the first century BC with Asclepiades, emphasis began to be placed on diet, exercise, baths, and temperance. The baths and exercise grounds were basic to the Greco-Roman life-style.

We know something of medicine in Palestine from rabbinic writings and scattered references in the Bible. Oil was a common remedy; often it was mixed with wine (Luke 10:25-37). Honey was put on open wounds and swallowed for a sore throat. Fig poultice, aloe, various herbs and root extracts, ferns, fish brine, and mandrake were used. Regular bleeding was common; eye salves were used; hot springs were sought after.

Proper treatment was not sufficient, however. Healing was bound up with the gods, especially Aesculapius. The ill went to a temple and offered a sacrifice, often a vo-tive offering. Lodgings were developed for these pilgrims, and eventually some of the temples developed into hospitals. The primary temple/hospital of Aesculapius was Epidaurus southwest of Corinth, with Pergamum and Cos following closely behind. His sanctuaries were established throughout the Empire.

Aesculapius (Latinized form of Asklepios) was the Greek god of healing. The wise centaur Chiron was believed to have been his teacher, for Aesculapius began as a mortal. Aesculapius was brought to Rome in 293 BC to halt a plague on the advice of Roman officials who consulted the Sibylline Books. His temple was built on Tiber Island. His attribute is the serpent-entwined staff, which still survives today in the symbol of the Hippocratic oath.

The infirm stayed in dormitories connected with these major centers of healing, where they gave an offering, prayed, and received visions that informed them of necessary treatment to be healed. The treatments sometimes were exotic; often they consisted of baths; often the application of medications was prescribed. Sometimes seemingly magical cures occurred. (See photos 456-470.)

Greek Medicine, Arthur J. Brock (New York: E. P. Dutton and Co., Inc.), 1929; *Travel in the Ancient World*, Lionel Casson (Toronto: George Allen and Unwin, Ltd.), 1974; *Life in Ancient Rome*, F. R. Cowell (New York: Perigee Books), 1980; *Daily Life in the Time of Jesus*, Henri Daniel-Rops (New York: Hawthorn Books, Inc.), 1962; *Philosophy and Medicine in Ancient Greece*, W. H. S. Jones (Baltimore: The Johns Hopkins Press), 1946; *Greek Medicine*, E. D. Phillips (London: Thames and Hudson), 1973; *The Hellenistic World*, F. W. Walbank (Cambridge: Harvard University Press), 1982.

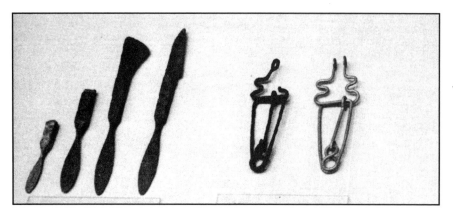

357, 358 Medical tools, from the Roman fort at Saalburg. Saalburg Museum, Germany. The instruments in photo 357 are, from left to right, 2 handles for scalpels, 2 scalpels with blades of different shapes (handles reproduced), a medical clamp, and a full reproduction of a clamp. Photo 358 shows, from left to right, an original and a reconstructed pair of medical pliers, and an original and a reconstructed pair of tooth pliers. Aesculapius became a favorite god, among others, with the military; each fort developed its hospital. The Roman army possessed a well-organized health organization with doctors, orderlies, and hospitals. In this respect it was vastly superior to most of the people around them.

359 Iron scalpels, from the province of Asia. Roman, first-third centuries AD. Roman-German Central Museum, Mainz. The blades have been partially reconstructed. Surgical procedures were widely practiced, including the cauterizing of wounds, lancing, setting fractures, trepanning of skulls, and even Caesarean delivery. Doctors who treated diseases were sharply distinguished from those who set bones, the latter being considered a much inferior trade.

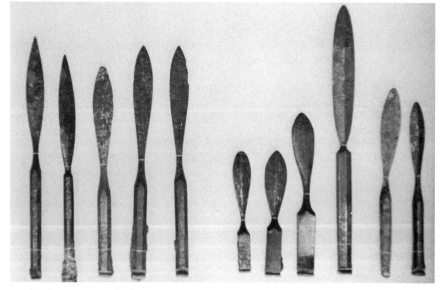

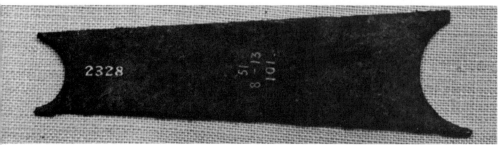

360 Bronze saw. British Museum. It has very fine teeth and was used for cutting through bones in amputations.

▲361 **Bronze medical spoons,** from Egypt, Roman period. Field Museum. The larger ones are for unguents, the smaller ones are earspoons.

▲362 **Bronze tongue depressor (above),** Roman, from Pompeii. Field Museum. It was used by physicians to hold down the tongue in order to cut out an abscess.

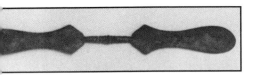

▲363 **Bronze double spatula,** Roman, from Pompeii. Field Museum. It probably was used by physicians to warm salve and pour it into the eye or other part being treated. Nutrition and hygiene was emphasized, operations even on internal organs were devised, and medical tools continued to improve.

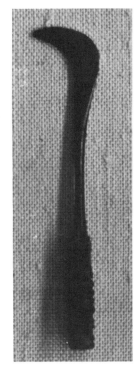

▲364 **Bronze forked probe (above left).** British Museum. It was used for extracting foreign bodies, including arrows, from a wound.

▲365 **Bronze surgical knife (above right).** British Museum.

▼366 **Tweezers,** various sizes and shapes. Roman-German Central museum, Mainz.

▼367 **Hooks and probe (below).** British Museum. The two left objects are hooks used for manipulating organs or tissues during surgery. The right object with spreading prongs is a probe used for extracting an object such as an arrow from a wound.

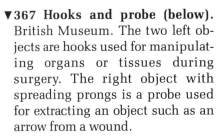

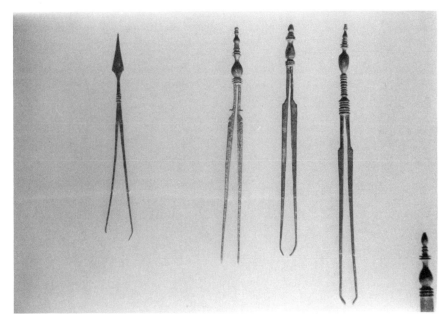

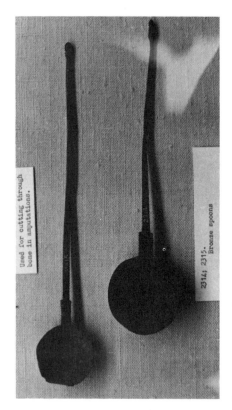

▲ **370, 371 Ointment pots.** Those in photo 370 are pottery; those in photo 371 are lead. Agora Museum, Athens. The pottery pieces date to about 300 BC, the lead pieces prior to the first century BC. Two of the lead pots are inscribed in Greek with the name of the maker or pharmacist and with the contents, *lukion ilukioni*, a purgative.

▲ **368 Bronze spoons,** the top one from Orvieto. British Museum. They probably were used for applying drops to the eyes or unguents to wounds. Note the small spout on the lower edge of each bowl.

▼ **369 Bleeding cup,** bronze. Field Museum. Some substance such as lint was placed in the cup and lighted to exhaust air from the vessel and so create a vacuum; then the cup was placed quickly over the place from which blood was to be extracted.

▼ **372 Drug box,** bronze. British Museum. The sliding lid is to the side of the box, which is divided into compartments, each with a hinged cover with handle. It is a portable container for drugs, probably from Cyrenaica, almost certainly used by a Roman physician. Similar boxes were used for surgical instruments.

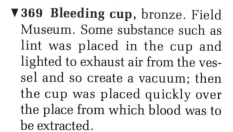

▼ **373 Trepanned skull.** Milwaukee Museum. This technique was widespread in the ancient world—central Europe, Greece, Egypt, and even in South America. The purpose was to drill or cut a hole in the skull to relieve pressure. The operation often was successful.

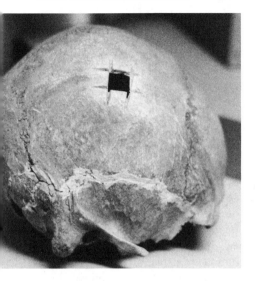

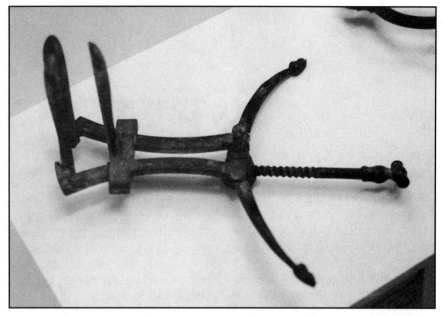

▲ **374 Vaginal speculum,** from Pompeii. Field Museum. The 4 prongs were inserted into the vagina and the handle was turned, spreading the prongs. Two of the prongs are fixed to the long bars, which are curved to work in conjunction with the third prong. It is attached to a crossbar which slides along the curved bars as the screwhandle is turned. The handle has a leaf design near its end.

▲ **375 Vaginal speculum,** from Pompeii. Field Museum. The 4 prongs were inserted into the vagina and the handle was turned, spreading the prongs. Two of the prongs are attached to the circle which extends in arms almost as long as the screwhandle. The other 2 prongs are attached to the shorter arms which are attached to the crossbar. The screwhandle passes through the crossbar to the circle to control all prongs evenly. Each end of the crossbar is decorated with a ram's head.

▼ **376 Rectal speculum,** from Pompeii. Field Museum. The 2 prongs were spread by the physician as he squeezed the handles together. Used to observe rectal diseases.

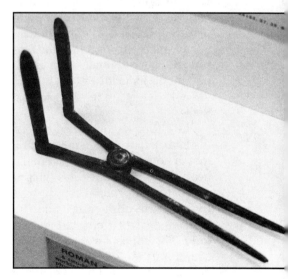

RELIGION

The religion of the first-century Romans was a blending of various elements comprised of ancient Latin agricultural beliefs, the Etruscan tradition, Greek religion, Asia Minor cults, and a wide range of other cults from the regions conquered by Rome. Even with the fairly developed amalgamation that had occurred by New Testament times, care should be exercised in considering what beliefs or deities lie behind a specific New Testament statement.

Judaism is the principal religion of the world of the Gospels; Greek and Asia Minor religions were the dominant ones of the areas to which most of the rest of the New Testament was written, yet it must be remembered that Romans lived in all of the areas. Not only did they take their Lares and other deities with them; the worship of the emperor's cult was part of the official observance throughout the Empire. Roman religion may be as important as Judaism as background to Paul's letter to the Christians at Rome.

The father was expected to lead his family in accordance with custom in honoring the goddess of the hearth (Vesta), the Penates (guardians of the family food supply, who lived in the cupboard), and the Lares (genii of departed ancestors). The concept extended to the community, so corresponding rituals were observed by magistrates on behalf of the community.

This simple explanation is basic, but the practice actually was much more complex. As Rome extended her rule, Roman gods, emperors, and the favorite deities of the emperors were added to local pantheons. In the first century every large city had several classes of priests.

An enormous array of worship patterns greets the researcher into Greek and Roman religion, to say nothing of the deities themselves. We have a number of descriptions of public ceremonies to provide some insights into the worship patterns. The *Bouphonia* of ancient Greece, for example, included 4 steps.

First, the ox was selected by having several of them mill around a table on which was placed certain foods; the ox which ate first was the one chosen by the god for the sacrifice. Second, the ox was killed, flayed, and the flesh eaten raw. Third, a mimicking of the ox returned to life was carried out by stuffing its hide with grass. Fourth, a trial was held for the one guilty of killing the ox, the resolution of which was that guilt was placed on the knife rather than the person wielding it; the reason for this need is part of the story of the sacrifice. The *Bouphonia* dates back into prehistory.

Another feast, the Magnesian, was observed annually to celebrate a peace treaty between Magnesia and Miletus. It, too, involved 4 steps. First, the finest possible bull was purchased and then exhibited to Zeus by means of a large procession and prayer led by a herald. Afterward it was fed by grain merchants for 9 months. Second, another large procession was held, which included images of the 12 gods. Third, 3 sacrifices were held using victims other than the chosen bull. Fourth, the bull was sacrificially killed and the meat distributed to the populace with no part of it being burned.

These 2 illustrations will suffice to indicate the variations that occurred in sacrifices. The typical sacrifice (*thusia*) followed a pattern of 3 steps, however. First came the preparation for and of the sacrifice. All of the participants washed their hands by lustration. Then grains of barley were either placed in a basket or scattered onto the altar, the sacrificial animal, and the earth; then the act was followed by prayer. A knife previously buried under the grain was used to slay the animal.

During the course of the praying a person officiating cut hair from the victim's neck or brow and threw it into the fire, an act which gave a "first-fruit" of the sacrifice to the altar ahead of time. Then the victim, which was adorned with wreaths and garlands, and perhaps its horns overlaid with gold, was killed as the women raised a piercing scream. The blood was caught and poured onto the altar (or if the animal was small it was held over the altar). A procession followed in which the parts to be burnt on the altar were carried around.

The second and central part of the sacrifice was the sacrifice (*thusia*) itself, the burning of the pieces on the altar. Fragrant woods and perfumes were thrown on the fire as the meat burned. The partici-

▲377 **Family offering sacrifice before an urn,** first century AD. Glyptothek, Munich. The family wears typical clothing. The father places incense on a small altar from a container in his left hand. A boy behind him holds a small dish, possibly a patera, in his right hand and an object now gone in his left; it possibly was an urceus. Such sacrifices took place in the home. *Texts: See photo 429.*

pants in the sacrifice then tasted bits of certain of the internal organs such as the liver and kidneys. In some sacrifices these organs were read by specially trained attendants. Third, the meat was cooked for a feast that involved all the participants; it was called a "holy supper." Libations were offered twice in the sacrifice, once when the portions for the deities were burned and once as the banquet began when a few drops were placed in and then poured out of each participant's cup. The banquet was concluded with music and dancing in which all participated.

Divination was another realm of religion. It was expressed in various ways. *Augury* was the interpretation of the flight and sound of birds, along with their manner of eating. The practitioner was the *augur*, and Rome had an official college of *augures* to advise courses of action. A variation was the use of chickens, taken along on military campaigns to observe their telltale eating patterns.

Haruspicina, inherited from the Etruscans, was the process of examining the entrails, especially the liver, of a sacrificial victim. This technique became popular enough to challenge the augures, but the 2 techniques were practiced side by side.

Other methods included the observation of lightning; involuntary movements of humans, such as sneezing; *geomancy*, which consisted of throwing earth onto a surface, or dust or sand into the wind, and observing the patterns; *pyromancy*, which was the observation of incense, flour, egg, etc. when thrown into a flame; use of water or a reflective object somewhat as a crystal ball is used; and other mysterious techniques.

Homo Necans, Walter Burkert, translated by Peter Bing (Berkeley: University of California Press), 1983; *Arcana Mundi: Magic and Occult in the Greek and Roman Worlds*, Georg Luck (Baltimore: The Johns Hopkins University Press), 1985; *Sacrifice in Greek and Roman Religions and Early Judaism*, Royden Keith Yerkes (London: Adam and Charles Black), 1953. Other sources are listed at the end of each subsection.

TEMPLES AND SHRINES

The earliest shrines were caves believed to be the home of a particular deity. Often these caves were believed to connect with the Underworld. Some of these ancient shrines developed over the centuries to become exceedingly famous and influential, such as Delphi, Eleusis, and Cumae. Delphi was the most significant international shrine in the Greco-Roman world. At such famous shrines, many temples were built to deities other than the primary one of the site. Patrons and cities built temples and shrines there to pay homage both to their own deities and to the one who owned the shrine. The small temples built for this purpose are referred to as "treasuries," because their primary purpose was to hold precious gifts given as offerings to the site's deity.

In Greek and Roman worship, the business concerning the people was done outside of the temple proper. A large temple consisted of 4 main portions: the *cella* was the walled room, the central portion of the structure. There stood the statue of the deity. A small altar for burning incense sometimes stood beside the statue; no other furniture was present. A light generally shone through a hole in the roof to reflect off of the statue, which was not white marble as we are used to seeing in museums, but was covered with gold, silver, precious stones, and appropriately painted.

One or more rooms were attached behind the cella for storing the treasures that the worshipers donated to the deity and its temple. The temple attendants also used the room(s) for their needs. At the opposite end of the cella was an anteroom which usually was open at the front. This basic form has varia-tions, such as rows of columns, shape, openness of the cella to the sky, etc., based on size and need. Greek temples usually were built on a low stone platform with 2 or 3 continuous steps running around all sides. Roman temples were built on platforms 9 or 10 feet high with steps on the front side. Greek temples had columns on all four sides; Roman temples had columns only supporting the porch (*pronaos*). The architecture and design of the temples themselves were very similar. The eastern temples built during this period were somewhat similar in design but the cornices, columns, and other design features were much more ornate.

By the first century, the Greek and Roman styles had been mixed in some structures. The temple, if it was large enough, stood in the precinct called a *temenos*, which often was entered through a monumental gateway (*propylon/propylaea*).

Entry to most temples was not closed to the populace as it was in the Jerusalem Temple, the exceptions being those deities whose priests and priestesses protected certain secrets. The devotee could enter into the presence of the deity, attach wax tablets which contained his prayer or vow to the statue, and pray standing, kneeling, or prostrate. When blood sacrifices were made, they were done on the altar which stood outside (see "Altars" below). It was placed at the entrance to the anteroom or at the bottom of the stairs.

Ancient Civilizations and Ruins of Turkey, Ekrem Akurgal (Istanbul: Haset Kitabevi), 1978; *Hachette World Guides: Greece*, Robert Boulanger (Paris: Hachette), 1964; *Women Leaders in the Ancient Synagogue*, Bernadette Brooten (Chico, California: Scholars Press), 1982; *Roman Sacrificial Altars*, Helen Cox Bowerman (Bryn Mawr College dissertation), 1913; *Ostia*, G. Calza and G. Becatti (Rome: Istituto Poligrafico dello Stato), 1977; *Larousse Encyclopedia of Archaeology*, Gilbert Charles-Picard, general editor (London: The Hamlyn Publishing Group, Ltd.), 1972; *Archaeology of the Bible: Book by Book*, Gaalyah Cornfeld (New York: Harper and Row, Publishers), 1976; *Qumran*, Philip R. Davies (Grand Rapids: William B. Eerdmans Publishing Co.), 1982; *Greek Votive Offerings*, William Henry Denham Rouse (Cambridge: The University Press), 1902; *The Architecture of Ancient Greece*, William Bell Dinsmoor (New York: W. W. Norton and Company, Inc.), 1975; *The Archaeology of the New Testament*, Jack Finegan (Princeton: Princeton University Press), 1969; *The Greeks and Their Gods*, W. K. C. Guthrie (Boston: Beacon Press), 1950; *The Oxford Classical Dictionary*, N. G. L. Hammond and H. H. Scullard, editors (Oxford: Clarendon Press), 1970; *Ancient Portraits from the Athenian Agora*, Evelyn B. Harrison (Princeton: American School of Classical Studies at Athens), 1960; *The Bible and Recent Archaeology*, Kathleen M. Kenyon (Atlanta: John Knox Press), 1978; *Cure and Cult in Ancient Corinth*, Mabel Lang (Princeton: American School of Classical Studies at Athens), 1977; *Nimes*, V. Lassalle (Paris: Art et Tourisme); *Greece: History, Museums, Monuments*, Leonidas B. Lellos (Athens: L. B. Lellos), 1972; *Everyday Life in the Roman Empire*, Joan Liversidge (New York: G. P. Putnam's Sons), 1976; *The Greek Stones Speak*, Paul MacKendrick (New York: New American Library), 1962; *Römermuseum und Römerhaus Augst*, Max Martin (Augst: Römermuseum Augst), 1981; "The Ark of Nabratein—A First Glance," Eric M. Meyers, James F. Strange, and Carol L. Meyers, *Biblical Archaeologist*, Fall 1981; "Synagogues in Palestine," Herbert Gordon May, *The Biblical Archaeologist Reader* (Garden City, New York: Anchor Books), 1961; "Ancient Synagogues in Galilee: Their Religious and Cultural Setting," Eric M. Meyers, *Biblical Archaeologist*, Spring 1980; *The Romans and Their Gods In the Age of Augustus*, R. M. Ogilvie (New York: W. W. Norton and Co.), 1969; *Roman Mythology*, Stewart Perowne (New York: Peter Bedrick Books), 1978; *Roman and Etruscan Painting*, Arturo Stenico (New York: The Viking Press), 1963; *Roman Art*, Donald Strong (New York: Penguin Books), 1976; *The Ancient Olympic Games*, Judith Swaddling (Austin, Texas: University of Texas Press), 1984; *Ephesus: Legends and Facts*, Cemil Toksoz (Cemil Toksoz), 1976; *Roman Art*, Helga von Heintze (New York: Universe Books), 1971; *Roman Art and Architecture*, Mortimer Wheeler (New York: Oxford University Press), 1964.

▶ **378 Antrum of the Sibylline shrine at Cumae.** Cumae was the earliest Greek colony founded in Italy (ca. 750 BC); it is located near Naples. The city had an important history in its own right, but it also was the seat of the Sibyl. The Sibyl, or priestess who uttered prophecies, was believed to be directly inspired by Apollo, whose shrine Cumae was. The cave was believed to communicate with the underworld. The Cumae Sibyl was the most famous among the Romans of 4 main ones, the others being on Mount Ida in western Turkey, Erythrae near Chios in Turkey, and the Sibyl of the Tiber River. Tarquinius, the ancient king of Rome, was believed to have purchased the Cumae Sibyl's books called the Sibylline Oracles. They became the sacred texts of the Roman state and were housed in the Temple of Capitoline Jupiter. It was through Cu-

mae that the Romans were brought into touch with the Greek mystery religions. Aeneas, Virgil's mythical founder of Rome, consulted the Sibyl at Cumae and communed with the beings of the underworld; from them he received instructions to found Rome. *Acts 16:16.*

◀ **379 Interior room in Cumae cave,** 1 of many. In these rooms worshipers came to receive oracles from the priestess. Her prophecies often were given in poetry and usually were purposely ambiguous so that they could be claimed to be fulfilled whatever the outcome. *Acts 16:16.*

▶ **380 Sanctuary of the Eleusian mysteries.** The photo shows a portion of the terrace which opened onto 2 caves. This is the Plutonion, Pluto's sanctuary, where Persephone disappeared into the underworld and then emerged. The sanctuary was complex, with many buildings used for different stages of the ritual. A huge Telesterion was to the left of the caves; it was the site of the initiation ritual and was the most important of the buildings. Located west of Athens, Eleusis was the ancient home of the worship of Demeter (see photo 472). This worship originally was a local one connected with the soil. Its influence spread throughout the Greek and Roman world; emperors were proud to be inducted into her mysteries. It dates at least to Mycenean times and probably earlier. The ceremonies, which are known to a degree except for the final ritual, were built around the cycle of the seasons in the form of Demeter searching for her daughter Persephone. The final ritual included

the granting of certain knowledge through a mystical experience. The religion became connected with immortality as a natural corollary to fertility (rebirth). The rites of purification, at least in Roman times,

had to do with raising the initiate to a divine (thus to an immortal) state. *1 Corinthians 13:2; Ephesians 1:9; 3:3-4,9; Colossians 1:26; 2:2; 4:3.*

▲ **381 Chapel of Mithra under Church of St. Clemente, Rome.** The chapel is typically subterranean and barrel-vaulted, with an altar at one end and stone benches

along the sides. No distinctions were made in the seating of people according to their stature as in most religions, but Mithraism was exclusively for males. It was especially

popular among soldiers. The cavelike nature of the chapels aroused feelings of terror, association with death, and a world of spirits. Its true symbolism, however, recalled the cave in which Mithra caught and slew the mystic bull. The devotees worshiped and ate in the chapel. The darkness was accentuated by selected uses of light, such as reflection from glass placed in a carving, or light from a hole shining on a particularly important point, object, or person, along with a number of other attendant mystical techniques. "Mystery" was familiar to Paul's readers. The altar shown has a typical bas-relief of Mithra slaying the bull. See photos 533-535 for a description of Mithra and Mithraism. *Ephesians 6:19; 2 Thessalonians 2:7; 1 Timothy 3:16; see also photo 380.*

▼**382 Mithraeum of the Seven Spheres, Ostia.** The benches (*podia*) for the devotees run along the sides, and a marble bas-relief of Mithra slaying the bull is attached to the far wall. This chapel was above ground and built of brick, but except for the window on the right wall it maintains the cavelike atmosphere. *Texts: See photos 380, 381.*

▲**383 Mosaic in Mithraeum of the Seven Spheres, Ostia.** The mosaic is 1 of 7 with 7 circles which symbolized the 7 planets; zodiac signs also are intact on the podium. *Texts: See photos 380, 381.*

▲**384 Mosaic in Mithraeum of the Seven Spheres, Ostia.** The tunic-wearing man holds a sacred (symbolic) object in each hand. The mosaic is on the end of the bench on the right side. *Texts: See photos 380, 381.*

◄**385 Lararium, House of Menander, Pompeii.** Roman houses typically had a lararium, a shrine for the household gods. Many lararia inside houses were cupboardlike and held small figures of the family gods, along with objects of value to the family.

◄386 Lararium mounted on villa wall, Augst. It is located on a wall of the inner court beside a door. The limestone niche is formed to represent a house with gabled roof. Two gods are on each side of the center figure, who is the household occupant, and their posture indicates protection over him. His head is covered and he is represented as sacrificing. The serpent below the figures is the symbol of earth power.

►387 House of the Lares, Ostia. Built by Hadrian, it dates to the second century AD, but illustrates the central place of Lares in Roman religion. The structure was a combination of house and market with small shops, which lined the courtyard in the openings separated by thick walls seen in the photo. The lararium located on one of the thick walls was made of colored brick. It is a deeper niche than the one in photo 386 and held small statues of the Lares.

▲ **388 Gallic gallery-temple,** wood model. Landesmuseum, Trier. Constructed after archeological findings in excavations in Trier, Germany. Roman temples were accommodated to local styles, as Roman gods were amalgamated with local gods.

◄ **389 Temple of Athena Nike, Athens Acropolis.** It is located just to the right of the Propylaea (monumental gateway). The small temple is only 27 by 18½ feet (8.23 by 5.64 m.), and 23 feet (7.01 cm.) high if the lost pediment is counted. Built in the fifth century BC, its construction lasted 30 years due to interruptions. The architect was Callicrates. It was dismantled by the Turks in 1685 and rebuilt by the Greeks after independence. Sculptured reliefs seemed to move with the pilgrim toward a central point in the temple where the worshiper performed a ritual act to Athena. The reliefs on the 4 walls celebrate Victory and may indicate that the temple was built a few years later than 426. A chamber (cella) housed the cult statue, a reproduction of an ancient wooden one.

390

391

392

390, 391, 392 La Maison Carré, Nimes, France. The "square house" is actually a temple that dates to the first century AD. Its design is called "pseudo-peripteral" be-cause of the half-round columns that run along the side of the *cella* (the enclosed part of the temple). They continue on line with the full columns of the *pronaos* (the open covered porch area). The Maison Carré is one of the best-preserved temples of ancient Rome and has been in continual use for one purpose or another throughout its history. Today it is a museum. Romans typically built their temples on a platform, as in this example. The capitals are Corinthian, with the curved leaves (photo 391) set at the top of fluted columns. The roofline and overhang decoration is exceedingly ornate (photo 392). The frieze is decorated with foliage, the cornice with medallions which contain Greek-fret, egg-and-dart, and rose motifs. The roofline has ogge-moulding with occasional lion snouts protruding. The roof, which cannot be seen in the photos, is tile. In ancient times an inscription was set on the main door, reconstructed as C. CAESARI AVGVSTI F COS L CAESAR COS DESIGNATO/PRINCIPIBVS IVVENTVTIS = To Caius Caesar, son of Augustus, consul, to Lucius Caesar, son of Augustus, nominated consul; to the princes of youth.

►393 **Gateway to outer court of Baal temple, Syria,** cast reproduction, Pergamum Museum, Berlin. The designs are mostly geometric, with scrolls predominating, but grape clusters and other fruits are set inside the patterns on the curve above the door, along with an occasional sunburst. A scroll design balances the lower part of the gable on each side and an image of a female deity with radiant is at the top of the curve.

◄394 **Propylon of temple to Athena Polias** that was in Pergamum, erected about 170 BC. Pergamum Museum, Berlin. The temple was erected by Eumenes II. On the architrave that rests on the lower columns is the inscription, BASILEUS EUMENES ATHENAI NIKEPHOROI (King Eumenes to Athena Bringer of Victory). The inscription (as well as the temple itself) was both an act of worship and propaganda for the king to celebrate his victory over the Gauls. The reliefs of the upper portico show arms and armor.

395 Treasury of the Athenians, Delphi. The reconstructed portions of the columns are clearly distinguishable. The panels above the columns feature the exploits of Theseus, a hero of Athens. Each event is separated by triple grooves (triglyphs). The treasury date is disputed but may commemorate the founding of democracy by Cleisthenes in 509 BC. Another series of reliefs, on the entrance facade, depicted the struggle of the Greeks and the Amazons, symbolic of Athens' battle against Darius. An inscription along the south terrace wall has: "The Athenians dedicate to Apollo the Persian spoils from the Battle of Marathon." Thus the purpose of the treasury is illustrated; it was built out of gratitude to Apollo, whose site Delphi was, for the god's help in this battle and events both earlier and later. Numerous inscriptions and gifts continued to be added into the Roman period as grateful acknowledgment was made to Apollo. The Treasury is 32 feet, 9 inches (10 m.) long and 19 feet, 8 inches (6 m.) wide.

396 Temple complex at Agina, a Greek island not far from Piraeus, Greece, reconstruction (see photos 397-398). Glyptothek, Munich. The monumental entrance (propylaea) is the structure in the center of the photo which extends on both sides of the wall. It was 24 feet (7.32 m.) wide, 20 feet, 6 inches (6.25 m.) deep. The buildings to the right of the entrance belong to the priests. The temple is Doric in style; various monuments face the temple along the wall. An ascending ramp runs up to the center of the temple entrance.

▲ **397 Agina temple dedicated to Aphaia,** a goddess with similar character to Artemis, reconstruction (see photo 398). Glyptothek Munich. The cult dates to the end of the Mycenaean period. The design of the temple is called hexa-style, with 12 columns running up each side; it is set on a 3-stepped base. A walkway runs inside the columns. A floral design with female figures stand on the peaks and griffins on the corners of the tiled roof. Well-executed sculptures decorate the pediments, the central figure being Athena. The scenes are from the Trojan War, due to the connection of the island with Achilles and Ajax. All of the sculptures were of marble. Aphaia was Britomartis who fled Crete.

▶ **398 Agina temple, cutaway to show the interior,** reconstruction (see photos 396, 397). Glyptothek, Munich. The temple was built of limestone, coated with stucco, and painted. The interior columns are set on 2 levels, the upper superimposed on the lower. Roof joists run from the outside columns, as do beams to support the ceiling. The cella walls support ceiling joists and a structure which adds support to the roof. The center aisle originally was open to the ceiling, but later galleries were added to which ladders gave access.

◄ **399 Theseum, Athens agora,** also called the temple of Athena and Hephaestus (see photos 400-401). Its identity with Hephaestus is secure, since numerous bronze-casting works have been found nearby; Hephaestus is the metal-workers' god. It is the best surviving example of the Doric hexastyle temple. Located on a low hill adjoining the west side of the agora, it dates to the fifth century BC. Its design resembles the Parthenon. It has a 3-stepped base. Most of the temple is made from Pentelic marble except for the sculptures, which were of Parian marble. Some, but not all, of the metopes (the horizontal structure between the columns and the overhang) were decorated with reliefs. The pediments once held sculptures. Three sides were decorated with a formal garden, the plants held in pots.

► **400 Cella of the Theseum, Athens** agora (see photos 399, 401). The part seen is the enclosed portion; the side walls extended on each end to include porches whose open fronts are supported by 2 columns each. A double tier of columns run along each side close to the wall. Bronze statues of both goddess and god stood inside.

▲ **401 Columned side of the Theseum,** Athens agora (see photos 399, 400). Six columns ran along each end, 13 along each side, counting the corner ones twice.

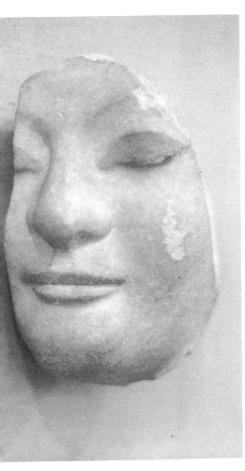

▲ **402 Fragment from temple of Diana, Ephesus.** The woman's face was part of a column drum relief dating to the sixth century BC, marble. British Museum. Diana was the Roman name for the Greek Artemis, who was the dominant deity of Ephesus for centuries. Only a few broken pieces of marble remain on the site. Ancient writers extolled the beauty of the temple, calling it 1 of the 7 wonders of the world. It was the largest edifice in the Hellenistic world, an achievement all the more impressive in that it was constructed entirely of marble. Blocks, columns, and other building material was reused in other buildings, including the Hagia Sophia in Istanbul. *Acts 19:23-41.*

▼ **403 Column drum from temple of Diana, Ephesus,** marble, about 340 BC. British Museum. The figures are, from left, Death (Thanatos), Alcestis or Eurydice, Hermes, and a female figure. The drum portion is 5 feet, 11 inches (1.8 m.) tall. The temple of the first century was the phase that was completed in the third century BC. It was set on a seven-stepped podium that was 8 feet, 9 inches (2.68 m.) high. The columns were 60 feet (18.29 m.) high and appear stouter than those of most other temples. Eight columns ran across the front and back of the temple, 21 along each side, counting the corner columns twice. Another row ran inside the outer row, and 4 sets of double columns supported the entrance porch. The figure of Artemis stood inside the cella. An altar stood in front of the temple. The marble-faced altar was horseshoe-shaped whose full dimensions were 105 by 72 feet (32 by 22 m.). *Acts 19:23-41.*

404, 405, 406 Relief from Arch of Titus, Rome. The arch was built in AD 81 shortly after Titus' death to commemorate victory over the Jewish revolt of the first century AD. A relief on an inner face of the arch shows Titus in a 4-horse chariot led by the goddess Roma, the emperor being crowned by Victory (not shown). The opposite face (shown) depicts the spoils from the Jerusalem Temple being carried in the

Triumphal processional, the menorah in the center, and the trumpets at the right. The triumphal arch through which the procession is about to pass is at the far right. The 3 plaques held on poles are tablets which identified by name the personifications of cities and rivers that accompanied the procession. Photo 405 is a closeup of the 7-branched menorah, photo 406 of the trumpets. The menorah was used in both synagogue and Temple. The relief is of Pentelic marble and is 7 feet, 10 inches (2.4 m.) high, 12 feet, 8 inches (3.85 m.) long. The relief is valuable for its picturing of the Temple menorah and trumpets. *Matthew 24:1-2.*

▼**407 Synagogue of Chorazin,** under reconstruction. It dates to the third century AD. A stone seat for "the ruler of the synagogue" ("seat of Moses," Matt. 23:2) was found in the excavations. The name of Yudan, the builder of the stoa and staircase, is inscribed on the back of the seat. The "stoa" was the synagogue hall; the steps likely led up to the Torah shrine. The outlines of the floor plan can be seen; the synagogue is 75 feet, 6 inches by 55 feet, 9 inches (23 by 17 m.) and had 3 entrances, all facing south toward Jerusalem. The outer walls were of basalt block. The inside was a sort of basilical design, with 2 parallel rows of basalt columns, with 2 additional columns along the back (near) wall. Benches ran along 3 sides. The structure had a columned porch before the entrance. *Matthew 11:21.*

408 Alexander Mosaic, from House of the Faun, Pompeii. National Museum of Naples. It was located in the same room as the Nile mosaic (photo 162). It is a copy of one of the great long-lost masterpieces of Greek painting that date to the fourth century BC. The mosaic style is *opus vermiculatum*; very small tesserae were used, which allowed the artist to blend colors smoothly. The composition shows the battle at the moment the tide had turned against Darius. The Persian king wears a large yellow tiara and flowing robes. He is attempting to turn and flee in his chariot, but his eyes are fastened on a favorite warrior or perhaps attendant who has fallen to Alexander (see closeup, photo 241). His army has formed a spear hedge of *sarissae* spears around him. Alexander is bare-headed and wears armor; he is driving his lance through Darius' warrior. The background is unlandscaped save for a shattered tree, which adds starkness to the battle scene.

409 Overview of Herculaneum. The arch at the upper right marks the main street, the Decumanus Maximus. The arch probably was the entrance to the unexcavated forum. On the center to lower right is a hall and across the street an entrance to the palaestra. Some remnants of the columned walkway and red-tiled roof still stand. On the left at the end of the street is the shop of A. Fuferus. The Trellis House (photo 143) is located among the buildings at upper left. The House of the Bicentenary, the House of the Beautiful Courtyard, and the House of the Neptune Mosaic (see photos 839-840) are in the top area of the photo. Mt. Vesuvius' lava flow froze time in Herculaneum at AD 79. *Matthew 9:35; 12:25; Acts 12:10; 16:12; 19:29, 32,41.*

410 Sacellum of House of Loreius Tiburtinus, Pompeii. The front of the room resembles a small temple. Inside, the decorations are in the Fourth Style, which dates to the time of Nero. A niche in the west wall once held a statue of Isis. On the south wall (left) in the photo is a small fresco of a priest. He wears the prescribed long white robe, has his head shaved, holds a sistrum (see photos 586-587) in his right hand, and holds the *situla* (bucket used for ritual lustrations) on his left arm. A Latin inscription under him is *amplus alumnus Tiburs* ("highly regarded disciple from Tibur"). Above the primary wall line the figures are more intricate, with thin lines, swirls, and figures inside frames. The roof has a beam effect but is plastered.

411 Cupids working on wedge press and stove. National Museum of Naples. The cupids are depicted making perfume. On the right, a cupid drives wedges into a frame, which forces the material being pressed under increasing pressure. On the left, a cupid stirs the liquid from the press over a stove. *Revelation 15:19-20.*

412, 413 Initiation of young girl in Dionysiac mysteries, from Villa of Mysteries, Pompeii, time of Augustus. The photos show the 2 side walls of the "Room of the Mysteries" in the villa (center wall not shown). The entire panorama has 29 figures. The first scene (photo 412) shows the reading of the liturgy by a boy who is being coached by a seated matron. Another woman, standing and richly clad, looks on, her hand resting on her hip with an air of a young woman who is about to go through the initiation experience. The woman on the right is a maidservant who holds a plate of food. The

▲ 408 Alexander Mosaic, from House of the
Faun, Pompeii.

▶ 410 Sacellum of House of Loreius
Tiburtinus, Pompeii.

▲ 411 Cupids working on wedge
press and stove.

▼ 413 Initiation of young girl in Dionysiac mysteries.

▼ 415 A woman and a man carrying food.

▲ 416 A man and woman carrying sacrifices.

417 Blue mosaic nymphaeum from triclinium.

▼ **418 Athena bowl centerpiece for table.**

next scenes (not shown) are of lustral purification, Silenus, the Panisca, scenes of the initiate in terror as she faces the prospect of flagellation. A damaged portion of the fresco showed Dionysus with Ariadne, an important part of the god's myth closely connected with the initiation ritual in which the initiate is "married" to Dionysus. Photo 413 shows the initiate stricken with fear, lying across the lap of another woman. She is nude, awaiting flagellation. Next to her on the right a maenad is performing an orgiastic dance, clapping cymbals held in each hand; behind her another woman holds a thyrsus. Another portion of the fresco shows the initiate opening a basket which contains a phallus, symbol of fertility, while a menacing figure with a whip stands by her. *Texts: See photos 380, 381.*

414 Venus and Priapus, marble, 24¹/₂ inches (62 cm.) in height. National Museum of Naples. The statue was found on a table in the *tablinum* of a house known as the Villa of Julia Felix, which included a brothel, in Pompeii. The goddess wears a see-through bikini which is gilded in gold and has gold bands on her arms, breast, and pubic area. Her eyes are inlaid with cement and glass paste. She is removing her sandal, preparing to bathe. Her left arm rests on the god Priapus (see photo 502), whose pubic area also was gilded with gold, and a tiny Eros sits by her foot and helps her with her sandal. Erotic frescoes also decorated the walls of the brothel in which this statuette was found. *Luke 15:30; 1 Corinthians 6:15-16; 1 Timothy 1:10; Revelation 17.*

415 A woman and a man carrying food. National Museum of Naples. Both are clad only in light tunics. The woman wears a lightweight veil and has let her tunic fall from her shoulder. She carries a small lidded bowl. The man carries a platter and an object in his right hand. Possibly they are taking offerings to Dionysus. The clothing recalls some ancient writers' criticism of Romans whose clothing was so thin that nothing was left to the imagination.

416 A man and woman carrying sacrifices. National Museum of Naples. The woman wears a very light see-through tunic which reaches to her wrists, over which she wears a peplos fastened at each shoulder and bound above her waist. She has belted it twice to arrange the tier effect. She wears a veil, has garlands in her hair, and carries a platter of gifts, including a silver box. The man wears a tunic and over it a himation; he holds a gift in his right hand. He also wears garlands in his hair.

417 Blue mosaic nymphaeum from triclinium. National Museum of Naples. The decorations are architectural except for the rooster scene at the bottom. Narrow columns rise on each side of the niche from well-proportioned rails and support cornices above; the effect provides an unbalanced depth to the scene.

418 Athena bowl centerpiece for table, first century AD or earlier. Glyptothek, Munich. The silver-gilt bowl is part of the Hildesheim Treasure. Roma, merged with Athena, appears in the dress of a Roman matron, but she wears the crown of Minerva (with whom Athena was identified) which is surmounted by a griffin. Athena leans her left arm on a shield and her right hand on a crook which may represent a ship's tiller. *2 Timothy 2:20.*

◄ **419, 420 Synagogue at Capernaum,** showing entrance and near interior (419) and back interior (420). It was built of white limestone, which stood in strong contrast against the black basalt of the region. For years illustrations of the structure have presented it as 2-storied, the upper of which was a gallery supported by the interior columns and which ran along the sides and back of the buildings. Current excavators, however, believe the building was 1-storied. This discovery, along with other evidence, raises the question as to how women were separated from men in synagogue worship or, indeed, if they even were (see source list, Bernadette Brooten). The structure had a basilical design, the columns being 16 feet, 3 inches (5 m.) high. The main entrance was from the south, thus facing Jerusalem; each side also had an entrance. The floor is paved with flagstones. Two rows of stone benches run along the lower walls on three sides, probably seating for the elders. People also sat on mats on the floor, facing a screen between them and the entrance. The "pulpit" where the lessons were read was located at the southeast corner, thus on the entrance side. The entrance led out to an unroofed porch. The east side of the synagogue had a trapezoid court with a portico. The ornamentation, the remains of which are extensive, was exceedingly ornate. The traditional fruit and geometric designs are found, but so also are reliefs of animals and signs of the zodiac. (The extensive use of the zodiac in synagogues has not been explained satisfactorily.) It dates to the early third century, but it apparently was built on the site of the older one. Near the steps which lead up to the platform at the southeast corner are lower ruins made of basalt; these ruins date to the first century. Additional excavations in 1981 under the floor of the synagogue revealed pottery that dates the previous structure to the first century. This synagogue likely was 1-storied but of similar floor plan to the standing ruins. It had a cobblestone floor. A trapezoidal structure is connected to the synagogue on the east side; it was a sort of community center and hostel for visitors. *Matthew 4:13; 8:5; 11:23; 17:24; John 6:59.*

▶**421 Relief of Ark of the Covenant, Capernaum.** The figure is a design on a frieze. The chest depicted has an arched roof which is supported by columns. Double doors are at the front and the ark is mounted on 4 wheels, which may symbolize mobility in the sense Ezekiel saw the vision of the Temple on wheels. However, the Ark in a synagogue during this period probably was on wheels and was rolled into place from its storage. The design of the Ark is similar to a mosaic of an ark found at Tiberias; it, however, did not have wheels. The circumstances of the loss of the ark are unknown. The most probable theory is that it was taken by the Babylonians when they destroyed the Temple in 587 BC. Synagogue "arks" housed Scripture scrolls. *Texts: See photos 419, 420.*

◀**422 Synagogue at Masada.** Located inside the northwestern wall of the fortress, it was built by Herod the Great, who placed the main entrance toward the east. It had an anteroom and a main room with 2 rows of 3 columns. The Zealots, still in the first century, enlarged the main room, added the benches along the walls, rearranged the columns, and laid a new floor. The rough stone structure (northeast corner) was added by the Zealots. *Matthew 4:23; 10:17.*

◄ **423 Synagogue at Herodium** near Bethlehem, built by Herod the Great. This structure, though slightly larger than the one at Masada, had only 4 columns, one at each corner. The main structure was of blocks. *Texts: See photo 422.*

▲ **424 Ark for Torah, Nabratein,** Israel. Rockefeller Museum, Jerusalem. The Torah was placed in the scallop shell, the top of which is the arch. The gable design represents the Temple. The block shown, of limestone, weighs about 1,000 pounds (453 kg.) and rested on stone pillars. A rosette appears at the inside peak of the gable and again at the lower left side. Egg-and-dart carvings run along the underside of the gable. A chain passed through a hole at the top of the scallop shell to hold an oil lamp which burned perpetually. A lion is on each side of the gable. It dates to the third century and may represent a development in which the Ark remained in a permanent location in the synagogue as opposed to the wheeled style which may have been used earlier. *Texts: See photo 422.*

425, 426, 427 Qumran. Photo 425 is a view from the tower at the northwest corner. The area with the low arched opening is a passageway with doorways at each end. Just beyond it is a vestibule with doors at each end and in the center of its far wall; it also had a stairway, which is the slanted ruin to the right of the doorway. The next room had stone benches running along its walls, recessed cupboards, and a niche which opened to each side of the wall. It may have been a meeting room. The room at the upper part of the photo with the square stone block against its rear wall was an annex (photo 426; another stone block can be seen in this photo, in the center of the room in direct line with the right side of the doorway) attached to the dining room, which runs horizontally just this side of it. In the annex were discovered stacks of tableware. At least some of the meals in the dining room were ceremonial in nature. The scriptorium (photo 427) lay just out of photo 426 to the left, running perpendicular in terms of the photo. Excavators discovered in it fragments of a table 16 feet (4.88 m.) long, 16 inches (40.64 cm.) wide, and 20 feet (6.1 m.) wide. When reconstructed (now in Rockefeller Museum) it was found to be a very large block of stone that, rather than having legs, tapered down to a 7-inch (17.8 cm.) bottom. A low bench on which the scribes sat to work at the table ran along the east wall. This scriptorium is where the Dead Sea Scrolls were written, its use confirmed by other discoveries in the room.

SACRIFICIAL SYSTEM

Several types of altars were used in the Greco-Roman world. The names were not used consistently in ancient times, but in general they were the *altare, ara, focus, foculus,* and *mensa,* plus the *scobes.* The large altar (Latin *altare,* Greek *bomas*) was dedicated to a major deity; a very large but good example is the altar to Zeus at Pergamum. The *ara* (Gk. *eschara*) also could be large, such as the Ara Pacis of Augustus, but it was devoted to a lesser deity. The domestic altar was the *focus* (Greek *estia*). Sacrifice also was made in pits for the deities of the Underworld; these were called *scobes* (Greek *bothroi*).

In practice, the word *focus* was used for both the *altare* and the *ara,* and in fact the word distinction between the *altara* and *ara* was lost by the first century. The word *foculus* was rarely used and apparently applied to a portable vessel or tripod. The *mensa* was the table on which sacred vessels were kept and offerings were placed.

The tops of altars essentially were in 4 forms: flat, with horns on the corners, with bolsters on the sides, or with shallow depressions (sometimes in combination with the horns or bolsters). The shapes of altars fall into 2 classes: those with curving profiles and those with straight sides. The shapes apparently were not influenced by their use but rather by their origins among various peoples long before the first century. The Greeks preferred round altars, while the Romans preferred 4-sided ones. The shapes do not appear to be connected with any particular cult. The flat ones are the most numerous.

Temples had posted on their premises the type of behavior expected of worshipers and the type of sacrifices that were and were not acceptable. Sacrifices varied by deity. Two distinct types of worship prevailed: the worship of deities such as those connected with Olympus and the worship of deities connected with the Underworld. The first type were joyous occasions whose observances occurred during the daytime, while the second were gloomy, particularly given to superstition, and occurred at night.

The place and function of priests in the first century varied. A priestly class was the pattern in the Near East, including Egypt; Greece and Rome had priestly functions, but anyone could be elected or appointed to the office. Dignitaries often performed the public priestly functions and held the important priestly offices. Indeed, some public offices carried with them the priestly assignment. Those in these positions wore the insignias of the priesthood.

Priests were organized into *collegia* or associations around the deity they served; the head of all of them in a community was the *pontifex maximus.* Anyone could serve in such positions; they were elected by the *collegia.* They were helped in various duties by others who kindled the sacrificial flames (*flamines*) or who danced the special dances, or who were assigned other rites. The *augures* were especially important, for they read the entrails of the sacrificial victims to forecast the future (the will of the gods). In the home, however, the father was priest. Sacrifices were performed in accordance with the religions' calendars and before an important event or by a person or group asking favors or giving thanks.

ALTARS AND OFFERING VESSELS

▼428 **Camillus with patera.** Roman, bronze, first century AD, 5 inches (12.7 cm.) in height. J. Paul Getty Museum. A camillus was an acolyte in the Roman cult. He had to be free-born and have both parents living. Often he was the child of an officiant of the cult. *Revelation 15:7; 16:1-17.*

◄429 Man offering sacrifice on small altar. Brussels Museum. He has a scroll in his left hand and holds a cake or small patera in his right hand over a small altar with flames. He wears a tunic folded over a belt with an outer cover clasped at the right shoulder. Upraised hands are at the top of the monument on either side of his head. *Acts 15:20; 10:7,14; 1 Peter 4:3; Revelation 9:20.*

▼430 Two altars with deities, relief. Capitoline Museum. The god and goddess are Serapis and Isis depicted as Zeus and Hera. Cerberus, a monstrous dog which guarded the underworld and came to be associated with Serapis, leans against his knee. A winged Eros holds a platter of sacrifices. A round altar on which a fire burns is set to the right of Serapis, who stretches his hand out toward it. As was common, it is decorated with garlands. Another small tiered cylindrical incense altar, which also holds a fire, similar to the one in photo 377 is at far right of the relief. Serapis held a staff, part of which remains over his left shoulder. Under his right arm is an animal, which appears to be a dog. Isis is beside him; she also holds a staff and her head is covered. Her right hand is outstretched in the same manner as that of Serapis. The outline of a temple is in the background. *Texts: See photo 429.*

▲431 Grave monument with sacrificial scene, about 160 AD. Roman-German Landesmuseum, Cologne.

The photo is a closeup of the relief; above it is an inscription:

DEAE   = For the god

VAGDAVERCVSTI = Vagdaver-
custis

TITVS FLAVIVS = Titus Flavius
CONSTANS AEF = Constans
erected this
altar

PRAET(orio) EM-
(mentissimus)V(ir) = his Emi-
nence the
Guard Pre-
fect.

The normal place for the officiating priest is at the right of the altar and the camillus on the left, which is the case shown in the photo. He is sprinkling incense onto the fire. His right hand and the object it held are broken off; he likely is pouring a libation from a patera; the wine for it came from the urceus in his left arm. The camillus holds an open box of incense. A musician beside the camillus plays a flute, while the worshipers stand beside the priest. *Texts: See photo 429.*

►432, 433 Two votive offering tripods. Roman-German Landesmuseum, Cologne. The essence of the votive offering was that it was voluntary; it was given for thanksgiving, for propitiation, or for a prayer to be answered. The tripod was widely used in the Greek and Roman cultures for both religious and utilitarian purposes. Photo 432 appears to represent a candleholder but may have held a container for incense or other offerings. The stand in photo 433 has a wide bowl and may have been either a brazier or portable altar. Braziers, in fact, sometimes were used as portable altars and vice versa. Tripods were dedicated often to the gods, and often in connection with victory in games. Very tall tripods were given as prizes in drama contests, for Dionysus was the god of the dramatist, in somewhat the same manner that the vase often is the form of a trophy today. *Texts: See photo 429.*

▼434 Incense stand. Brussels Museum. The 3 legs end in deer hooves and the shaft begins with a maid holding a mirror. Above her head a cat and a fowl climb the shaft. Doves face inward from each corner of the platform on which incense was placed. *Philippians 4:18; see also photo 429.*

▶435 An Altar for Jupiter and the Genius of the Caesars. Roman-German Landesmuseum, Cologne. The inscription is:
I(ovi) O(ptimp) M(aximo)
ET GENIO
IMP(eratoris)
L(ucius) PACCIVS
NONIANV
(centutio)LEGIONIS
I M(inerviae)
It translates:
The Best and Greatest Jupiter
and the Genius
of the Emperors
(dedicator of this altar is)
Lucius Paccius Nonianus
Centurion of the First Legion
Minerva
The sides of the altar are decorated with reliefs of cloth, garlands, and laurels. The dedication is to the highest god of the Empire, Jupiter, and the protective goddess of the legion, Minerva. *Texts: See photo 429.*

◀436, 437 Altar to Cybele, located in the House of Attis and Cybele in Glanum, France. A nearby bench might have been for the gathering of the faithful. The altar is for votive offerings and was dedicated to the "ears" of the goddess by her "pious servant Loreia." The inscription is above the wreath; the ears symbolizing the goddess' hearing are carved inside the wreath. An offering table stands in front of the altar. Its inscription reveals that it was dedicated by the priestess Attia Musa to Cybele. Photo 437 shows the top of the altar; the side receptacles probably were to hold a grate or brazier in place. The center receptacle was used for libations and drink offerings. *Texts: See photo 429.*

▲ 438 Funerary altar from Caesarea Maritima. Rockefeller Museum, Jerusalem. It belonged to a military man, whose figure is on the left side in the photo. Below the image of the Roman legionary eagle is an inscription identifying the deceased person's legion as the XIIth. To the upper right of the eagle is a personification of Victory. The figures stand inside carved columns supporting arches, inside of which are conch shells. *Texts: See photo 429.*

▼ 439 Altar to Zeus at Pergamum, the greatest altar in the Greco-Roman world. Now reconstructed in the Pergamum Museum in East Berlin, it stood on the second terrace of the Acropolis overlooking the wide valley below. It was built by Eumenes II (197-159 BC), who set it on a podium 17 feet, 6 inches (5.33 m.) in height. The lowest step of the podium was 119 feet, 6 inches by 112 feet, 3 inches (36.45 by 34.21 m.; podium not shown in photo). The frieze, which runs below the columns, is 7 feet, 6 inches (2.32 m.) high. Following it from beginning to end, the devotee could recall the story of the battle between the gods and the giants (the *Gigantomachy*). The widest steps on the bottom are 68 feet, 2 inches (20.75 m.) wide; the stairs between the wings are 30 feet (9.14 m.) wide. The altar stood in the court at the top of the stairs; if the columns across the front of the court (top of the stairs) are placed in error, as some believe, the sacrifices would be open to the plain far below. *Texts: See photo 429.*

► **440 Lar holding patera and offering,** bronze statuette. Brussels Museum. The Lar has radiants encircling his head. The patera was a shallow dish used for pouring liquid sacrifices onto an altar. Wine libations were poured to seal a contract; food libations of milk, honey, oil, and wine were poured in funerals. Water sometimes was used as a libation. Often a formal libation was preceded by a procession, a prayer, and an ecstatic cry. Libations also formed a part of many types of sacrifices; they could be poured from other vessels, such as a pitcher or amphora. *Texts: See photos 428, 429.*

▼ **441 Effigy of deceased holding patera.** Etruscan sarcophagus lid, from Etruria, Italy, third-second centuries BC. Field Museum. The Etruscans were an advanced civilization in central Italy defeated by Rome early in its history. The Romans always poured a libation during meals to honor the family Lar. Libations were common in all types of worship, in sacrifices, at tombs, before a journey, before retiring at night, at marriages, and at any event which called for purification. *Texts: See photo 428.*

SACRIFICING

▶ **442 Sacrificial scene,** fresco from Pompeii, 76¼ by 57 inches (188.6 by 144.8 cm.). National Museum of Naples. The scene is the myth of Jason appearing before Palias, but it reflects then-current dress and private sacrifice. Palias and two women stand on the steps of a temple, which can be faintly seen in the background. A man leads a bull, holding a garland on its head, to a sturdy sacrificial table called a *mensa,* by which Jason stands with an attendant. The attitude of the bull was important as it approached a sacrifice. If he went to the altar willingly the omen was good, but if he resisted the omen was bad. At the bronze table, the bull would be sprinkled with water and a word spoken to him. If the bull nodded the omen was good, but if he shook his head the omen was bad. A large vessel is under the table; a small bottle is on top of the table; and the attendant with a garland on his head places a shallow bowl onto the table. All of the people in the scene wear garlands except Jason. *Texts: See photo 429.*

◀ **443 Youth leading pig to sacrifice,** small bronze relief, Roman, first century AD. British Museum. The pig was the special victim of Persephone and the Bona Dea, though it was used in other sacrifices as well. *Texts: See photo 429.*

▶ **444 Sacrificial scene.** Bergama Museum, Bergama, Turkey. The relief shows a bull tethered to a ring fixed in the ground, a priestess holding a patera and torch, and a horned altar on which a flame is burning. Another torch balances the composition on the right. Beyond the bull is a pillar that ends in a head of grain. The priestess wears the himation over a tunic and has a garland on her head. The altar has in relief the figure of a garland with streamers. The bull stands on the two small platforms. *Texts: See photo 429.*

▲ **445 Bacchic procession,** marble relief from Rome, AD 100. British Museum. It was found in the Villa Quintiliana on the Appian Way. The style followed dates to the fourth century BC. A maenad in front plays a cymbal; she is followed by 2 satyrs, 1 of whom plays the double flute. The other carries a thyrsus and walks with a partner, commonly associated with Bacchus. Both satyrs carry animal hides across their shoulders. *Romans 1:22-29; Galatians 5:19-21; Ephesians 5:18.*

▲446 Bacchic procession, sarcophagus. National Museum of Naples. Various symbols of Dionysus/Bacchus are included in the relief. From right to left: a faun carrying a curved pipe (aulos); behind him a devotee carrying a box from which projects a phallus symbol; at bottom, Dionysus as an infant riding a lion and playing a lyre; drunken men and women leaning on and supporting one another, the last one carrying a club; 2 centaurs, 1 playing double pipes and 1 a lyre; an Eros on the near centaur's back; a snake in a basket and a panther under the centaur; and a chariot, pulled by the far centaur, carrying Dionysus and Silenus. *Texts: See photo 444.*

▼447 Sacrificial procession of freedmen, marble, period of Tiberius. Copy from Roman-German Central Museum, Mainz; original in Vatican Museum. The relief was found beneath the Palazzo della Cancellaria; it was on 1 side of a large monument and is 3 feet, 6 inches (1.05 m.) in height. The frieze shows a procession of freedmen who were responsible for leading in the worship of the Lares of the City of Rome. From 7 BC onward the ritual led by these freedmen came to be associated with the worship of the Genius of Augustus. Lictors, musicians, and victims for the sacrifice (bull, steer, and heifer) form the procession. Statuettes of the Lares are being carried by 4 bearers. The first figure from the left with covered head (fourth on front row) holds an image of the emperor wearing a toga. The 2 figures to the right of him carry images of Lares. When the sacrifice took place, the entrails were examined to determine if any defect was present which would render the animal unfit for sacrifice. Every word and act had to be precisely accurate; any mistake meant that the whole procedure had to begin again. The entire rite was conducted in strict silence except for the flute player(s) whose music drowned out any evil or unlucky sound which might affect the sacrifice. *Acts 22:28; 1 Corinthians 7:21-24; 2 Peter 2:19; see also photo 429.*

▶ **448 Sacrifice to Dionysus,** fresco from Herculaneum. National Museum of Naples. Dionysus is seated, recognized by the thin pole he holds, called a thyrsus, and the cup in his right hand. Three women wearing garlands and expensive chitons that are flounced at the waist carry offerings to him. One of the women is placing a laurel wreath on Dionysus' head and holds a ritual dish in her other hand. The other 2 women wait, and a little girl stands at far left.

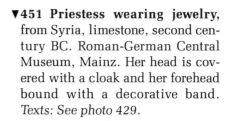

▼ **451 Priestess wearing jewelry,** from Syria, limestone, second century BC. Roman-German Central Museum, Mainz. Her head is covered with a cloak and her forehead bound with a decorative band. *Texts: See photo 429.*

▲ **449 Priest in act of sacrificing,** found in Yugoslavia, bronze, first or early second century AD. Roman-German Central Museum, Mainz. He holds a patera in his right hand and the fragment of an *urceus* (container for wine used in the libation and poured into the patera). His head is covered as was the custom. *Texts: See photo 429.*

▲ **450 Woman offering sacrifice,** funerary relief. National Museum of Naples. Her head is uncovered, her hair is fixed in a bun but full around the sides, and she wears a himation over a tunic, one end draped across her arm. Both hands are extended and she holds an offering in her right hand and reaches toward a tall, narrow incense stand. *Texts: See photo 429.*

▲ **452 Priest of Serapis,** marble, about AD 180, height 2 feet, 7¼ inches (79.5 cm.). J. Paul Getty Museum. The priest wears on his head a gilded filet to which is attached the 7-pointed star of Serapis. *Texts: See photo 429.*

► **453 Priest of Isis,** 40 BC. Agora Museum, Athens. The sculpture was influenced by the Egyptian style. It is 11³⁄₈ inches (23.6 cm.) in height. *Texts: See photo 429.*

▲ **454 Priest from Athens,** first century AD. National Museum, Athens. He wears a braided headband. *Texts: See photo 429.*

commemorate birth, coming of age, or marriage; weapons for victory in war; clothing; toys long-used by children when they grew up; domestic implements from grateful wives; models of tools, deities, wheels, or animals; or replicas of arms, legs, internal organs, or other healed parts of the body. They were given to induce a deity to accomplish some action or in gratitude for a deity having done so. *Texts: See photo 429.*

▲ 455 **Olympian sanctuary staff list for years 28-24 BC.** Olympia Museum, Greece. The marble tile came from the temple of Zeus. The temple was completed in 456 BC; ancient writers extolled its beauty. The altar, which may date as early as the tenth century BC, was 27 feet (25 m.) or so to the north side of the temple. It consisted of a rectangular mound with 5 steps; on top of it was a huge conical mound from accumulated ashes of sacrifices which had been made into plaster after each sacrifice. The structure rose to a height of 22 feet (6.71 m.). *Texts: See photo 429.*

MAGIC

456, 457 **Clay votive food offerings.** Corinth Museum. The concept of feeding the gods dates to prehistory and was continued both for that purpose and for giving first fruits to the gods. Models of food sometimes accompanied the real food, not given in its place, as reminders to the god that the food was given. Votive offerings took every conceivable shape and size, large and tiny, of precious metal or clay. Locks of hair might be given to

▲**460, 461 Clay votive offerings of eye and ear,** Etruscan, third century BC. British Museum. Representations of body parts generally have been found in healing sanctuaries and represent prayers or thanksgivings for cures. Some votive offerings were won in contests, while most were purchased in the market; in either case such offerings represented value. Sometimes the value was great; for those offerings the priestly staff kept inventories. Many temples became repositories of great wealth. The original excavator of the Aesculapeion at Corinth estimated that the mass of votive offerings that represented parts of the body amounted to a 13-cubic-yard (10-cubic meter) pile. *Texts: See photo 429.*

▼**458 Amulet with phallus and vulva,** made from deer horn. Roman-German Central Museum, Mainz. The phallus symbol is common in many religions; in some it is the principal symbol. The herm (see under "Gods and Goddesses") in its original form was a phallus symbol. The symbol represented reproduction and possibly aggression, a view supported by 462. The "phallus-bird," well known to classical scholars, was a large wooden phallus with wings attached that was floated out to sea in what apparently was a symbol of restoration after death. *Acts 8:11; 15:20; Colossians 3:5.*

◄**459 Two rings with phallus symbols,** gold, Roman Imperial period. British Museum. They likely were worn by children for good luck and to ward away evil spirits. *Texts: See photo 458.*

462-466 Amulets with phalli and vulvas, bronze. Roman-German Museum, Cologne. Photos 462-465 show phallus amulets, photo 464 being a double phallus with a clenched fist on the left projection; 466 (below right) shows a disk with a phallus stamped on it, a winged phallus, two phallus amulets, and a cluster of vulvas. See description in photo 458. *Texts: See photo 458.*

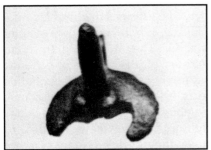

462

463

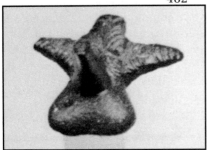

464

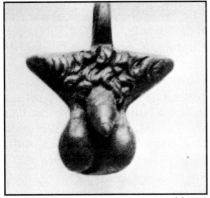

465

466

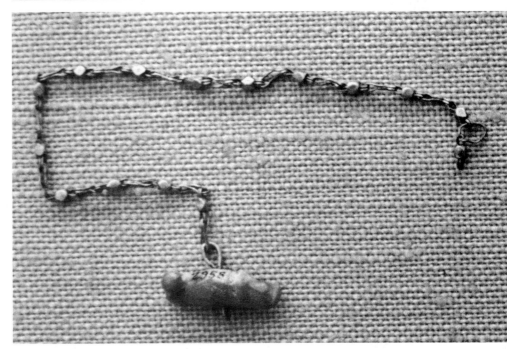

▲ **467 Coral phallus on gold chain,** Roman, second century AD. British Museum. Amulets could be made of cheap material, but those made of precious stones were believed to have special powers. They were worn by both sexes as necklaces and as rings. Roman children wore bulla necklaces (see photo 743). *Texts: See photo 458.*

◄ **468 Phallus relief in bakery,** Herculaneum. The bakery belonged to Sextus Patulcus Felix (see photo 834). The relief, fixed to the wall in the dough room, is ceramic. The large phallus has the hind legs of a donkey, which has its own smaller phallus. They were put in the room to ward off the evil eye or bad luck in mixing the dough. The phallus was the symbol of the god Fascinus (among others), who had the power to ward off the evil eye. In this context, the phallus symbol was not considered obscene. Phallus reliefs were common in public places, set into brickwork of houses and into paving stones. The practice continued into medieval times; phallus reliefs have been found on churches of the period. *Texts: See photo 458.*

◄ **469 Gold amulet case and chain,** Roman, second-third centuries AD, from Petelia in south Italy. British Museum. It contained an Orphic (see photos 503-504) inscription on gold foil that dated several hundred years earlier. *Texts: See photo 458.*

▼ **470 Pendant with magical inscription.** Carnelian in gold mounting, third-fourth centuries AD, place of discovery unknown. Roman-German Central Museum, Mainz. Every Roman child wore a talisman called a *bulla* around his neck to ward off evil spirits. Names of gods and demons appear along with magical formulas. *Texts: See photo 458.*

GODS AND GODDESSES

An adequate study of the gods and goddesses of the New Testament world would occupy a great many pages. The problems are more numerous than that of space, however. Rome and Greece had different religious heritages; while they overlapped and became somewhat amalgamated, any application to New Testament passages should take into account the nature of the worship in the particular locality under study. While generalizations are valid, sometimes local distinctions may be quite important.

Greek religion is much better known than Roman religion; the Greek deities can be traced through their myths in such a manner that conquests and the movement of peoples can be identified to some degree. Roman deities were linked more to functions than to personalities, and persons and families had their personal gods. Other gods were Etruscan, some were from Gaul, and others came from the Greek colonies long established in the West. By the New Testament period, many of the gods had indeed become thoroughly identified one with the other, yet Greeks did not worship all of Rome's gods and Rome did not worship all those of the Greeks.

Each city had its own festival observances; of those deities worshiped in common with other cities the dates were compatible, but other feasts, sacrifices, processions, and observances were dear to the hearts of citizens. All of these put together meant that the ancient gods were legalized and integrated into the lives of the communities. The standard Roman city would have temples to the major deities of Rome—Jupiter, Juno, and Minerva—perhaps combined with the local or Greek deity, perhaps kept separate; additional temples would exist to Apollo, Mercury, Isis and Serapis combined, Hercules, Hephaestus, Ceres, Mars, and perhaps others. Philippi had perhaps 25 temples, Nicomedia over 40. MacMullen indicates that the frequency of deity worship was in this order: Zeus (by $2^{1}/_{2}$ times more often than any other), Apollo, Athena, Dionysus, Artemis, Hera, Aphrodite, Aescalapius, Tyche, Hercules, and the Great Mother. The compilation of references includes worship by other identifications.

The mystery religions were of a different sort. They appealed to the individual's need for conversion, moral standards, special knowledge, fellowship, purification, atonement, and immortality. Such imposing gods and goddesses as Cybele, Mithra, Isis, Sabazios, and Dionysus stimulated the emotions and produced a freedom, especially for women, that Greek and Roman society did not allow. The knowledge granted to those who rose high enough was inexpressible and involved mystic union with the deity; often ecstatic behavior was part of the union.

In fact, Romans had ceased to worship their gods; the temples had fallen into such disrepair that Augustus made their renovation and the revival of Roman religion one of his priorities. Educated Romans had turned from the cold impersonalness of their deities to philosophy.

The common people found outlet elsewhere. The deities that were closest to their lives were the lesser ones, those that had to do with luck, protection, and the underworld. The *manes* were spirits of the dead; magic was accomplished by lining up an earthly known object or factor with its corresponding structure in the unknown; foretelling by a wide range of methods as diverse as reading intestines or the flight of birds could help a person avert disaster; astrology could do more, and many people lived by it. The phallus symbol, and sometimes the vulva, were magical symbols which could overcome evil because of their creative and life-giving power. The gods were functional; the ancient god Janus who faced both ways not only was protector of the gate and door, but somehow he was inherent himself in the gate and door.

Gods had different functions, each one designated by a name, such as Apollo Doctor; the proper appellation had to be used or the god would not answer. As confused as the picture is to the Western mind, the ancient believer was surrounded all his life by gods of every type. Bas-reliefs and statues, brightly colored and larger than life, showed him how each divine being looked; bas-reliefs told stories, too, of the gods' exploits. The objects the figures held or wore told their characteristics. Temples lined the marketplaces and streets and processions carried the divine effigies among the people. Philosophers, poets, dramatists, preachers, priests, guilds, friends, and parents talked of gods and goddesses, of greater and lesser beings, of the ones most apt to help a tradesman or a traveler. Gods to many were the substance of life in the Empire.

Not surprisingly, the ancient equivalent of the hospital was connected with a deity. Aesculapius

(Latinized form of Asklepios) was the Greek god of healing. The wise centaur Chiron was believed to have been his teacher. His main sanctuary was at Epidaurus in the Peloponnese, but he also had important centers at Athens, Pergamum, and Cos. Aesculapius was brought to Rome in 293 BC to halt a plague, heeding the advice of those who consulted the Sibylline Books. His temple was built on Tiber Island. His attribute is the serpent-entwined staff, which still survives in the symbol of the Hippocratic Oath.

Emperor worship was added to the elaborate and confusing (to us) array of worship. Scholars have made various proposals regarding the nature of emperor worship. Some have proposed that the people really were not so naive as to believe the emperor was divine, that the so-called worship was more a political act of loyalty. Others, enamored with Roman culture over Greek, or Greek over Roman, have attributed baser motives to the less-favored culture. Some have supposed that the Greeks used emperor worship to gain political favors, others that the worship was genuine.

Recent scholarship generally has sought to interpret emperor worship in the social context of Greek and Roman life. S. R. F. Price (see source list following) argues that the ruler cult arose in Asia Minor when city-states came under the domination of kings who were not city citizens. The psychological outlook of the people was such that they could not cope with an outsider's rule without some device; they could not submit to such rule by a man not their own, but they could submit to a god.

This view appears reasonable and is worthy of consideration so long as it is not forgotten that the divine-ruler dynamic had been present as far back as the Mycenean period in Greek lands and was common in other regions much earlier. The Homeric myths have heroes—all of them ruler class— each of whom had one divine parent. The cities they founded or came to rule boasted of the divine origins of their rulers; hence the city itself shared in the heritage.

Divine birth, to be sure, was used by the rulers to enhance their rule, but they surely believed themselves that their heritage was true. The concept was fully ingrained into the fabric of Greek peoples on both sides of the Aegean Sea. (Ruler cult in Macedonia, however, was extremely rare.)

Greeks also worshiped heroes, the most notable being Herakles (Hercules), who even became a god. Later, as the power of the cities declined in the wake of empire builders such as Mithridates and Rome itself, cults arose that were dedicated to powerful citizens, benefactors, and even athletes. Early in Roman rule in Asia Minor, cults to the goddess Roma and to Roman officials developed.

Augustus' rise marked the end of new cults dedicated to any other individual. Asia Minor viewed the new emperor as the savior of the world who brought it out of the chaos it had suffered for several decades of destruction of cities, piracy on the seas, kidnapping for slavery, slaughter of mass numbers of people as punishment for supporting a rival king, and warfare which drained the populace from the land so drastically that large areas were virtually uninhabited.

Gratitude to Augustus was genuine, and the Greeks' background of ruler worship made proclaiming him to be divine quite natural. The earliest known proclamation came from the province of Asia in 29 BC (Bithynia also established a cult to Augustus in the same year). The provincial assembly voted to offer a crown to whoever devised the greatest honors for the god, meaning Augustus. Worship of Augustus differed from earlier Greek ruler cults in some important ways, pointed out by Price.

First, spontaneous gratitude arose to Augustus for bringing peace and prosperity in general rather than a city honoring a benefactor for some specific action. Second, earlier cults were city cults; this one and the succeeding ones were province-wide, determined by provincial councils of all the member cities. Third, the same provincial councils had the responsibility of representing their province's interests to Rome; thus arose the marriage between emperor worship and favors (which should not be interpreted oversimply as manipulation). Fourth, regular festivals celebrating the divine emperor were inaugurated with an imperial high priest.

Cities competed aggressively for the honor of being the *neokoros* (temple warden), the city which was granted the privilege of building and maintaining the temple and cult. Pergamum won the honor in Asia.

The imperial priests were not professionals; they were appointed from the most important local families of the host cities. Sometimes they served a short time, sometimes all their lives. The populace expected them to grant lavish gifts of festivals, food, and even buildings.

Rome encouraged these developments through the governors; most emperors sought to appear humble and aloof. Gaius (Caligula) was an exception. He ordered a temple built to himself at Miletus and the Jerusalem Temple to be rededicated to him (see "Caligula").

The ruler cult was not so familiar an idea to the Romans, but the emperors saw the potential in the concept to aid their rule. Such a divine connection was not impossible in the context of Roman religion (see Apotheosis, photo 527 and Genius, photo 526). From Julius Caesar on, the emperor was the highest priest, the Pontifex Maximus. Augustus was cautious in accepting the title of god in the West, though he did follow the Ptolemys' previous identification as a god when he conquered Egypt (he could do little else). Emperors after him increasingly encouraged such worship. Domitian was the first to accept the title, "lord and god."

The title of the imperial high priest in Asia Minor was "high priest of the goddess Roma and of Emperor Sebastos son of god." After Augustus, who had emperor cults dedicated to him in 34 cities, the cult gradually became generic for the living emperor. *Sebastos* was another name for the deified emperor; temples to the *sebastoi* were for all emperors past and present.

Emperor worship in the eastern provinces was limited almost exclusively to the Hellenized areas. Temples, statues, priests, and altars are extremely rare in rural and non-Greek areas such as Mysia, Paphlagonia, Cappadocia, the Troad, Phrygia, eastern Lydia, and Pisidia. The rituals also followed Greek patterns; the Roman colonies followed Roman rituals and used Roman terms such as *flamines*.

The festivals connected with emperor worship involved the entire city. The procession generally began at the forum with sacrifices and followed a prescribed route with great pomp and celebration. Households sacrificed on small altars outside their homes as the procession passed. It ended at the imperial temple which was decorated with garlands. There animals were sacrificed and food—especially meat—was distributed to the people, and spectacles such as horseraces, gladiator battles, animal fights, and various competitions were held.

Emperor worship had 2 aspects: worship of the living emperor and worship of his apotheosis or genius. Caligula and Domitian apparently were the only rulers of the New Testament period who required their worship; the others, even Nero, only welcomed it.

The Romans indeed brought order into the world. "The imperial cult stabilized the religious order of the world. . . . along with politics and diplomacy, [emperor worship] constructed the reality of the Roman empire" (Price, p. 248). New Testament writers and especially the early church fathers were painfully conscious of the dominant power of emperor worship as a challenge to their belief that only Christ is Lord.

The Orphic Hymns, Apostolos N. Athanassakis (The Society of Biblical Literature), 1977; *Cults and Creeds in Graeco-Roman Egypt*, H. Idris Bell (Chicago: Ares Publishers, Inc.), 1957; *Gods and Heroes in the Athenian Agora*, John McK. Camp II (Princeton: American School of Classical Studies at Athens), 1980; *The Mysteries of Mithra*, Franz Cumont (New York: Dover Publications, Inc.), 1903; *Caesar and Christ*, Will Durant (New York: Simon and Schuster), 1944; *Mystery Religions in the Ancient World*, Joscelyn Godwin (San Francisco: Harper and Row, Publishers), 1981; *The Greeks and Their Gods*, W. K. C. Guthrie (Boston: Beacon Press), 1955; *The Oxford Classical Dictionary*, edited by N. G. L. Hammond and H. H. Scullard (Oxford: Clarendon Press), 1970; *National Museum*, Semni Karouzou (Athens: Ekdotike Athenon S. A.), 1980; *Everyday Life in the Roman Empire*, Joan Liversidge (New York: G. P. Putnam's Sons), 1976; *Paganism in the Roman Empire*, Ramsey MacMullen (New Haven: Yale University Press), 1981; *Römermuseum und Römerhaus Augst*, Max Martin (Basil: Römermuseum Augst), 1981; *The Romans and Their Gods in the Age of Augustus*, R. M. Ogilvie (New York: W. W. Norton and Co.), 1959; *Pompeii: AD 79*, John Ward-Perkins and Amanda Claridge (Boston: Museum of Fine Arts), 1978; *Roman Mythology*, Stewart Perowne (New York: Peter Bedrick Books), 1983; *The Harvest of Hellenism*, F. E. Peters (New York: Simon and Schuster), 1970; *Larousse Greek and Roman Mythology*, Joel Schmidt (New York: McGraw-Hill Book Co.), 1980; *Roman Imperial Sculpture*, D. E. Strong (London: Alec Tiranti), 1961.

▶**471 Zeus/Jupiter,** Roman, first century AD, found at Lyons. British Museum. The bronze statuette probably is a miniature replica of a Greek statue of about 300 BC. He once held a thunderbolt in his right hand and a scepter in his left. A small chlamys or scarf is draped over his left arm. His eyes were inlaid with silver. In early Greece Zeus was the god who illumined the sky and provided the clouds, rain, thunder, and lightning. Long before Roman times he had become the head of the Greek pantheon. He lived on Mount Olympus with the rest of the 12 principal gods. He fathered many deities through a complex web of unions. He came to be identified not only with Jupiter, the primary god of Rome, but with the primary gods of many lands and peoples as the Empire spread, who retained, however, their own distinct characteristics. Zeus came to be associated with virtually every area of life and was considered to be the father of all. He often is portrayed seated to symbolize his seat

of power, his upper body unclothed to symbolize that men can see him through his thoughts and through the universe, and his lower body often is clothed to symbolize that he is invisible in his appearance on earth (Menander). *Acts 14:12-13; 19:35.*

▲472 Jupiter Dolichenus and Juno Regina, bronze, third century AD. Copy in Roman-German Central Museum, Mainz; original in Kunsthistor. Museum, Vienna. The statuette was found in a wall at Url, Austria. Jupiter, the Roman power of the sky (who manifested himself in various ways), was identified with Zeus. Like Zeus, he was associated with the thunderbolt and with rain. Jupiter Optimus Maximus, the best and greatest of all the Jupiters, had his major temple in Rome. He was closely associated with various deities, but especially with Juno and Minerva. He was a god of war but also of peace and treaties. Jupiter Dolichenus was a local god of Hittite origin in Commagene. Dolichenus became associated with Jupiter as the cult spread west. The depiction in the photo is typical; he wears Roman military dress, holds a thunderbolt and a double axe (both missing), and stands on a bull. Juno, shown holding a staff in one hand and a patera in the other and standing on a deer, was an ancient Roman goddess who became identified with Hera, Zeus' primary wife. She was the goddess of women, particularly their sexual life and childbirth. Each woman had her own Juno, sort of a guardian angel. She was worshiped much more comprehensively, however, and became an important state goddess, one of the Capitoline triad with Jupiter and Minerva. Hera was somewhat similar to the Greeks; she was Zeus' legitimate wife and the guardian of marriage; these attributes were dominant during the Roman period. Earlier, she was connected with the moon, and in addition she probably in more ancient times was an earth-goddess whose power over procreation included agriculture as well as childbirth. *Texts: See photo 471.*

▼473 Poseidon with trident, sometimes identified as Zeus with thunderbolt. National Museum, Athens. The bronze statue was found in the sea off Cape Artemision where it had sunk with its ship along with other treasures some Roman had raided along with other spoils. It dates to the fifth century BC, is $82^{1}/_{4}$ inches (2.09 m.) in height, and is the work probably of the Attic sculptor Kalamis. He is about to throw the trident and is caught in the moment of pause, legs apart, shoulders balanced. He has curls on his forehead and his hair is tucked back in a plait. Poseidon was Zeus' brother, and as Zeus was god of the sky, Poseidon was god both of the sea and of fresh water. The Romans identified him with Neptune. His symbol was the trident, or 3-pronged fish-spear. Earthquakes were his work, and he was the god of horses for some reason probably connected with the people who introduced him into Greece; horses, in fact, were sacrificed to him along with bulls. Another brother was Hades (Pluto), god of the underworld. Demeter often was associated with him. Poseidon vied with Athena as the chief deity of Athens; the city worshiped him on the acropolis but his chief temple was on Cape Sounion, the first sight an Athenian saw as he approached his homeland by sea. His consort was Amphitrite.

▼474 Apollo with lyre. National Museum of Naples. His principal home was Delphi, with the island of Delos next in importance. He was god of beauty as seen in light, music, poetry, youth, moderation, prophesy (he caused the ecstatic frenzy that accompanied his prophets and prophetesses). He was considered by the Ionian Greeks to be their founder. As such, he was the embodiment of the Greek spirit. In fact, he was related to higher civilization. Originally, however, he may have come from Asia Minor; a number of important shrines to him existed there. He also was god of shepherds, archery, medicine (he fathered Aesculapius), and was Averter of Evil (though he also was believed to be the one responsible for sudden deaths). As god of prophecy he had several important shrines, but Delphi was the most important one. He revealed his secrets through the medium, who was possessed by him in ecstatic fashion. The Delphi priests considered a stone there, the *omphalos*, to be the center of the earth. In the photo Apollo is seen, characteristically, sitting on it.

▲475 Nude Apollo, found at Zifeth, Egypt, bronze, Roman, first century AD. British Museum. Apollo was made by Lucian to be the principal guide of Aeneas in his journeys to establish Rome, and Augustus claimed descent from him. Artemis was his twin sister and he often is associated with her. His youthful beauty brought him into many amorous liaisons, each of which likely reveals something about ancient history. As god of the arts he was called Apollo Musagetes. His bird was the swallow.

◄476 **Diana the Huntress,** whom the Romans identified with the Greek Artemis. National Museum of Naples. She was an Italian wood-goddess associated long before the first century with Artemis. Her cult was widespread through the Greco-Roman world. She was goddess of women, including childbirth. Artemis was an ancient Greek goddess of the earth, especially the forests, hills, and uncultivated areas. She, too, was goddess of women and also of fertility (yet a virgin goddess), and a huntress and goddess of hunters. The apparent conflict between her identity as a fertility goddess and a perpetual virgin is reconciled by the ancient belief that her virginity could be renewed by lustrations. She was protectress of all young, a logical assignment in light of her fertility aspects. Her special animal was the stag, 2 of which accompany her in the photo. She often was pictured with bow and arrows; the statue in the photo shows her with a fragment of a bow in her hand and the quiver can be seen over her shoulder. She was perhaps the greatest goddess worshiped in Greece, Asia Minor, and Crete. Larger animals generally were not sacrificed to her; goats and birds were common. She developed into a city goddess with her most important shrine being at Ephesus. Her earlier representations have her wearing a long dress, but by the first century she generally wore a short tunic as in the photo. Often she appears with Apollo. *Acts 19:24-41.*

◀477 **Artemis of Ephesus,** statue of the time of Domitian. Ephesus Museum. Her worship at Ephesus was different from the norm; there her surrender to love without restraint predominated over her perpetual chastity. The photo shows her in her Ephesian representation with many breasts (a few scholars identify them as eggs) which could succor those who were born through her gift of fertility. Her animal, the stag, is well represented, with one on each side of her and 3 rows of them running from her ankles to her waist and others on her headdress. Reliefs of other animals cover the statue: bees (her symbol), rams, crabs, bulls, and griffins. She performed miracles, cured the sick, regulated commerce, and aided in good decisions. She was identified with many local goddesses throughout the Roman world and often was confused with Hecate and Selene. Phrygia worshiped her as Cybele, Cappadocia as Ma, Crete as Britomartis. Her cult was closely associated with Demeter and Persephone, who also had fertility aspects. Artemis statues similar to this one have been found in many sites, including Caesarea Maritima (second century AD. *Acts 19:24-41.*

◄**478 Athena Parthenos,** second century AD. National Museum, Athens. It is a Roman copy of a fifth century BC lost original by Phidias which stood in the Athens Parthenon. The statue shown is of marble and is 3 feet, 3⅝ inches (1.007 m.) in height. The statue is not well done, but it is the closest representation we have to the original, in which more than a ton of gold was employed. Athena is wrapped in her peplos and wears on her breastplate the aegis symbol (see photo 479). Her helmet has 3 crests; the center one is mounted on a sphinx, while the outside ones are mounted on griffins. Her left hand holds a shield, which rests on the ground, and by which the sacred Acropolis snake is poised. Her right hand supports a winged Nike, symbol of victory. The serpent symbol is due to her earlier worship as a snake goddess. Two other symbols not in the statue shown were the olive tree and the owl, both prominent in her worship connected with the Athens acropolis. The owl was her symbol of wisdom. She had another name, Pallas, which probably means "girl." This Pallas likely was a warlike figure which combined with Athena. Thus, she was protectress of Athens, having won her role as that city's patron deity by defeating Poseidon for the honor. She also was a goddess of arts and crafts, weavers and potters, protectress of households and health, goddess of literature and arts, and ensurer of the impartiality of law. She was worshiped extensively. She was identified with Neith in Egypt, and the Romans identified her with Minerva, a logical melding since war was her primary attribute. Other attributes of Minerva were compatible with Athens as well: embodiment of elevated thought, wisdom, intelligence, literature, arts, and music.

See color photo 418.

► **479 Athena with aegis,** Archaic period, 530-520 BC. Acropolis Museum, Athens. Athena has across her shoulders and down her arms the *aegis,* which was an attribute but also an object. It is a goatskin bordered with snakes and sometimes with a Medusa head in the center (see photos 1, 478). With it she aided her heroes and dispersed her enemies. In the statue shown, she holds the snake's head outstretched toward a now-lost opponent that was impaled on her lance.

6.

▲482 **Hermes,** marble head of first century BC-first century AD. Excavated at Narona, Dalmatia. Ashmolean Museum, Oxford. He was an ancient god of the countryside. In ancient times he was represented by a pile of stones at a road juncture or other significant place; later an upright pillar replaced the pile; then a phallus was added to the stone to promote fertility; and eventually he emerged as a full figure. His promotion of fertility caused him to be linked with Aphrodite. Often he is pictured, even in New Testament times, by a pillar surmounted by a head and with a phallus protruding. He became the deity who guided travelers and, logically, dead souls to Hades. In full form he is pictured with winged sandals, staff, and broad-rimmed traveler's hat. He was the god of simple folk, especially of shepherds, the marketplace, assemblies, literature, inventor of the alphabet, music, the lyre, astronomy, and was servant and messenger of the gods. He also was god of doorways (as he was of road crossings), so his image or herm often was set up next to entrances. His cleverness gained him the honor of being the patron god of thieves. He was identified with the Egyptian Thoth and the Roman Mercury, who was strongly connected with commercial activity. Thoth was the god who weighed souls at death, and he invented writing.

▲480 **Athena, Aphrodite, and nymph,** gilt-bronze mirror back. Roman, from Asia Minor or Syria, first-second centuries AD. British Museum. Athena at left leans on her shield and spear. She is dressed in a sheer garment and wears a crested helmet. Behind her is an owl perched on a stand on which are carved various symbols including a lobster and serpents. Aphrodite is seated and conversing with a nymph. A sacred tree grows between them. In the space below the ground is a torch, doves, and a mirror.

▶481 **Mars,** from Tivoli, Hadrian's palace, from an original of the fifth century BC. Tivoli Museum. The statue in photo 483 shows Mars as a bearded figure in accordance with early tradition; this statue has him young and nude as he generally was depicted later. He wears a helmet, supports a shield on a tree stump, and once carried a sword in his right hand.

▼ **483 Mars,** second century AD statue of type image that stood in the temple of Mars Ultor (Avenger) in the Augustus Forum, Rome. Capitoline Museum. Only the head and torso are ancient; the rest is poorly restored. Mars was identified with the Greek Ares. He was not worshiped widely in Greece, but the Romans held him in high esteem; he was chief god next to Jupiter. His festivals came at the beginning and end of the campaigning season. His sacred animals were the wolf and woodpecker; dogs were sacrificed to him. His offspring who appear in mythology are vicious and ferocious fighters. Along with his war image, he also was associated with agricultural functions. He was associated with Aphrodite in a passionate love affair.

▲ **484 Serapis,** Alexandrian god assimilated to Zeus. Bronze, first century AD after a style that dates to fourth century BC Greece. British Museum. The god's origins are disputed, but his principal worship appears to have arisen from the temple in Memphis, Egypt which was over the tombs of the Apis bulls. The name Serapis likely is a shortened form of Osorapis (Osiris and Apis). The Ptolemies apparently established the cult of Serapis as part of their plan to rule Egypt. Serapis thus was an imperial deity; he was worshiped along with Isis and Harpocrates (Horus). The Serapeum in Alexandria was considered to be one of the wonders of the world. The worship, essentially created by the Greeks, combined attributes of both Greek and Egyptian deities. His facial features resemble those of Zeus and sometimes he was depicted with a staff or scepter as Zeus carried, and other names attached to Zeus such as Helios and Amon-Re were attached to him. He absorbed Aesculapius' healing powers, and he also was identified with Dionysus and Helios. He also took some of Osiris' features, and so was a savior god of healing, oracles, and the future life. His worship became widespread throughout the Greco-Roman world; a large Serapeum has been excavated at Puteoli.

▼486 Demeter, Persephone, and Triptolemus, votive relief from the Telesterion of Eleusis, about 440 BC, 7 feet, 11 inches (2.413 m.) in height. National Museum, Athens. The relief depicts an ancient fertility myth. Demeter is giving wheat ears to Triptolemus while Persephone puts a wreath on his head. Originally the relief was covered; the ears of wheat were of metal, probably gold. Various fertility goddesses who once were local became identified with one another as civilization spread. Demeter was one of these; in New Testament times she was identified particularly with the Egyptian Isis and the Roman Ceres. Eleusis wanted to believe she was Zeus' wife, so she also was identified with Hera. Demeter's fertility function came to identify her as well as a goddess connected with death and the underworld (*chthonioi*), as was typical. Hence, the animal offered to her in sacrifice was the pig, along with honey and fruits of the earth. She was foremost the earth goddess; the myth reflected in the relief includes an annual life-death cycle. Her followers came to believe she also had the power to grant immortality. To that end believers went through mystery rites of purification and initiation.

▲485 Serapis, clay, from Asia Minor, second century AD. Roman-German Central Museum, Mainz. He often is depicted with the modius (basket) on his head, which is a symbol either of fertility or of an opening into the highest part of the body. In full-figured representations of Serapis he is shown seated with the underworld 3-headed dog Cerberus beside him, attributes from Hades. Perhaps the fact that his major temple was in Alexandria, a port city, accounts for his becoming the protector of sea travelers. His was a mystery cult, and cult meals figured prominently in his worship.

◄487 Isis, Roman, first century BC-first century AD. British Museum. An Egyptian goddess, she was the wife of Osiris and the mother of Horus; but she became the most widely worshiped goddess in the Greco-Roman world. Identified with many fertility goddesses, one hymn addresses her as "O Thou of countless names," while another asserts that people in various lands call her Astarte, Nanaia, Artemis, Leto, Great Mother, Hera, Aphrodite, Hestia, Rhea, and Demeter; it was, of course, a hymn of a devotee. Her worship became thoroughly Hellenized in terms of architecture and language, but the Eastern mystery rites remained with her, including holy water from the Nile, individual rituals, and the public fertility cult drama. She had many temples, including Rome, Corinth, and a well-preserved one at Pompeii. She apparently unseated Serapis as the chief deity in the temples where they both were worshiped. A fresco from Pompeii shows a worship ceremony of Isis. It takes place outside of her temple. A choir is arranged ascending the steps on each side of the priest, who descends down the steps toward an altar at the bottom. The sacrifice did not include animals, but rather milk, honey, and herbs. The sacrifice was followed by a sacred dance or perhaps drama. One of her symbols was the sistrum, a musical instrument (see photos 586-587), which is represented on many funeral monuments. The representation in the photo has her with Greek features (cf. photo 489) of a curl on each side of her face, without a headdress, and with Greek clothing. Isis religion stimulated strong emotions among devotees.

▲488 Isis, with Greek and Egyptian symbols. Marble, 150-180 AD. Bode Museum, Berlin. This representation is more Egyptian than photo 487, which is Greek. Here she wears a long garment with an Egyptian-style knot at the breast. Her headdress is a Sabazios hand (see photo 526). She holds a cobra in her right hand and entwined around her arm, and she carries a basket in her left hand. Her priestesses dressed as the goddess herself dressed, and as they walked in procession they shook the sistrum, whose vibrations represented all the world's vibrations, those powerful creative forces. In the other hand was carried a milk pitcher or a model of a breast to represent her nurturing power. Devotion to her was easy, for she was warm and represented the best aspects of a lover, wife, and mother.

▼ **490 Nimes Venus.** Maison Carée Museum, Nimes. She was an obscure goddess who was connected with kitchen gardens but was not, apparently, a fertility goddess. Before the New Testament period she became identified with Aphrodite. The photo shows her just after she has arisen from the foam (an Aphrodite myth) and is pulling her clothing around her, her hair already bound. Augustus claimed descent from her, part of his propaganda campaign that involved Virgil's Aeneas myth, and her cult spread widely. She absorbed the cult of Ariadne.

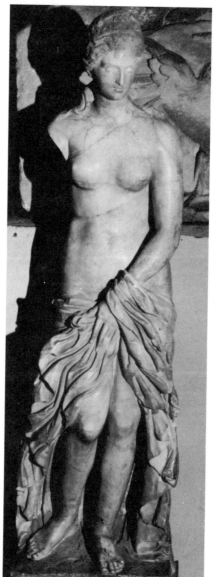

▲ **489 Ceres,** relief on Jupiter column. Roman-German Landesmuseum, Cologne. The column portion has 1 side unfinished where it was against a building; the other 3 sides contain representatives of various gods and goddesses. A figure of Jupiter stood on top. These columns often were pillars in the open. They may have been tied to the veneration of sacred trees. Ceres was an Italian corn goddess early identified with Demeter and for most of the Greco-Roman world completely absorbed into her. Ceres' principal temple was in Rome. She holds in her right hand sheaves of grain and in her left a voyager's staff.

▲ **491 Venus with jewelry,** bronze. Römerhaus Museum, Augst, Switzerland. The goddess wears a high diadem and gold wire jewelry around her neck and wrists. Other jewelry adorns her upper arms. Overall height, 7⁵/₁₆ inches (18.7 cm.). She was often portrayed with her clothing tied in a knot low on her hips. Aphrodite was a powerful goddess who protected marriages, maintained harmony between spouses, granted fertility, and aided in births. Her promotion of fertility was unpredictable, however, and the passion she aroused often could not be stopped, causing infidelity, revelry, and every kind of vice connected with sex. Multi-seeded fruit were dedicated to her. She herself was caught in the web, for she was passionately in love with Adonis.

▼492 Aphrodite/Venus with her dove symbol worn as a hat. British Museum. Copy of Greek original of about 100 BC. The dove was a symbol of marital fidelity; other such symbols attached to her were the swan and pigeon. One of her principal sanctuaries was at Corinth. Prostitutes considered her to be their patron deity. Her domain differed some at various shrines; at some locations she was associated with seafarers, or with war, but generally she was disassociated with war.

494 Aphrodite, Pan, and Eros, found at Delos, marble, 4 feet, 4 inches (1.32 m.) high, about 100 BC. National Museum, Athens. The sculpture is from a group that was carved for a Syrian merchant on Delos. Aphrodite, whose hair is bound with a cloth, fights goat-footed Pan off with her sandal, while Eros has his hand on Pan's horn pushing him away. Eros was assimilated with the Roman Cupid.

See also color photo 414.

▲493 Aphrodite/Venus of Rhodes, first-century BC copy of famous work of Doidalsas, 19⁵/₁₆ (.49 cm.) high. Rhodes Museum. She is portrayed either at the moment she has been disturbed by a noise or while taking a bath. She holds her hair parted and turns her head. The statue is not considered to be an excellent sculpture, but it is effective nonetheless. It is polished to a sheen and was of the type that adorned public gardens or those of wealthy homes. Representations of her emerging from the sea, often with attendants holding a tunic, are common due to the myth of her origin from the sea's foam.

◄**495 Herm,** bronze, end of second century BC, 40¾ inches (103.5 cm.). J. Paul Getty Museum. The herm, produced by the Greek artist Boethos, reflects an intermediate stage in the development of Hermes (see photo 482). The herm originally was a pile of rocks, then a pillar; then a phallus was added to the pillar somewhat as protrudes from this example. Then a head was added. Finally, a herm's features were more fully developed. Sometimes a herm had Pan's features (Hermes was Pan's son). Pan typically had the head (or sometimes human head with goat ears and horns), legs, and hooves of a goat. Hermes' head here is fully developed and shows features of divinity. Sometimes shoulder projections were added to hold wreaths.

▲**496 Pan with a he-goat,** mirror cover, bronze. Benaki Museum, Athens. Pan has a man's body and a goat's legs. He pushes against the goat's head with his left hand. He wears a cape and carries a wine bucket. The tree behind him represents the woods, his domain. Due to his name (*pan* = all) he came to be perceived as a universal god.

▲**497 Cave of Pan**, relief from second half of fourth century BC. National Museum, Athens. Pan has been given the attributes of Zeus; thus his worshipers asserted him to be the universal, or head, god. His shrines were caves scattered throughout Asia; the one shown in the photo represents his cave in the acropolis of Athens above the agora. Pan was capable of inducing panic and terror and he sent nightmares, but his domain was mountains, caves, and lonely places, which he loved. This association was proper, since he was associated with shepherds. The flute, which also is associated with shepherds, was his instrument. He was a fertility god with brutal sexual power, but also was physician and prophet, and represented the power of nature.

▶**498 Young satyr with goat**, second century AD copy of a Hellenistic prototype. Agora Museum, Athens. The satyr wears a goatskin, thus maintaining his mythical connection with the goat, and he holds a goat by the horns. The goat origins can also be seen in his face. Ancient writers often confused satyrs with sileni, whose traits were similar but more often associated with the horse. Sileni were pictured as perpetually drunk and often as companion to Dionysus. The Roman name for the satyr was faun.

▲499 Dionysus on satyr's shoulders, Naples Museum. Dionysus holds cymbals while Satyrus is eating grapes. Satyrs were wildlife spirits who roamed the woods and hills; Dionysus was associated with such areas (see photos 502-503). They generally had animal characteristics, more often the goat characteristics of Pan, but later were almost fully human. They were mischievous and were considered to be brothers of the nymphs (see photos 504-506). Dionysus is depicted as a young boy.

▼500 Faun from House of the Faun, Pompeii. Photo is of copy in courtyard of house, bronze. National Museum of Naples. The Romans identified fauns with satyrs; though their mythology differs, their characteristics are virtually the same. Though a human figure, this faun shows goatlike characteristics of budding horns, pointed ears, and short tail. He throws back his head, snaps his fingers, and moves his feet as though dancing the special dance of the satyrs. The satyr personified abandon and pleasure.

◄501 Priapus, erotic god of fertility. Bronze, $4^{13}/_{16}$ inches (12.3 cm.), first-second centuries AD. J. Paul Getty Museum. Priapus' attributes are fruits and his phallus, the sources of life. His phallus always is depicted as very large. He is shown here wearing a thick skull cap and a long, loose tunic. The fruit is supported by his excessively large phallus. Due to his mythology, he usually was portrayed as misshapen. He was especially loved by simple people, and his figure was prominent in brothels. He was the son of Dionysus and Aphrodite; he also was identified with Pan. His statue often was placed in gardens where his powers would influence their fertility.

See also color photo 414.

▼**502 Orpheus among animals,** clay dish. Roman-German Landesmuseum, Cologne. Orpheus is the central figure. He is dressed in a short tunic and wears a mantle thrown back as a cape, a Phrygian hat, and boots. He is leaning back and a tree is beside him. His left hand rests on a lyre which is set on an altar. He is surrounded by many animals; they were subject to his charm: lions, cattle, sheep, dogs, horses, deer, boars, a centaur, an eros (called Phanes, an important figure in Orphism), and various other symbols. The animals are the same ones seen in Dionysiac celebrations, but with Orpheus they are tamed and calm; with Dionysus they are wild. Orpheus' origin is disputed, but he is thought to be from Thrace or perhaps was a Greek living in Thrace. It is his figure that most directly affected Christian art representation of the Good Shepherd theme, though the symbol is widespread through the ancient world. He was a poet and singer who set forth the Orphic views in his songs. A collection of Orphic hymns, which may have been dated from the fifth century BC to the fourth century AD, extol Orpheus' virtues and apparently were used in a mystery initiation. The hymns reveal a close affinity between the Orphics and Dionysus, who eventually became the chief Orphic god. Some scholars feel that Orpheus actually was a reformer of Dionysiac religion.

▲**503 Orpheus floor mosaic,** out of a house in Miletus. Pergamum Museum, Berlin. The top register shows Orpheus as poet and singer holding a lyre and surrounded by animals (see photo 502), while the lower register shows Eros figures hunting the wild animals. The 2 contrasting registers may picture the contrast between Orphism and Dionysiac worship. Orphism arose in the Greek Archaic period and evolved as both a philosophy and religion. Orphism likely reflected little of Orpheus himself, however. Out of the Greek myths they constructed a view that included the concept that people have within them both a divine spark (the soul) and an evil nature (the body); the body is a prison of the soul. This view apparently lay behind their abstenance from meat. Upon death, those who were not purified on earth entered the Nether World; the initiated entered a realm of happiness. These fortunate ones were taught the proper words to speak upon arrival in the afterlife. Orphic beliefs, in fact, had several important similarities to Christianity, including communion with the god, purity of life, and immortality. Orphism, however, projected the Path of Knowledge as the way to happiness, and Orphics believed that the uninitiated were reincarnated, while the initiated went on to "Lethe."

▶505 Hercules and a nymph, a bronze mirror cover from Corinth, about 300 BC. British Museum. Nymphs generally were depicted nude or nearly nude, as was Hercules. The nymph has a light tunic thrown across her shoulder; Hercules holds his symbol, a pelt, across his arm (see photo 516). Nymphs were good, but they also had the characteristics of the satyrs and were associated with Pan. Artemis, too, often was accompanied by nymphs. They could inspire men and women to prophesy, grant fertility, and aid in great accomplishments.

▲504 Nymph seated on a rock, Rhodian work, first century BC. Rhodes Museum. Nymphs were female spirits that inhabited trees, streams, woods, and even cities and regions. They were mortal though long-lived, young, and beautiful; they were deities who may be compared to fairies. In addition to the local nymphs, whose names reflected their localities, there were nymphs named by function. The Nereids were sea nymphs, the Naiads inhabited fresh running water, the Dryads were forest dwellers, the Alceids lived in swamps, the Oreads lived in mountains, and the Hamadryads lived in woods; the list could continue.

▼506 Nereid riding a sea monster. National Museum of Naples. The Nereids lived in a palace in the depths of the sea with their father, Nereus, an ancient sea god who was depicted in ancient art with varying shapes and characteristics. The Nereids each personified a form of the sea's surface but they were usually perceived in mermaid form. The most famous Nereid was Amphitrite, Poseidon's wife.

▼507 Cybele on chariot pulled by lions, bronze. Metropolitan Museum, New York. She was the great Anatolian mother goddess who granted fertility, cured diseases, protected in war, provided oracles, and generally cared for her people. She became associated with Demeter by the Greeks and all the other attendant associations followed (see photos 486-489).

The photo shows her characteristically seated on a throne on a four-wheeled wagon pulled by lions. She wears a crown with three towers that represent her protection of the cities, and carries a patera in her left arm, a cymbal in her right hand.

Her cult was officially taken to Rome and included in its worship about 205 BC. Her young lover Attis (see photo 524) was incorporated into her worship, which was a mystery religion of which we know little. It included a ritual meal, a descent into an underground chamber, and the genitals of a bull. The *taurobolium* was performed with initiates, who went into a pit or ditch over which a grate was placed. A bull was sacrificed on the grate and its blood released to fall onto the initiate below. This procedure was part of other mystery religions as well. Her worship was orgiastic and ecstatic; it involved the worship of the female principle in nature. Due to similar functions in some areas, Cybele worship became associated with Dionysus. Dionysus' devotees considered her to be a servant to him, while worshipers of Cybele had her clearly the superior to her lover Attis. Her worship also became entangled in Mithraism; she appealed to women, while Mithra appealed to men. In imitation of the myth of Attis, male devotees of Cybele sometimes castrated themselves while in the throes of ecstatic possession, after which they became her priests or attendants and dressed ornately in women's clothes. At least in Rome, her annual procession had her lifesized figure being carried to the noise of musical instruments and with libation bowls. Pessinus in Phrygia was her main sanctuary.

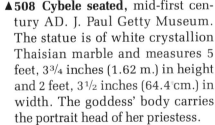

▲508 Cybele seated, mid-first century AD. J. Paul Getty Museum. The statue is of white crystallion Thaisian marble and measures 5 feet, 3¾ inches (1.62 m.) in height and 2 feet, 3½ inches (64.4 cm.) in width. The goddess' body carries the portrait head of her priestess.

▶**509 Dionysus enthroned,** fresco from Pompeii. National Museum of Naples. Called Bacchus by the Romans, the god sits on the throne nude except for a cloth laying across his legs. He is crowned with an ivy wreath and holds a wine cup in his right hand, a thyrsus in his left. His feet rest on a footstool. The throne is flanked on its left by a dog and on its right by a tambourine. The rise of his worship in Greek and Roman lands is an enigma to scholars; the myths seem to indicate that he forced his way into people's lives against the opposition of regional leaders. His celebrations took place both during the day and at night; they were joyous at times but gruesome at other times; they included wild revelry and sexual license, ecstatic behavior, and thanksgiving for the earth and animals. Women were the most frequent worshipers, perhaps because the utter freedom Dionysus granted was a release to Greek women, whose lives were confined. Participants in a revelry wore fawnskins and each carried a thyrsus, Dionysus' emblem. It was a long rod with a tip of ivy, vine, or pine cone on its end. Some carried snakes on their arms or entwined in their hair. The beat of the tympanum and the strain of the flute aroused their passions, further aroused by their own cries and shouts. They had a sense of union with the divine; this fact was crucial to the Greeks, for they believed deity was the only way to immortality. The ecstatic worshipers saw visions and, using their bare hands or thyrsi, they fell onto animals, tore them apart, and ate their raw flesh. The scouring of women was part of the ritual. The priest of Dionysus chased "maenads," who were women under the throes of ecstasy; if he caught one she might be treated violently. Plutarch recorded that one was killed in his lifetime (an act more common in ancient times). The wine,

which was so important that Dionysus/Bacchus was considered to be the god of wine, was representative of all life-giving fluids, whether blood, sap, or semen. Dionysiac religion was spread throughout the Empire. Many of the celebrations lacked the violence toward animals and humans that was common in earlier worship (local authorities purged them out),

but the other elements were retained. As Cybele was identified with other earth goddesses, Dionysus was identified with Thammuz, Osiris, and others. Shorn of his wilder elements but retaining the sexual license and revelry, he became associated with joyous living, games, festivals, and the patron god of the theater. His processions displayed the phallus.

▶**510, 511 Portion of Dionysus floor mosaic,** Roman-German Landesmuseum, Cologne. The insets show scenes from myths and stories about Dionysus. Photo 510 shows, from left to right, Dionysus with wreath and cape playing a flute with a maenad who is draped with a cloth and holds a lyre; Dionysus with thyrsus wearing a wreath and with an animal skin thrown back across his shoulders, sitting on a stool drinking wine from a large cup; and bearded Dionysus wearing a wreath and an animal skin across his shoulder as he dances with a maenad, perhaps an initiate (compare figure in color photos 412-413). Photo 511, from top left clockwise, shows a dove (animal figures run around the perimeter of the mosaic); the infant Dionysus with thyrsus riding a horse, a common theme; a drunken Dionysus leaning against a Silenus who carries a thyrsus hooked to the handle of a wine bowl; a faun or Pan with a wine bucket on a pole leading a goat (Pan often is depicted having sexual intercourse with a goat); the infant Dionysus as a cupid riding a lion; a tiger; and Dionysus with thyrsus holding a bunch of grapes which a boy reaches for while a maenad plays the double flute. He probably originated in Thrace. Thracian and Macedonian women were strong devotees.

◀**512 Janus, the double-headed god.** *Aes grave* coin, ca. 240 BC. Milwaukee Museum of Art. He was a major Roman god whose two faces reflect his ability to see both past and future and exercised power over both heaven and earth. He was the door god (doors look both ways) and was the protector of Rome. The doors of Janus' temple were left open during any period in which Rome was at war since he was out fighting for Rome, and closed during peacetime since he was protecting the city.

▲513 Hephaestus, god of metalworkers, bronze statuette, second century AD, from Mainz region. Roman-German Central Museum, Mainz. He is shown bearded, with long tunic, the blacksmith's oval cap, and metalworking hammer. Called Vulcan by the Romans, Hephaestus' largest temple stood next to the workers' district of ancient Athens on the edge of the Agora (see photos 399-401). His early history was as god of fire, especially volcanic fire; the connection with the forge is readily apparent. He became the god of metalworkers and eventually of all craftsmen. He was both god of craftsmen and craftsman to the gods of Olympus. The fact that he was lame in mythology and often is pictured that way may indicate that in early Greek society lame men often became craftsmen. Aphrodite sometimes is considered to be his wife, due to the connection between good craftsmanship and beauty. Vulcan was the ancient Roman god of volcanic fire; he was worshiped especially in great craft centers and may have been the chief god of Ostia.

▶514 Tyche, goddess of the city, second century AD. Brussels Museum. The monumental statue shows Tyche (Roman Fortuna) in characteristic pose dressed as a matron and holding a cornucopia in her arm. Her headdress represents a walled city. Sometimes she was depicted holding a rudder, to signify guidance. Her name means luck or fortune, which may or may not include skill. The Greeks and Romans held varying views of her; some considered her capricious, a reflection of life itself, while others sought her good graces. Her protection was especially sought by people about to engage on risky ventures, such as traveling. Every person had a Tyche, but cities also had them. The earliest city Tyche seems to have been connected with Antioch and Alexandria; by the New Testament period the city tyche was common, especially in Asia Minor and the East; they had surnames of the city under the tyche's protection. Fortuna was an ancient Italian goddess who brought fertility. At times, and especially later in the Empire, she was identified with Isis.

▲515 Victoria, Greek Nike, bronze statuette, 24³/₄ inches (63 cm.) in height, third century AD. Römerhaus Museum, Augst, Switzerland. She holds aloft a shield which carries the bust of Jupiter/Zeus in relief. The victorious goddess stands on a globe of the heavens on which are stars and a half-moon inset in silver. The goddess guided gods and heroes to succeed in their exploits. She is shown as winged, with another wing attached to the hem of her short tunic. She often was associated with Athena, and sometimes their names were combined to Athena Nike. She was distinct from Athena, however, and was associated with Mars more often than Jupiter. The army was especially devoted to her, as were emperors and athletes, for obvious reasons; but others who sought victory in other endeavors such as craftsmanship or beauty also worshiped her.

▼516 Hercules as young man, gold-gilt bronze colossal statue, second century AD Roman version of original from theater of Pompey. Vatican Museum. Hercules is shown with his characteristic attributes of club, lion skin, and apples of Hesperides, which were connected with his myths. He is one of the better-known group of deities who were mortals or semi-mortal offspring of the union between deities and mortals, the heroes of myth. "Hercules" is the Roman pronunciation of the Greek Heracles; the name connects him with Hera. He may have been a historical figure whose exploits formed the basis for much elaboration into the twelve labors famous in mythology. He was the most widely worshiped of the heroes; his shrines appear throughout the empire. Strictly speaking, heroes were worshiped differently than deities, but sometimes he was worshiped as a god and sometimes identified with local gods. His successful exploits brought him renown as a conqueror of evil, a fighter for justice, and a model of courage. Many cities and peoples believed he was their founder and fathered their ancestors. Roman merchants gave him homage due to Hercules' wide travels in which he overcame incredible obstacles; indeed, they often paid him a tithe of their profits. His unusual popularity is due in part to the fact that he, a mortal, succeeded through courage, strength, wisdom, and cunning to be admitted to Olympus; thus he offered hope to the ordinary Greek. The fact that he is depicted as a sexual athlete, a glutton, and a heavy drinker only endeared him to the people. In some worship centers, women were excluded. His cult was the first foreign one in Rome.

world, second century AD copy of a Hellenistic original, marble. National Museum of Naples. Called Atlantas by the Romans, Atlas supports on his shoulders the celestial globe. A bas-relief of the signs of the zodiac encircle the globe. The appearance of the universe as a sphere indicates the progress of science, influenced by astrology, in ancient Greece. Atlas was an ancient Titan who was cursed to hold the sky up. The Atlas Mountains in North Africa took their name from him. *Matthew 24:14; Luke 4:5; Revelation 16:4.*

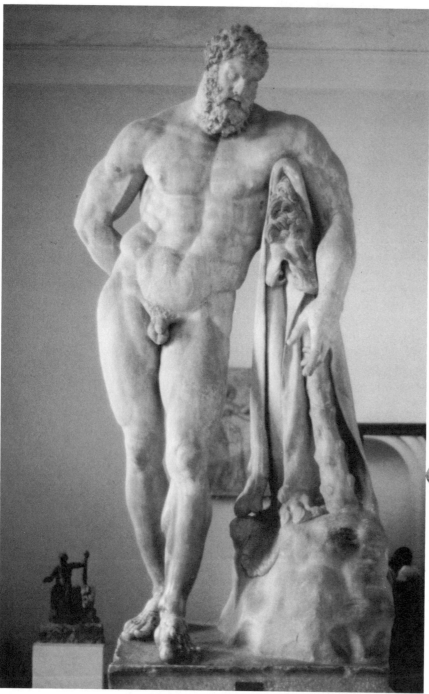

▲**514 Farnese Hercules,** marble, 10 feet, 5 inches (3.17 m.) in height. National Museum of Naples. The gigantic statue, found in the Baths of Caracalla, is a version by Glykon of Athens (1st century BC) of an earlier work by Lysippos (340-320 BC). Part of the extremities are restored. Hercules, weary from his labors, rests on his club over which is draped a lion skin. ("Farnese" refers to collector, Pope Paul III.)

▼519 **Oceanus, father of the river gods.** Capitoline Museum. Though various rivers, streams, and other bodies of water each had their own local deities, all of them were connected subterraneously by Oceanus. His water source was believed to exist where the sun sets and at the outer reaches of the world. Earlier than the New Testament period his cosmic power was more greatly emphasized; by the New Testament period his power was more focused on the oceans. The representation of the river god as reclining came from an ancient Greek tradition which was elaborated by artists in Egypt who developed the flowing style for the Nile god. The pattern became attached to all river gods and Oceanus.

▲520 **Centaur being tamed by a baccante,** from Villa of Cicero in Pompeii, third style of art, Augustan period. National Museum of Naples. By the New Testament period, centaurs had become connected with Dionysiac worship, as they represented the animal desires and barbaric behavior. The baccante flies in the air above the centaur's back as she clings to his hair. She holds a thyrsus in her right hand.

▼521 **Centaur, half horse, half man;** Roman, AD 90, height 5 feet, 3¾ inches (1.62 m.). J. Paul Getty Museum. The statue is made of rosso antico and stood in a palace of Domitian. Centaurs roamed the woods and mountains of parts of Greece; they were lustful and loved wine. Most scholars believe their myth arose due to the horsemanship of the Thessalians who seemed to be one with their mounts. Some centaurs were famous in the ancient world, the best-known of which was Chiron, a wise teacher of philosophers who also knew medicine.

▼523 Men, bronze statuette from Anatolia, probably second century AD. Museum of Art and Archaeology, University of Missouri—Columbia. Men was a lunar god, often represented on horseback, who was worshiped widely in Anatolia. Here he wears a Phrygian peaked cap, pants tucked into his boots, a sleeved tunic over which is a heavier outer garment belted at the waist and below the waist to hold a fold. His cape is attached by a clasp on the right shoulder, and the two horns or a crescent moon is shown over each shoulder. Men evolved into a mystery religion with affinities to Mithraism and with a sacred marriage (to the god) ceremony. Men was "the man in the moon" who was responsible for the impregnation of women. He became assimilated to Attis, the inferior consort of Cybele, but earlier he had been an important god in a number of localities. His symbols, which represent fertility, were the peacock, pomegranate, and pinecone, one of which he holds in his right hand. He also was a god of healing, gave oracles, and protected tombs.

▲522 Luna, Roman moon goddess. Bronze, first-second centuries AD, provenance unknown. Roman-German Central Museum, Mainz. She is dressed in a long Greek belted tunic, stands on a celestial globe, holds a torch in one hand and a cloth in the other. The cloth forms a sky canopy over her head and gives the impression that she is floating. She has a crescent on her head, and her face is radiant. She was identified with the Greek Selene, whose love affairs were frequent; both sometimes were identified with Diana-Artemis. Her waxing and waning depicted her dual nature of presiding over birth and death, growing and blighting crops; and she was the stopping-place after death from where the dead either went on to a higher world or fell back to earth in a new life.

▲ **524 Attis with wings,** bronze statuette with pupils inset in silver, from Anatolia, first-third centuries AD. Museum of Art and Archaeology, University of Missouri—Columbia. Attis was the inferior consort of Cybele. Here he is shown in a long garment that is slit so that parts of it can be pulled around the legs and clasped to fit like pants. He is shown here not as her consort but as her youthful attendant. He is described in various ways in the myths. He meets a violent end and is resurrected in the typical fertility cycle. Sometimes he castrates himself; he was the prototype of the Cybele eunuchs (see photo 507). In the photo his tunic is pulled open to reveal that in his reborn state his self-mutilation has been reversed; as a child his sex drive no longer is a source of suffering. He was given official status during Claudius' reign and by AD 150 had equal status with Cybele. The worship included eating and drinking from the sacred implements of tambourine and cymbal.

▼ **525 Sabazios hand.** Roman-German Central Museum, Mainz. Sabazios, a Thrace-Phrygian deity who was known to the Greeks at least by the fifth century BC, often was identified with Attis. Gifts of this hand, giving the "benedictio latina" sign, often were made to him. The numerous symbols are to avert the Evil Eye. The hand shown in the photo is fairly simple, with only a serpent (Sabazios' symbol), two animals, and a yoke. Some hands are covered with various animals, divinities, and symbols such as cornucopias, cymbals, vessels, etc.; some have Sabazios seated in the palm of the hand and wearing a tunic, trousers, and a Phrygian cap. Each symbol belonged to a deity, but in this context they probably were emotional appeals to magic. Additionally, to some devotees at least, he was a loftier god; and the symbols had to do with his transporting them to eternal heights after death.

▲ **526 Genius or Lar,** bronze statuette, provenance unknown, second century AD, Roman-German Central Museum, Mainz. The Genius often was portrayed in the form of a serpent, but this one is in the pose of a Lar. While a Lar was the spirit of the dead ancestor (see photos 385-387), the Genius was somewhat like a guardian angel. Every person had a Genius, but the Genius of the head of the family was honored as the principal one of the family. Great people, especially the emperor, had correspondingly great Geniuses, and even the gods had their Geniuses. *Romans 8:38; Colossians 2:18.*

► **527 Apotheosis of Emperor Antonius Pius and Faustina,** bas-relief on the pedestal of a pillar of Antonius Pius (AD 138-161), from Rome, marble. Original in Vatican Museum; photo is of copy in Roman-German Central Museum, Mainz. The emperor and his wife are the figures being carried on the wings of the deity. They hold scepters and are flanked by eagles, symbol of the empire. The male figure at lower left is a personification of the Campus Martius; he holds an obelisk. Roma, showing some of the characteristics of Minerva, is at lower right. Though the second century, the relief illustrates the concept of the divinization of the emperors. Though the identification of kings with gods was foreign to Italy, it was a common feature of Eastern religion and culture. The emperors, beginning with Julius Caesar, adopted the practice and used it to enhance their reigns. The belief

and this representation had some affinities with the belief in the emperor's genius. *Texts: See photo 526.*

◄ **528, 529, 530, 531 Coins showing the Graces.** Milwaukee Museum of Art. These allegorical deities originally numbered only three (Splendor, Abundance, and Jollity) but increased over the years. *Fides* (528), Good Faith, is shown standing, with a plate of goods in her left hand and a grain in her extended right hand. Her common symbol was a pair of gloved hands, which represented solemn agreement. *Hilaritas* (529), Rejoicing, is seated and holds a branch in her right hand. *Concordia* (530), Harmony, is standing with a child holding to her; she holds an olive branch in her left arm and a pomegranate in her outstretched right hand, symbols of fertility and peace. She personified agreement between citizens, cities, etc. *Indulgentia* (531), Mercy, is seated on a throne of power and holds a symbol of mercy outstretched. *1 Corinthians 13:2, 13; James 4:16; 5:11.*

◄ **532 Mithra slaying the bull,** bas-relief, second century AD. Vatican Museum. Mithra is in Persian dress and Phrygian cap. He plunges his knife into the bull's neck; the blood brings regeneration. A dog, companion to Mithra, is seen; a serpent and a scorpion, representing unclean demons, are sucking the bull's blood and the life from its vitals. Thus all of the life-giving fluids represented by the bull's death are under attack by Evil to steal them from mankind.

► **533 Mithra slaying the bull,** bas-relief. Capitoline Museum. Mithra is shown in his cave with the common animal symbols described in photo 532. In addition, the Genius of the Day is seen faintly at the left with lighted torch; the Genius of the Night is at the right with his torch extinguished and pointing downward. In each upper corner is a head representing the sun and the moon. The killing of the bull indicates the victory of the day (Mithra is the sun-god) over the night (the bull).

▼ 534 Mithra slaying the bull, large statue somewhat undersized. Capitoline Museum. Portions of the sculpture have been broken away. Mithra seizes the bull by the left horn, while in photos 532-533 he seizes it by the nostril and throat. Mithra was an ancient Iranian god allied with Ahura Mazda. Imported into the West, he became a major god with such titles as Lord of Light, God of Truth, Savior, Victorious, and Warrior. His promise of immortality struck a note among Romans. Mithraism was a mystery religion, but it was thoroughly transformed from its Eastern origin into a Latinized version. It had 7 initiation levels: Raven, Bride, Soldier, Lion, Persian, Sun Courier, and Father. They practiced the taurobolium ritual (see photo 507). Metrical texts and hymns have been discovered in the Mithraeum under the Church of Santa Prisca in Rome. Mithraism had some gnostic views and astrology was interwoven in its beliefs. Boundless Time, called by various names, was at the top of the pantheon of Mithraism.

Mithra, the god of light, occupied the middle position between hell and heaven, so he was an accessible mediator. The origin of the earth was explained by means which sounded scientific at the time; the various deities of the Greco-Roman world were woven into its theology; it taught a heaven and a hell, which also was had its pantheon of deities, some of whom escaped from

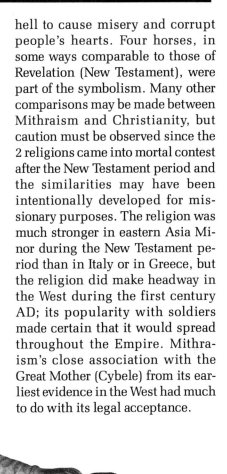

hell to cause misery and corrupt people's hearts. Four horses, in some ways comparable to those of Revelation (New Testament), were part of the symbolism. Many other comparisons may be made between Mithraism and Christianity, but caution must be observed since the 2 religions came into mortal contest after the New Testament period and the similarities may have been intentionally developed for missionary purposes. The religion was much stronger in eastern Asia Minor during the New Testament period than in Italy or in Greece, but the religion did make headway in the West during the first century AD; its popularity with soldiers made certain that it would spread throughout the Empire. Mithraism's close association with the Great Mother (Cybele) from its earliest evidence in the West had much to do with its legal acceptance.

535 Bull-slaying Nike (Victory). Glyptothek, Munich. The fragment is from Trajan's forum. Some scholars believe the representations of Mithra slaying the bull came from this Hellenistic theme. Another Nike is to the right, kneeling; both Nikes are winged. A candelabrum is on the left. Victory often was associated with the army, as was Mithra; sometimes she carried a legion's name as her own surname.

536 Animal circle relief, from Rome, marble, first century AD. Copy from Roman-German Central Museum, Mainz; original in Staatliche Museum, Berlin. The circle was associated with Zeus, whose image sometimes was in the center, indicating his power over the entire universe, his creation. The figures are signs of the Zodiac.

◄537 Epicurean skull mosaic, found in the garden of a large tannery near the Stabian Gate, Pompeii. National Museum of Naples. It was a tabletop which stated something of the Epicurean view of life. The skull hangs as a plumb bob from an A-frame level. Below it is a butterfly (the fluttering soul) on a wheel (time's flight). On the right is a traveler's staff from which hangs a wallet and tattered clothing; on the left is a scepter from which hangs a purple robe. The composition asserts that Fate eventually equalizes everyone. Philosophy was a form of religious expression among the educated that probably aroused more intense and competitive feelings than did any of the deities among their worshipers. Several philosophies developed thorough and comprehensive views of life and death. Stoicism and Epicureanism were 2 of the strongest. *1 Corinthians 15:32.*

►538 Scene from *Iliad*. Roman Museum, Malta. The marble relief is low and probably was produced in a provincial workshop during the first century AD. Called the "Doloneia," the scene is of the Trojan Dolon about to be killed by the two Greek warriors Diomedes and Odysseus. Homer's *Iliad* and *Odyssey* formed the basis of the religious beliefs of the Greek world and influenced Rome in a major way. Homer's writings were virtually canonized, and so many commentaries had been written on them by the New Testament period that the myths had been reinterpreted as allegories of great spiritual truths in ways that were compatible with first-century world views. They were the basis for much of the education of the period. *1 Timothy 1:4; 2 Peter 1:16.*

LEISURETIME

The use of leisuretime in the first-century Greco-Roman world is impossible to reconstruct; it differed by region and by class. A number of writers described Rome, but that city was unique and should be used as an example of other cities only with caution.

Many terra-cottas and other art forms depict many activities both of work and leisure; they include depictions of barbershops, laborers, craftsmen, banqueting, gossiping, sports, farming, worshiping, bath activities, toilet, laundering, and a host of other subjects. Yet putting the information together for a composite picture of any given class or region outside of Rome is virtually impossible. Indeed, archeology is only just now developing techniques for recovering the life of the common people; history is the tale of kings.

Many leisure activities became common, with some local variations. These are described in the subheadings that follow. The bath was popular throughout the Empire; the theater was more popular and tamer in the eastern than in the western provinces; spectaculars that included gladiatorial combat and naval battles were more popular in the western than in the eastern provinces; and the more a given city contained Roman citizens, the more leisuretime activities (we may reasonably assume) were provided.

►**539 Men's *caldarium*, Forum Baths, Pompeii.** This hot room was entered from the warm room (photo 544). The circular opening above was fitted with a door which could be adjusted to control the temperature. Bathers stood naked around the round basin to wash themselves with hot water. Soap was not used; cleansing was done by use of strigils (see photos 611-612), curved instruments for scraping the skin. Personal slaves or bath attendants aided the bathers. The opposite end of the hot room held a large marble bathtub. The women's baths were attached but had a separate entrance. A short corridor led to a room which served both as a dressing-room and the cold room. The women patrons went from there into the warm room and last to the hot room. Pipes often were installed in the ceilings of hot rooms to increase the temperature more.

◄ 540 Fresco, theater scene from Herculaneum. National Museum of Naples. The painting probably depicts or drew its inspiration from a scene painted on the stage wall of a theater. The elaborate and delicate designs are of the so-called fourth style. The entrance represents a propylaeum (monumental gate), which is supported by slender columns topped with crown capitals. A tragic mask is set above the propylaeum in its center; on either side, faintly seen, is a bull. The clearer darker figures are winged horses representing Pegasus. Between the capitals which support the propylaeum hang 2 shields from which garlands are draped. Other monumental buildings are faintly represented beyond the propylaeum. The propylaeum interior is shown as richly ornamented in stucco and fresco. On the right side a whimsically narrow candelabra column takes the eye to the curtain at the top, which is reminiscent of the draping below the porch-stage; it is capped by another tragic mask in its center. The colors include gray, gray-blue, carmine, red, and white. The painting indicates the rich nature of scene design in the Roman theater.

See also photo 540.

BATHS

The word for bath is the Greek *thermae*; the Greeks knew them as early as the sixth century BC (Sybaris). It was the Romans, however, who developed them into the magnificent public utilities they became, uniting cleanliness with bodily exercise and intellectual pursuit into a daily social event. Some baths were public ones, owned by the state, while others were privately owned.

Most towns had at least 1 bath; 17 have been excavated at Ostia, which had a maximum population of 50,000 (though they did not all date to the same period); 2 at Herculaneum; 4 at Pompeii. The prices varied depending on the clientele, but were very low; the ones provided by the state allowed all but the very poorest to maintain proper hygiene. Some private baths may have catered to certain clienteles, but the public baths were attended by wealthy and poor alike, where they intermingled freely.

Many baths have been excavated; the most impressive ones, such as the Baths of Caracalla in Rome, date beyond the New Testament period and are more monumental than the ones known in the first century AD. However, Trajan's Baths, early in the second century, were very well appointed; so we may assume that if the earlier baths were not as great in size, they were luxurious nonetheless.

The patron first went to the exercise area and engaged in whatever sport he fancied. After a good workout, he went to the sweating-room (*sudarium* or *laconicum*); after encouraging the sweating process he went to the room for undressing (*apodyterium*), which had clothes-lockers set in niches. The first room for bathing was the cold bath (*frigidarium*); the next was the warm bath (*tepidarium*); the last was the hot bath (*caldarium*).

The process could go the other way around, depending, one would assume, on whether a patron wanted to be invigorated or relaxed. Tub baths could be taken, and swimming pools often were provided. After the bath the patron often had himself scraped with a strigil (see photos 611-612) by his slave or paid an attendant to do it, was massaged, and had perfume applied. Then he might go into the garden to converse with friends, or attend a poetry recital, or read in the library.

The bath was a great contributor to architecture in general due to the multiplicity of types of rooms and uses of the bathhouse. The first dome constructed, for example, was that of the *frigidarium* of the Stabian Baths in Pompeii, dating to the second century BC. In addition to the rooms for bathing, baths generally provided latrines; rooms for lectures, music, or the reciting of poetry; libraries; gardens; food; and fountains. Beautiful statuary, paintings, and music were abundant.

Mixed bathing prevailed in the major cities until Hadrian stopped the practice in the early second century AD. Women wore light clothing and men wore loincloths; however, the practice apparently caused considerable scandal. In the other cities men and women either had separate baths, or separate times of the day were allotted to each sex. The baths normally opened at noon and, according to ancient sources, closed at sunset; however, the multiplicity of lamps found in baths may indicate that some of them at least stayed open into the night.

With the variety of activities and social atmosphere, they were noisy and boisterous, with laughing, singing, brawling, and advertising of food, drinks, and hair removers. Ancient writers both praise and condemn the baths. Sometimes brothels were connected with them; sometimes they apparently were basically wholesome.

Daily Life in Ancient Rome, Jerome Corcopino (New Haven: Yale University Press), 1940; *Herculaneum*, Joseph Jay Deiss (New York: Harper and Row, Publishers), 1985; *The Architecture of Ancient Greece*, William Bell Dinsmoor (New York: W. W. Norton and Co., Inc.), 1975; *Cities of Vesuvius: Pompeii and Herculaneum*, Michael Grant (New York: Penguin Books), 1976; *The Zealots of Masada*, Moshe Pearlman (New York: Charles Scribner's Sons), 1967; *Roman Art and Architecture*, Mortimer Wheeler (London: Thames and Hudson, Ltd.), 1964.

▶541 **Bathhouse at Saalburg Roman fort,** model. Saalburg Museum, Germany. The part of the model in the photo shows the western side where the furnace was located. The man on the right stokes the furnace with wood or charcoal. The cutaway floor shows the path of the air forced under the floors which are raised on hypocausts, pillars made from tiles. This bath was arranged so that when the patron entered the dressing-room, he had a choice of a latrine to the left; then he entered the cold room and could choose the sweatroom on the right or go into the cold bath itself on the left. From there he went to the warm baths (there were 2 rooms) and then to the hot baths, a portion of which is shown on the left side of the photo. This bath perhaps had 3 furnaces. The hypocaust installation could

▲ **542 Hypocaust system, Masada.** The pillars, made of rounded clay bricks, supported the floor of the caldarium of Herod's private bath in his palace at Masada. It measures 33 feet by 36 feet (10 by 11 m.). Hot air was channeled up from an outside stove into the hypocaust and then into flues which ran up inside the walls to surround the room with heat. The bath complex included a cold room, warm room, dressing room, and court.

raise the room temperature by 30 degrees; flues in the walls could increase it another 30 degrees. Baths were common to life in the Empire.

◄543 *Frigidarium* at Jericho, Herod's palace. It was about 26 feet, 3 inches (8 m.) in diameter and had four niches. The floor level was even with the floors of the niches. The round center column and circular wall around it probably were foundations for a large basin which was above floor level; the channels did not hold water since there is no evidence of waterproofing. The brickwork that makes up the wall with the niches is called *opus reticulatum*, a Roman style (see photo 167). This bath was arranged differently than the one in photo 541. The entry was 2 rooms to the right (east) into a dressing-room. From there the bather could turn to his left into a *tepidarium* and thence to the *frigidarium* shown, or turn to his right into another *tepidarium* and thence to a *caldarium*. The bath was a private one, part of Herod's palace, which was extensive.

►544 Men's *tepidarium*, Forum Baths, Pompeii. A long brazier (inside the iron grill) provided heat. Benches lined the walls; 2 of them are on either side of the brazier, also inside the iron grill. A ledge runs around the wall, formed into niches by the placement of terracotta *telemons*. They are topped by a cornice, above which the vaulted ceiling begins. The decorations included both designs in stucco and paintings in fresco. The Forum Baths included a section for men and one for women; 11 shops ran along 2 outside walls of the complex. The men entered through a corridor and into a changing-room, from where they could turn into the cold room or the warm room. The hot room (photo 539) lay beyond the warm room.

◄ **545 Women's *apodyterium*, Forum Baths, Herculaneum.** Women apparently did not care for cold baths. The woman patron entered a larger vestibule from the street, then came into this waiting-room. Niches are provided for clothes, with benches for sitting while waiting to enter the warm room next door, and after that the hot room. The ceiling is vaulted and has a fluted design; the floor is a black on white mosaic of a nude Triton and various sea animals. Several graffiti were discovered in this room; a salute to Ovid (whom Augustus banished for writing *The Art of Love*), a naked girl, several phalli, and part of the Latin alphabet.

► **546 Men's *apodyterium*, Forum Baths, Herculaneum.** The entrance from a corridor is at the near end. At the far end can be seen set in a niche a basin for washing hands, and on the left next to the side door a low basin for washing feet before entering the cold room through that door. The door on the end wall at right leads to the furnace and water tower areas. The darker door on the right side wall leads to the hot room, which was furnished in the same manner as in photo 544. Men's and women's baths were inaccessible one from the other, but some shared common exercise grounds, at least at certain hours, since 1 entrance to them is near the entrance to the women's baths. Hadrian's action was due to an increase in prostitution; the problem may or may not have existed during the first century.

▲**547, 548 House of the Thermopolium, Ostia.** The thermopolium entrance is under the arched porch in photo 547. It was located in a long block of shops, which can be seen to the left of the roofed area, which is the thermopolium. Chairs were available under the arch for loitering. Small baths such as these combined bath and bar. The oven is the marble structure at left in photo 548; shelves for supplies and display of wares are on the small facing wall. Such small baths were neighborhood meeting places.

►**549 Two women bathing,** gilt mirror back, reverse is silvered; mid-first century AD, from Asia Minor or Syria. British Museum. A statue of Aphrodite stands on a pedestal in the background. The women wash from a basin, while the one on the left bends over holding a cord which runs into the mouth of a large jar. A pitcher stands at the foot of the woman on the right, who holds an object in her hand, perhaps a sponge.

LIBRARIES

Libraries existed throughout the Empire. Augustus encouraged their development along with that of literature, undoubtedly as part of a propaganda campaign which worked quite well; he exercised some control over the contents of libraries, though many private libraries must have contained such banned books as Ovid's. Trajan's Forum (see photos 115-118) included small separate Greek and Latin libraries behind the basilica. In the library square stood the famous 100-foot-high column of Trajan, which had a series of 155 scenes which spiraled up the column to read like a scroll to depict Trajan's two campaigns against the Dacians. Public libraries established in Rome and their royal support caused scholars to flock to the capital city and helped make Rome into a major city of learning.

The word "museum" originally referred to a place associated with the muses. They were focal points of learning, homes for scholars. Alexandria was the prototype of such centers; it was established by Ptolemy I about 284 BC. Its library became renowned, housing perhaps 500,000 scrolls (estimates vary from 100,000 to 700,000) which averaged 20 to 30 feet (6 to 9 m.) in length. They were stored in pigeonholes, each scroll having a tag to identify its contents. Due to political differences, Ptolemy VIII in 145 BC repressed the scholars, who fled to other cities along with their experience and there established other libraries. Antioch of Syria and Pergamum were principal beneficiaries; other major libraries were housed at Rome, Athens, Teos, Cos, Smyrna, Ephesus, and other cities. As today, a large city might have several.

Many libraries were attached to gymnasia and baths. Private libraries were highly prized (one unearthed at Herculaneum had 1,756 scrolls), some of them gained by Romans as they pillaged the conquered Greeks. Some of the more enlightened Romans allowed scholars, many of whom were captured Greeks forced into slavery, access to their collections. Scrolls became so highly prized that dealers sprang up. Some of them mass-produced books by having slaves write new scrolls as a reader dictated to them.

Education in Ancient Rome, Stanley F. Bonner (Los Angeles: University of California Press), 1977; *From Alexander to Cleopatra*, Michael Grant (New York: Charles Scribner's Sons), 1982; *The Mute Stones Speak*, Paul MacKendrick (New York: W. W. Norton and Company), 1983; *A History of Education in Antiquity*, H. I. Marrou (Madison, Wisconsin: The University of Wisconsin Press), 1956; *Inscriptions from the Athenian Agora*, Benjamin D. Meritt (Athens: American School of Classical Studies), 1966; *Pergamon; Archaeological Guide*, Wolfgang Radt (Turkish Tourist Bureau), 1978; *Ephesus: Legends and Facts*, Cemil Toksöz (Tarik Uzmen Ofset Basimevi), 1976.

▼**550 Library of Celsus, Ephesus.** Currently undergoing reconstruction, the library was built in AD 135 by Julius Aquila in honor of his father, Celsus Polemeanus of Sardis. Access was through a beautiful yard paved with marble and up nine steps flanked by statues. The facade seen in the photo, 2 stories high, stands at 53 feet (16.15 m.) and held rich sculptures. Four statues, now in Vienna, celebrated the virtues Wisdom, Character, Knowledge, and Understanding. The reading room was 36 by 55 feet (10.97 by 16.76 m.) and contained on one end a niche for an offering box. The inner walls were separated from the outer walls, making the building moisture-proof. The large open space in the lower part of the photo is the area of the agora. *Luke 4:17,20; Acts 1:1; 19:19; 2 Timothy 4:13; Revelation 3:5.*

▼552 **Rules, Library of Pantainos, Athens,** dated about AD 100. Agora Museum, Athens. It reads in Greek capital letters without spaces: "No book shall be removed for we have taken an oath. Open from the first hour to the sixth." The library was located just south of the Stoa of Attalos (now rebuilt and home of the Agora Museum). *Texts: See photo 550.*

▲551 **Library at Aesculapeion, Pergamum.** This smaller library was for the benefit of the patients and others who visited the hospital-temple at Pergamum. The famed library, much larger, was on the acropolis next to the temple of Athena, its patron deity (see model, photos 107-110). It was at Pergamum that parchment was developed from sheepskin due to an embargo of papyrus by Ptolemy V, who sought thereby to cripple competitors to the Alexandrian library. Parchment was more expensive, but other sides could be written on and it was much more durable. The large niche in the end wall held a statue of the emperor Hadrian, who rebuilt the Aesculapeion structures after an earthquake. Rectangular niches line the other walls; they held the pigeonholes for the scrolls. *Texts: See photo 550.*

▲**553 Greek Library, Tivoli.** Greek and Latin libraries often were separate and adjoining, as at Tivoli. The Greek library was larger than the Latin one. It was built on a quadrant consisting of a large central room with adjoining alcoves entered by large, high arches. The high arched ceiling rose to the roof of the second story, which contained smaller alcoves. *Texts: See photo 550.*

◄**554 Latin Library, Tivoli.** The Greek and Latin libraries were part of Hadrian's palace, the Latin one being smaller than the Greek. It had a high arched ceiling in the central hall and adjoining alcoves. The second story was smaller and contained a porched and an apsed window—somewhat like a large bay window—supported by pillars. *Texts: See photo 550.*

THEATER

The theater had a long history by the New Testament period, beginning with the Dionysiac festivals in Athens. Roman theaters developed distinctive features to accommodate the type of performance favored by Romans. The theater never was as popular with Romans as with Greeks; the first permanent one in Rome was built by Pompey. In Greece the theater was intricately woven with religion, the worship of Dionysus, and developed under the watchful care of the city fathers of Athens. In Roman lands it followed the popular taste of the masses, which caused it to become much more coarse. The Roman stage moved into the orchestra area closer to the audience, and the wall behind the stage was built to accommodate increasingly ornate and even baroque backdrops.

Theater forms developed systematically in Athens: The epic developed first, the story of the gods and stories of Homer; lyric poetry was next (seventh-sixth centuries BC), stories drawn from myth and sung to the lyre; and drama came last (sixth century), influenced by the others. The dance of maenads in the worship of Dionysus made certain that such dancing would be important in Greek drama; but since only men could appear in public life, men danced the part of maenads.

The early theater forms included scenes that reflected Dionysiac religion, with the drinking, sexual involvements, and ecstatic behavior common to the devotees. The dress of the characters reflected those themes; the phallus was common in Greek comedy and often pronounced with emphasized artificiality. New Comedy modified this custom (see photo 573).

A great many representations of actors and scenes are available to provide information about the Greek and Roman theater: vase paintings, terra-cottas of characters, statues, bas-reliefs, and frescoes. Many tragic masks—stereotypical masks which represent specific characterizations—are known; terra-cottas especially reveal the comic characters who generally wear short tunics with nothing below the hips and whose faces are grotesque, buttocks and phalli pronounced.

Music was important to the theater in ancient times as now. Lyres, cithera, flutes, clappers, tympana, auloi, and other instruments were used. The dance continued both as part of dramas (though its role was reduced) and as a separate entertainment. Farce developed on its own track. Originally the actors and chorus members were citizens participating in a civil and religious ceremony. While tragedy developed from only one to include more actors (see below), the number of actors in comedy was not limited.

The great Greek poets so well known to modern students gained their fame through writing plays for competition in the annual Dionysiac festivals. Thespis, the sixth-century BC founder of Greek tragedy, gave his name to the term "thespian"; with him, too, the term "hypocrite" (answerer) was applied as he stepped out to answer the chorus. His plays had one principal character; Aeschylus (525-456 BC) added the second actor and also made the role of the chorus less important. He decorated the theater, developed the use of theatrical devices, and codified the dress into mask, sleeved robe, and

buskins. The actor, then, was completely covered so that his personality could be completely lost in his character. He had to project his voice, enunciate clearly, sing and recite, and change from character to character in both demeanor and voice.

Sophocles (496-406 BC) invented scene painting, differentiated the roles of the persons involved in drama, and established a firm pattern for the drama. Other important dramatists include Euripides (484-406) and Aristophanes (about 457-385 BC).

The theaters evolved from stands cut into hillsides with the earth floor at the bottom serving as a stage into elaborately designed buildings of the Empire period. Originally the orchestra at the foot of the semicircular seating was a place for dancing around the altar of Dionysus, who was god of the theater and of its participants (later, actors and others).

The design had excellent acoustics; Greek architects were aware that sound moves in concentric circles and so designed the theater seating to receive the sound. The design was perfected by the Romans. The Greeks, however, discovered the amplification qualities of vases arranged by size and shape to pick up and amplify specific notes. The vases that picked up the highest notes were set toward the edge of the seating; those that picked up the lower notes were set toward the center. Vase selection also was made from bottom to top of the theater seating to accommodate specific sounds. The full result was that these vases ensured that the sounds from the stage could be heard by all the audience.

Many theater tickets have been

found in excavations, made of bronze or lead and decorated with Athena heads or other figures and symbols, along with the location where the holder was to sit.

Vitruvius, who lived during the time of Julius Caesar, wrote a treatise on the proper architecture of a theater. From him we know the design the Romans considered best, and from other sources we know something of the scenery and devices used in performances. Scenes painted on panels held by wooden frames might be placed one in front of the other so that the scene could be changed simply by pulling one frame away and revealing the next. Other theaters allowed for 3-sided wooden constructions on wheels to be rolled into place for scene changes simply by turning the prism to the next scene; these structures may have been set into holes cut into the stone so they could pivot. Cranes hoisted actors aloft so they could appear to fly, and actors could appear suddenly from underground passages as apparitions.

Guilds of actors developed in the third century BC. They were headed by a leading actor or musician, who often was a head priest of Dionysus; they were religious as well as professional organizations. All people connected with the theater in all its manifestations could belong. These guilds traveled throughout Greek lands, and later the empire, and aided greatly in the expansion of Hellenistic thought.

The theater developed somewhat differently in Italy. The mime provided drama without the chorus common to Greek theater. The mime moved away from the myths of Homer to a use of the myth forms in a farcical way. The crude costumes of older Greek comedy continued in use. Their use, it must be remembered, was due to their religious connection to Dionysus and not only for their intrinisic crudity. The farce developed into shorter

and simpler forms for the convenience of the traveling troupes. This development was the dominant influence for drama during the New Testament period.

Roman drama had a much less auspicious beginning than did Greek drama; it was minor and so crude that laws eventually had to be enacted to keep it within acceptable bounds. The Oscan region (which included Pompeii and Herculaneum) was a major contributor to the development of Roman theater. Greek literary forms were made over to Roman tastes. Theater was used for political propaganda, but it also catered to the lower classes by parodying politicians. Plautus (born 254 BC) was the first important Latin playwright. He was influenced by Menander's New Comedy but made his own contribution, which included story lines of interest to Romans and the use of music, without chorus but with songs and flute or double pipe. Other Roman writers continued the distinct direction Plautus began, some more and some less refined. By the first century BC the Roman mime was given its literary form. With various degrees of influence and independence shown by Roman writers, Roman theater was extremely varied.

The Romans were great admirers of acting skill, so major "stars" of the stage developed, each with his own specialty. Aesopus was famous in Rome for playing tragedy, while Roscius was famous for comedy. Pantomime developed during the time of Augustus, a pattern in which a seated man held a mask that represented the character and an actor mimed the character without speaking.

Roman theater was given to "show business" spectacles; whether the accommodation to base public taste hastened the decline of the theater or simply was a reaction to reality, the people's interest became more and more directed toward the spec-

tacular. Gradually the circus and amphitheater eclipsed the theater. By the New Testament period Roman theater had virtually left behind the more classical themes and catered to the lower types of drama. Much evidence exists that the better forms still were popular at least with the upper classes: frescoes in Pompeii, Herculaneum, and elsewhere, expanding of theaters, and participation of emperors in theatrical productions beginning with Nero. Even so, the texts we have and descriptions of plays indicate that the sensational elements prevailed. The music was loud and sensual; the bizarre was introduced (such as use of deformed people or dwarfs as musicians). Women who appeared in pantomimes were considered wanton.

Romans enlarged the orchestra pit in order to use the theater for gladiatorial shows and wild beast contests.

The odeon was a smaller roofed building, sometimes in the shape of a theater and sometimes not. It was used for musical competitions, poetry recitations, and other types of performances. Occasionally, however, the word "odeon" was applied to theaters, such as the theater of Herodes Atticus in Athens.

Another common use of the odeon probably was for delivering the diatribe, a form of oration highly respected by Romans, who modified the Greek form, and was used by philosophers to present their views.

The History of the Greek and Roman Theater, Margarete Bieber (Princeton: Princeton University Press), 1961; *The Architecture of Ancient Greece*, William Bell Dinsmoor (New York: W. W. Norton and Co., Inc.), 1975; *Great Treasures of Pompeii and Herculaneum*, Theodore H. Feder (New York: Abbeville Press, Inc., Publishers), 1978; *Cities of Vesuvius: Pompeii and Herculaneum*, Michael Grant (New York: Penguin Books), 1976; *Qedem: Roman Caesarea*, Lee I. Levine (Jerusalem: The Hebrew University of Jerusalem Monographs of the Institute of Archaeology), 1975; *Art and Thought in the Hellenistic Age*, John Onians (London: Thames and Hudson, Ltd.), 1979.

▲**555 Odeon, Thessalonica.** This odeon is located along the east side of the Roman agora of Thessalonica; it dates to the period of Diocletian and Galerius. An odeon (or odeum) was a small theater, sometimes roofed hall, used for musical competitions, declamations, recitations, and other events. The one shown is designed in the basic form of a small theater, semicircular and with rising tiers of seats. Marble-faced deep doors flank the side of the odeon which faces onto the street. *Acts 17:1; 1 and 2 Thessalonians.*

▶**556 Odeon, Pompeii.** Originally the building was roofed; it could seat up to 1,500 spectators. Roman in style, it was built about 75 BC by the same city magistrates who built the Amphitheater. The wide bottom rows were for movable seats on which sat the city council members and other people of honor. In the lower right of the photo can be seen remains of a parapet above the fourth row; it separated the seats of honor from the walkway (the fifth wide row) which gave access to the gallery. A covered corridor also ran along the top to give access from above to the seats. The straight wall behind the stage was richly painted in fresco. At the edge of the seats on each side, 5 rows up, was set a male figure, barely discernible in the photo next to the arched doorway. The odeon lies southeast of and adjoins the larger theater (see photo 557), part of a public complex that includes a palaestra, forum, temple of Isis, and other buildings.

557, 558 Large theater, Pompeii. It was a Greek theater converted to the Roman style. Photo 557 shows the stage area, photo 558 from the palaestra behind the stage area. This theater is older than any of the Roman theaters; it dates to the third or second century BC in a durable form. It would seat about 5,000 persons. During Augustus' time, the auditorium was rebuilt, the corridor was covered, and boxes were installed for the tribunes. The seating is arranged in 3 galleries; a covered corridor was located above the 2 galleries that can be seen. It followed the curve of the seating, and 6 doors opened onto the stairs that are visible in the photo. The third gallery once was above the corridor and was entered from 4 outside doors. The lower rows seen in both photos are broader and were honorary seats for important persons. Special boxes for magistrates who provided for the plays were set above the arched entrances, one of which can be seen in photo 557.

557

The wall which stands behind the stage is the third plan, built after the earthquake in AD 63, probably during Nero's time. The previous plan dated to Augustus; it had straight walls. The wall shown backs a low stage and was richly decorated. An apse-like niche in the center, from which a back door opens, is flanked by rectangular niches which also had back doors. Dressing rooms were behind these doors; the low ruins in 558 was the outside wall. The 3 niches opened onto the stage through various openings, richly ornamented with columns, paintings, reliefs, and statuary, through which the actors descended dramatically by steps onto the stage. Compania, the region in which Pompeii was situated, was the primary shaper of Roman theater. Both theaters successfully merge Roman, Italian, and Greek elements. Most performances held in it were of baser expressions of life.

558

▲559 Theater of Dionysus, Athens. Located at the foot of the acropolis on the southeast side, it was part of a sacred area of Dionysus. The present form dates to the second or perhaps first century BC, but the theater itself began in the sixth century BC. An ancient annual festival dedicted to Dionysus included dramatic and musical contests from which Greek tragedy developed. It is distinctly Greek in style, in which the plays were fitted to the high wall behind the stage (the stage itself was adapted to the Roman style). A large masonry block, unseen in the photo, was set in the stage wall to support a crane which allowed actors to appear to be in flight. A porch supported by pillars projected out between the first and second floor, providing an additional level on which action could take place. Reliefs can still be seen, carved during Nero's reign, of scenes from the myths of Dionysus. Dedicatory monuments and statues won by the dramatic contestants lined the entrances and the streets leading to them. The paving of the orchestra, seen in the photo set up for a modern presentation, was done by Nero. A famous altar to Dionysus stood in its center. Holes were placed in appropriate places in the stage to support wooden pillars so that the set could be designed to accommodate specific needs; this pattern was common in theaters. Dressing rooms were on the sides. The steep seating of the auditorium is in three levels separated into sections by landings and steps; the normal capacity was about 17,000 but as many as 30,000 could be seated. A wide bottom row held 67 seats for the honored attenders; the one for the priest of Dionysus was set in the center. Statuary of emperors, benefactors, famous actors, and others were scattered throughout the auditorium. *Acts 17:15-34.*

▼560 Theater, Caesarea Maritima; located on the southwest part of the city, it looks out to the sea. Herod the Great constructed the theater, cutting the seating out of a hill. It measured some 328 feet (100 m.) in diameter and seated about 4,000 spectators. The orchestra floor was decorated with frescoes in geometric design, the only such design from the early Imperial period. The theater underwent various alterations over its lifetime of 4 to 5 centuries. Judah had other theaters, too, at places such as Samaria, Beisan, Gadara, and—as some archeologists believe—at Jerusalem southwest of the Temple Mount. *Acts 8:40; 9:30; 10:1-22; 21:23,33.*

561

564

562

565

563

561, 562, 563, 564, 565 Theater, Miletus. Photo 561 shows the overall dimensions of the massive theater. It was built in the fourth century BC and modified at various times until it reached its largest proportions in Roman times: 469 feet (140 m.) wide and probably 131 feet (40 m.) high, able to seat over 15,000. (Ephesus had the largest theater, 493 feet, 150.3 m.) Photo 562 shows the foundations of the stage, which was 2-storied with a porch between the first and second, similar to the structure in photo 559. A series of 7 large openings separated only by piers allowed the space behind them to be adapted to various depths, depending on the need for the scenes, or it could be closed by use of panels painted to fit the scenery. The openings were larger in the center and successively smaller toward the sides. Entrance to the seats was through arched doors such as those seen in 561. Wide corridors led to other interior entrances such as the marble-faced one in 563; these doors opened onto corridors (564) which gave access to the rows of seats. Photo 565 shows fragments of the seats of honor which occupied the first row by the orchestra; their heights indicate that cushions were added. Two pillars, which can be seen in 561 and one of them at far right bottom in 562, were part of a series that supported a canopy. *Acts 20:15-17.*

▲566 Fresco depicting stage setting, from Boscoreale villa, about 50 BC. National Museum of Naples. The painting, from a dining room, is 4 feet, 9 inches long (1.45 m.) and is painted in the so-called second style. Its design apparently was based on a Greek stage of the Hellenistic period. Contrasted with photo 540, this style has a central focal point, the center door. The door is flanked by 2 columns on each side, the outside ones fluted. A winged figure, possibly Mercury, is above the door, while tragic masks are set on the cornice outside the fluted columns. The cornice is supported by figures of deities who stand on projections. Candelabra, the one on the left seen more clearly, stand on the floor outside the fluted columns. Scenes are depicted above the door and top left. The depth of the painting and the intricate detail is excellent and probably reflects the more classical approach of the Greek theater over the more baroque of the Roman.

►567 Sculpture of tragic mask representing a king, Roman, first century BC to first century AD. Ashmolean Museum, Oxford. The sculpture is companion to 568. The costume of the theater was set, types of characters wearing the same garb for quick recognition. The masks varied slightly but not much; they were clearly and instantly recognizable for the type of character depicted, whether god, slave, freedman, comic, or king. Masks in the Roman theater were coarser than in the Greek, as was true of the theater styles in general. Roman masks have wide openings for eyes and mouth, as in this photo and 568. The hair styles, of course, are not first century.

▲**569 Decorative relief of tragic mask of Silenus,** small ivory. Agora Museum, Athens. Silenus, usually shown drunken, was closely associated with Dionysus, god of drama and actors.

▼**570 Relief of dancer,** from the theater at Arles, France. Musée Lapidaire, Arles. The figure could be a winged victory, since the fragment was found in secondary use south of the theater, but it appears to be part of the theater decorations. Dance is much older than the theater and became intricate with the theater as well as following other forms of entertainment. Acrobatic dancing is depicted on many vases and other objects; ballet was popular, including water ballets performed in waterproofed orchestra pits; chorus was both common and ancient; and dancing was integrated into the story lines of dramas.

▲**571 Dancer in a mime,** bronze figurine, Greco-Roman date. Museum of Art and Archaeology, University of Missouri-Columbia. The mime developed during the Hellenistic period in Syracuse and spread both to Greece and Italy. The form did not use masks, the clothing was not stereotyped but reflected life, and women as well as men performed in them. The mime left behind the repetitious themes and forms of tragedy and represented real life. Mimes were not silent (pantomime developed during Augustus' time), they were short, and usually they were comic. The mime became much more popular in the Roman world than the older forms, partly because the audience liked seeing the actors' and actresses' faces and partly because the themes were taken from life and politics. Some of the mimes developed into burlesque, with themes of adultery, ridicule of the gods, and nudity becoming common. As with theater of today, great variety existed. *Ephesians 2:3; 5:3.*

▲572 **Three actors appearing before Dionysus.** National Museum, Athens. The relief probably is connected with the famous *Baccae* of Euripides. Dionysus holds a rhyton in his left hand and a shallow wine bowl in his left, while a female companion sits on the edge of his bed. The first actor, facing Dionysus and saluting him, holds a tragic mask which representation is debated; the second man faces the other way and holds a tragic mask of an older man with beard. The second and third men also hold tympana. The relief from Piraeus reflects the clothing worn by actors, the long smyrma with sleeves. In the classic forms of drama the audience could tell who the characters were by the type and color of clothing they wore: white clothing was an old man, multicolored was a young man, yellow was a courtesan, purple indicated wealth, red indicated poverty. Different lengths of tunic or use of mantle or hat indicated whether slave, freedman, aristocrat, or parasite.

▲573 **Menander, poet of New Comedy,** portrait head. Rhodes Museum. The face is gaunt and the brow furrowed, the hair is disheveled, and the poet appears lost in thought. Menander (about 343-291 BC) was the most important writer of New Comedy, which began to replace previous drama forms during the fourth century BC about the time of Alexander the Great. It dealt with themes of daily life, principally of rich Athenians, and was influenced by the rising philosophies of Stoicism and Epicureanism. Menander wrote over 100 comedies, but during the New Testament period his fame, which was perhaps second only to that of Homer, was due to collections of anthologies of philosophical sayings taken from his plays. One result of his work was the discarding of indecent costumes and the influence of drama costuming more toward everyday life (though the patterns became stereotyped); the earlier ones remained, however, in characters of lower classes. *Romans 1:14; 1 Corinthians 1:19-26; 2:1-6; 3:18-20; 1 Timothy 6:20.*

MUSICAL INSTRUMENTS

Music was an integral part of Greek life; Homer even has Achilles playing a lyre. Marriage, funerals, religious processions, harvest festivals, gatherings of friends, and virtually every other facet of Greek life contained music. Musical contests were common alongside athletic ones; poetry and music were virtually inseparable. Since various musical instruments were associated with various deities, music and the instruments on which it was played were thoroughly integrated with religion and religion with music.

Education included music; music theory was part of the study of mathematics, but practical study in the playing of music was emphasized as well. Ancient writers believed music to be so important to the development of the soul that only the better forms of music were encouraged for study. Some forms were considered to be Hellenic, others foreign; some warlike, others soft; some manly, others effeminate. During the Hellenistic age, attempts even were made to assign musical properties to food and drink and organize meals around the harmonies. The Greeks organized music forms according to their regions of origin: Dorian, Ionian, Aeolian, Lydian, and Phrygian.

Musical theory began in the seventh century BC. Greek writers provided books on music theory (e.g. Aristoxenus, Euclid) and some of the music systems are known to us. Some of them were either developed or popularized by philosophical schools because a system of scales or tones fitted a particular philosophy (e.g. Pythagorianism).

Conservative Romans, on the other hand, had little use for music, which they considered to be effeminate, other than the music that accompanied their religious observances. More and more into the Empire period, however, Romans became addicted to music and enjoyed it as Hellenism became popular. The mystery religions generally included musical instruments in connection with their worship, a fact which aided in the spread of some religions. The eventual wide acceptance of music by Romans is clear in that Plutarch, the Roman historian, wrote a treatise on music.

Music declined in importance, however, so far as its being taught in Greek schools, from the second century BC onward. It still was a required subject but no longer was on a par with the study of literature or even of gymnastics. The change came partly because of the increasing specialization of education and partly because music had become highly technical.

This development was in regard to education only; in life itself music was as popular as ever; it was simply left to the professionals to entertain the rest. These musicians were considered to be in the same class as actors and actresses; they were tradespeople, whose lifestyles were suspect. With some exceptions in which the best-known artists were honored, this attitude continued throughout the Greco-Roman period. Learning music was considered a reasonable accomplishment for girls, but not a manly course. Strangely enough, emperors and other aristocrats were influenced sufficiently by Hellenistic customs and its concept of the ideal man that they learned to play instruments as part of their boyhood education; some of them became quite proficient.

As with the theater, the Roman common folk tended to be fond of forms of music considered base by the aristocrats. Dio Chrysostom (second century AD) decried the shrill, riotous, discordant, motley music and the lascivious dancing that accompanied it.

Instruments included string, wind, and percussion. The most common stringed instruments were the lyre, cithara (a more elaborate lyre), and barbiton. The lyre and cithera are shown below; the barbiton was similar to a lyre but with longer strings, resulting in a lower tone. The harp and lute (similar to a modern guitar) were also used. The flute and double pipe, or aulos, were common wind instruments, along with pan pipes, or syrinx, which could be a single pipe or up to a series of 7 pipes joined together. "Flute" is a mistranslation; an aulos is more like a clarinet. They usually were played in pairs, held in place by a band that passed around the cheeks and head. The flute-like horizontal pipe was the *plagiaulos*. The bagpipe, made of an animal bladder, was known, and the organ was popular. The lyre, cithera, and aulos were the favored instruments of music as art.

Mystery Religions in the Ancient World, Joscelyn Godwin (San Francisco: Harper and Row, Publishers), 1981; *The Oxford Classical Dictionary*, Second Edition, N. G. L. Hammond and H. H. Scullard, eds. (London: Oxford University Press), 1970; *A History of Education in Antiquity*, H. I. Marrou (Madison, Wisconsin: The University of Wisconsin Press), 1956; "Musical Instruments of the First Century," David W. Music, *Biblical Illustrator*, Winter, 1982, pp. 77-80; *Art and Thought in the Hellenistic Age*, John Onians (London: Thames and Hudson, Ltd.), 1979.

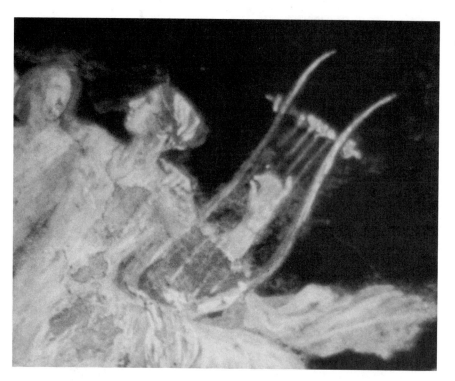

▲574 Lyre, part of fresco of a centaur being tamed by a baccante. From Villa of Cicero, Street of the Tombs, Pompeii, third style, Augustan period. National Museum, Naples. Lyres had from 3 to 12 strings or even more and varied in size from those small enough to be held to those with 18 strings, so tall that they required the player to stand. The strings were of gut or sinew; the soundbox at the bottom was of tortoise shell or hide stretched over a wooden frame. *1 Corinthians 14:7; Revelation 5:8; 14:2; 15:2; 18:22.*

▼575 Woman playing lyre, painted on *lekythos* (oil bottle). British Museum. *Texts: See photo 574.*

►576 Cithera, part of statue of Apollo, Roman copy of a Hellenistic Greek statue found in the temple of Apollo at Cyrene, marble, first century AD. British Museum. The cithera was plucked both by hand and with a plectrum (see photo 474). Some plectrums were simpler and made of shell. The cithera dates to the third millennium BC in the Orient, Egypt, and Crete. *Texts: See photo 574.*

▲577 Cowherd playing single syrinx, or flute, part of mosaic of pastoral scene from Roman villa in Corinth. Corinth Museum. From ancient times, the flute was associated with mystical and orgiastic rituals. *Matthew 9:23; 11:17; Luke 7:32; 1 Corinthians 14:7; Revelation 18:22.*

▲578 Roman clarinet, from Italy. Field Museum, Chicago. The tube has 10 fingerholes, which can be closed with movable metal bands. This instrument was a more advanced form of the aulos.

▼580 Aulos and pipes (syrinx), from Farnese statue of Dionysus and a satyr. National Museum of Naples. The aulos is turned up at the end. The syrinx might be a single pipe or a series. It was especially associated with Pan and sometimes was referred to as Pan pipes. A poet, Theocritus, wrote a poem in Greek and dedicated it to Pan which was arranged in lines equal to the varying lengths of the pipes in a syrinx such as the one in the photo. *Texts: See photo 577.*

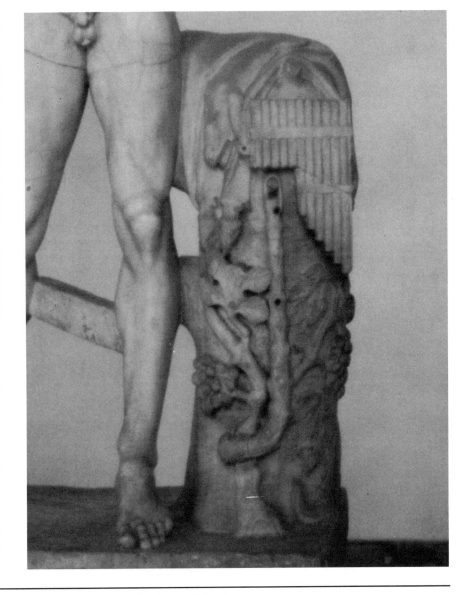

▲579 Cherub playing auloi (double pipes); one aulos has a curved-up end, the other straight; from a sarcophagus. Brussels Museum. The larger aulos with curved bell made a lower sound than the smaller straight type. The sound was somewhat like that of a bagpipe. The instrument often is translated as a flute, but it was more like an oboe. Because of the disfigured appearance of the face as it was being played, the lyre became a more popular instrument. *Texts: See photo 577.*

▲ **581 Maenad and satyr with aulos and tambourine *(tympanum)*,** closeup of marble relief of a Bacchic procession, about AD 100. British Museum. The relief is from the Villa Quintiliana on the Appian Way, Rome. The style is derived from fourth-century BC Attic prototypes. The satyr plays double pipes (auloi) that are straight, while the maenad beats a large tympanum. The auloi often were bound together at the top and held to the head by a band, which allowed the player to blow harder; it is not known whether they were blown simultaneously or separately. The double pipes sometimes had belled ends with bulblike mouthpieces. *Texts: See photo 577 for pipes.*

▲ **582 *Lituus,* a form of trumpet.** Roman-German Central Museum, Mainz. The 2 fragments in the forefront are authentic; the 2 complete ones in back with straps are models. The *lituus* was an Etruscan instrument adopted by the Romans. Other horns included the *cornu,* almost circular and large, and the *tuba,* a straight trumpet. Horns, more typically Roman, were used primarily for military purposes. The *salpinx* (tuba) is mentioned often in the New Testament. Brass instruments were blown through a bone mouthpiece. Romans apparently made no contribution to music theory. *Matthew 6:2; 24:31; 1 Corinthians 14:8; 15:52; 1 Thessalonians 4:16; 1 Timothy 4:16; Hebrews 12:19; Revelation 1:10; 4:1; 8:2,6,13; 9:14; 18:22.*

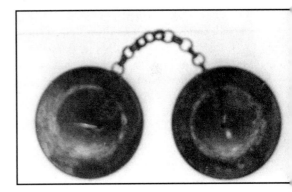

◄ **583 Bronze cymbals with ancient linen cord,** Egypt, about 200 BC. British Museum. This instrument probably is the *kumbalon* of 1 Corinthians 13:1.

▼ **584 Cymbals,** Roman, from Italy. Field Museum, Chicago. *1 Corinthians 13:1.*

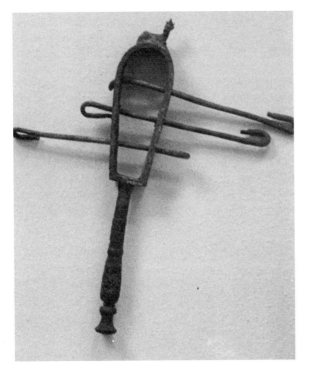

◄ **585, 586 Two sistrums,** from Italy. Field Museum, Chicago. A sort of rattle, sistrums originated in Egypt in connection with the worship of Isis and were introduced into the Roman world during the first century as the Isis religion spread. The shape of the sistrum represented the sacred enclosure (temenos) within which the 4 bars rattle. The rattles represent the interplay of the 4 elements which Isis worshipers believed were involved in the world; the rattling sounds represented the interplay of alchemy and vibration which control the organization of the world.

GAMES AND AMUSEMENTS

Games and amusements of many varieties were popular throughout the Greco-Roman world. Many bronze and clay animals and other toys have been excavated; baby rattles, dolls, tiny pots and pans, doll furniture, whips, spinning tops, wheeled toys, marbles, knucklebones, and dice all were popular.

Gambling was quite popular; some emperors engaged in it excessively. Knucklebones and dice were used for a variety of gambling games, but wagers were made then, as now, on virtually any contest.

Eroticism in the Empire was discussed briefly under photos 458-470 in context with magical properties of phallus and vulva symbols. Eroticism also for the sake of sexual stimulation and expression was prominent in both the Greek and Roman worlds. Sexual activity was highly visible during the New Testament period. A number of Roman writers discuss the promiscuity of both men and women, especially married ones; their remarks were about the aristocrats, however, and should be used with some caution in applying them to general culture. Nevertheless, the frequency of brothels, graffiti in public places, widespread use of nudity in every type of artwork, and other evidences indicate that promiscuity (both heterosexual and homosexual) was common. Owners, both men and women, took sexual advantage of slaves, men who could afford it had courtesans whom they escorted in public, and the attendant results of both sadism and divorce were commonplace.

In Romans 1:18-32 Paul described the nature of the "reprobate mind." Thus he provided us with a glimpse of the kind of world in which he sought to proclaim the gospel. Excavations throughout the Mediterranean world have continued to reveal how pervasive and thorough-going was the preoccupation with sexual pleasures.

Erotic art appeared in every form, including statuary, frescoes, and household objects. Scenes of explicit sex were common in homes. Statuary found in the villas destroyed by Mount Vesuvius include fountain statues with large phalli and sculpted and bronze human, animal, and mythological figures engaging in erotic lovemaking. Frescoes include erotic scenes that depict numerous positions and acts, Priapus (see photo 501) weighing his huge phallus, romping nude satyrs, and Dionysiac figures. Bas-reliefs, painted to add detail, had the same themes. Furniture design often had ithyphallic satyrs or other figures as legs; mirrors and even dinnerware had etchings or reliefs of sexual scenes.

No book that attempts to clarify the nature of the New Testament world would be complete without some revelation of this part of the life of Greece and Rome. The information and pictures in this section are intended not to sensationalize but to inform. Museums in Europe typically display erotic artifacts in their historical contexts, while those in the Mediterranean world usually lock them in rooms to which access is gained by requests to guards. Once the scholar becomes aware of the extensive holdings related to these subject areas, he is soon convinced of how completely ancient society was permeated with erotic statuary and paintings, some of which was not considered obscene by the people of the day and some of which clearly was.

"Rome's Reprobate Mind," David E. Garland, *Biblical Illustrator*, Fall, 1983, pp. 18-26; *Erotic Art in Pompeii*, Michael Grant (London: Octopus Books, Ltd.), 1975; *Pompeii: AD 79*, John Ward-Perkins and Amanda Claridge (Boston: Museum of Fine Arts), 1978; *The Athenian Agora*, Dorothy Burr Thompson (Princeton: American School of Classical Studies at Athens), 1971.

▼587, 588 **Bone gaming counter and dice.** Museum of Art and Archaeology, University of Missouri—Columbia. The counter shows a muse holding a double flute (see photos 579-581); from Alexandria, first century AD. The dice are of bone, Late Roman period. Dice were used as counters for various games and for gambling. Each die was numbered 1-6 and, as today, various combinations had different values. Two die were used; the gambling games were popular with both Greeks and Romans, men and women, and were especially popular with Augustus.

GAMES AND AMUSEMENTS

589 Knucklebones and dice, Roman, first-fifth centuries AD. Agora Museum, Athens. Knucklebones were used for dice; each side had a name. They were used in various games, just as dice are today, including tossing them into the air and catching them on the back of the hand. Knucklebones were from joints of sheep or goats or were made of terra-cotta and other materials. An ancient form of dice, knucklebones continued in use unabated and were used for gambling, too; four pieces were used and the various combinations of "faces" had their own meanings and values. *Matthew 27:5; Mark 15:24; Luke 23:34; John 19:24.*

590 Girls playing knucklebones. Drawing of a monochrome fresco in the National Museum of Naples. Reproduced from *Pompeii: The City, Its Life and Art,* Pierre Gusman (London: William Heinemann), 1900. The name of each lady is written in Greek by her portrait. *Texts: See photo 589.*

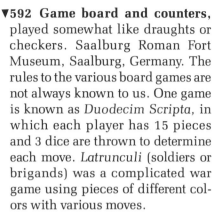

▼592 Game board and counters, played somewhat like draughts or checkers. Saalburg Roman Fort Museum, Saalburg, Germany. The rules to the various board games are not always known to us. One game is known as *Duodecim Scripta,* in which each player has 15 pieces and 3 dice are thrown to determine each move. *Latrunculi* (soldiers or brigands) was a complicated war game using pieces of different colors with various moves.

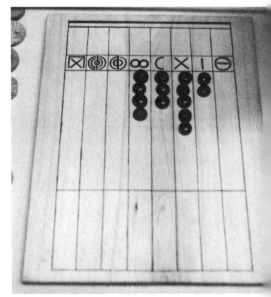

▲591 Game carved into floor of Antonia fortress, Jerusalem, often called the Lithostratos. The carving is in the convent of the Sisters of Zion. The small square on the left is called "The Mill," an ancient game popular throughout the ancient world. Three concentric squares are incised in the stone and are connected by 4 transverse lines that form points of intersection (see at left side of the stone block). Two contestants had 9 stones each; they took turns placing the stones on the intersections; then they took turns moving the stones, each player seeking to place stones on 3 points in a row, thus forming a "mill." Each success allowed the player to take a stone from his opponent, the object being to reduce the opponent to 2 stones or the inability to play.

▲593 Game board and counters, played somewhat like draughts or checkers. Saalburg Roman Fort Museum, Saalburg, Germany.

▶594 Two men probably playing a game, sandstone relief. Landesmuseum, Trier. The men sit on stools and hold an object between them which is not absolutely identifiable. Likely, it is an abacus (see photo 240) or a board game.

►595 **Advertisement for brothel, Ephesus,** carved in sidewalk. The symbols are disputed, but the upper one appears to represent a pubic area; the footprint advises the customer to make his way to the brothel; and the figure of a woman has a sign across her chest which reads "Follow me." The sign is carved into a marble slab that makes up part of the sidewalk across and down the street a few yards from the brothel. Cicero argued that affairs with courtesans were and had been for ages common practice (*Pro Caelio* 20.48). *Luke 15:30; 1 Corinthians 6:15-16; Ephesians 5:5; Revelation 17.*

See color photo 414.

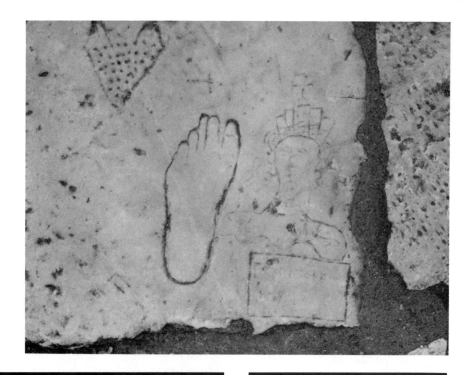

▲596 **Aphrodite with Priapus,** ornamental silver dish, second century AD. Glyptothek, Munich. The goddess sits on a rock in a rustic shrine and feeds grapes to a goose. She wears a light tunic and jewelry; one breast is exposed. On the right edge of the dish above the broken place is the head of a small Eros; a herm of Priapus beyond her is framed by a sacred tree on the left hand and a column on the right. The god of eroticism has an erect phallus, as he is usually shown; the herm is an advanced type with only the legs portion in the form of a pillar. *Mark 7:21; Acts 15:20; 1 Corinthians 5:1-11.*

▼597 **Lamp with erotic scene,** first century BC-third century AD, Roman. Roman-German Landesmuseum, Cologne. Eros, who is Love personified, the principle of generation, appears in human form to engage in a sex act with a woman on her bed or couch. The theme was common on lamps, especially those for the bedroom. *Texts: See photo 596.*

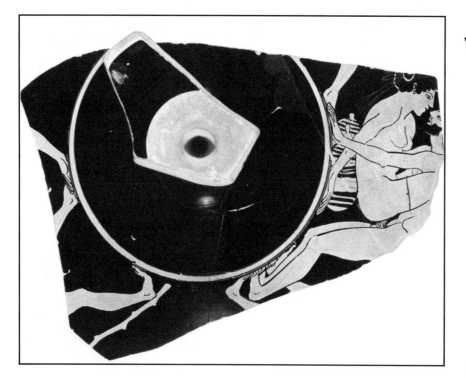

▲598 Erotic scene on cup fragment, about 500 BC. J. Paul Getty Museum. The Type B cup is attributed to an artist named Onesimus. Such public display of eroticism did not begin with Rome; it was wide-spread for centuries among both Greeks and Etruscans. One reason erotic scenes were so common on pottery was the common Greek practice of banqueting with *hetaerai*. *Texts: See photo 596.*

▼600 Antinous, homosexual lover of Hadrian, early second century AD. Vatican Museum. The young man, whom Hadrian had deified, appears here as Bacchus. He holds a thyrsus in his left hand and his head is decorated with other Dionysiac symbols. Marble is from Hadrian's villa. Homosexuality was an integral part of Greek life; it was rejected earlier by the Romans but became widely practiced by them by the New Testament period. *Romans 1:24-27; 1 Corinthians 6:9; 1 Timothy 1:10; 2 Timothy 3:3.*

◄599 Erotic scene on plate. J. Paul Getty Museum. The work of the best-known artists of ancient Greece included erotic scenes, and their ware was widely marketed. Similar scenes on pottery continued into the Christian era. *Texts: See photo 596.*

SPORTS

The origin of sports lies in warfare. Early in Greek and in Roman culture, the actions required of a good soldier were developed in childhood through training and celebrated in manhood through contests.

Officially established in 776 BC on a more ancient base, the Olympic Games were held every 4 years after the summer solstice at the time of the full moon. It was the hottest time of the year, and the games lasted 5 days. By Roman times both Greeks and Romans were allowed to enter the events; slaves could attend but not compete. Married women, except for the priestess of Demeter Chamyne, were strictly forbidden to attend; apparently virgins were allowed entrance. Women had their own games, however, the Games of Hera which were celebrated in Olympia along with the Olympic games for men. By Roman times, all women were allowed to attend (so said Dio Chrysostom), and by or shortly after the first century events for women were included in most of the great Greek games.

On the first day of the Olympics, sacrifices were made to the gods and athletes took oaths. Victors were crowned with a branch of the sacred wild olive which grew by the temple of Zeus and their names were inscribed on stones, honored by poets, and, if they won 3 times, sculpted by artists. Events included running, boxing, wrestling, chariot races, horse races, discus, javelin, jumping, foot races, the *pankration* (all-out wrestling), racing in armor, contests for heralds and trumpeteers, orations of poetry and philosophy, musical contests, communal singing, feasting and revelry, processions, and private

▲601 **Overview of Olympia,** model, British Museum. The view is to the north-northeast; the dates of construction are in parentheses. The near building (third century BC) is the Leonidaion, a hostelry for distinguished guests; to its left is Phidias' workshop (fifth century BC); the next building to the left at the edge of the photo is the Palaestra (third century BC), beyond which out of the photo is the Gymnasium and Field of Mars. The next row of buildings, from the right, are: the South Portico (fourth century BC); the Bouleuterion, the building with circular end walls (various stages, sixth-second centuries BC); the temple of Zeus (fifth century BC); the circular structure left of the Zeus temple and right of

the Palaestra is the Philippeion (fourth century BC); the Prytaneum (fifth century BC), which has a temple of Hestia, is just north (above) it; the long building to the right of the Philippeion is the Heraion, the temple of Hera (seventh or sixth century BC); the row of small buildings to the right of the Heraion are treasuries dedicated by various Greek cities during the sixth-fifth centuries; the entrance to the stadium (long field at upper right of photo) is at the end of the row of treasuries; the long building which runs perpendicular to the stadium is a portico, at the right end of which is a complex of buildings, among which is included a house built by Nero. Mount Kronion rises in the background.

---

and public sacrifices. Different cities emphasized different types of events; at Delphi, for example, music contests were the most important.

The Olympics remained the

most important of the great panhellenic athletic festivals, but 3 others developed to comprise the circuit: the Pythian Games at Delphi (to Apollo, every 4 years), the Isthmian Games at Corinth (to Po-

▲602 Temple of Zeus, Olympia, model. British Museum. The temple was built in the fifth century and assumed its final form in the fourth century BC. It is Doric in style and was decorated with 21 gold shields, gold basins, bronze and marble statuary (a number of which were famous in their own right), statues of victors, and the colossal statue of Zeus inside. It was carved by Phidias and was 40-45 feet (12-14 m.) high. He was in the center of 3 aisles separated by columns and was beyond the fifth column. A large square marble basin was in front of him; it held the oil with which the statue was anointed (to keep the ivory from cracking). The statue itself was of chryselephantine; Zeus held a Victory of the same material in his right hand and a scepter surmounted by an eagle in his left. His throne was made of ebony and bronze with ivory and gold veneer, with numerous precious stones inset. Such was the veneration of the Olympic games. Here and Dodona were Zeus' favorite sites.

▼603 Platform to Zeus temple, Olympia. The worshiper ascended the stairs to the vestibule (pronaos), from which he could view the colossal statue of Zeus. The ancient altar lay to the right.

seidon, second and fourth years of the Olympic cycle), and the Nemean Games at Nemea (to Zeus, same years as Isthmian but different months). Any athlete who won his event in all 4 games was afforded special honor. Milon of Croton, a wrestler, was perhaps the most famous ancient athlete of them all, having won some 33 wreaths in the 4 Panhellenic games from 540-516 BC.

Victors were crowned with olive (Olympian), the laurel (Pythian), the fig-wort (Isthmian), and the fir (Nemean). The wreaths were more than a simple recognition of victory; the belief was that the god represented by the branch gave his special protection to the winner.

Other cities such as Delos, Plataea, Piraeus, Athens, Cos, and Cnidus followed by establishing games, some of which were well established by Roman times. Some had a full slate of events while others celebrated only a single one or group to commemorate a special historical event, such as at Marathon. Athletes for most events competed in the nude, especially in pre-Roman Greek states. The body itself was celebrated as well as the event in which it competed; moreover, nudity was a statement of freedom and culture, for neither slaves nor barbarians were allowed to compete in the events.

During the fourth century BC amateur participation in the games diminished and sports were taken over by professionals. The most spectacular events, such as the *pankration* and boxing, went to professional athletes first. Strength became more important than the proportioned body, a change which is reflected on many of the pieces of art that survive. With the spread of Hellenism and the involvement of more peoples into that culture, the desire for athletic prowess among the populace in general grew once again, as demonstrated by the importance of the bath, palaestra, and gymnasium. Nevertheless, professional athletics continued in importance.

The Romans had their own history of sports. As with Greece, the events were connected with expertise in warfare; many of the events were much the same. Etruscan sports (from which Rome received considerable influence) included women, even events such as wrestling between men and women. Etruscan games also included the performance of prisoners of war (who were later executed as human sacrifices), organized combat, and games involving animals; all of these are reminiscent of the Roman amphitheater games.

While the Greeks gloried to show their nude bodies, Roman culture was the opposite. The higher classes wore rich clothing as marks of distinction when they competed; the lower classes competed in the nude. Greece had its influence on Rome, but the nudity generally was seen in events such as running. The Roman games were by the first century meant for entertainment. The tamer Greek athletic events did not gain popularity among the Romans, while the more violent and spectacular events became more so. More events were added, sometimes by rich private citizens. During the first century AD Rome (the city) had 88 days of celebration per year. Special events were arranged as well, such as a series of games organized by Titus in AD 80 which lasted 100 days. The special status of the city of Rome, however, should not be applied as the norm throughout the Empire.

Greece, Robert Boulanger (Paris: Hachette World Guides), 1964; *Classical Greece,* C. M. Bowra (New York: Time Inc.), 1965; *Greece: History, Museums, Monuments,* Leonidas B. Lellos (Athens: Approved by General Direction of Antiquities and Restoration of the Ministry of Culture and Sciences), 1972; *Sports and Games in the Ancient World,* Vera Olivova (New York: St. Martin's Press), 1984; *The Ancient Olympic Games,* Judith Swaddling (Austin: University of Texas Press), 1980.

▲604 **Palaestra, Olympia.** Each side of the square measured 219 feet (66.75 m.); it contained a square court inside. The building and grounds were used for training in wrestling, boxing, and jumping.

▲605 **Entrance to stadium, Olympia,** called the *Krypte.* The passage was made into a vaulted tunnel in the first century AD, 105 feet (32 m.) long, to be used by competitors and umpires. The stadium beyond could seat about 40,000 and was decorated throughout with dedicatory shields and bronze works of art. About midway on the edge of the seating stood the altar to Demeter Chamyne. The stadium was 630 feet, 9 inches (192.27 m.) long; the stands, rather than being on a straight line, bowed outward at the center so spectators on either end could have a better view. *1 Corinthians 9:24-27; Galatians 5:7; Philippians 2:16; 3:14; Hebrews 12:1.*

▼607 Statue base with inscription to winner, first century BC. Olympia Museum. In the form of a Doric capital, it supported a statuette of Charops of Elis; the inscription reads: "Charops of Elis, son of Telemachus, victor in the horse race." *Texts: See photos 605, 606.*

▼608 Funerary stele of Olympian boxer who prayed to Zeus to give him either victory or death, third century AD. Olympia Museum. The boxer's name was Camelos; the inscription reads: "Agathos daimon, Camelos of Alexandria, boxer and winner in the Nemean Games died here in the stadium while he was boxing, after he prayed to Zeus to give him either crown or death. He was 35 years old. Farewell." *Texts: See photo 606.*

▲606 Victorious athlete, the Getty Bronze, second half of fourth century BC, 4 feet, 9⅞ inches (1.47 m.). J. Paul Getty Museum. The artist was Lysippus, the last of the great sculptors of the Classical period. His style caught the athlete in a moment of action, as here he adjusts his victory wreath. Lysippus' work was built on by the Hellenistic artists. *2 Timothy 2:5; see also photo 605.*

▲610 Victory procession, athletes with shields, marble, base for victory statue. The procession moved to the temple where victors were crowned. Acropolis Museum, Athens. *Texts: See photo 606.*

▲609 Inscription of an athlete named Lycius. Roman, marble statue base from Geronta, near Didyma in Asia Minor, height is 31½ inches (80 cm.). British Museum. It commemorates his achievements and reveals that he was a winner at the Great Didymean games. The inscription states that Lycius won at the Didymean Games and competed at Olympia and at all the other games in a manner worthy of victory. Such honors were afforded many athletes by their home cities. *Texts: See photos 605, 606.*

▲611 Athlete's toilet set, aryballos and two strigils linked by a chain to a ring for hanging on the wall. Roman, first-second centuries AD. British Museum. The objects were found in a stone coffin near Dusseldorf. Before exercise, the athlete owner of this set rubbed olive oil onto his skin, which he took from the flask (aryballos); the oil prevented sunburn and kept dirt from getting in his pores. After exercising, the oil and dirt were scraped off with the strigil. *Acts 24:16; 1 Timothy 4:7-8; Hebrews 5:14; 12:11; 2 Peter 2:14.*

▼**613 Statue of boxer,** from Sorrento. National Museum of Naples. Almost any type of hand blow short of gouging was allowed, even hitting the opponent while he was down. Contests lasted sometimes for hours. It was the most violent of the Greek games. More ancient gloves were simple leather thongs, but they evolved into a sort of glove that left the fingers free. *1 Corinthians 9:26-27.*

▲ **612 Athlete scraping himself with a strigil,** Etruscan, about 500 BC, from Arezzo. British Museum. *Texts: See photo 611.*

▲**614 Statuette of boxer.** Rockefeller Museum, Jerusalem. *1 Corinthians 9:26-27.*

▼615 Boxing scene, oil lamp, from Roman fort at Vindonissa. Windisch Museum, Switzerland. Most blows were struck to the front of the face and the neck. Increasingly, especially with the rise of the *caestus*, boxers began to wear helmets and ear covers. *1 Corinthians 9:26-27*.

▲616 Boxing scene, mosaic from Forum of the Corporations, Ostia. *1 Corinthians 9:26-27*.

►617 African boxers, terra-cotta, second-first centuries BC, possibly made in Italy, height 10³/₈ and 9³/₄ inches (26.3 and 24.4 cm.). British Museum. The younger boxer on the left has struck a telling blow to the older, balding boxer on the right, who staggers from the uppercut. The wrappings of their gloves around the wrist can be seen on the near forearm; the type of glove is the Roman *caestus*, which had lead balls attached to add to the brutality. They are wearing loincloths and are barefoot. *1 Corinthians 9:26-27*.

◄618 Two wrestlers, from series of Palaestra scenes that included photos 626 and 627. National Museum, Athens. The bas-relief measures 12¼ inches (31.12 cm.) in height, 26½ inches (67.31 cm.) in width. The relief decorated the base of a kouros statue found in the so-called Wall of Themistocles. Traces of red paint remain on the relief. *Ephesians 6:12.*

▼619 Two wrestlers, bronze statuette. Roman-German Landesmuseum, Cologne. The standing wrestler has an armlock on his opponent's arm and shoulder. Two types of wrestling were known, the stand-up type and the ground type; different holds were allowed in the 2 events. As a pure event, only the stand-up type was allowed; ground wrestling was part of the *pankration. Ephesians 6:12.*

▲620 Boy wrestler, 1 of 2 from garden of Villa of the Papyri, fourth century BC in origin. National Museum of Naples. The bronze statue has eyes of glass paste, and traces of red paint remain on his lips. *Ephesians 6:12.*

▲621 Male figure lunging, Roman, bronze, first century AD. British Museum. *Ephesians 6:12.*

▲622 Jumping weight, Archaic. National Museum, Athens. The *haltere* was used by athletes in the long jump to give more distance. The long jump was the only jumping event observed. The jumper thrust them forward as he jumped to gain extra propulsion and then swung them backward just before he landed to add a few more inches. It was the most difficult event. *Texts: See photo 605.*

▶624 Discus thrower, first century AD. British Museum. Roman marble copy of lost Greek *Diskobolos* bronze by Myron (460-450 BC); height is 5 feet, 7 inches (1.69 m.). One of the best-known and most frequently copied works of the ancient world, the marble statue was found in Hadrian's villa at Tivoli. The head may be restored in the wrong position. (See photo 243.)

◄623 Parts of starting line from Olympia stadium. Olympia Museum. The grooves are for the runners' toes. The short race, the *stade,* was the most ancient Olympian event; it determined the length of the stadium. Later the double length race was added, then a long-distance race (20-24 lengths). Apparently all of the Panhellenic games had these races. The runner who won all 3 was called a "tripler"; the greatest of all was Leonidas of Rhodes, who won 4 triples from 164-152 BC. The race in armor was added last, in 520 BC. Other minor races were included in various games. *Texts: See photo 605.*

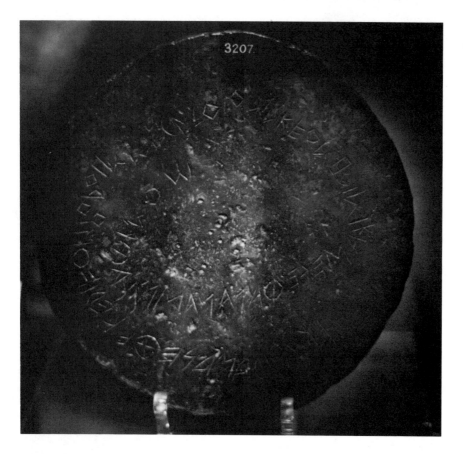

▼627 Ball players, about 500 BC, from series of palaestra scenes that included photos 618 and 626. National Museum, Athens. Outside of the photo to the left a youth prepares to throw the small, hard ball, while the rest of the athletes wait either to catch the ball or to tackle the one who does catch it. This game, *phaeninda*, had some aspects of modern rugby and was a favorite recreation of older teenage boys.

▲625 Bronze discus with inscription, Greek, sixth century BC, probably from Kephallenia. British Museum. It was thrown by the athlete Exoidas in a contest he won at Kephallenia, after which he dedicated it to Castor and Pollux. The inscription is written from right to left; the discus weighs .52 pounds (1.15 kg.). Most surviving discuses are of bronze, some are marble or lead, with an average of 1.13 pounds (2½ kg.). Official Olympic ones, however, were even.

▲626 Dog and cat fighting, held on leashes by 2 youth, each of whom has an onlooker behind him, about 500 BC, from series of palaestra scenes that included photos 618 and 627. National Museum, Athens. This entertainment afforded a good opportunity for gambling and were not part of the games.

628, 629, 630 Hunting scenes, from a synagogue mosaic in Apamea, Syria. Brussels Museum. The scenes appear on the mosaic bottom (628), center (629), and top (630). The lowest register has a hunter with hunting dogs chasing 2 hares; he holds a spear and has a game bag over his shoulder. To the right is a hunter with spear and shield attacking a leopard, which in turn attacks a boar. In the next register above a lion is shown devouring a deer it has just caught. Photo 629 shows 2 mounted hunters with spears attacking a tiger whose attention is turned from an animal it is devouring; perhaps the dead animal was bait. Photo 630 shows a hunter with shield and spear, which he is about to thrust into the throat of a leopard. To his left is a hunter with bow and arrow drawing aim on a lion which is about to attack another hunter on horseback. The bowman has just killed a bear. The horseman in the upper register also is a bowman and is shooting a second arrow into a deer. The mosaic shows both the dangers and thrills of the hunt. A sport from primitive times, hunting during the Empire became big business due to the demand for big game to supply the amphitheater.

▼ **632 Hunter and his dog, oil lamp.** Roman-German Landesmuseum, Cologne. The hunter and his dog are running after their game. The hunter carries a spear and wears only a tunic or light mantle which is blowing behind him.

▲ **631 Mounted hunter with rabbit,** bas-relief from grave monument found at Neumagen, third century AD. Landesmuseum, Trier. He has just returned from his hunt and shows his game to another man. His hunting dog looks up at the rabbit. The hunters in photos 628-630 wear light clothing; this hunter wears a hooded mantle over a long tunic.

CIRCUS AND AMPHITHEATER

The principal event in the circus (hippodrome) was chariot racing, and the circus was designed for that event. It was a long enclosure with 1 end semicircular to allow for the horses' turning. The other end was for stables, where the competitors gathered to prepare for the race. A divider (spina) sometimes ran down the center; always a pole (meta), sometimes quite elaborate, was at each end to mark where the horses turned. Teams were designated by colors and competing horses were grouped in even numbers from 2 to 10 or even 12.

Chariots were not used any longer by the first century for warfare, but the sport was enormously popular. The chariot was an attribute of Jupiter; chariot races earlier were a religious as well as secular event, but by the Imperial period their religious significance was minimal. Earlier the sport was socially exclusive, but by the first century charioteers were professionals for the most part, usually slaves or freedmen. They were idolized and became wealthy if successful. The competition could become dangerous; on the turn around the spina the chariots could become entangled, and many charioteers carried knives to cut themselves free from tangled reins.

The circus shows included all kinds of equestrian events, such as ordered marches on horseback, acrobatics on horses, and performances of horses, but horse races as such were not observed. Some types of Greek athletics were observed in the circus but, except for boxing, were not highly popular with Romans.

The Circus Maximus in Rome measured 1,968½ feet (600 m.) in length by 492 feet (150 m.) in

▲633 **Amphitheater at Pompeii,** exterior. It is the oldest amphitheater in existence and dates from 80 BC. All of its levels are above ground, though the floor was sunk into the ground; no underground passages lead into the arena for either spectators or participants. The outer staircases led to the higher seats.

width. Rome had 3 hippodromes during New Testament times (the other 2 were the Campus Martius and Circus of Nero). Other cities had hippodromes; those in the East included Constantinople, Alexandria, and Antioch of Syria.

Three types of performances were held in the amphitheater: gladiatorial combats, wild beast hunts, and naval battles. The most popular were the wild beast hunts, which included battles between animal and man and between animal and animal. The men condemned to fight the animals were condemned criminals; they were allowed weapons or had to fight barehanded depending on their sentence. Such condemned men were not necessarily criminals; they might be unfaithful slaves, political offenders, or even debtors. Survival might bring pardon. The

Spectator behavior was a problem at such public gatherings; a riot between Pompeiians and visitors from nearby Nuceria in the Pompeii amphitheater in AD 59 over a gladiatorial contest resulted in its closing by the Senate for 10 years, and other actions were taken against the city. Hebrews 12:1.

gladiators who fought wild animals were called bestiarii.

Gladiatorial combat was next in popularity, and the lines crossed over that of animal battles. Some gladiators were professionals; others were slaves who sought the better life even a slave could lead if he were good; others were condemned criminals or prisoners of war. A good gladiator was a good investment. They were trained carefully in gladiatorial schools, which included doctors, armorers, and other specialists. One school was in Pompeii; part of its grounds can be seen in the background of photo 558 behind the large theater.

Four types of gladiator are known: (1) the Mirmillo was armed with a helmet with visor, a short sword, and an oblong shield; (2) the Samnite was armed like the Mirmillo, the significant difference being the fish crest on the Mirmillo's helmet; (3) the Retiarius wore no armor but only a light tunic and fought with a net and trident; and (4) the Thracian fought with a sword or dagger and round shield. Variations within these types developed with the years, such as the Briton who fought in a war chariot. Guilds for gladiators were formed later than the New Testament period, toward the close of the second century. Later, in fact, women gladiators are known. Naval battles were rare due to the cost and difficulty of waterproofing and flooding the amphitheater.

A contest ended when a gladiator was wounded or killed. If wounded he could lay down his arms and ask the crown for mercy by raising his right index finger. The crowd made its decision known by a thumbs up or down sign. The thumbs down signal brought the death thrust from the winner.

Between the principal events spectators were treated to various types of entertainment such as athletic contests or circus acts. Outside the amphitheaters were peddlers who hawked food, drink, and other goods.

Amphitheaters were built throughout Italy and the Western provinces; they were rare in the East, where the spectacles were not so widely accepted.

Debate exists as to whether early Christians were forced to their deaths in amphitheaters, particularly in the Colosseum in Rome. While no early evidence exists for the location of the persecutions, the amphitheater is the most likely arena for such persecution to have taken place. The dates of construction, however, must be considered; so far as we know, all of the apostles except John were dead when the Colosseum was dedicated. Other amphitheaters existed in Rome prior to that time, though. The earliest one of stone dates to Augustus' reign.

Roman Construction in Italy from Tiberius Through the Flavians, Marion Elizabeth Blake (Washington, D. C.: Carnegie Institution of Washington), 1959; *Cities of Vesuvius: Pompeii and Herculaneum*, Michael Grant (New York: Penguin Books, Ltd.), 1971; *The Oxford Classical Dictionary*, Second Edition, eds. N. G. L. Hammond and H. H. Scullard (Oxford: Clarendon Press), 1970; *Nimes*, Victor Lassalle (Paris: *Art et Tourisme*); The Flavian Amphitheater, Giuseppe Lugli (Rome: *Bardi Editore*), 1971.

▲634 **Amphitheater at Pompeii,** interior. The end corridors are for participants in the games to enter the arena. The lower seating was for city authorities and dignitaries; the upper gallery was for women. Graffiti scratched into the walls recall the horror of the contests (e.g. "3 killed, 6 spared, 9 victorious"). Shop walls in Pompeii announced the contests and advertised awnings, free gifts, and other inducements to attend. *Amphitheater* means "a place for viewing from all sides." *Hebrews 12:1.*

635, 636 Arena of amphitheater at Puteoli, chief seaport of Rome prior to the development of Ostia. Paul disembarked his ship at Puteoli on his trip to Rome. The structure was begun as prosperity came to the city after it supported Vespasian's bid for the emperorship. Its construction was long in duration and it may not have been completed until Trajan's reign. The construction technique is much the same as that of the Colosseum in Rome. The Puteoli amphitheater retains the floor, which is missing in the Colosseum. In photo 635 can be seen the many openings to the subterranean rooms and passages for the entry into the arena of animals and gladiators. Photo 636, shot near ground level, shows the inset around each opening into which the trap doors fit. The brickwork of the supporting walls can also be seen. The long wall which runs around the arena floor provided protection for the spectators (see discussion for photo 641). Volcanic dust was used to make very strong waterproof cement. *Hebrews 12:1; Acts 28:13.*

►637 Puteoli amphitheater, corridors leading to galleries. Local volcanic stone was used to construct the amphitheater. The weight-bearing portions of the structure were made from stone that was fastened into place with clamps rather than mortar and faced with brick; the relieving arches and spans were of concrete faced with brick. The arrangement of springers and arches created rooms, which later were used for shrines by various guilds. *Hebrews 12:1; Acts 28:13.*

▼638 Colosseum, Rome. Officially the Flavian Amphitheater, the name "Colosseum" became attached to it possibly due to the colossal bronze statue of Nero which stood in his Golden House across the street from the amphitheater. It was built by the Flavian emperors after AD 64, the year Rome burned under Nero's rule. The niches apparently were designed to hold statues, but it is debated whether they actually were ever added. The inauguration took place in June, AD 80, under Titus. The exterior of the structure measures 617 by 513 feet (188 by 156 m.) and is 159 feet (48 ½ m.) high. The first 3 stories are of strong arcades of 80 arches each, all of which are 13 feet, 9 inches (4.19 m.) wide. Their heights are 23 feet, 1 inch (7.04 m.; first story) and 21 feet, 2 inches (6.45 m.; second and third stories). The fourth story held 40 windows alternated with 40 shields of gilt bronze; small windows under the shields provided light to the inside corridor. The entire design of the building was to provide a structure strong enough to support the spectators the amphitheater would hold and to provide well-organized movement of both spectators and participants. *Hebrews 12:1; Acts 19:21; 28:15-16; Romans.*

▶**639 Colosseum, Rome, corridors** leading to galleries. Two ambulatories such as this one ran side by side all around the amphitheater on the first 3 floors, one on the fourth floor. Other corridors are placed appropriately in the structure, and vaulted corridors running in right angles connected the various passageways. Built on marshland, the structure required advanced engineering. *Texts: See photo 638.*

▼**640 Colosseum, Rome, galleries.** When complete, it had 6 tiers, the first 5 of stone, the highest 1 of timber. The seating began 12 feet above the arena floor, which is the walkway-appearing oval in the photo above the subterranean chambers. The emperor's box was at the south end, near which sat the consuls and the Vestal Virgins; opposite, on the north end, the City Prefect had his box, and various magistrates and priests sat near him. A wood standing area, covered, ringed the top above the third tier. The seating capacity is debated, ancient sources suggesting 87,000 while modern scholars would claim 50,000. Inscriptions cut into the seats designated the type of citizen who could sit in it; thus various classes sat separately in different parts of the amphitheater. Senators and knights sat on the top 2 or 3 rows of the lowest tier. Common women were not allowed in the first 2 tiers of seats. The processions began at the west end; the dead were carried out the east end. *Texts: See photo 638.*

▲641 Colosseum, Rome, subterranean chambers. The arena floor which once covered the chambers was of waterproofed masonry with portions of wood (see photos 635-636). Some sections were removable for cleaning, movement of materials, and erection of temporary scenery such as hills, lakes, etc., as required during the games. The chambers were used for caging animals, storing weapons, etc. Trap doors may have existed, such as at Puteoli, for the release of animals at the right moment. The depth and complexity currently seen date from Diocletian; the chambers existed in simpler form when Titus dedicated the structure. A portion of a low wall which once ran all around the arena floor can be seen in the lower right. The walkway outside of it allowed attendants and others to pass and kept beasts from getting too close to the spectators. A higher temporary wall could be raised for certain events. Archers sat in the niches that can be seen in the wall on that level; they were to shoot any animal which tried to leap from the arena. *Texts: See photo 638.*

►642 Amphitheater, Nimes, exterior. Built soon after 30 BC, it measures 437 feet, 8 inches (133.4 m.) long, 332 feet, 8 inches (101.4 m.) wide, and 68 feet, 10 inches (21 m.) high. The local stone was difficult to work, so the reliefs are simple. It was used for races and gladiatorial battles. *Hebrews 12:1.*

◄**643 Amphitheater, Nimes, interior.** It was able to accommodate 24,000 spectators in 24 tiers of seats arranged to accommodate various classes. The upper rows have grooves cut into the seating every 15¾ inches (40 cm.) to mark space assigned to each person. An awning once stretched over the audience. The structure was used in typical ways, but 2 lead counter-weights found there evidence some theater use. It is built with various vault types of construction, with passageways arranged to give easy access to all parts by the spectators. Two underground galleries cannot be seen. The arena area itself measures 225 feet, 6 inches (68.75 m.) long and 124 feet, 8 inches (38 m.) wide. The seating shown is for a modern performance. *Hebrews 12:1.*

▼**644 Chariot race in circus,** relief, third century AD. Vatican Museum. The race is over and the charioteers approach the emperor's box in the hippodrome. The winner extends his hand to a well-wisher in the emperor's box, while the emperor holds a scepter. A Victory and an equestrian statue are mounted to the right of the emperor's box. Each chariot is 4-spoked, shallow, and pulled by 2 horses. The winning charioteer still wears his helmet; the others have removed theirs. The chariot race was the favorite sport.

645 Victorious charioteer, mosaic, from the Emperor's Baths in Trier. Landesmuseum, Trier. The charioteer's name, Polydus, is inscribed at the top. He drives a 4-horse team whose lead horse has his name, Compressor, inscribed at the bottom. The driver holds a whip in his right hand and a victory branch in his left. The harnesses run around the chest and lower neck of each horse. The white horse on the right has a decorative band around its upper neck. A chariot race had 7 laps, noted by movable markers.

646 Two-horse chariot, bronze model, Roman, first-second centuries AD, found in the Tiber River. British Museum. Only 1 horse remains. The chariot wheels have 8 spokes and the chariot itself was made of wood, wicker work, and leather. The end of the harness pole has a decorative ram's head. *Revelation 9:9*.

▲647 **Charioteer leading a horse**, from the Circus Monument, third century AD, from Neumagen. Landesmuseum, Trier. He wears low boots and holds a whip in his left hand as he leads the horse with his right. His hair is short and curly, and he wears a tunic bound tightly about his waist.

▼648 **The Cologne Gladiator Mosaic.** Roman-German Landesmuseum, Cologne. The mosaic was found in a Roman house. The portion in the photo shows somber gladiators standing in the arena wearing their mantles. The gladiatorial contests began with a magnificent procession, made famous in Rome with the greeting to the emperor: "Those who go to their deaths greet thee."

◄649 **Gladiator, a Samnite;** ivory clasp. Roman-German Landesmuseum, Cologne. The Samnite carries a short, straight sword and an large, oblong shield. His helmet is visored and covers his neck as well as his head.

▲ **650 Gladiator,** ivory clasp. Roman-German Landesmuseum, Cologne. He carries the oblong shield of the Samnite but wears only light armor. His left leg and right arm are protected and he wears a loincloth, probably of leather. His weapon is a curved, pointed stave.

▼ **651 Gladiator,** ivory. Louvre. He carries the oblong shield of the Samnite and wears a visored helmet which partially protects his neck. He is nude but his left leg and right arm are protected, and he carries a short sword.

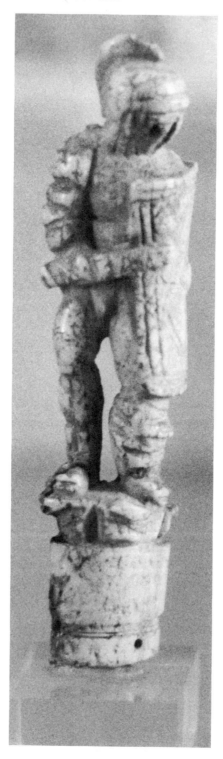

▲ **652 Samnite gladiator.** Louvre. He is fully armored, his visored helmet covers his neck, he carries an oblong shield, and his weapon is a curved blade, probably a scimitar.

◄**653 Gladiator, *retiarius*,** marble, from tombstone of a gladiator. Museum of London. The tombstone probably came from Smyrna. He holds a trident in his right hand, a dagger in his left, and has a shield on his left shoulder. He wears a leather cap and loincloth. The protection is a variation on the usual dress of a Samnite, who relied on his net to capture his opponent before dispatching him.

▼**655 Gladiator scene on oil lamp,** third century AD. Roman-German Landesmuseum, Cologne. The combatants wear the same light protection—leather caps and loincloths—and carry the same weapons of short sword and small oblong shield. The man on the left has the better of his opponent. He holds his shield high and is about to plunge his sword, while his opponent apparently has lost his weapon and is kneeling on his shield.

◄**654 Victor and defeated gladiators,** mosaic from the Roman fort at Augst, Switzerland. Römerhaus Museum, Augst. The scene is from the same mosaic as photo 647. The victorious Mirmillo on the left is fully armored with visored helmet that covers his neck, greaves, oblong shield, and short sword. The wounded Thracian also is fully armored with a similar helmet and greaves. He has dropped his shield, which is smaller, and holds a scimitar in his right hand. The defeated one can raise his index finger to the crowd who then sets his fate.

◄**656 Victor and defeated gladiators,** mosaic from the Roman fort at Augst, Switzerland. Römerhaus Museum, Augst. The scene is from the same mosaic as photo 645. The victorious gladiator is a Mirmillo, who wears a helmet, greaves, loincloth, and a protective covering on his left arm, which holds a sword. He carries his shield on his right arm. His fallen opponent is a retiarius, who wears a loincloth and a protective covering on his left arm. His net appears to be on his head and shoulder. *Luke 21:35; Romans 11:9; 1 Timothy 3:7; 6:9; 2 Timothy 2:20.*

▼**658 Gladiator scene on oil lamp,** third century AD. Roman-German Landesmuseum, Cologne. The 2 opponents approach each other warily. The retiarius on the right holds a trident in his left hand and a sword in his right; his net is across his back. The gladiator on the left wears a helmet, greaves, and protection on his sword arm. He carries an oblong shield and a short sword. *Texts: See photo 656.*

◄**657 Gladiator scene, Thracians, oil lamp,** third century AD. Roman-German Landesmuseum, Cologne. The combatants are similarly protected with full armor including helmets which flare out widely at their brims to deflect downward blows, greaves, and body armor. Both probably are Thracians, as noted by the scimitar held by the man on the left and the round shield held by the man on the right. The kneeling man holds a small rectangular shield similar to the Thracian in photo 654.

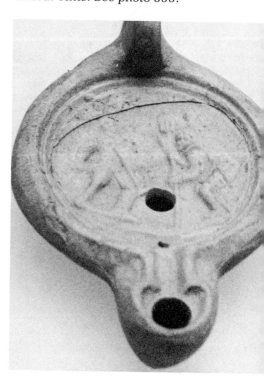

▲659 Grave monument of the gladiator Aquilo, early first century AD. Roman-German Landesmuseum, Cologne. It is inscribed:

AQVILO C(ai) ET
m(arci) VERSVLATI
  L(iberti)
H(ic) S(itus) E P(atroni)
F(aciendum) C(uraverunt)
ET MVRANO L(iberto)
The inscription means: "Aquilo, previously a slave of Gaius and Marcus Versulatius, lies buried here. His former masters released him and granted him his freedom, which this gravestone records." The slave praised his master for granting him freedom after a succession of contests. The opponents are similarly armed with crested, unvisored helmets which have deflectors for the back of the neck, greaves, and loincloths. Their missing swords presumably were short. The shields are somewhat different, the one on the left being longer and curved at the top for added protection (and weight). Slave gladiators were valuable property.

◄660 Gladiators, Mirmillo or Samnite against Retiarius, water bottle. Roman-German Landesmuseum, Cologne. The heavily armed Mirmillo on the left carries a sword and shield, is helmeted, and wears armor and greaves; the lightly armed Retiarius carries a knife and trident and wears a leather headdress and loincloth. He has lost or is not using his net.

►661 Samnites, equally matched and fully armed, relief from Ephesus, third century AD. Pergamum Museum, Berlin. The inscription above the heads of the figures is AXTERIOPIOS DRAKON. The combat is close quarters and to-the-death. Both men wear helmets with neck protectors, greaves, and loincloths, probably of leather with bindings about their midsections; their thighs and upper bodies are bare. The man on the left thrusts a knife into the side of his opponent.

▲662 Victorious gladiator kneels over fallen opponent. Both are Samnites or Mirmillos (the only difference was the type of crest on the helmet), water bottle. Roman-German Landesmuseum, Cologne. Both gladiators are fully armored, with wide neck protectors on their helmets. The victor pulls a knife out of his fallen opponent. Their 2 shields are laying on the ground on either side; other gladiatorial combats still are in progress in the background.

▼663 Mirmillos in combat, oil lamp. Roman-German Landesmuseum, Cologne. Both gladiators carry small shields and short swords. One man is on his knee but still battling, while the other warily watches him. Both are fully armored.

►664 Hunting scene in amphitheater, oil lamp. Roman-German Landesmuseum, Cologne. The scene could be a hunting scene in the open, with the fence on the left a snare, but it likely is an arena scene (the wall at the bottom of the circle appears to be an arena wall). If so, the props are temporary ones that are set up in the arena according to the event. A hunter is hidden behind a rock blind and waves his arms to run the rabbits into the snare, where they will be killed with clubs. A seated man is at the upper end of the snare. *Romans 11:9.*

◄**665 Gladiator fighting a bear,** beaker fragment. Roman-German Landesmuseum, Cologne. The gladiator is armed with a spear and has his head and body protected with spiked armor or mail, and he wears greaves and heavy gloves. Bears, lions, panthers, elephants, and rhinoceri were popular fighting animals in the arena. *1 Corinthians 15:32.*

►**666 Gladiator fighting a bear,** bas-relief. Bergama Museum, Turkey. The gladiator wears only a leather covering over his shoulders and loins and has only a knife for the battle. When prisoners were put into the arena with wild animals, sometimes they had no protection and were quickly torn to death, as in "thrown to the lions." At other times they were clothed and made to act out a myth, such as the story of Orpheus, which climaxed in their deaths.

◄**667 Gladiator fighting a bull,** bas-relief. Bergama Museum, Turkey. The gladiator is dressed like the one in photo 666 but has a shield and short sword, which he plunges into the back of the bull's neck. Bullfighting was introduced from Thessaly; the fight was conducted from horseback or on foot, with the *bestiarii* usually leaping onto the bull's back and bringing it to the ground before killing it. *1 Corinthians 15:32.*

HOME AND HEARTH

▶ **668 Funeral monument of a family,** from Neumagen, third century AD. Landesmuseum, Trier. The father holds his last will and testament in his left hand and grips his wife's hand with his right. Their small son stands between them. The scene is one of stability and love, but whether it is a statement of an ideal or of reality is debated. The need to picture family life in such a manner, though, at least reveals the desire for closeness and order. The family is clothed formally, with all 3 figures wearing the inner tunic, visible above the feet and under the outer garment, and the himation, which is arranged differently on all 3 figures. The woman has a narrow band under her breasts and the boy appears to be wearing a tunic with long sleeves over which his outer garment hangs. *Ephesians 5:22 to 6:4; Colossians 3:18-21; 1 Timothy 3:4-5,11-12; 5:8.*

▲**669 School scene,** from a relief column, Neumagen. Landesmuseum, Trier. The man who erected the gravemarker wanted to remember the teaching periods conducted in his house. Two boys sit opposite one another in high-backed chairs which have ball-shaped legs. Each one holds a partially unrolled scroll in his hand. The embarrassed looks on their faces and their averted eyes reveals that they have not answered the schoolmaster's question properly. He sits between the 2 boys on his cathedra, a high-backed chair set on a low dais and with a footstool. The style of his hair, beard, and eyes reveals that he is a Greek grammarian. A younger brother to the students stands nearby on the right of the relief. He carries a handled box that holds writing slates and awaits his own turn to take a lesson. Such tutoring was for the well-to-do. *Acts 19:9; Galatians 3:24-25; 4:2.*

◄**670 Woman wearing himation over tunic,** terra-cotta, Hellenistic, second-first centuries BC, discovered at Myrina. Bergama Museum, Turkey. She is dressed much as the woman in photo 718 but has pulled her himation over her head. *Texts: See photo 683.*

CHILDHOOD AND EDUCATION

Children were heavily involved in religious rituals in both Greece and Rome, possibly due to emphasis on their sexual purity in more ancient times. An unmarried daughter began the singing in some types of family rituals; a child announced after a family meal that food offered to the family's gods was acceptable; boys and girls sang in choirs during public religious observances; and in some public rituals children carried the sacred objects.

Schooling began among the Romans at the age of 7; before that a child remained with his mother and other women. The ancient view was that his father then took charge of his training. If this ever was completely true in practice, by the first century both parents were involved in their children's education. Though a child normally attended school, a father was expected to share his insights with his son on a range of subjects which were as diverse as the father was capable of discussing.

Some Greek cities long had sponsored education for their citizens, but the Romans did not have public education. The earlier Romans had built their training to service their military skills; Greeks, who started somewhat the same way, had come much farther.

Greek education had its origin in military needs; part of its distinguishing mark was to encourage love between men. As with nudity in athletics, Greeks considered the education-linked homosexuality to be a distinguishing mark of Hellenism which set it apart from barbarianism. Two factors may aid in understanding the Greek mind in this regard. First, the Greeks were convinced that the bonds estab-lished between male lovers bode well in battle; a warrior would fight harder to protect his lover and to gain his admiration.

Second, early Greek education was built on the concept that an adult male should take a youth (15-19 years of age) under his wing to teach him. This pederastic relationship (paiderasteia) that developed was the closest in Greek society. The elder was responsible for the youth's education and was held accountable by Greek society to do the work well (Sparta even required good educational efforts by law).

By Roman times the homosexual relationship between older male and youth had disappeared, but the influence of the special relationship and commitment of teacher to youth and youth to teacher remained in several areas: the pedagogue, who was not to be emulated but who had a sense of caring about his charge; the better teachers of rhetoric; and the role model whom a Roman youth chose to follow. (That is not to say that homosexuality had died out, only that it was not a major factor in the educational process.)

Greeks held school in such places as gymnasiums, though specially designed rooms probably were not used. Many teachers probably taught wherever they could find space. Among Romans, teachers made do with what they could find. The best space, for advertising purposes, was near a forum. The open-air teaching was the least satisfactory due to competition from shops, passersby, and other street noises, so only those teachers who could afford nothing else taught in the open air. Conversely, only those parents who were too poor to afford anything else sent their children there. The alternative for such a teacher was not attractive; if he found a secluded spot few people would learn of his teaching. Only by attracting more students could he ever afford rented space.

The more fortunate teacher found space wherever he could (the evidence for school locations is spotty): in his own home, a loft, a converted shop or warehouse, or if he was fortunate in a pleasant area of a villa or in a room above a busy colonnade.

By the New Testament period, Roman schools had learned much from Greece. Education was influenced heavily by Hellenism; indeed, the goal of Greek education had become the norm throughout the Greco-Roman world: to achieve *arete*, the fullest and most perfect development of all a person could be (cf. Eph. 4:13, "unto the measure of the stature of Christ"). The process of education toward this goal was *paideia*, and the goal of *paideia* was to become *paideia*, a word the Romans translated *humanitas*. Devotion to this ideal was an integral part of the policies of the various Hellenistic rulers and was adopted by the Romans as well.

The Romans were a more practically oriented people than the Greeks; that fact would not change and had its influence on Roman education, regardless of their love of Hellenism. They adopted the Greek educational structure by and large, and they were taught by Greek teachers, but success in a Roman world was the continuing goal. Within those parameters, *arete* was sought.

Greek language and literature, formal argument techniques, and philosophy were included in first-century education, along with music, physical training, the history of Rome, and Roman law. The well-educated Roman was expected to be proficient in both Latin and Greek; the Greeks, on the other hand, generally were not concerned to learn Latin.

School had 3 levels: primary, grammar, and rhetoric. It began at the crack of dawn; statuettes survive of pedagogues carrying lanterns and even a child. The schoolmaster sat on his cathedra (see photo 669) with his cylindrical box of scrolls beside him. The students usually sat on backless benches, often working in dark spaces with the aid of oil lamps. The master often dictated, for many students could not afford the scrolls from which he read; the students wrote exercises on wooden or wax tablets held on their knees. The older students sometimes coached the younger ones in exercises. A school might consist of a very few or perhaps several scores of students.

The schools were anything but well-mannered places; it is no wonder that those who could afford it brought tutors into the home. Ill-behaved students, along with teachers who often had bad reputations, gave rise to the general truism that "morals are corrupted in schools." Primary education was conducted in the home if at all possible. Ancient educators debated the advantages and disadvantages of attending a grammar school; boys often attended but girls received that level of education at home. There were exceptions. At Greek Teos, for example, girls received the same education as boys; and primary schools were spread throughout Greek lands.

Philosophers and poets, who also were teachers, had their schools indoors or outside by the street according to what they could afford. Some teachers worked as tutors, going into the homes that could afford them. The quality of education was as wide as the quality of teachers, some of whom were quite good and some of whom were quite poor. The tutor carried with him his scroll box (capsa) into the home. Many tutors, the better ones, are known to us. Some became quite well off. But the range of success was wide, and being a teacher probably was a difficult life for most.

Education was augmented by the surroundings in virtually every city. Homer was virtually the Bible of education, and his stories were painted and carved in fora and monuments, along with myths and famous people. Some public walls had maps painted on them, adding to general public knowledge and used by teachers.

A large number of educated Greeks were brought as slaves into wealthy Roman households to teach their children; they laid the foundation for Roman scholarship (though private schools had existed in Rome at least since the sixth century BC). School was serious business, and we might wonder why the Neumagen relief (photo 669) recalls it with apparent fondness or if its builder had other reasons. A fresco from Pompeii depicts a boy being stretched out and whipped; a school tablet in the Berlin Staatsmuseum has the words, "Work hard, boy, lest you be thrashed," which the teacher had required the boy to write four times. Corporal punishment was the order of the day. The ferule, similar to a cane, was used; more serious offenses called for the whip made of leather thongs, or the even more serious for a whip made of a series of pliant rods tied together (this is the whip shown on the Pompeii fresco).

Many slaves received educations at the grant of their masters, sometimes attending school alongside the household's own children. Not only did they make good companions; they often became the guardians (Latin, custos; Greek, pedagogus) of the next generation when they grew up, escorting them to and from school, palaestra, and gymnasium where the various types of education took place. The pedagogue's service as escort included protecting the children from danger, seeing that they learned their lessons, instilling correct moral behavior, and punishing when necessary. He was not the teacher, but he was a strong and continuing influence. He taught the Greek or Roman child to ignore street activities by walking with his head slightly bowed. The child remained under the pedagogue until he put on the toga of manhood. At that time the pedagogue often was granted his freedom and he sought work then as a paid pedagogue, which work he might find in a training school called a paedagogia connected with a wealthy household. These schools existed to train slaves in various kinds of skills in demand, from waiting tables to keeping books.

From primary school, where the basic skills were taught by rote memory and recitation, at about the age of 12 (depending on proficiency) the boy or girl went on to grammar school, somewhat of a misnomer just as it is today. There the primary subject was literature, especially the writings of the poets. A man of letters, in fact, was called a grammatikos. The term is apt in that the teacher on this level felt that a basic understanding of grammar, including etymology, was an essential base for further education. The grammatikos also was called "professor." Grammar school came to include 3 basic areas: linguistics, mythology, and poetry. However, this broad truth is not what it seems. Mythology, for example, was not taught for its own sake but for moral values, with allegorical meanings that taught moral truths attached to events and statements in Homer and other writings.

The earliest Greek grammar was written by Dionysius Thrax, who taught in Rhodes about 100 BC; the earliest Latin grammar was by Palaemon in the first century AD.

The Roman boy wore a child's purple-edged toga along with a talisman called a *bulla* around his neck until he was 15 or 16. At that time he stopped wearing the *bulla*, which was dedicated and put with the family gods and heirlooms, and he took on the toga of manhood. (Only Romans were allowed to wear the toga, on penalty of death.) At that time the young man entered specialized training for his profession, whether military, oratory, or otherwise. He also chose a role model whom he would seek to emulate in manner and speech (cf. 1 Cor. 4:16; 11:1).

Those who sought further education entered the third school level, rhetoric (a manner of oratory). Developed by the Greeks, it comprised 5 divisions: invention, arrangement, style, memory, and delivery. Famous speeches were studied, analyzed, and repeated; voices were trained for modulation, power, projection, and control; gestures and delivery skills were practiced. The goal was to develop a person's ability to perform in the lawcourts and before public assembly to present his case in such a way that he would win either the case or the audience. Declamation was the term applied to speeches made on a standard theme. Styles of oratory developed differently in different regions. Asiatics spoke rapidly; Greeks spoke with fluidity and sometimes with vehemence; Romans spoke loudly. Success in rhetoric was the key to success in high places in the Roman world. Those young men who could afford it preferred to study in a major Greek center until they were in their early twenties. Athens long had been a favorite place, and still drew many; but the fashionable places were Marseilles, Rhodes, Alexandria,

Carthage, Antioch of Syria, and Ephesus; a number of other cities had famous schools, including Rome itself.

The Roman primary schools, then, concentrated on basic reading skills, the grammar schools on grammar and literature, and the schools of rhetoric on declamation. Greece had long emphasized alongside those subjects arithmetic, geometry, astronomy, and music. (They were, to be sure, part of the study of philosophy, variously emphasized by different schools.) The Romans, in fact, were especially gifted at engineering, so obviously related subjects had to be taught somewhere; their practical bent would presuppose a major interest in such "practical" subjects. Many Roman and Greek children did study these subjects, but they received that training from specialists by paying additional fees.

After rhetoric, a few students went on to study philosophy, some with the intent to become philosophers and others to answer various personal needs. (Justin Martyr joined himself to several philosophers one after the other in his search for meaning, which he finally found in Christian faith.) The path of the philosopher brought radical change to the learner's life; he accommodated his dress, food, and behavior to that of the philosopher he chose to follow. Some students had conversion experiences in which they dedicated themselves totally to the philosophy they chose. Some philosophers were itinerate preachers of their doctrine, seeking converts in the marketplace as Paul did in Athens.

Education in Ancient Rome, Stanley F. Bonner (Berkeley: University of California Press), 1977; *Greek Society*, Frank J. Frost (Toronto: D. C. Heath and Co.), 1980; *The Oxford Classical Dictionary*, eds. N. G. L. Hammond and H. H. Scullard (Oxford: Clarendon Press), 1970; *Paideia: The Ideals of Greek Culture*, Vol. I, Werner Jaeger, 2nd edition (New York: Oxford University Press), 1945; *Rhodes Museum I: Archaeological Museum*, Gregorios Konstantinopoulos (Athens: E. Tzaferis), 1977; *A History of Education in Antiquity*, H. I. Marrow (Madison, Wisconsin: The University of Wisconsin Press), 1956.

▶**671 Child from sarcophagus of Two Brothers**, Hikesios and Hermippos, from Smyrna, Roman period. Ashmolean Museum, Oxford. The boy's father grasps his mother's hand. The boy is barefoot and wears a belted tunic with short sleeves. He appears relaxed and daydreaming. *Romans 8:17; Galatians 4:1-7; Colossians 3:20.*

▼ **673 Boy eating fruit from tunic**, Hellenistic. Rhodes Museum. The plump child is using the folds of his clothing to carry fruit. His himation has short, full sleeves. A trace of sandal can be seen on his feet. Children were favorite subjects for sculpture during the late Hellenistic rococo period. *Matthew 18:1-6,10; 19:13-15, 1 Corinthians 13:11.*

▲**672 Child from sarcophagus**, same as in photo 671. The man in the tunic which covers only 1 shoulder is an attendant. The boy peers from around the man to watch his parents. His dress is the same as his brother's, a tunic with short sleeves and belt. *Texts: See photo 671.*

▲**674 Boy carrying fruit in tunic.** Bergama Museum, Turkey. This boy also is plump and wears a short tunic with sleeves and sandals. *Texts: See photo 673.*

HOME AND HEARTH

675

676

677

675, 676, 677 Scenes of children from Sarcophagus of the Two Brothers, fourth century AD. Vatican Museum. Early Christian sarcophagi frequently depicted biblical scenes. In photo 675, the child carrying the bed represents the healing of the paralytic; it is useful for knowing clothing and other styles since the depictions are anachronistic. The clothing styles of children appear to have changed little from the first century. Photo 676 depicts the sacrifice of Isaac; photo 677 is a portion of the scene that depicts the feeding of the 5,000. The boys in 675 and 676 are dressed the same, barefoot and with long-sleeved belted tunics. The boy in 676 wears a sleeveless tunic which crosses only one shoulder; it, too, is belted.

▼**678 Boy jockey on horseback,** third-second centuries BC, bronze. National Museum, Athens. The boy's height is 32 inches (81.3 cm.), that of the horse is 90½ inches (2.3 m.). They were found separately in a shipwreck off the coast of Cape Artemision, so dispute continues as to whether they belong together. The boy, who has negroid features, is intent on his goal of racing his mount. He is barefoot and wears a short sleeveless tunic that is belted, with the full cloth folded over it.

▶**679 Boy working in a warehouse or shop,** one side of a sandstone grave marker from Hirzweiler, Germany. Landesmuseum, Trier. The peaceful scene reveals a portion of a boy's life. He either is helping handle drapery in a warehouse or selling it in a shop connected with the family. He is dressed in a long, full tunic with long sleeves and unbelted.

680, 681 Scenes of children playing, relief. Vatican Museum. The scenes are 2 panels of 1 side of a Roman sarcophagus. Children and Puttoi are playing together. The *putto* is a purely ornamental figure that replaced the Eros in Roman art. On the left of photo 680, several winged Eroi roll disks or small wheels with sticks; on the right 2 teams of boys playing "horse" attempt to pull one another down. They wear short tunics with short sleeves. On the left of photo 681 children are eating fruit, and in the center a ball game played with "hockey sticks" is going on. The children on far right perhaps are playing that they are shopping. Photo 681: *Matthew 11:16.*

MEN AND WOMEN

The much-heralded and notorious breakup of family life in the early Roman Empire applied much more to the upper classes. The morals of the people in general were decried by Christians (e.g. Rom. 1). Though family life may have been more intact among the wider populace than among the wealthy, poor moral conditions were common. Both in Greece and Rome, unwanted infants were exposed; more often they were girls. Abortion was common, but it was dangerous, considered to be murder, and the woman had little public sympathy.

Women were freer in Roman life than in Greek and freer in northern Greece (Macedonia) than in southern Greece. The evidence about status of women in Greece is mixed, and the scholar has the difficult task of avoiding anachronistic views. Kitto, for example, states that the opinion accepted by virtually all scholars is that women in classical Athens were repressed, yet he feels uneasy about the interpretation and argues that they had more freedom than normally believed. But how much freedom? And how much change occurred in Greece as a result of Roman conquest?

Ancient Greek literature, vase paintings, and funeral monuments are the primary sources for our knowledge. Greece in its heyday was fundamentally a military society in which the male role was predominant. Though many examples can be cited of women who competed well in that world, the only areas where they could excel consistently were as priestess and prostitute.

The priestess of a female cult was a respected person who competed in influence and prestige with the priest. Women were perceived as being less intellectual than men but capable of a higher spirituality.

The *hetairai*, the female companion, mixed freely in male company at the price of providing sex. She was a Greek figure, however; Romans had no such courtesans. Their prostitutes had to be licensed and wore dyed hair and distinctive dress.

The average Greek woman of the Classical period (ca. fifth century BC) was expected to be faithful in the duties related to the household: care for the boy until age seven and the girl until marriage; she was to cook, spin, weave, and direct any household servants the family might have. She was not supposed to leave the house unchaperoned, she was required to spend most of her time in the Women's Quarter of the house, she ate with other females, and she is depicted in writings as given to gossip, intrigue, and unfaithfulness.

In the Roman world of earlier times the Roman mother had no inheritance rights, either from her husband or her son unless a will clearly stated her inheritance; moreover, the family line was recognized through the male only. The Empire, which brought so many changes throughout the Greco-Roman world and beyond, saw family practices changing as well. The father's absolute rule over wife and family was under attack. By the second century AD that absoluteness had disappeared; during the New Testament period it was in transition.

Exposure of infants still was practiced in the first century. They were placed on refuse dumps and only survived if someone rescued them.

Discipline by the father in the Roman home was rigorous, yet Pliny the Younger, writing early in the second century, revealed a liberal atmosphere. The delegation of parental responsibility to others such as pedagogues was common. Marriage, too, apparently followed much the same pattern of change as mates came to be chosen more for love rather than by arrangement; the old custom of a father "selling" his daughter to her new husband died out. Among Romans—the upper classes, at least—betrothal became almost trivial, somewhat like moderns "going steady."

In addition to the revolution of marrying for love, and of women taking advantage of a law by which she could designate a male relative other than her husband or father as her legitimate guardian, Augustus himself generated some of the change in the status of women by his law designed to bring more Roman children into the Empire. Any woman who had 3 children was exempt from guardianship by either husband or father, which meant that she could own property and dispose of it in her own will at death; indeed, she now lived in her husband's home as an equal. Carcopino claimed, in fact, that Roman women were as much or more emancipated than contemporary feminists claim for themselves (p. 85; he wrote in 1940).

The changing social conditions brought changing moral conditions as well. Promiscuity and concubinage were common; but other problems developed such as families remaining childless. Women became active in many activities and businesses previously reserved for men. How far down the social ladder this freedom continued is difficult to say, and how widespread beyond those of Roman citizenship is even harder.

There is no doubt about the upper classes; literary evidence clearly shows the freedom enjoyed by women of wealth. Funeral monuments provide some evidence that such freedom extended to the rising middle class (by which is meant those freedmen who gained wealth through business endeavors). Many of them apparently died childless. The assumption is reasonable that citizens and freedmen all could and did take advantage of laws to their benefit.

Poverty, however, is a serious handicap to freedom. In those rural homes where clothing had to be spun from wool rather than purchased or in poor city homes where rough cloth had to be purchased for making clothes, and other chores also had to be done by the household rather than through purchased labor, the choices were fewer. The division of labor into "women's work" and "men's work" was a necessity.

The marriage age in earlier times was as young as 12 for girls, with 14 being the norm; during Augustus' time women waited until their late teens or early twenties to marry. This fact alone allowed for a climate of freedom for women.

Some writers, Carcopino for example, believe that most women who had adequate leisure for additional activities devoted themselves to music, to mastering various subjects such as law or philosophy, or to sports but were not interested in becoming involved in business. New Testament evidence of Priscilla and Aquila, however, calls this conclusion into question. Carcopino cites statistics of women who earned wages in various activities ranging from secretary to fishwives and compares their numbers with those of men in such occupations. Obviously, using this technique men come out much more active; a more adequate measurement would be to compare the evidence of one period with another to measure increase or decrease.

The laxity of parental discipline noted above may not have been true at all for those families who were seeking to ascend the social ladder. They had strong reasons for training their children to study hard and succeed. Many reliefs from various regions of the Empire depict a well-ordered homelife. They reflect either the ideal which Romans wished for or the family life of lower and middle classes which did not allow the family to disintegrate as much as the high classes.

By the first century divorce was no longer only the province of Roman men; consent by both parties was the norm. The more immediate result was an epidemic of divorces throughout the New Testament period, at least among the upper classes (whose behavior is better documented). Augustus placed some restrictions on divorce, and he allowed women to reclaim their dowries, which kept some greedy men from divorcing their wives.

This libertarian view of Roman family life must be balanced by what is known of the Roman Republican period. Change began during the second century BC, but it did not come overnight; and every age has those who hold on to the old ways. Prior to the Empire, the Roman matron was absolute head of the household as her husband was of the outside affairs and of the family in general. She raised the children and attended to the house, but she also accompanied her husband to social affairs. She shared quarters with her husband (she had no separate "women's quarters" as in ancient Greece). She was highly regarded in public and wore the special clothing of a matron with pride. Criticisms of women, especially of wives, are common in ancient literature; the fact that men were the writers and that little corresponding complaint about men from women exists provides a clear statement of male dominance even amidst the touted freedom of Roman women. The old ways, nevertheless, were passing away.

Greek dress, which the Romans essentially adopted since the toga was difficult to wear, was quite simple but had many variations. It consisted of rectangular pieces of cloth draped in various ways. The cloth was dyed in many colors and embroidered. The styles were a merging or variation of the Doric and Ionic tunic (see glossary below), the Doric being the oldest and more likely to be found in rural than in urban areas during the first century.

Glossary of clothing terms

Burrus: Rectangular cloak with hood (cucullus) made of heavy wool for bad weather.

Calceus: Roman footwear always worn with the toga. It was a leather boot which reached above the ankle. It was bound on with thongs which were fastened to the sole and heel, wound around the leg, and tied in front in pairs, the number and their arrangement dictated by rank. Senators had 2 pairs of ties, their boots were red, and they had an ivory crescent on the toe.

Caliga: Roman military boot, bound up with leather thongs but more sandallike than the calceus.

Capitum: A sort of corset.

Chiton: See "tunic."

Chlamys: A small rectangular mantle, longer than it was wide, held around the neck by a brooch. It was worn especially by horsemen and travelers. A short tunic was worn under it.

Cidaris: Conical cap worn by Medes and Persians, sometimes with a sharp point on top, usually ornamented heavily.

Cucullus: Hood of a cloak (see "burrus").

Diplax: A long peplum, a shawl

long enough to be wound twice around the body and pulled over the head for a covering.

Fascis: Brassiere, same as strophium.

Himation: Long cloak, an outer covering worn over the tunic. It came in various sizes but was always rectangular. Sometimes it hung over the left shoulder and under the right arm; sometimes it was wrapped around the entire body and pulled over the mouth and back of the head.

Kausia: A traveling hat similar to the petasos (see below) but flatter.

Mantle: A wide range of outer garments. Women sometimes wore mantles over their upper bodies. See also "pallium" and "paenula."

Mamillare: A sort of brassiere, also called strophium.

Mitra: A cap worn by Parthians, it was cylindrical, wider at the top than the bottom, and often ornamented.

Palla: Roman outer garment essentially like the himation worn by women (see "pallium"). It was a large shawl which could be pulled over the head and could extend to the knees.

Pallium: Essentially the same garment as the palla but worn by men.

Paenula: A cape with a hood, used for traveling by both men and women and also by common folk. It was of wool or fur, sleeveless, and had a hole for the neck. When worn over armor it was called a paludamentum.

Pantaloons: Dress of Asiatics such as Medes, Assyrians, Persians, Parthians, Amazons, Phrygians, Lycians, and Syrians, all of whom influenced Asia Minor. The dress included a long-sleeved vest. The pantaloons were trousers which, like the vest, were sometimes loose, sometimes full, often richly ornamented. A wide, sleeveless tunic held at the shoulders by a clasp and at the waist by a belt sometimes was worn over the vest and pantaloons.

Peplos: The same as the Doric chiton but made from a shorter cloth which gave more of a column appearance to the dressed figure (see "tunic").

Peplum: Outermost covering of the body, worn by both men and women. It is similar to a shawl and could be of heavy material for protection or very light material for style. It was virtually the same garment as a pallium. See also "diplax."

Petasos: This hat (not shown in photos) was for traveling and riding. Somewhat like a "coolie hat," it had a wide, stiff brim with a raised crown. A similar hat but with a high point in the center of the crown was worn by women.

Phrygian bonnet: A cap with a high crown and sometimes with flaps that fell to the shoulders. It was made of pliant material, leather, or even metal. The pliant material, most common, resulted in the top of the bonnet bending forward and is shown this way in many reliefs; it is the bonnet worn by Mithra.

Pilos: A conical cap, made from felt, worn by sailors and workmen.

Sandals: Generally thongs, many varieties were available. See also "calceus" and "caliga." Soles of sportsmen and travelers were quite heavy, those of others similar to modern soles. Leather, cork, or wood covered with bronze was used for soles, depending on the need. The material was held in place by iron nails, which sometimes were arranged to leave religious or other symbols in the footprint. A particularly intriguing one on a woman's sandal found in Egypt was "Follow me."

Stola: Outer tunic worn by married women, similar to the regular outer tunic or chiton but fuller and with a colored border. (See tunic.)

Strophium: A sort of brassiere, also called fascis and mamillare.

Toga: Dress which only Roman citizens were allowed to wear, on penalty of death. In its simplest form it was a cloth in the approximate shape of one-third of a circle. The straight side was about 6 yards long, and the widest point of the outer curve was about 2 yards. One end was thrown over the left shoulder from back to front with its point almost touching the ground in front. The larger part of the toga then was pulled from the back under the right arm, across the front, and thrown again over the left shoulder, again with the point almost reaching the ground. Sleeves often were added to the toga. By the first century the manner of wearing the toga had become stylized by doubling the part that came under the right arm in such a way that a bow was formed across the front of the body; the point near the ground on the front was pulled up from inside the folds and hung over the bow. The toga continued then to be wound across the top of or behind the head, behind the right arm to reappear in front of the right knee, then up and across the left shoulder to hang down behind. Children's togas had purple stripes along the edge; at age 15 the stripe was removed and they wore the standard adult white toga. Knights and senators both had a purple stripe on their togas; those of the knights were narrow, those of the senators were broad. Togas were white, except sometimes dark ones were worn at funerals; triumphant generals and later the emperors wore the purple toga. (Purple is a broad term; it includes deep and bright reds, blues, and purples.) The toga was difficult to wear and Romans preferred the Greek clothing except when occasion demanded the formal Roman dress. Originally all Romans, men and women, wore the toga, but its difficulty caused women and then lower classes to abandon it long before the Imperial period.

Tunic, long: Essentially, the

Latin word for Greek chiton, a long or short garment of different weights worn under the himation and sometimes alone. The earliest form of Greek clothing represented in art is the style sometimes called the peplos. It was of 1 piece, slightly taller and about twice the arm span of the woman wearing it. It was first folded over from the top of its width and then wrapped around the side and back of the body. The result was that 1 side was closed, 1 side open, and an apron covering the upper body was formed by the first fold. It was pinned at the shoulders and sides, with the arms coming through the holes left on either side of the clasps at the shoulders. Sometimes the open side was sewn up, and a girdle or belt held the clothing at the waist. This is the earliest form; variations followed. It was made in earliest times of wool, then of flax, and finally of flax mixed with silk or pure silk. The Ionic tunic was

not folded over before being wrapped around the body; it was folded around the body and clasped at the shoulders, leaving a draped appearance. Variations of these styles developed, including sewing up the open side or adding long or short sleeves, and adding ribbons across the chest or as belts set high or low. The Ionic tunic was of thinner material than the Doric and sometimes was very thin. It came to be called a stola in the first century BC.

Tunic, short: Worn by men for everyday wear. It was arranged similarly to the Doric tunic but reached only to the knees or was even shorter. Boys, workmen, and slaves also wore the short tunic. When fastened on one shoulder only to allow more freedom for the right side it was called the exomis. The soldier also wore the short tunic underneath his armor. Women sometimes wore an inner short tunic somewhat like a shirt, with or

without sleeves. The tunic, either long or short, also was used for sleeping.

"Girding Up the Loins," Jimmy Albright, *Biblical Illustrator,* Summer, 1985; *Roman Women: Their History and Habits,* J. P. V. D. Balsdon (New York: The John Day Co.), 1962; *A Guide to the Exhibition Illustrating Greek and Roman Life* (London: British Museum, by order of the trustees), 1908; *Daily Life in Ancient Rome,* Jerome Carcopino (New Haven: Yale University Press), 1940; *Greek, Etruscan, and Roman Art,* George H. Chase, revised by Cornelius C. Vermeule III (Boston: Museum of Fine Arts), 1963; *Greek Society,* Frank J. Frost, second edition (Toronto: D. C. Heath and Co.), 1980; *The Oxford Classical Dictionary,* edited by N. G. L. Hammond and H. H. Scullard (Oxford: Clarendon Press), 1970; *Costumes of the Greeks and Romans,* Thomas Hope (New York: Dover Publications, Inc.), 1962; *The Greeks,* H. D. F. Kitto (Baltimore: Penguin Books, Inc.), 1957; "The Fuller," J. W. Lee, *Biblical Illustrator,* Summer, 1985; *Rome in the Augustan Age,* Henry Thompson Rowell (Norman, Oklahoma: University of Oklahoma Press), 1962; "Greek Women's Dress," *Biblical Illustrator,* Winter 1986, p.17, Paula A. Savage; *Ante Pacem: Archaeological Evidence of Church Life Before Constantine,* Graydon F. Snyder (Macon, Georgia: Mercer University Press), 1985.

▲682 **Bas-relief showing duties of women.** Capitoline Museum. The 3 women in the center probably are goddesses connected with the home. The central figure holds a balance scale in 1 hand and a cornucopia in the other, indicating the values of justice and prosperity. She is flanked by one figure holding wool-spinning tools and another holding a tiny infant. The 3 women, who either represent the duties of women or the goddesses who watch over women as they perform those duties, are adored by a female (left) and a male (right) figure. *1 Corinthians 14:34-35.*

▼684 Funerary statue of matron of Herculaneum type, Roman period. National Museum, Athens. Copy of a Greek work of the fourth century BC attributed to Lysippus. The name was given to the type because the best example is from Herculaneum. The hairstyle with covered head is similar to that of a portrait statue of the mother of Balbus, a proconsul, in the National Museum of Naples, though that woman is older. A companion statue, of Balbus' daughter, has the same hairstyle but uncovered. She wears an inner tunic, which is seen at her lower legs, over which is a himation. She is shown barefoot; men and women generally went barefoot in their homes. *Texts: See photo 683.*

▲683 Draped female figure of the "personification-of-modesty" type (*pudicitia*), probably period of Tiberius. Malta Museum. She wears a tunic, seen at the bottom of the statue, and a himation over it wound around her body and across her shoulder. *Mark 11:7-8; Acts 9:39; Hebrews 1:11; 1 Peter 3:3; Revelation 3:4-5.*

▲685 Old woman in himation. Vatican Museum. Her tunic hangs off her right shoulder and she has her himation arranged about the lower part of her body and held there at the waist by a knot made by pulling the material up from behind and draping it over the edge of the wrapping. Knots at the waist sometimes indicated that one was from a province. The himation continues around her back and covers her head. She holds an ointment bottle, probably for oil, in her left hand. *Texts: See photo 683.*

686, 687 Head of woman, from Appian Way near Rome, about AD 100. Glyptothek, Munich. The woman's hair is fixed tightly with 2 bands on her forehead, the bottom band swept down and the upper band swept up. Most of her hair is braided around the crown of her head, with some strands combed tightly to the back of her neck. Woman often wore wiglets to attain the various styles. *1 Corinthians 11:15; 1 Peter 3:3.*

688, 689 Head of a woman with a diadem, about AD 100-110. Glyptothek, Munich. She may be Plotina, wife of Trajan. Her hairstyle is similar to that of the woman in photos 686-687, except that the diadem is added and tresses are arranged in circlets along the base of the diadem. *Revelation 12:3; 13:1; 19:12; see also photos 681,682.*

691, 692, 693, 694 Female statues, bronze, National Museum of Naples. All of the women wear chitons (tunics) with outer upper coverings. The fold of the inner tunic, which can be seen just below the outer upper covering in photos 692-

691

▲ **690 Two women waiting on Dionysus,** portion of fresco from Pompeii. National Museum of Naples. The 2 women are awaiting their turn. One woman carries a ritual dish with offerings and a small child at bottom left also waits with offerings. The 2 women wear garlands and are dressed in expensive chitons bound at the waist and flounced below the hips. Each woman wears flowers in her hair, a frequent depiction in frescoes of Pompeii. The rod in the background at right is a thyrsus. *Matthew 5:40; Acts 9:39.*

694, was formed by pulling the cloth up above the belt and dropping it over the belt. An additional belt and fold sometimes was added. The statues show the Ionian tunic, which was of fine linen rather than the wool of the Dorian tunic. To compensate for the thinness of the material, the women wear mantles over their upper bodies. It is pulled around the body and fastened at the shoulders much like the tunic but reaches only to the waist or somewhat shorter. The Ionian tunic also was fuller than the Dorian and the upper foldover was not done (see glossary). The open side was sewn up and buttons or clasps were fastened at the shoulders. *Texts: See photos 683,690.*

694

692

693

▼695 Seated woman, wearing chiton and himation. Found in the gymnasium, second half of first century AD. Olympia Museum. A bird is on her right thigh. *Texts: See photos 683, 690.*

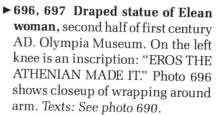

►696, 697 Draped statue of Elean woman, second half of first century AD. Olympia Museum. On the left knee is an inscription: "EROS THE ATHENIAN MADE IT." Photo 696 shows closeup of wrapping around arm. *Texts: See photo 690.*

698, 699, 700 Woman in Greek dress, with closeups. British Museum. Her hairstyle is typically Greek, full and bound about the crown with a band, with tresses falling down her neck to her shoulders (see 699) and 3 thick curls hanging just behind her ears. She also wears earrings. She is dressed in an inner long tunic, which is seen about her feet, over which she wears a himation. Photo 699 shows the himation sleeve arranged to reach her right elbow, while 700 shows the sleeve reaching her wrist. Both sleeve openings are closed by means of buttons (see photo 701). What appears to be thinner material over her breast is not the tunic but the himation which has heavier folds falling from the shoulders. *1 Timothy 2:9; 1 Peter 3:3; see also photo 678.*

▲701 **Closeup of arm fastenings,** marble, second half of first century AD. Olympia Museum. The photo is from the statue of the Elean woman of Herculaneum type, "Albertinum," Dresden. Under the right knee is the inscription: "AULOS SEXT(I)OS ERATON THE ATHENIAN MADE IT."

▼702, 703 **Portrait bust of aristocratic Elean lady,** second half of first century BC. Olympia Museum. The hair on the back of her head is pulled tightly and finished in a bun; the front is combed up in tiara fashion, either combed over a form or perhaps this part of her coiffure is false. *Texts: See photos 686, 687.*

704 Portrait head of lady, first century BC. Olympia Museum. She wears a low tiara over 2 rows of curls over her forehead. Her hair flows narrowly down the back of her neck and ribbon ends trail below and behind her ear. A fourth-century BC style of Aphrodite that was much copied by Romans may have inspired her hairstyle. *Texts: See photos 686, 687, 688, 689.*

▼**706 Portrait bust of young woman,** period of Tiberius. Agora Museum, Athens. Her hair is cut short, parted in the middle, and waved. A Pompeiian mosaic shows a portrait with a similar hairstyle but longer and held by a ribbon. The preponderance of hairstyles shown on Pompeiian frescoes are either short or, more often, long but pulled up and held with ribbons or bands. Greek hairstyles in representations generally seem to be longer than Roman styles but are pulled up and away from the neck and bound in various ways. *Texts: See photos 686-687.*

▲**707 Woman's head, Roman.** Bergama Museum. Her hair is long, parted in the middle, and flared out from her forehead and face. Ringlets trail down the sides of her neck. She wears a tiara, behind which is a veil. A similar style was worn by Queen Arsinoë II of Egypt in the second century BC. *Texts: See photos 686-687.*

▲**705 Full portrait of a woman,** AD 130-150, marble. British Museum. It was found in the temple of Aphrodite at Cyrene. Her hair sweeps up from her forehead and braids are wrapped around the crown of her head. She wears a tunic over which she has a himation, arranged to cover fully both shoulders. *Matthew 27:32; Acts 2:10; 6:9; 11:20; 13:1; see also photos 678, 681-684.*

▶**708 Woman wearing mantle with hood** pulled partway up on her head, terra-cotta, Roman period. Bergama Museum, Turkey. Her hairstyle is similar to the woman in photo 707, but instead of a tiara she wears a band or ribbon and earrings. Portraits of Eastern women, such as Syrian, are shown with head covered while those of Roman women generally are not except as they are sacrificing or depicted as old-fashioned matrons. Greek portraits are mixed, with some heads covered and some without. *Texts: See photos 686-687, 698-700.*

▲**709 Woman with Dionysus,** closeup of photo 573 showing woman sitting on edge of the god's bed. About 400 BC. National Museum, Athens. She wears a light tunic with a ribbon running under her breasts and crossed between them over her shoulders. *Texts: See photo 690.*

▶**710 Head of barbarian woman,** first-second centuries AD. Corinth Museum. Her wavy hair is parted in the middle, pulled back, and reversed upward. The head and the one in photo 711 served as an embellishment on the second story of "The Facade of the Colossal Figures" that was in the agora west of the propylea. *Acts 28:2; Romans 1:14; 1 Corinthians 14:11; Colossians 3:11.*

▲**711 Head of barbarian woman,** first century AD. Corinth Museum. Her hairstyle is similar to that shown in photo 710, with wavy hair pulled back tightly and braids wound about the crown of her head. An Etruscan sarcophagus dating to about 290 BC shows a similar style. *Texts: See photo 710.*

712, 713, 714, 715, 716 Terra-cotta heads of third-first centuries BC. Ceramicus Museum, Athens. The woman in photo 712 wears large earrings and has her hair fixed in long curls which are pulled back and up and held in place with a band. Photo 713 shows a woman with her head covered. The woman in 714 has her hair parted in the middle and pulled back gently in large waves. She wears earrings. Both women in photos 715 and 716 wear hats of different styles, but both set caplike on the backs of their heads. Their hair is fixed similarly, parted in the center, but the woman's hair in photo 714 is more curly. She also wears large earrings. *Texts: See photos 686-687, 698-700.*

712

713

714

715

716

◄717 Woman wearing tunic bound below the breasts with a ribbon, terra-cotta, Hellenistic, second-first centuries BC, discovered at Myrina. Bergama Museum, Turkey. The lower fold was formed by pulling the material up and letting it drape over a belt or girdle underneath the fold. Her hair is curled and loose except for the ribbon tied at the top of her head. The dove on her shoulder may indicate that the statuette represents Diana, who usually is shown with a second fold to hold the tunic high enough to leave her legs free for hunting. *Texts: See photo 690.*

▼718 Woman wearing himation over tunic, terra-cotta, Hellenistic, second-first centuries BC, discovered at Myrina. Bergama Museum, Turkey. The inner tunic is visible above her feet. She has pulled the himation around her right arm and grips it from underneath. She wears earrings and her hair is curled tightly and held in place by a band. *Texts: See photos 683, 698-700.*

HOME AND HEARTH

▶**719 Woman in Greek dress,** probably of the Imperial family. Ephesus Museum. She holds up the hem of her himation with her left hand, revealing more of the inner tunic. *Texts: See photo 683.*

▼**720 Sarcophagus scene showing clothing styles,** Brussels Museum. The man on the far left with scabbard and the fourth man from the left wear hooded mantles closed at the front and without sleeves. The clothing is common to Gaul; it is the basic sleeved tunic worn by both men and women of all social ranks. The cut might be full or the sleeves long or short. Sometimes it was worn over a thinner inner tunic. Scarves were worn as well, and women sometimes wore large, tasseled shawls. The second man from left and the falling man both wear long tunics. The man holding the ladder and the man at far right wear short tunics with short sleeves and belt, while the man to the right of the ladder holder wears a loincloth called a licium which is tied around his waist. *Matthew 3:4; 5:40; Mark 1:6; 6:9; Hebrews 1:12.*

See color photos 415-416.

▶721 **Shepherd holding ram, wearing short tunic,** pre-Constantinian sarcophagus. Pio-Christian Museum, Vatican. The tunic, arranged as the shepherd has it off the shoulder to allow for more freedom of movement, is called an exomis. He wears supple boots which are bound high on his calf. *Luke 6:29.*

◀722 **Fisherman wearing short tunic,** from pre-Constantinian sarcophagus. Pio-Christian Museum, Vatican. The significance of the fisherman on early Christian sarcophagi is not known, though various possibilities easily come to mind. The man wears the short tunic on both shoulders and bound at the waist. His cap is the pilos. *Luke 6:29.*

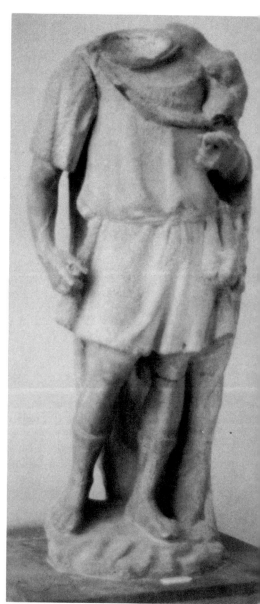

▼ **724 Hunter, wearing short tunic and cape,** copy of a Hellenistic original. National Museum of Naples. His tunic has short sleeves and is belted. His mantle is the pallium, held at the right shoulder by a clasp. He holds a bag of small game on his left arm. *Luke 6:29; 2 Timothy 4:13.*

▲ **723 Man and boy cooking pig,** Roman adaptation of a Hellenistic original, possibly a painting rather than statuary. National Museum of Naples. Both workers wear the *licium,* a simple loincloth knotted at the waist. The loincloth was of various shapes, sometimes a long piece of cloth shaped somewhat like a shawl, sometimes following a more precise pattern. The Boston Museum of Fine Arts has a loincloth cut from the hide of a deer into which has been cut tiny holes so closely placed that the material has a net effect. The leather loincloth is shaped smaller at the middle where it passed between the legs and has ties on each corner. It dates to about 1490 BC and shows both the ancient nature of the loincloth and the variety that developed from early times. The typical poor man's loincloth was wrapped around the waist, pulled between the legs, and tucked into or fastened at the waist.

He probably is Regillus, youngest
son of Herodes Atticus, a well-
known Roman consul and philan-
thropist of the second century AD.
At the boy's left foot is a lockbox.
He wears a tunic pulled tightly
about his waist (unless the point of
the toga is visible, a tunic and toga
appear much the same on statuary).
Matthew 5:40; 10:10; Mark 6:9.

▼ **726 Youth with toga,** AD 69-76.
Malta Museum. The toga is pulled
across the waist and a fold draped
over from underneath as described
in the glossary. The fragment of a
box for scrolls, called a *capsa* or
scrinium, is at his feet.

▲ **727 Roman with toga,** first century AD. Ashmolean Museum, Oxford. The inner tunic is visible from
the neck down the man's right side.
The point of the tunic can be seen
between his feet. The difficulty in
wearing the toga can be imagined
from its convolutions.

▲728 Man wearing mantle, bronze, probably a ploughman. Landesmuseum, Trier. The height of the statuette is 4¾ inches (12 cm.). The way the hands are held suggests reins for a team of oxen. His mantle reaches his hips and is thick and stiff. This mantle was worn by the common people of Germany, but similar ones, made of felt or leather, were worn throughout the Empire. *2 Timothy 4:13.*

▼729 Man wearing heavy mantle, bronze statuette. Landesmuseum, Trier. *2 Timothy 4:13.*

▲730 Portrait bust of young man, perhaps member of Imperial family, first century AD. Agora Museum, Athens. His hair is cut short and combed down toward his forehead.

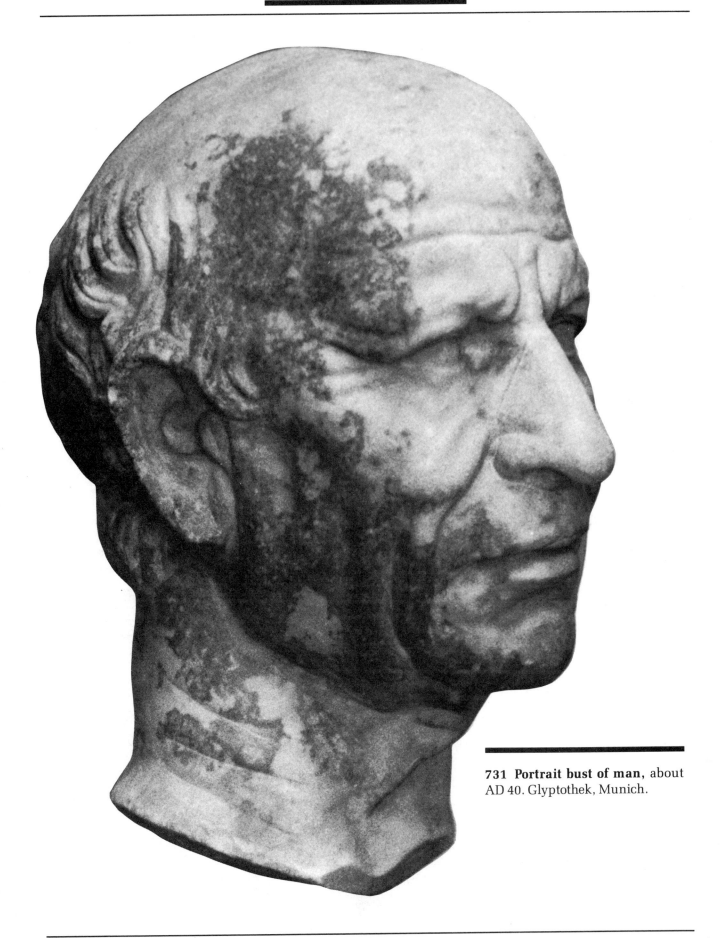

731 Portrait bust of man, about
AD 40. Glyptothek, Munich.

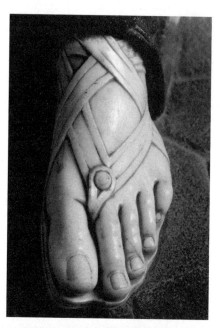

(see photo 474)

▼ **733 Sandal on statue of Apollo with Cithera** (see photo 474), second century BC. National Museum of Naples. The typical sandal was a thong, with straps arranged various ways. The sole of this sandal follows the contours of Apollo's toes and is bound on the foot with wide bands. The thong itself is held in place by a button. *Matthew 3:11; Luke 3:16; 10:4; 15:22; Acts 13:25.*

▲ **732 Calceus worn by Marcus Nunius Balbus,** a first-century AD aristocrat from Herculaneum. National Museum of Naples. The leather boot reaches above his ankle and is held on by leather thongs fastened to the heel and sole and wound around the leg, then tied at the front. The arrangement shown is with two ties, which designated a senator. If his calceus is the normal design for a senator, it would be red and with an ivory crescent on the toe.

▶ **734 Sandal on Farnese Hercules** (see photo 517), found in Baths of Caracalla, Rome. National Museum of Naples. The sandal has a sort of net arrangement surrounding the toes and heel, but it is a thong, which comes between the toes under the button. The shoe is substantial, with a fairly thick sole, a wide band across the instep, and held around the ankle by straps. *Texts: See photo 733.*

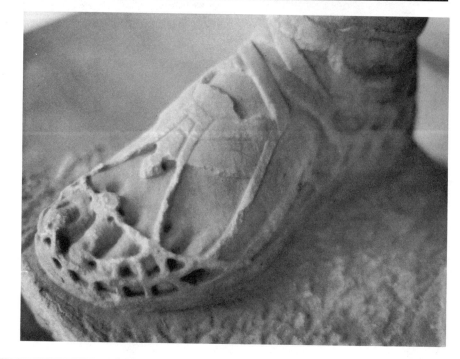

▼736 Leather thongs, Roman. Glyptothek, Munich. The thong passes from the sole to a wide band which encircled the instep and ankle. *Texts: See photo 733.*

▲735 **Soles from hob-nailed Roman boots,** from the Roman fort at Saalburg, Germany. Saalburg Museum. They survived the centuries because they had been thrown into a well with a number of other leather goods. The nails held several layers of leather and also provided traction.

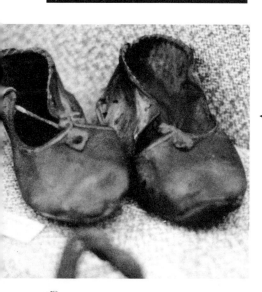

◄737 **Leather shoes, Ptolemaic-Roman** periods, Egypt. British Museum. The shoes have soft soles, are fully enclosed, and are held on the foot by a leather string which passes from the center of the upper shoe to each cuff where it was tied.

▲738 **Sandal on Farnese statue of warrior,** restored with head of Apollo, from an original of fourth century BC. National Museum of Naples. The sandal is a simple thong with closed heel. Straps pass from the 2 levels of the upper heel and from the sole in front of the heel to join the thong at the top of the instep where they are tied. *Texts: See photo 733.*

JEWELRY

The jewelry cases of the ladies of Herculaneum contained necklaces, bracelets, bangles, anklets (not worn by respectable women), brooches, pins, buckles, diadems, hairpins, and rings. There is nothing surprising about jewelry of the first century. Its designs contained precious jewels as they would today, and semiprecious jewels sometimes carved intaglio with images of deities, mythology, or emperors. Gold, silver, bronze, ivory, and other materials were used, and the workmanship was excellent, often intricate. Opals, sapphires, emeralds, sardonyx, jasper, topaz, beryl, onyx, diamonds, and especially pearls were used in jewelry.

Rome was a comparative latecomer to the manufacture of fine jewelry. After Rome began her various second-century BC battles in the East, and particularly after Sulla's victories in the early first century BC, precious metals, stones, and jewelry flowed into Rome. Not only jewelry, but riches such as silver plate became exceedingly popular. Even middle-class families possessed full sets of silver plate along with various extra showpieces. Any successful businessman valued his collection and displayed it with great ostentation. A collection excavated in a villa at Boscoreale, one of the destroyed towns in the Bay of Naples, included 109 pieces. Another collection from Pompeii included 118 pieces.

During Augustus' time so many goldsmiths were at work making jewelry and other objects in Rome that they were divided into 2 guilds, 1 for those who worked in plain gold and 1 for those who worked in leaf. Craftsmen worked

▲739 Gold bracelet, Hellenistic, fourth-first centuries BC. Benaki Museum, Athens. The bracelet ends in a well-fashioned ram's head, below which is intricate filigree work. *Revelation 18:12.*

throughout the Empire, usually selling their wares in their own shops. Some jewelry, though, was sold at large; Alexandria and Antioch of Syria were major centers. Silver shops also sought to meet the demand for such luxury goods. During the New Testament period, Roman silver goods were found throughout the Empire, even on its environs.

Signet rings were worn and used to seal documents, and a ring sometimes contained a small key. Both men and women were fond of rings and usually wore several.

Eastern women wore much more jewelry than Roman or Greek women, if the funerary monuments are a valid indication.

British Museum: A Guide to the Exhibition Illustrating Greek and Roman Life (London: Trustees of the British Museum), 1908; *Waterworks in the Athenian Agora,* Mabel Lang (Princeton: American School of Classical Studies at Athens), 1968; *Everyday Life in the Roman Empire,* Joan Liversidge (New York: G. P. Putnam's Sons), 1976; *Rome in the Augustan Age,* Henry Thompson Rowell (Norman: The University of Oklahoma Press), 1962; *The Athenian Agora,* Dorothy Burr Thompson (Princeton: American School of Classical Studies at Athens), 1971.

▲740 **Bronze bracelets, from Egypt,** Greco-Roman period. Field Museum. The child's pair on the left end has a lily pattern. The adult bracelets on the right imitate twisted metal but are solid cast. *Revelation 18:12.*

▼741 **Earrings with pendants, from Egypt,** first-fourth centuries AD. Field Museum. The earrings are made of bronze, silver, and gold. *Revelation 18:12.*

EARRINGS WITH PENDANTS

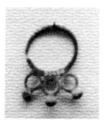

▲742 **Earrings, from Egypt,** Greco-Roman period. Field Museum. The top 2 rings are decorated with 4 circles and balls; the rest have 3.

▲743 **Earrings, first century AD.** British Museum. They are made from emeralds held by thread. The design was a common one and done with various materials such as pearl, stone, or glass. *Revelation 18:12.*

◄744 **Ring, from Tarsus,** AD 200-300. British Museum. The setting is nicolo bezel set in well-executed gold design. *Luke 15:22; James 2:2; Revelation 18:12.*

► **745 Earrings, from Samsum in Asia Minor,** AD 200-300. British Museum. The larger round objects at the bottom are in the shape of miniature bullae, which in New Testament times was a symbol of free birth (later freedmen were allowed to wear them). The design here may or may not have been intended to represent the bulla (a child's neck charm). *Revelation 18:12.*

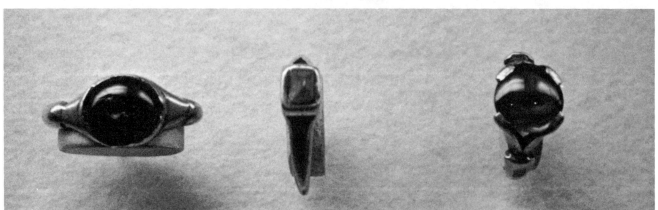

▲**746 Three gold rings,** British Museum. The one at left is a garnet with intaglio image of a bird, about AD 200. The center one is a finger ring of emerald bezel, AD 200-300. The one at right is a finger ring of sapphire bezel, AD 200-300. *Revelation 4:3; 21:19; see also photo 740.*

◄**747 Two gold necklaces,** AD 100-200. British Museum. The center one with shorter neck chain contains an image of Medusa, AD 100-200. The longer one has alternating amethysts and emeralds, about AD 200. *Revelation 4:3; 18:12; 21:19-20.*

▲**748 Bracelet, from Tunis,** AD 200-300. British Museum. It is of gold set with sapphires, emeralds, and pearls. *Revelation 4:3; 17:4; 18:12; 21:19.*

▲**749 Belt buckle, Italic,** fourth century BC. British Museum. The fastening hooks are in the shape of 2 men who wear caps with very high crowns. Portions of the belt are attached.

TOILET

▼ **752 Toilet scene, woman with 2 servants,** funeral monument. Landesmuseum, Trier. The woman sits on a padded stool and rests her feet on a footstool. One servant holds a mirror while another arranges her hair.

▲ **751 Toilet scene, woman with 4 servants,** from Eltern grave monument from Neumagen, third century AD. Landesmuseum, Trier. The woman sits in a wicker chair with a footstool while her servants attend her needs. One holds a mirror while another arranges her hair. A servant on the right holds a bottle that probably contains oil.

▲753, 754, 755, 756, 757 **Toilet scenes from silver bucket.** National Museum of Naples. The bucket (height, 12 inches, or 30.4 cm.) shows 5 scenes from the life of a woman of leisure at her toilet. The scenes indicate a large room with roof supported by arches springing from columns. All of the women are nude until photo 757. Photo 753 shows a servant with her hair fixed on top of her head who carries a large vessel of water. Photo 754 has 2 servants rubbing the mistress with oil; the standing servant hands her mistress a small bottle of oil or perfume. Photo 755 shows the mistress more clearly; she is sitting on a large stool, supporting her weight by her left arm as a servant behind her combs her hair. Photo 756 shows 2 servants conversing as they go about their tasks, the one on the left carrying a small

▲758 **Roman bronze bathtub,** found in Boscoreale, first century AD or earlier. Field Museum. The tub was found in the entrance court of the villa; tubs typically were located near the entrances of homes. It was made from 5 pieces: sides, ends, and bottom. Tubs were made in various ways: hollowed out of rock, made from terra-cotta, built of small stones or brick and waterproofed, or made from bronze as in the photo.

▼ **759 Bronze mirror with bone handle, Etruscan,** 350-330 BC. British Museum. The side seen in the photo is the back side; it is decorated with an engraving of a mythology scene, a representative of Peleus overcoming Thetis. *Texts: See photo 760.*

pail, the one on the right holding her mistress' tunic. Photo 757 has a servant helping the one in the previous photo straighten the cloth of the tunic. The foundation for makeup was a substance made from the sweat of sheep's wool, applied before bed. The next morning the makeup was applied, which consisted of various concoctions described by Ovid in "On Making Up a Woman's Face." Unguents and perfumes came from various areas; the East furnished the most exotic, but a perfume called *seplasium* from Capua was highly admired.

▲**760 Bronze mirror from Etruria, Italy.** Field Museum. It has a long handle for grasping it comfortably. The side seen in the photo was highly polished; the other side was decorated with a scene of the Dioscuri and 2 women. The arrangement was a typical one with ancient mirrors. *1 Corinthians 13:12; 2 Corinthians 2:18; James 1:23.*

▼**761 Silver mirror, from Roman hoard.** British Museum. *Texts: See photo 760.*

▼**762 Bronze slab mirror, from Chiumi, Etruria, Italy.** Field Museum. Made from an alloy of copper and tin (speculum, a variety of bronze), it has been polished for use as a mirror. *Texts: See photo 760.*

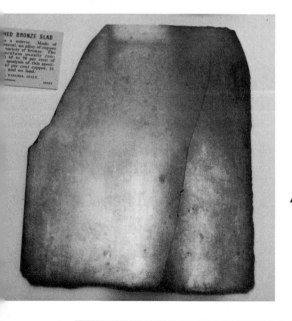

▲**763 Bronze mirror from Thebes,** 1300 BC. British Museum. Though it is much earlier than the New Testament period, it shows how highly polished a bronze mirror could be. The ivory-handled mirror was found in the tomb of Ani, a scribe. *Texts: See photo 760.*

▼765 Earpicks and nail cleaners, Roman. British Museum. The object on left combines a nail file with serrations along its side. The lower ends of both objects are for cleaning the nails, while the upper ends have tiny spoons for removing wax from the ear.

▲766 Various toilet articles, Roman period. Milwaukee Museum. The photo includes bottles, scissors, tweezers, a hairpin, and a small spoon.

▲764 Bronze cist for toilet articles, from Praeneste, Latium, Italy, fourth century BC. Field Museum. The cist was used as a case for the mirror, perfume, rouge, and small objects used in the toilet. It has 3 feet in the form of lion's claws, each one surmounted by a bust. Eight human figures decorate the body of the cist, with a band of palmettes below and ivy wreath above. The figures are involved in a Bacchus dance. On the left is a woman playing a double flute, while on the right a woman with sword drawn has seized another woman by the hair. The handle is in the form of 2 dolphins, each one of which has animal and mythological figures incised.

ROMAN BRONZE TWEEZERS
For the removal of superfluous hair from the face for cosmetic purposes.
POMPEII, ITALY

▲767 Roman bronze tweezers, from Pompeii. Field Museum. Tweezers were used to remove unwanted hair from the face.

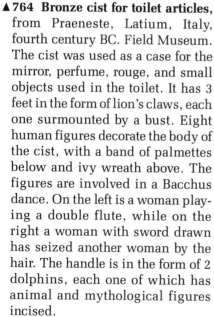

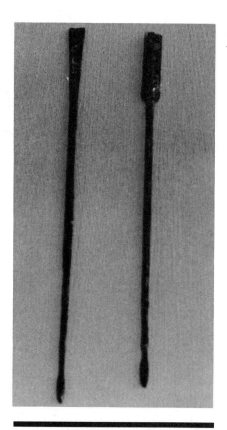

◄**768 Cosmetic spatulas.** The Archaeological Museum of The Southern Baptist Theological Seminary. Each spatula has a larger and smaller end for applying cosmetics and eyeshadow.

▼**769 Bronze spoons, from Egypt, Roman** period, first-third centuries AD. Field Museum. The larger spoons are for unguents; the smaller 2 are ear-spoons.

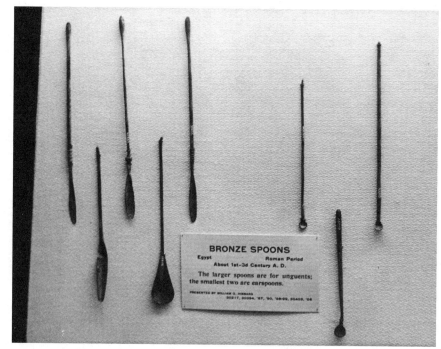

►**771 Bronze makeup box with 5 compartments,** bronze, from Cologne. German-Roman Landesmuseum, Cologne. The lids to each compartment are hinged and have small handles. Many cosmetic boxes have been found; some of them are of exquisite design, such as a woman's head, swimming duck, crouching boar, a shoe, etc.

◄**770 Cosmetic dish with dispensing spout.** Museum of Archeology, Nimes.

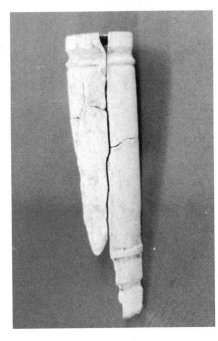

▼773 Bone salve or ointment container. The Archaeological Museum of The Southern Baptist Theological Seminary. The hollowed-out ivory container is very small and had a stopper.

▲772 Cosmetic palette. National Museum of Naples. The fractured palette is held together by a modern frame. Various components were mixed together on the palette.

▲774 Bottles for ointments, perfume, and oil. Roman period. Milwaukee Museum. Two rings and a pair of dice can also be seen. The larger bottles were for oil, the smaller ones for perfume. *Matthew 26:7-9 and parallels; Luke 23:56; John 19:39; Revelation 18:13.*

◄775 Perfume bottles, Roman period. German-Roman Landesmuseum, Cologne. The unusual bottle on top is a "donut" with small feet and a neck to which is attached thin metal handles that become a band to encircle the bottle. The 2 lower bottles are squat with wide rims and stout handles to match the design. Perfume was popular with both sexes. In antiquity, it was made by boiling down the petals of flowers (see photo 353). By the eighth century BC perfumes were imported from the East; they included such incenses as frankincense and myrrh. *Texts: See photo 774.*

►776 Long-necked spherical ointment bottle, German-Roman Landesmuseum, Cologne. *Texts: See photo 774.*

▼778 Tiny perfume bottle. National Museum of Naples. This bottle is shaped like a tiny amphora, with curved bottom and side handles. *Texts: See photo 774.*

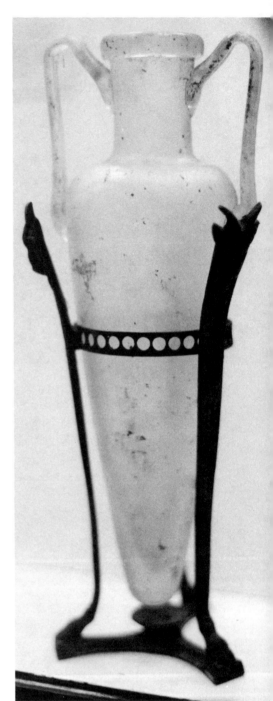

▲777 Tiny perfume bottle. National Museum of Naples. These tiny bottles were used to hold precious perfumes. This one is long-necked, of clear glass, and has 3 tiny feet. *Texts: See photo 774.*

▼780 Silver cosmetic box, from Roman hoard. British Museum.

▲779 Perfume bottle, alabaster. Rockefeller Museum, Jerusalem. The so-called "tear-drop" bottle in which the ancients supposedly caught and kept tears is a myth. The small bottles allowed the perfume to be poured in drops. *Matthew 26:7; Mark 14:3; Luke 7:37; see also photo 774.*

▲781 Glass amphora, from Pompeii, first century AD. Field Museum. The stand is modern but is designed in accordance with ancient style. The medium-sized bottle probably held some liquid used in the toilet, such as oil with which to rub the skin.

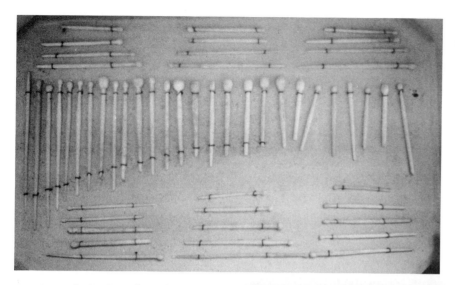

▼783, 784 Collection of hair objects, from in and near Pompeii. National Museum of Naples. At right photo, top right is a comb. Most of the other objects are ivory hairpins, each with a decorative top: The woman's head in the center is a female deity; the full woman at the right is Pudicitia, the personification of modesty and chastity (bone); the woman just below her is Aphrodite tying her hair. In left photo is a pinecone, hands, knobs, heads, statues, and a rooster. Combs were made in ivory or wood.

▲782 **Bone hairpins,** found in Roman villa at Malta. Malta Museum. The style is simple and had been in use from ancient times. They are in various lengths and the heads are of different sizes, but the design is the same. The design is much like a thorn, which probably served the purpose of pins in primitive times.

▼785, 786 **Bronze fibulae, from Italy.** Field Museum. These decorative "safety pins" were used to fasten the tunic at the shoulders and sometimes along the sleeves. The simplest fibulae were of one piece of wire bent to the proper shape, but all kinds of designs were added, with a thicker bow to accommodate the decorations. The spring was strengthened by doubling it. Romans used fibulae more than did Greeks; their designs evolved into the brooch.

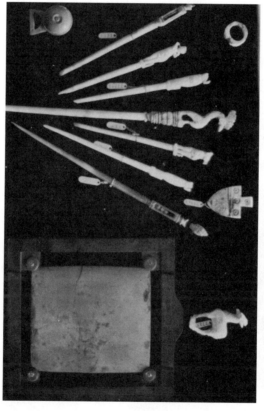

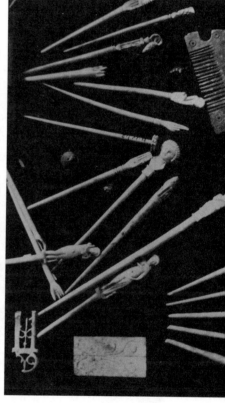

BRONZE FIBULAE

ANCIENT ITALY

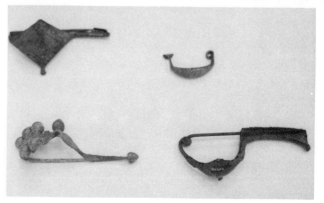

FURNITURE

Furniture was sparse in the Roman world. The bed or couch was the most important piece; the Roman slept on it, napped on it, and reclined on it for leisure or to receive company. It might have been of wood or bronze, or for the poorer simply a slab of masonry attached to the wall. Single and double beds were used, and triple beds (or even larger) sometimes were placed in dining rooms. The bed covering was sparse. A mattress usually was used, on which was placed one cover on which the sleeper lay and another for covering himself. Bedrooms generally were small and contained only a bed, chair, chest, and chamber pot.

Chairs were for most of the population stools or benches without backs. Folding stools often were carried about to be used whenever one chose to sit. The high-backed throne-chair was used for state occasions and divinities, and the sloped-back chair was especially popular with women of leisure or for people of stature such as teachers or leaders of religious ceremonies. The man of leisure sometimes sat in one to read the poetry he was fond of writing to a group invited for the occasion. His chair was on a dais, while his audience sat on backed chairs or benches.

The primary difference in the furnishings of the wealthy was not the amount but the richness. Their furniture was of exotic woods inlaid with ivory or tortoise shell, or of bronze with silver or gold designs. Citrus wood was especially popular for tables, and marble was quite popular for tops, pedestals, and bases.

Daily Life in Ancient Rome, Jerome Carcopino (New Haven: Yale University Press), 1940; *Cities of Vesuvius: Pompeii and Herculaneum*, Michael Grant (New York: Penguin Books), 1971; *Corinth and Its Environs in Antiquity*, Savas E. Kasas (Athens), 1974; *Führer durch das Landesmuseum Trier*, Von Reinhard Schindler (Trier, Germany: Selbstverlag des Rheinischen Landesmuseum Trier), 1980; *Greek and Roman Technology*, K. D. White (Ithaca, New York: Cornell University Press), 1984.

◄**787 Roman woman of leisure.** Pompeiian room reconstructed in Metropolitan Museum of Milwaukee. The woman reclines on a couch of the type used as well for dining. A pillow footstool is at the foot of the couch, a padded stool is in the foreground, and a 3-legged rectangular table containing fruit is nearby. A planter with a fern is set on a higher 3-legged table against the wall near her foot, and to its left is another padded stool. Behind her in the corner is a floor stand for hanging lamps. The floor is marble and the walls are richly adorned with frescoes. She holds a small wine cup in her hand and wears a long tunic with a light shawl around her shoulders and upper body. *Mark 10:17-31; Luke 12:16-21; 16:19-31; 1 Timothy 6:6-10.*

▼**788 Sitting stool**, third century AD, funeral monument. Landesmuseum, Trier. The stool is a cylinder with designs on its side and a cushion for padding. The matron rests her feet on a footstool. (See full scene in photo 752.) *Matthew 21:12.*

▲**789 Bedroom in villa**, Augst, Switzerland. The reconstructed villa houses the museum with its finds from excavations of the Roman fort at Augst. The bedroom shown has furniture reconstructed from finds at Pompeii. The bed consists of a frame onto which has been stretched wide straps which support the mattress and pillow. The legs and feet of the bed are well designed and turned on a lathe, and the bed has a headboard. Room furnishings include a chest with nailhead-like design, a round tripod table, a wicker chair, and a floor lampstand. Greek styles formed the basis of Roman furniture, except that the rounded-back chair and the floor lampstand (earlier, candlestand) were Etruscan contributions. *Matthew 9:2,6-7; Luke 5:18-26; 8:16; 17:34; Acts 5:15.*

◄**790 Woman on couch**, terra-cotta. Benaki Museum, Athens. The couch is Roman; Greek couches did not have backs. Couches were used for both dining and sleeping. *Texts: See photo 789.*

▲791 Funeral monument of Longinus, AD 80-90. Roman-German Landesmuseum, Cologne. The inscription in Latin reads:
LONGINVS BIARTA

BISAE F(ilius)
BESSVS EQ(ues)
ALAE SVLP(iciae)
AN(norum) XXXXVI
DE suo F(aciendum) C(uravit)

The deceased person's name was Longinus Biarta, son of Bisa, family of Besser. Longinus is a Roman name, while Biarta is Thracian. He was a rider in the cavalry of Galba in AD 46 and probably came to Germany to serve Galba and decided to remain. Longinus reclines on a cushioned dining couch, and he holds a cup in his right hand and a napkin in his left. Two additional cups are on the tripod table by his couch. Both cups have opposing handles. His servant stands at his foot to wait on him, holding a dipper in his hands to refill his master's wine cup. The 3-legged table, which legs end in lion claws, was common in Greece and Rome and may originally have been designed to accommodate uneven floors. The bed legs are ornately turned and the bed has both a headboard and a footboard. Longinus reclines on a thick mattress and pillows. *Texts: See photo 789.*

▶792 Woman on couch, funeral relief. Corinth Museum. The deceased is shown reclining on a couch of the same style as shown in photo 791, with well-turned legs, a headboard and footboard, and with mattress and pillows. The ever-present 3-legged table stands beside the bed and another woman sits nearby on a folding chair with a footstool. Below the inscription above the deceased is a design of connected rosettes from the center of which hangs a disk which may represent a plumb bob (see photo 296). Stools were common for household use and were of various designs as box-shaped, with legs, or folding. *Texts: See photo 789.*

◄793 Funeral marker of cavalry-man Marcus Sacrius, end of first century AD. Roman-German Landesmuseum, Cologne. The inscription in full reads:
MARCVS SACRIVS
SECVRI F(ilius) PRIMIGENIVS
eqVES ALAE NORICOR(um)
TVR(ma)
pAterCLI CIVES REMVS
ANN(orum)
XXVI stIP(endiorum) XI H(eres)
F(aciendum) C(uravit)
"Marcus Sacrius Primigenius, son of Securus, was a rider in the northern cavalry division, squadron of Paterclus, of the region of Reims. He died at 26 years of age after 11 years of service; thus he served from age 15. His heirs allowed this gravestone erected." His pose is virtually the same as that shown in photo 791, with wine cup, 2 bowls on the 3-legged table, and a servant ready at the foot to pour more wine.

◄794 Deathbed of a married couple, fourth century BC. Corinth Museum. It is 6 feet, 9 inches (2.06 m.) long and 3 feet, 4 inches (1.02 m.) wide; it was found in a Macedonian vault-grave in Cleliotomylos. The artifact provides a view of the double bed. The 4 legs done in relief on each corner would be free-standing in a real bed. *Texts: See photo 789.*

►795 Bed in House of the Charred Furniture, Herculaneum. The wooden slats and portions of the turned legs are intact. Usually beds were made of wood, which sometimes was inlaid with rare woods and fitted with metal intaglios of silver or gold. Legs were of wood or bronze. Rope or other material sometimes served in place of the slats, on which were placed mattresses and pillows. Chamberpots were placed close by. The walls were paint or fresco on plaster. *Texts: See photo 789.*

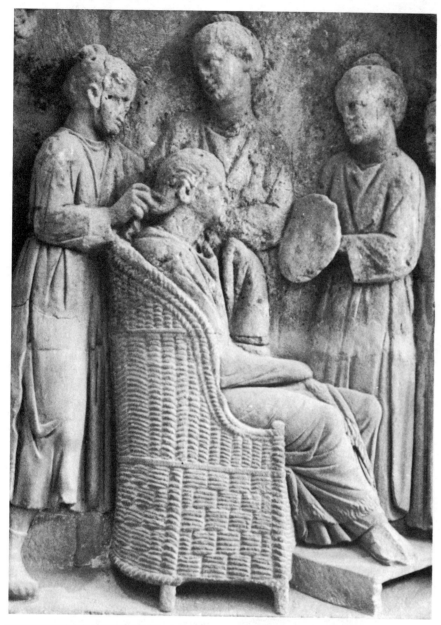

◄ **796 Woman in wicker chair,** grave monument from Neumagen, third century AD. Landesmuseum, Trier. The deceased, an aristocratic woman, is shown at her toilet with 4 attendants (one at extreme right). One servant fixes her hair while another holds a mirror. The wicker chair is a common style, woven in wicker around a wood frame and with a curved back. A footstool normally was used, as in this photo. (See photo 751.)

► **797 Man in curved-back chair** collecting rent, grave monument from Neumagen, third century AD. Landesmuseum, Trier. The landowner or official sits and holds a codex with several leaves (see photo 201). The material of the chair is not wicker; perhaps it was made of leather or wood. The feet are round balls and the man sitting does not use a footstool.

▲ **798 Venus sitting, Mars and Eros nearby,** fresco from Pompeii. National Museum of Naples. The scene is an erotic one, with Eros playfully watching at the side as Mars caresses Venus' breast. Venus sits on an elaborately turned throne-chair of a type usually used in state occasions. It is covered in fine upholstery on the seat and back; the legs are substantial but taper to a narrow line just above the feet, which flare out again to wide proportions. The arms are round and supported above the legs with small statuettes. *Matthew 5:34; Acts 2:30; Colossians 1:16; Revelation 3:21.*

FURNITURE

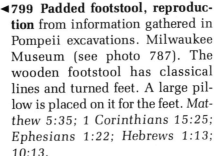

◀**799 Padded footstool, reproduction** from information gathered in Pompeii excavations. Milwaukee Museum (see photo 787). The wooden footstool has classical lines and turned feet. A large pillow is placed on it for the feet. *Matthew 5:35; 1 Corinthians 15:25; Ephesians 1:22; Hebrews 1:13; 10:13.*

▼**800 Pedestal table, from House of the Charred Furniture, Herculaneum.** The table has been partially reconstructed from broken pieces. The top and base are marble, and the pedestal is in the form of a man in Phrygian dress, possibly representing Attis. Pedestal tables were the most common type; they were used to display prized possessions and often had tiers of shelves. Tables such as the one shown have been found in first-century AD homes on the Western Hill in Jerusalem; thus they were common throughout the Empire.

▼**802 Stone bench in House of the Wooden Partition, Herculaneum.** The wooden partition divides the living room from the atrium. This house, along with many others in the region, was converted from luxurious villas to apartment houses after the earthquake of AD 62. The pool once had an open skylight directly above it to catch rainwater which augmented the house's water supply. Flowerpots were set around the lower and sometimes upper ledge. The small pillar supported a flowerpot or small statue. The bench, which in appearance is similar to stone benches today, provided a relaxing place to sit. The plastered walls were decorated with frescoes. Romans invented window glass, and its use spread rapidly among those who could afford it.

▼**801 Table with offerings,** closeup from photo 442. National Museum of Naples. The rectangular table is substantially built with a thick top supported by squared legs and a shelf below. The objects on the table are offerings to be used in the ritual.

▲803 Family meal, Roman period, gable of grave monument from Neumagen. Landesmuseum, Trier. Women sit in chairs at each end of the table and another in the center, and men are between them. They partake of wine and food. Two platters of food are on the table and each seated woman holds a basket of fruit in her lap. The woman at left hands a cup of wine to the man beside her while the next man and woman pass food from one to the other. A food table or cabinet in the right corner of the gable has a wine bowl on top with a ladle standing in it. A wine container with ladle stands on the floor in the right gable corner. The chairs are of different design; the one on the left is enclosed and has a slightly curved back and small ball feet, while the one on the right has a pronounced curve for the back and is open, made of wood, and with the front legs straight and the back ones slanted. Each chair has a footstool. The table is stoutly made with 6 legs joined by rungs.

►804 Cherubs working at a table, fresco from Herculaneum. National Museum of Naples. Each cherub sits on a stout 4-legged stool and works at a stout rectangular table with 4 legs connected by rungs. A shelf attached to the wall above them holds containers, and a large cabinet stands open beside them. The cabinet has ornate short legs and double-hinged doors. The work they are doing cannot be determined. The cherubs wear loincloths. *Matthew 15:27; Mark 11:15-19; Acts 6:2; Romans 11:9.*

◄805 Brazier, in reconstructed Pompeii room. Milwaukee Museum (see photo 787). Though some wealthy homes were heated by pipes which ran from furnaces through floors and walls, most homes were heated by open braziers in which charcoal was burned. This one is of iron supported by lions' feet. The sides are decorated with theatrical masks between which is an animal over a kill. A handle is provided at each end and the top is decorated with high crenalations. The brazier, with various modifications, was used for both heating and cooking.

▲806 Brazier, iron, from Etruria, Italy, about 500 BC. Field Museum. The brazier is supported by legs with false wheels, each of which is surmounted by a hippocampus, which is a mythical seahorse with a fishtail. Bowl-shaped braziers also were placed on tripods for height.

LAMPS

Lamps have a long history and seem to have originated in the East. By the seventh century BC they were being produced in Greek lands and by the third century in Roman areas. Mold-made lamps appeared during the third century BC, and during the first century AD Roman lamps dominated the market.

The forms of lamps varied widely during the New Testament period, from primitive pinched spouts to multiple spouts, made of clay, bronze, or even of gold, standing or hanging, with simple or elaborate design and artwork. Stands had platforms or arms for setting or hanging lamps. Reliefs depicting mythology, religious symbolism, daily life and work, and erotic scenes were common.

A small lamp burned for an average of 2 to 3 hours and provided a little more light than a candle. The oil used was the same as for cooking except that a bit of salt was added to provide a brighter and yellower flame.

The Oxford Classical Dictionary, edited by N. G. L. Hammond and H. H. Scullard (Oxford: Clarendon Press), 1970; *Lamps from the Athenian Agora*, Judith Perlzweig (Princeton: American School of Classical Studies at Athens), 1963; *Pompeii: AD 79*, John Ward-Perkins and Amanda Claridge (Boston: Museum of Fine Arts), 1978.

807, 808 Two pinched-spout lamps, found in the Roman villa, Malta, reconstructed to house the museum. Malta Museum. Lamps with pinched spouts are primitive in design. *Matthew 5:15; 25:1-13; Luke 8:16; 15:8; Revelation 4:5; 8:10; 18:23.*

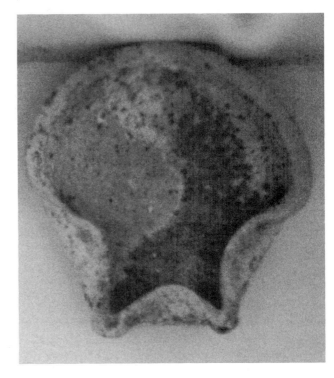

▲809, 810, 811, 812, 813 Five single-spout lamps from Palestine, Roman period. Milwaukee Museum. Photos 809 and 810 are the most typical type and were used throughout the Empire. The oil was poured into the large hole to feed a wick which extended through the small hole. The first one is designed simply with raised lines; the second design is a more intricate use of spirals and tendrils, and it has a thumb knob on the back. Photo 811 is a more circular and flatter design and has a small hole

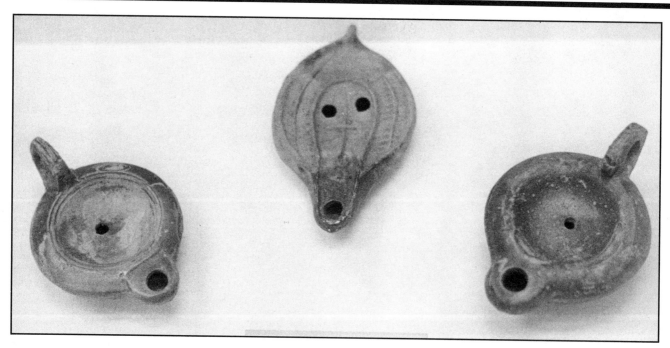

▲814, 815, 816 Three single-spout lamps, from Pompeii, first century AD. Field Museum. The lamp on the left is shallow, without decoration except for the handle, and has a small oil hole set in a top that is somewhat more recessed than most; the recess was to avoid spilling oil while pouring. The lamp in the center has 2 offset oil holes. A raised band runs around the oil holes and the wick hole, and a cross runs from between the oil holes toward the end of the lamp. (Crosses have a history independent of the Christian symbolism.) The result is a sort of face, though that design may not have been intended. Other bands with radiating lines are on either side, and a pinched handle is provided on the back end. The photo on the right is similar to the one on the left except that it has 2 circles at the edge of the recessed middle. This dish type, Italic, was developed in the first century AD. *Texts: See photo 807.*

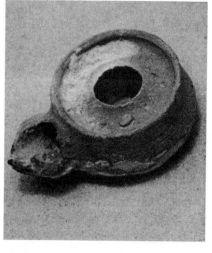

▼818 **Single spout lamp with relief.** Museo di Villa Giullia, Rome. The recess contains a bas-relief of two gladiators fighting. The oil hole is small and the wick spout is flared out. *Texts: See photo 807.*

for oil. The remaining space contains a relief. Photos 812 and 813 are quite simple and unadorned but with a somewhat larger chamber for holding oil. This style devel-

oped during the first half of the fourth century BC. These molded lamps were superceded by the dish type in the photos that follow. *Texts: See photo 807.*

◄817 **Lamp with manufacturer's stamp,** first-third century AD. Roman-German Landesmuseum, Cologne. Commercial lamps are commonly found in the western provinces of Rome, with the name of the manufacturer stamped on the bottom. They generally have a simple form; decorations with theater masks, busts or heads of deities, and the like are not usual. *Texts: See photo 807.*

▼**820 Hellenistic clay lamp,** fourth-first century BC. Benaki Museum, Athens. The oil bowl is deep and has holes through which the oil flowed to a smaller recess in the spout. Three pinches have been built into the spout but, judging by the burn marks, only the front pinch held a wick. *Texts: See photo 807.*

▲**819 Mold-made clay lamp with Silenus.** Museum of Art and Archaeology, University of Missouri-Columbia. Silenus, the constant companion of Dionysus, is shown holding a wine bowl. A thyrsus is behind him. The dish style made possible relief designs such as this one and much like the one in photo 818. Both have a flared wick spout. Museum photo. *Texts: See photo 807.*

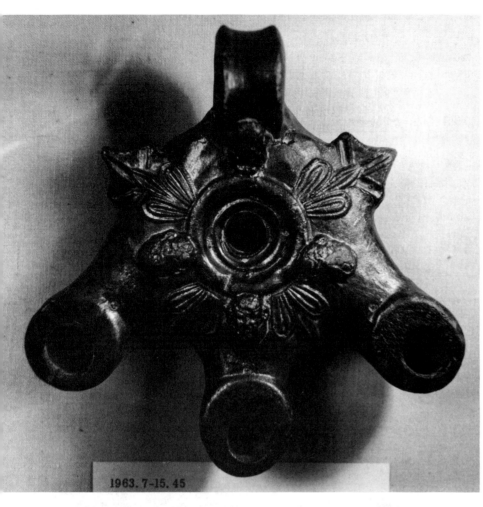

▼**822 Eight-spout lamp,** from Roman Egypt, second-fourth centuries AD. Field Museum. *Texts: See photo 803.*

▲**821 Three-spout lamp,** late first century AD. British Museum. Of clay, it was mold-made in central Italy by the lampmaker A. Paccius. Four Silenus and satyr heads, interspersed with stylized leaves, decorate the body. *Texts: See photo 807.*

▼**823 Seven-spout lamp,** from Roman Egypt, first century AD. Museum of Art and Archaeology, University of Missouri-Columbia. The figure on the thumbpiece is Zeus Amun. The oil hole is decorated with incised heavy lines running to circles. Curves ending in spirals artistically join the various nozzles to the center of the lamp. Museum photo. *Texts: See photo 807.*

▲ **824 Relief of a candelabrum,** Roman, from Smyrna, second century AD. Ashmolean Museum, Oxford. The candelabrum has a heavy, very ornate base with Egyptian design features from which rises a palm tree, complete with trimmed fronds, dates, and upper fronds, on top of which is a candleholder.

▼**825 Table stand for lamp.** Photo courtesy of Kelsey Museum of Archaeology, The University of Michigan. The iron stand has a 2-nozzle lamp on top. The shaft is an elongated fluted column design, the 3 feet end in horses' hooves, leaves alternate between the legs, and an iron tool for lifting the cap from the oil hole hangs down the side of the stand. Designs of similar nature but taller were used as floor stands. Small tripods or other stands only 3 or 4 inches high also were used for table tops. *Matthew 5:15; Mark 4:21; Hebrews 9:2; Revelation 1:12-13,20; 2:1,5.*

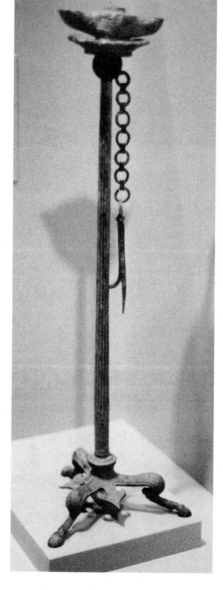

▲**826 Bronze oil lantern,** Roman, from Oplontia, first century AD. British Museum. A small lamp burned inside the lantern, which was for outside use. Some kind of transparent or translucent material, perhaps horn, bladder, or linen was held in place by the metal frame. During the Imperial period glass began to be used. The domed top could be raised for access to the inside. Several such lanterns have been found. *John 18:3.*

►**827 Two-spout hanging lamp with cover.** Photo courtesy of Kelsey Museum of Archaeology, The University of Michigan. Lamps often were hung either from holders attached to walls or from table- or floor-lampstands. The iron mouse on the lid perhaps served to frighten real mice from attempting to steal the oil. *Texts: See photo 807.*

◄**828 Bronze oil lantern.** National Museum of Naples. A candle was burned in the container at the bottom of the base or an oil lamp could be placed inside the lantern. The apparatus on top is the handle, which is attached by chains, and which also provides various ways of hanging the lantern. *John 18:3.*

FOOD AND DINING

Bread, wine, and olive oil provided the basic diet of the common people, both Greeks and Romans. Bread was of wheat or barley, barley being the inferior of the 2. It sometimes was supplemented by cheese, honey, or other simple foods. Wine was the only beverage of significance; both beer and milk were considered barbaric. Those who lived in a city, even a small one, purchased the oil and wine in shops and the bread at bakeries. Porridge was common; fish was an important supplement to the diet, and many varieties were eaten. In addition, Greek writers mention cake, figs, grapes, olives, goat meat, fruit, honey, grain, lentils, cummin seed, game such as hare and boar, and a variety of other dishes.

The Roman common diet was somewhat broader; in addition to the foods mentioned above, poultry, hunting game, and eggs were important. Some Romans were vegetarians and preferred a wide range of vegetables and fruit. The Roman loved the evening meal and added as much variety to it as they could afford. Sauces, condiments, and herbs were important to the Roman kitchen; they apparently disliked the natural tastes and preferred strongly spiced preparations.

With the rise of a middle class during the early Empire, the evening meal took on more and more of a culinary experience. Ironically, the cooking arrangements bordered on the primitive. Chimneys were unknown (the 2 examples so far found are disputed), so smoke from the hearth and oven had to escape through a window or an opening in the loft. The oven was for baking pastries; the hearth was for other cooking. The hearth provided an open charcoal-burning surface.

Romans observed 3 meals a day, but the first and second meals, somewhat similar to breakfast and lunch, consisted of small amounts ranging from a simple drink of water to bread with a little cold meat, vegetables, cheese, or fruit washed down with wine. The evening meal was the celebrated one and the table was well set. The frequent picture of the Roman glutton reflects the image of the evening meal, when all the work was done, and does not recognize the sparcity of food partaken the rest of the day.

Romans and Greeks ate the evening meal reclining on couches or the couch-shaped *triclinia*, both for comfort and as a mark of social distinction. During the first century, both Roman men and women ate reclining, while their children ate in chairs by the couches. Slaves, travelers, and customers at *tabernae* ate in chairs. Tablecloths were not used until Domitian's time; prior to that the marble or wooden top was simply wiped off as necessary. Along with the spoons, food was eaten with the hands as well, so that handwashings were needed after each course; servants stood by with water and towel. The full meal consisted of 7 courses.

The wealthy delighted in new and exotic recipes, and several ancient writers caricatured the lengthy dining experience of the aristocrats. Though wide application is not appropriate, the records reveal much of the Roman diet. A cookbook has survived as well which contains a great many recipes by a celebrated Roman cook named Apicius; his book is available today (see bibliography following). Hosts sometimes served good and poorer wines to guests according to their station in life. A full banquet included entertainment of music, dancing, acrobatics, poetry, or comics between courses. Belching was considered an act of politeness.

One more typical dinner by an aristocrat was described by Pliny the Younger (*Ep.* I, 15) as consisting of oysters, chitterlings, and sea-urchins, with entertainment of Spanish dancers. A middle-class meal for a guest is recorded as including mallows, lettuce, leek, mint, eggs, lizard-fish, mutton, meatballs, beans, sprouts, chicken, ham, apples, and wine (*Martial*, X, 48). Honey was used for sugar, and the typical Roman house was built around a garden plot. The garden, for both flowers and food, was a major factor in Roman life.

Daily Life in Ancient Rome, Jerome Carcopino (New York: Yale University Press), 1940; *Herculaneum: Italy's Buried Treasure*, Joseph Jay Deiss (New York: Harper and Rowe), 1985; *A Short History of Technology*, T. K. Derry and Trevor I. Williams (New York: Oxford University Press), 1961; *Amphoras and the Ancient Wine Trade*, Virginia R. Grace (Princeton: American School of Classical Studies at Athens), 1961; *The Oxford Classical Dictionary*, N. G. L. Hammond and H. H. Scullard, editors (London: Oxford University Press), 1970; *Römermuseum und Römerhaus Augst*, Max Martin (Augst, Switzerland: Römermuseum Augst), 1981; *Führer durch das Landesmuseum Trier*, Von Reinhard Schindler (Trier, Germany: Selbstverlag des Rheinischen Landesmuseums Trier), 1980; *Ante Pacem: Archaeological Evidence of Church Life Before Constantine*, Graydon F. Snyder (Macon, Georgia: Mercer University Press), 1985; *Apicius: Cookery and Dining in Imperial Rome*, Joseph Dommers Vehling, editor and translator (New York: Dover Publications, Inc.); *Pompeii: AD 79*, vol. II, John Ward-Perkins and Amanda Claridge (Boston: Museum of Fine Arts), 1978; *Roman Art and Architecture*, Sir Mortimer Wheeler (New York: Oxford University Press), 1964; *Country Life in Classical Times*, K. D. White (Ithaca, New York: Cornell University Press), 1977.

▲829, 830 **Progress of meal**, reliefs. From a frieze once attached to a burial monument in Neumagen. Landesmuseum, Trier. Photo 830 shows 2 women and 2 men eating around a rectangular table covered with a cloth (which developed during Domitian's reign). The women sit in wicker chairs at each end, while the men recline in Roman fashion behind the table. The men pass drinking cups to the women, and a platter of fish is seen on the table. The back wall of the dining room is equipped with curtains, and a serving room is off to each side. The room to the left is a liquor room where beer and wine are kept to serve the table (beer would not be included in Greek or Roman houses). A high table with legs in the shape of a lion's head tapering to a lion's foot holds vessels of various shapes, while other vessels are on the floor under the table. One servant holds a vessel under his arm and reaches for another on the table, while another servant pours wine or beer from a long-necked jar into a bowl. Wine was stored and shipped in large amphorae and was quite strong; anyone who drank it full strength was considered abnormal. The wine was poured into a bowl and mixed with water at a rate of one-third up to four-fifths; sometimes the wine was cooled with snow or heated for special types. The room to the right of the dining room is more weathered and part of the scene is outside of the photo; the scene has servants working at a wood sideboard handling large plates and dishes. Photo 829 shows a kitchen scene. The left side is weathered, but a servant can be seen cleaning a large plate. The next servant to the right works at a long wood table cutting food with a large knife (see photo 321), another servant works with a mixing bowl at a small wood table, and 2 cooks work on an oven top preparing food.

▼ **831 Kitchen in Roman villa, Augst,** Switzerland. From right to left is seen an oven, a handmill, and a hearth. The oven is raised on a platform for convenience. The handmill is turned by the long handle that is attached to one side of the upper stone by a peg and runs through a large hole in the upper crosspiece, which allows the handle to turn with the upper stone. Other handmills are on the floor beside the mounted one. The top of the hearth is used for cooking, while the oval opening holds a supply of wood. The wood is burned on the hearth top until a bed of hot coals is formed; then cooking vessels are placed over the coals using a variety of holders and grates. A grappling hook (see photo 888) hangs on the wall between the mill and the hearth, and chains for attaching vessels hang above the hearth. A wall shelf and a table on the left wall hold utensils and provide work space. The kitchen is typical for a villa. The hearth is modeled after one found in the House of the Veteii in Pompeii. The fire burned on a masonry base covered with flat tile, and gutter tile was attached to the inside walls. The oven was not connected to a chimney; the rising smoke escaped through some other opening, such as a window in the loft or high roof. The oven is reconstructed from one found in Augst, which is quite similar to a much larger commercial one found in Herculaneum. (An unusual feature of the one found in Augst is that it served also to furnish heat for a hypocaust system.) The iron grate on the hearth was fashioned after a find in Augst. Cooking utensils typically included bronze or sometimes clay pots, saucepans, 3-legged bowls (legs allowed for coals to be put underneath; otherwise a grate had to hold the vessels), casseroles, specially shaped vessels, spoons, scoops, knives, sieves, utensils, and mortar and pestle. The latter was essential in the Roman kitchen for grinding grain and spices to prepare the sauces widely used in food. The cook took great pride in developing new tastes for food, which was enjoyed in its richness not only by the wealthy, but by all Romans. *Luke 10:38-40*.

▲ 832 **Oven in Herculaneum villa,** in the House of the Atrium and Mosaic. The supporting blocks are made from brick which is plastered over. The cooking surface is of flat tiles. Wood was stored in the open space under the cooking top. Hot coals were prepared on the tile surface, and cooking utensils were set above the coals on various types of grill and raised platforms. Smoke escaped through the window above. *Matthew 6:30; Luke 12:28.*

▶ 834 **Commercial oven in Herculaneum,** in the bakeshop of Sextus Patulcus Felix. The oven is of the same design as the one in the Roman villa at Augst (see photo 831). Two phalli above the oven door ward away evil, particularly that which would ruin his baked goods. The modern pizza oven is similar to the same design. A baker's palette with a long handle was used for placing the bread and other goods in the oven. Felix had an assembly line of sorts; another room contained 2 grinding mills turned by small donkeys and areas for mixing the recipes. *Matthew 6:30; Luke 12:28.*

▼ 833 **Cooking pot on stand,** from Roman fort at Saalburg, Germany. Saalburg Museum. Coals were placed inside the clay stand, which has various openings for the circulation of air, and the cooking pot was placed on top. Such stands allowed the cook to vary the type of heat to various dishes. The iron grill in the foreground was to set in the coals so that pans and other utensils could be set on top of it.

▼836 Dining room in Roman villa, Augst. The reconstructed dining room is part of the reconstructed villa which houses the museum at Augst, Switzerland. It opens off onto the peristyled garden and boasts a mosaic floor. The dining room, *triclinium*, received its name from the built-in 3-couch arrangement, the *triclinia*. A door leads directly from the kitchen to the dining room, which has eating couches arranged in the form of three beds in a U-shape. Diners reclined on pillows and covers, so that they ate on their stomachs or sides with their freshly washed feet not straight downward but crosswise. The host sat in the center, alone if he asserted his privilege or with a guest whom he sought to honor. The seating arrangement was set and symbolic, the highest position being to the right of the host. A small round table also is built into the arrangement to hold the food, which was kept supplied continuously by servants. A candlestand is nearby to provide light, and a wicker chair is ready for company. The floor of the room is decorated with a mosaic which measures 10 feet, 4 inches by 15 feet, 5 inches (3.15 by 4.7 m). The mosaic, which has geometric designs and bright rosettes, was found in an estate house at Holstein. In the back wall of the room is a painting of the Homeric story of a Trojan kidnapping Helen, an enlargement of a fresco found at Pompeii. *Matthew 11:18-19; 26:20-25 and parallels; Acts 2:46; Revelation 3:20.*

▲835 Cooking surface in small bath, Ostia. The thermapolium in which this oven was excavated was a small private establishment where friends could meet, bathe, visit, and eat. The oven has a large working surface, with shelves above and a large area for storing wood. The surface of both the working area and the shelves connected with it is of marble. The cooking was done with stands such as the one in photo 833, since snacks rather than large meals were prepared.

837, 838 Dining room in Pompeii, Villa of Julia Felix, located next to the amphitheater. The area includes the *triclinia* seating arrangement and a nymphaeum. The seating is similar to that shown in photo 836 except that the table is somewhat larger and the couch on the right side has a built-in bolster at the near end. The fountain is typical; it is decorated with a brightly colored mosaic and has a pedestal for a statue. Water was piped to it, and musicians stood by it during formal dinners to play, sing, or dance. The area is covered by a pitched roof supported by round plastered-brick pillars and the nymphaeum, and it is open to a large walled garden area. *Texts: See photo 836.*

▼839, 840 Nymphaeum in Herculaneum, House of Neptune and Amphitrite (wine merchant's house).

Photo 839 shows the nymphaeum itself; photo 840 shows a mosaic on the wall to the right of the nymphaeum. The nymphaeum is similar to the one in photo 838. It has smaller rectangular niches on each side of the arched one; the arched one held a statue, and the smaller ones held marble pedestals. The stone structure is covered with marble mosaic. The 2 scenes on either side of the arch are the same, a dog chasing a stag, with a peacock looking down from flowers tied in place with ribbons. The side borders are delicate scrolls and festoons of leaves and fruit; the upper border alternates with vases and winged seahorses connected with scrolls. The style is classical and was rare during Roman times. Above, the design has disappeared but may have been stucco with figures or decorations in relief. Theatrical masks cap the structure. Photo 840 shows Neptune and his wife Amphitrite framed in large borders. Neptune is nude except for a shawl draped across his shoulders, and he holds his trident in his left hand. Amphitrite is draped in a traditional goddess manner, with clothing off her shoulders and covering, in an improbable manner, only her lower thighs. She wears a necklace, teases her hair with her right hand, and holds a thyrsus in her left. The two figures are set in a gold background. The wide side borders are festoons of fruit and leaves connected by delicate scrolls. They support a wide radiating sconce-shell arch. The outside mosaic borders are square columns with classical bases and capitals; they support a band of geometric designs. The extensive mosaics and bright colors (blue and gold predominate) compensated for the fact that the dining room did not open onto a garden area. There is a small place for musicians to perform to the left of the nymphaeum. The house is a simply designed 2-storied one, the front lower part of which was a shop.

◄841, 842 **Eucharist scenes from Christian sarcophagi.** Vatican Museum. The 2 fragments are from Christian burials during the Roman period. The early Christian implications are debated among the options of agape love feast, meal for the dead, a meal connected with eschatology, or an amalgamation of various purposes. That debate is important for early church history, but the styles of dressing and eating also provide evidence for earlier patterns. In both photos the table is curved; the style is called a *lunar sigma*. The most important persons reclined at the ends; the table normally accommodated 7 or 8 people. In photo 841 the open space in front of the table contains a small table on which a fish has been placed. The diners all are reclining in the traditional manner and are dividing round loaves of bread. They wear tunics, mostly off the shoulder, but at least the man second from left has his arm covered. Photo 842 has only the round loaves of bread, but a servant dressed in a belted tunic serves the diners out of a woven basket. They do not appear to be reclining, but the artist may have made the figures more upright simply to show them better. *Texts: See photo 836.*

►843 **Bowl of ancient wheat.** British Museum. During the Ptolemaic period wheat increasingly replaced barley and emmer as the chief cereal crop grown in Egypt, especially when Rome made Egypt the primary supplier of grain for the city's dole. *Matthew 3:12; 12:1; Luke 16:7; Acts 27:38; Revelation 6:6; 18:13.*

◄**844 Fresco of birds and mushrooms,** from Herculaneum. National Museum of Naples. Part of a 4-part panel that includes photo 847; they were joined at the museum but originally were separate. On the left, top shelf, are 3 thrushes; below them is a collection of 6 pink mushrooms. On the right, top shelf, are 2 partridges (probably); below are 2 eels. Paintings of dead birds, animals, and fish were popular themes for frescoes; it was customary to send uncooked foods to friends.

►**845 Fresco of hens and grain,** from Herculaneum. National Museum of Naples. The hens have not yet been killed, though the feet are tied. The grain in the baskets may represent their food or may be for the meal; the staff probably was used to catch the hens. Apicius has recipes for chicken fricassé, boiled, creamed, stuffed, cold, with various sauces, chicken broth, and others.

◄**846 Fresco of squids and fish,** from Pompeii. National Museum of Naples. Various types of fish are represented; two hang from a nail on the left, others are laid on the top and bottom shelves, and a squid and shellfish are depicted between the shelves. *Matthew 7:10; Mark 14:17-20; Luke 24:42.*

▲847 Fresco of fowl, rabbit, and fruit, from Herculaneum. National Museum of Naples. On the left is a plucked chicken hanging by its feet and a rabbit hung up by one forepaw. On the right is a partridge strung up by its beak and beside it a pomegranate and an apple.

▼849 Fresco of food, from Herculaneum. National Museum of Naples. The bird is a kingfisher; it stands on the handle of a silver pitcher. Two scuttlefish (top shelf), a crayfish, shellfish, and murex are visible, and credit is given to Neptune with the addition of his trident.

▼848 Fresco of fruit, seafood, and fowl. National Museum of Naples. A silver bowl on the top shelf holds fruit, the platter on the center shelf holds small fish, and the bottom shelf holds 2 geese.

▲850 Fresco of seafood, from Pompeii. National Museum of Naples. Various types of seafood are pictured, the centerpiece being the 2 fish in the basket on the bottom shelf. Shellfish, squid, and a platter are set on the shelving.

VESSELS
AND COOKING UTENSILS

►**851 Reconstruction of Hildesheim silver room.** Landesmuseum, Trier. The Hildesheim Treasure, a collection of silver plate that dates to the early first century AD, was found in Hanover, Germany and now is in Berlin. It was taken as booty from Quinctilius Varus. Only a few pieces and part of the room are shown; the reconstructions are plated, whereas the originals were solid silver. The floor contains a mosaic with geometric designs, and the side table has a slate top supported by massive columns with spiral designs. The pieces shown include a large bowl, vases, dishes, and ladles. Romans generally ate from round plates and shallow dishes, but they had special dishes and bowls shaped to particular kinds of food. Knives and forks were not used, only spoons of 2

shapes: one with a circular bowl and a point on the handle for extracting shellfish, and a pear-shaped dessert spoon for eating cereals and other foods. *2 Timothy 2:20-21; Revelation 18:12.*

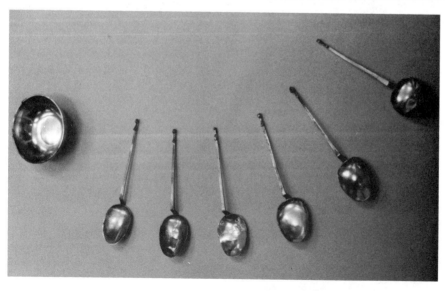

▲**852, 853 Silver table service,** from Tivoli (ancient Tiber), about AD 100. Field Museum. Eight of 20 pieces are shown; photo 852 has 6 spoons and a small bowl, and photo 853 shows an oval vessel

shaped for a special dish. Each piece is inscribed with the name of the silversmith, SATTIAE.L.F., along with a slightly exaggerated weight as was customary at the time. *Texts: See photo 851.*

See color photo 418.

▼855 **Skyphos with erotic scene** in relief, second-third centuries AD. German-Roman Landesmuseum, Cologne. A skyphos was a 2-handled drinking cup; it was in common use from antiquity.

▲854 **Silver serving spoons,** Roman period. Milwaukee Museum. A wide variety of decorations was used in silverware, which has been found in all parts of the Empire. Manufacturing centers or at least suppliers included the coastlands of Asia Minor, Antioch of Syria, Rhodes, Mitylene, and Alexandria. *Texts: See photo 851.*

▲856, 857 **Megarian bowls,** third century BC, made in Attica. Agora Museum, Athens. This type of bowl was used for drinking wine and was particularly popular during the third-second centuries BC. They are similar in design to bowls found in large quantities in Pompeii which were manufactured in Gaul. Thus the style continued in use, though Italy and Gaul replaced Greece as primary suppliers.

▲858 Glass plate, first century AD. Leyden Museum, Netherlands. It was made by blowing molten glass into a mold (see photo 859). Blown glass began to be manufactured during the first century AD. Its place of discovery probably was Syria. Before that, various methods of glass-making were employed. In very ancient times 2 methods were used: Fritting was the process of heating the ingredients of glass—soda, lime, and sand—and raking the material to eliminate the gasses and to mix the ingredients properly; the melting and annealing process fused the ingredients into a vitreous fluid, then cooled or annealed the mixture slowly to avoid cracking. Glass made from pure ingredients is colorless, but even small amounts of impurities add color, a fact the ancient workmen used to advantage. Alexandria produced a fine colorless glass, due probably to pure silver sands used in their process. The early glass objects were shaped in clay molds or by grinding the glass as if it were stone; some of the results are impressive. The most common method, however, was to dip a sack of sand into molten glass, remove it with the glass clinging to the sack, roll it on a stone table to shape it as it cooled, add decorations as desired, then pour out the sand from the center of the vessel after it cooled. During the Ptolemaic period, Egypt devised mold-pressed ware. In this process, colored rods (called canes) were fused together, then cut transversely to make multicolored glass. The mosaic glasses and bowls used by patricians during the Roman period were made from this method. Recent excavations in Jerusalem uncovered evidence of a thriving glass industry, with many rods found *in situ*. Both mold and glass-blowing processes were discovered.

▶859 Plate of thin molded glass, Roman, first century AD. Leyden Museum, Netherlands. Like the plate in photo 858, this plate was made by blowing molten glass into a mold, the early process of glass-blowing. As skills developed the molds were discarded. The glass-blowing method that followed was essentially the same as today.

► **860 Ribbed plate of cast glass,** Roman, first century AD. Leyden Museum, Netherlands. To cast the plate, soft glass was pressed into a mold; then the interior was wheel-polished and the exterior exposed briefly to fire. This type of plate was made in both multicolored and monochrome glass and was especially popular during the first century AD.

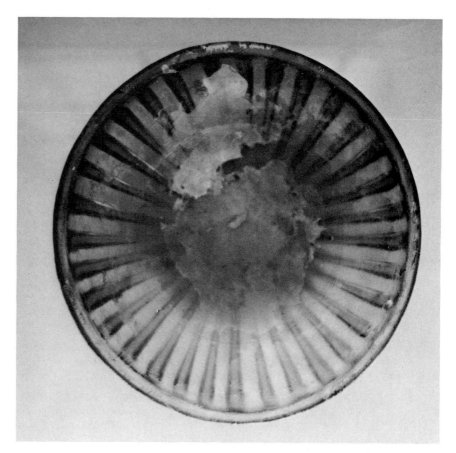

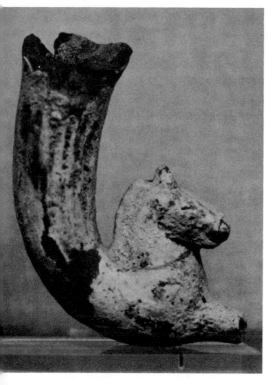

▲ **861 Terra-cotta drinking rhyton,** Roman period, from Egypt, first-third centuries AD. Benaki Museum, Athens.

▲ **862 Clear glass drinking cups,** Roman, first-second centuries AD. Field Museum. Thin-walled, clear glass goods were manufactured in Egypt at Alexandria and possibly at Karanis.

863   864

865

866

863, 864, 865, 866 Pottery, various types, from Egypt, Roman period, first-fourth centuries AD. Field Museum. The cup on the left in photo 863 is smooth; the one on the right has corrugations made by the potter's wheel. The handle was added separately. Photos 864 and 865 show several styles and sizes; most have the corrugation design and, like the cup, the handles were added later. The small bottles in photos 865 and 866 are shaped like the glass bottles of the period and are meant to imitate them. Photo 866 also shows 2 serving bowls and 2 jugs.

▲867 **Pottery cup,** first century AD. Agora Museum, Athens. The height of Greek pottery production came during the sixth and fifth centuries BC at Athens. With Athens' decline in the early fourth century, other regions vied for the trade through various designs and approaches. During the first century BC the Romans developed their famous Arretine bowls by the relief-molding process that essentially had been developed by Athens. The glaze added to the Arretine was a coral red, giving the archeologists their name for it, *terra sigillata*. The Romans also produced a blue-green glazeware, which was a lead glaze applied by dipping the vessel to coat the outside and applying a thinner coating inside. Much pottery was used, however, that was left unglazed. The cup has projections alternating with dots, two horizontal recessed lines at top, and a base.

▲869 **Pottery dish,** Roman. Milwaukee Museum of Art. The dish is deeper than a plate.

◄870 **Pottery bowls** from Malta, found in Roman villa. Malta Museum. The same style of pottery, but red, has been found in great quantity at Pompeii and evidently served as the regular earthenware table setting. The Pompeii pottery is decorated, while these bowls are plain.

▶**871 Group of amphorae,** from Cologne, Roman period. Roman-German Landesmuseum, Cologne. Amphorae were among the most common containers in the ancient world. They were used for measuring, storing, and for shipping after being packed in protective material. Amphorae usually were made from clay, occasionally from glass. For the manufacturer, they were useful to ship wine, fruit juices, oil, honey, vinegar, figs, medicine, grain, and even money. For the home they held the food supply and water. Poor people used them for urns, and they were placed along the streets for urinals. Their tops were so designed that they could be sealed with corks, which for shipping often was covered with wax; they had 2 opposing handles; and the pointed bottom usually had a tip or knob that also served as a handle. The shape not only made their manufacture more

economical; they were easier to handle. When transported they were packed in protective material such as rope (see photos 193-194); in homes and shops they were set upright in sand or in stands made for them, or sometimes simply were leaned against a wall.

▲**872 Pottery of various types,** found in Augst. Römerhaus Museum, Augst, Switzerland. On the left are amphorae set upright in sand and one in a stand of the ancient type. The shelves contain jugs, pitchers, bowls, and dishes of various sizes and shapes. Four jugs hang on the wall.

▲873 Large storage jars in commercial kitchen, hanging from a rod. Römerhaus Museum, Augst, Switzerland.

▼874 Heavy, flat-bottomed jug, from Malta. Malta Museum. The heavy design may have served to keep its liquid cool.

▼875 Mosaic of bird and basket. National Museum of Naples. The bird is pulling a mirror from a basket. The basket is woven from fine, thin material with different colors to create a design. The top is carefully matched and has a handle. The weave appears to be soft.

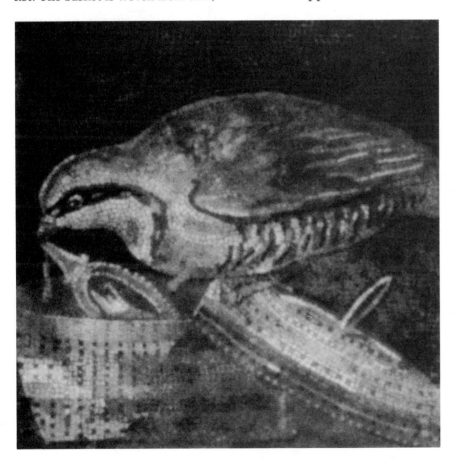

▲876 Basket with lid, from Egypt, Roman period. Field Museum. The basket is woven and coated. It had various uses, one of which was to protect small jars during transport.

◄ 877 **Cat stalking birds on a bird-bath.** National Museum of Naples. The birdbath is a finely wrought vessel with 2 handles. The parrots are at home; the pigeon is pictured as an intruder. He looks at a leaf or his reflection in the water. A cat crouches hungrily at the base and some fruit is placed at the lower left of the mosaic. The bowl style was common for birdbaths. This one has scallops around the rim.

▲ 879 **Large copper vessel shaped like a *krater*.** National Museum of Naples. The krater was a deep drinking cup that was popular for many centuries, from Mycenean times into the Roman period. It was used for mixing water with the wine at mealtimes. The bottoms varied; they did not always have a base.

▲ 878 **Large 2-handled vessel shaped like a kylix,** a shallow drinking bowl. National Museum of Naples. It may have been used for a birdbath or may have been a cultic vessel. The kylix was a favorite shape for banquets, *symposia*, and drinking parties.

◄**880 Bronze saucepan,** from Pompeii, first century AD. Field Museum. It has a straight handle with a hole in the end for suspension from a hook. Its bowl is deeper than the one in photo 881.

▲**881 Bronze saucepan,** from Pompeii, first century AD. Field Museum. This pan is similar to the one in photo 880, but the handle has sleeker lines and the hook-hole is more decorative.

◄**882 Bronze stewpan,** from Pompeii, first century AD. Field Museum. The pan has incrustations of earth and pumice from the volcano that destroyed the city. Its bowl is shallow and it has a hole at the end of a straight handle for hanging from a hook.

▶**883 Bronze strainer,** from Pompeii, first century AD. Field Museum. Incrustations and rust have closed the holes in the bottom. Its purpose was the same as for strainers today.

◀**885 Bronze strainer,** from Pompeii, first century AD. Field Museum. Some of the holes can still be seen; they are arranged in patterns. The handle has a hole for suspension from a hook.

▼**884 Bronze strainer,** from Pompeii, first century AD. Field Museum. The holes are large compared to those shown in photo 885. The handles were missing and have been reconstructed.

▼**886 Bronze spoon,** from Italy, Roman period. Field Museum. The spoon was used as a ladle.

▼**887 Bronze baking pan,** from Pompeii, first century AD. Field Museum. It was used for baking pastries or cakes in the shape of a pie slice. Pans of various shapes were used.

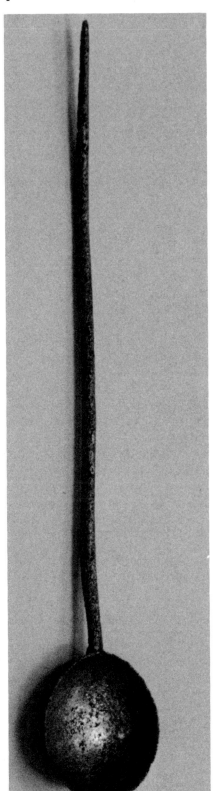

▲**888 Bronze grappling hook,** from Vulci, Etruria, about 500 BC. Field Museum. The hook was used for catching and pulling cooked meat from a pot. A wooden handle was inserted into the socket.

DEATH

Greek and Roman views about death and the afterlife were varied. The earlier beliefs can be traced, but a number of strains competed for attention during the first century, ranging from mythical beliefs to absolute denial of afterlife by philosophy.

Death practices were somewhat uniform, in contrast with afterlife views. Proper burial was essential, and to that end many Romans and Greeks—craftsmen, merchants, and even slaves—belonged to guilds which were primarily burial societies.

The primary function of a Roman guild was to finance the funerals and burying of its dead members. Under the Empire they were carefully watched and generally new ones were not allowed to organize, since they easily could become political organizations. The old ones, however, were allowed to continue. The members paid dues to their guild, which then saw to the expenses connected with death. The guilds were clubs, too, for the living, and members who had made good in life celebrated various functions by supplying banquets or other activities to the members. Often slaves and citizens, especially freedmen, belonged to the guilds together.

Greeks and Romans practiced cremation during the New Testament period, though both had used inhumation earlier in their histories. Views of the afterlife apparently had little to do with the choice, which was based on other factors such as economics. Burial, it was believed, was essential for the departed to enter the underworld of death. Criminals sometimes were not buried for this reason; thus, their suffering continued in the uncertain world of the shades. Roman law, however, allowed for burial of animals with few exceptions.

When death came to a person, a loved one closed his eyes and placed a coin in the mouth to pay Charon, who charged a fee to ferry the departed across the Styx River (Acharon is the name of the river for Greeks). The deceased was dressed in clothes he or she would wear in life and placed on a couch to be viewed. In the Roman house, the body was placed in the atrium with feet to the door; outside, cypress or pitch-pine was hung to indicate that the house was taboo, thus warning certain religious figures to avoid approaching. After the funeral the heir used a special broom to sweep the death pollution from the house.

Depending on ability to pay, a procession of the dead person carried on a litter passed through the streets, preceded by flutes for the young or trumpets for the older deceased; the litter was followed by hired mourners, and in the procession were actors (or others) wearing likeness masks of dead ancestors to indicate their attendance at the funeral. At the end of the procession speeches were made about the departed, after which the body was inhumed or placed on a pyre and burned. The pyre was as elaborate a structure as could be afforded.

The ashes were gathered up and placed in a cinerary urn, which was placed in a niche in a tomb. Gifts, belongings, furniture, and other objects might be burned on the pyre with the body or placed unburned in the tomb. Cremation was the only method used during the first century; inhumation did not begin until Trajan's time. A banquet was held immediately after the funeral at the burial place, and again during the year—for Romans once on the ninth day after burial; for Greeks 3 times on the third, ninth, and thirtieth days, or on the third, seventh, and fortieth days. Thereafter, banquets were held annually.

Greek and Roman belief in an afterlife was nebulous, contradictory, and varied; this condition is due to a wide range of belief bases, with no particular belief dominating, and to preoccupation with this life. Plato had taught that the soul survived in eternity by being absorbed into a great whole. Aristotle believed that only the reason survived. Philosophers who followed them believed any inquiry into an afterlife was a foolish waste of time, so most of Greek philosophy simply ceased to deal with the subject. Epicurius, however, taught outright that there was no existence of any kind after death, thus freeing people—so he believed—from any such concern so they could live in tranquillity. The enormous power of philosophy from the Hellenistic period beyond the first century thus gave its weight to the denial of any afterlife.

Neo-Pythagoreanism was an exception. The ancient philosophy of the Pythagoreans had almost died out. It survived as a minor view whose adherents were more a cult than a philosophical school. When just prior to and during the Empire period the view arose again, its adherents had absorbed some Orphic and Eastern views. They claimed that the soul was immortal and was trapped in an earthly body. The soul must take care in this unhappy life not to allow the body to influence it too much. At death, the soul hovers for some time on earth but then ascends to the moon, the first dwelling of the blessed. The "shade" of the soul remains there, while pure reason ascends to the sun.

The philosophers' teachings had great impact on the educated, but the common people continued to concern themselves with whatever followed death as best they could. When the mystery religions and then Christianity appeared, both found people ready to accept their promises of life after death. The mystery religions promised immortality to those persons who became identified (deified, immortalized) with the god through secret knowledge and rituals. The abode of the blessed is in the bowels of the earth (so taught Dionysus and Sabazios), where the kind of bliss attained in the drinking festivals on earth continue in an eternal banquet.

The devotees of Cybele, the Mother Earth goddess, were absorbed into her (who had given them birth). This ancient Hades-type view, however, became akin to the Dionysiac view as the 2 cults became closely identified. Serapis and Isis worship followed the same development. Mithraism taught differently. The soul of the just, according to Mithra, rose to the sky to enjoy eternal bliss. The souls of the wicked would roam the earth or be dragged into the earth's depths. The place in the sky to which the blessed ascended was variously believed to be the sun, planets, or stars, depending on the type of Mithraism that was followed.

Generally speaking, Greeks believed that any existence without the body was an unhappy one, so death in any case was worse than life. Though this view was prevalent, Greeks also believed in a certain manner of life after death. While the better people went to the Elysian Fields, the undeserving went to the prison Tartarus (some-times the word is used as an equivalent of Hades).

In earlier Greek history, the Elysian Fields was the special abode of the high-born hero; as time passed it became the abode of the just. Tartarus, in contrast, was surrounded by a river of fire; infallible judges determined who would take that left turn and who the right one into punishment or reward. (Some later, but pre-Roman, writers placed these regions above ground in the southern hemisphere, which was uncharted.)

Whether the general populace actually believed the myths about the subterranean regions is debated. Tomb inscriptions seem to indicate that the stories were believed, but the use of language could be poetic. Ancient writers can be quoted to indicate that almost no one believed the stories anymore; other writers can be cited who indicate that such belief not only was held by many but was beneficial.

Romans especially but Greeks also worshiped the spirits of their dead ancestors. They continued well into the Empire period to follow the practice of having intimate family banquets in the tombs of the deceased. Many of these areas, painted with frescoes and otherwise decorated, have been excavated in catacombs and tombs. A common belief, in fact, was that the deceased continued to live on inside the tomb (hence the veneration of the tombs of dead heroes) and was able to enjoy the congeniality of the banquets held in the tomb. (Banquets sometimes were held in guild halls or homes.) The practice of celebrating the dead with banquets in the tombs was one reason why the tombs were located on main streets and as near the gate as possible; Romans tried to locate them in convenient places.

Greeks and Romans believed in ghosts more or less in the modern sense; one who remained unburied, or who was too much caught up in life with bodily pleasures, or who was murdered and his murder unavenged, might have difficulty passing on into the realm of the dead. Added to these unfortunate people were the shades identified earlier of all the deceased (except perhaps for Neo-Pythagoreans). In spite of the nearly unanimous views of philosophies that there was no existence beyond death or that such could not be determined, a surprising number of highly educated persons who were committed to philosophy believed in manifestations, apparitions, and other communication with the dead. The tomb was the door to the nether-world, by which the departed spirit would come and go; hence the tomb was a logical place to communicate with the dead.

The first century, then, knew a variety of beliefs in life after death: complete denial of any form of afterlife; salvation by identification with the deity through secret ritual or knowledge; mythological cross-ings of the River Styx and assignment to Tartarus or the Elysian Fields; belief in a tripartite human (body, soul, and shade); an unconscious union with deity; a rising of the reason to astral realms; belief in ghosts, apparitions, and magic; or a combination of elements from each view. By the New Testament period, Greek and Roman views had become so thoroughly amalgamated that little or no difference can be discerned between them.

Life in Ancient Rome, F. R. Cowell (New York: Perigee Books), 1980; *After Life in Roman Paganism*, Franz Cumont (New Haven: Yale University Press), 1923; *The Archeology of the New Testament*, Jack Finegan (Princeton: Princeton University Press), 1969; *Cities of Vesuvius: Pompeii and Herculaneum*, Michael Grant (New York: Penguin Books), 1971; *The Oxford Classical Dictionary*, edited by N. G. L. Hammond and H. H. Scullard (Oxford: Clarendon Press), 1970; *Jewish Ossuaries: Reburial and Rebirth*, Eric M. Meyers (Rome: Biblical Institute Press), 1971; *Glanum*, Francois Salviat (Paris: Caisse Nationale des Monuments Historiques et des Sites), 1977.

▲ 889 Scene of funeral pyre. Capitoline Museum. The scene, a shallow relief from a third-century AD sarcophagus, probably represents a mythological death, such as that of Achilles or Meleager. A nude body is carried by 2 men, one under his back and one holding his legs over his shoulders. He is followed by a figure which wears a long, flowing tunic, has long hair that falls free, and may be winged. The woman in front staggers as if in grief while the next woman looks back. These 3 women may be mourners or some or all may represent divinities. The one at the far right is dressed in the style of Diana and, as Diana would, holds a dog. The figure who appears to be rising from the pyre is in the style in which Aphrodite rising from the foam often is portrayed. The figure at far left may be a Victory. The funeral pyre is prepared with wood stacked in alternating rows. A man prepares a fire in a stove on the top of which sets a large pot. The funeral has all the elements of an ancient one, with attendant deities, mourners, procession, and pyre.

▶ 890 Street of the Tombs, Pompeii, looking toward the Villa of Mysteries from the Herculaneum Gate. Burial was not allowed inside Roman cities, so roads leading into the city became lined with tombs; the closer to the city gate, the better. The same custom was practiced among the Greeks. The nature of the tombs is seen better on the right side of the road than the left. They vary greatly in design, depending on the tastes and wealth of the owners. The entrance to a villa appears occasionally along the road, which indicates that "graveyards" were not fearsome places to Romans and Greeks.

◄891 **Tombs with resting place for travelers, Street of the Tombs, Pompeii.** The tomb roads were busy and noisy, frequented by pedestrians; they did not have the gloomy image associated with cemeteries in the modern world. The photo shows a semicircular architrave with a bench for passersby to rest; it was provided for that purpose by the builder. Cicero, in fact, rested in this hemicycle (*De Amicitia*).

► **892 Interior of a tomb, Street of the Tombs, Pompeii.** The interiors were beautifully painted with fresco on plaster and sometimes contained extensive furniture and other items. They were lit by lamps or vents in the walls. Urns were placed in the niches. Sometimes a flat area was provided for placing offerings to the dead. Family meals were eaten in tombs on anniversaries to honor the dead ancestors. *Romans 3:13.*

▲893 Tomb of the Julii, Glanum, near St. Remy, France. The 3-storied mausoleum of Caius and Lucius Caesar dates to about 40 BC. Their 2 togate statues can be faintly seen within the rotunda at the top of the monument. The full height of the structure is 59 feet (18 m.); its design is of a type found in other places in the region. The monument sets on a square pedestal of dressed stones. The bas-relief scenes on the first floor can be seen in closeup in photos 49-50. The next story is square, with a Corinthian column and capitals at each corner, with arched openings between. The frieze above the columns contains mythological figures. The third story is a rotunda with Corinthian columns topped with a cone-shaped roof. The inscription is SEX. L.M. IVLIEI. C.F. PARENTIBVS SVEIS = Sextius, Lucius, Marcus, sons of Caius, of the family of the Julii, their parents. They may have been nephews of Julius Caesar.

▼894 Tomb of Zechariah, Kidron Valley, Jerusalem. The tomb appears to be independent, but it is connected inside by a passage which leads to the so-called Tomb of James to the north (left), which is a complex of several rooms. The monument is cut from rock of the hillside; it is 29 feet, 6 inches (9 m.) high and 17 feet (5.2 m.) wide. The top is in the form of a pyramid which is visually supported by reliefs of pilasters topped with Ionic capitals. It dates to the second half of the first century BC and shows a union of Greek and Egyptian architectural styles.

▲895 Tomb of Absalom, Kidron Valley, Jerusalem. The monument (the name is legendary) dates to about AD 50 and is cut out of the rock of the hillside. It is 54 feet, 1 inch (16.5 m.) high and 19 feet, 8 inches (6 m.) wide. It has the same type of pilasters and Ionic capitals as the monument in photo 894 but has in addition an architrave, frieze, and cornice. Above that entablature is a large square stone block which supports a superstructure comprised of a cylinder and a conelike top similar to the one in photo 893 but without the statues, which would not be appropriate in a Jewish monument. The structure contains a burial chamber with 2 arcosolia (niches in the wall for placement of the bodies). The opening is on the south side above the cornice. The opening behind and left of the tomb is the entrance to the so-called Tomb of Jehoshaphat, which contains 8 rooms and dates to the same time as the Tomb of Absalom.

▲896 Child's ossuary, Judea. The Archaeological Museum of The Southern Baptist Theological Seminary. The 6-lobed rosette decoration was the most popular style of decoration during the New Testament period and was widely used throughout the Near East, in Parthian, Nabatean, and then Christian burials. The prevalence of the pattern over Greek styles may indicate a resurgence of Eastern art forms over Hellenistic among Jews. The ossuary was for the storage of bones after the body decayed. The Jewish pattern of burial was inhumation, in contrast to the Greek and Roman cremations. The body was placed in the tomb, usually in body-sized niches called arocosolia, or sometimes on ledges. When it had completely decayed, the bones were gathered and placed in an ossuary which might be left on the tomb floor or buried under the tomb floor of the room which contained several niches, thus freeing the niches to be used again.

▼898 Funerary mask for mummy, period of Trajan. Photo courtesy of Kelsey Museum of Archaeology, The University of Michigan. In earlier Egypt the image of the deceased was painted on the mummy case. In Roman Egypt, at least in the Fayum region, likenesses were painted on wood and placed in a "window" in the mummy over the face of the deceased. The process is called encaustic; it consists of colors impregnated into wax. The images are not really likenesses; a number of types were prepared for general use and only certain changes were made at the wish of the family, such as addition of jewelry worn by the deceased, as is the case with this image, which also includes gold.

▲897 Funeral monument for holding urns, first century AD. Vatican Museum. It belonged to the miller P. Nonius Zethus. The marble block has conical hollows to hold the cinerary urns. The bas-reliefs at each side of the inscription show scenes from his life as a miller and flour merchant. The block, with the urns, would be placed inside the family tomb.

SCRIPTURE INDEX

Bold face type refers to photo numbers; regular face type refers to page numbers. The references are not exhaustive. Additional information may be found by referring to appropriate headings in the Subject Index.

SUBJECT INDEX